'Walsh, Oxburgh, Redlich, and Myklebust have provided two invaluable resources for the field of forensic interviewing and interrogation. Researchers, students, practitioners, and policymakers now have at their fingertips the most up-to-date information from countries around the globe on methods of questioning victims, witnesses, and suspects. Simply put, these two volumes are a fascinating and enlightening foray into the variety of international interview and interrogation practices.'

Gail Goodman, *Distinguished Professor of Psychology, University of California, Davis, USA*

'With chapters from over 25 countries, this book brings together everything there is to know about contemporary practices of investigative interviewing all over the world. For forensic psychologists, criminologists, and law enforcement professionals alike, this unique collection of chapters—on how to interview and interrogate crime victims, witnesses, and suspects—provides an invaluable resource.'

Saul Kassin, *Distinguished Professor of Psychology, John Jay College of Criminal Justice, New York City, USA*

International Developments and Practices in Investigative Interviewing and Interrogation

Techniques in the investigative interviewing and interrogation of victims, witnesses and suspects of crime vary around the world, according to a country's individual legal system, religion and culture. Whereas some countries have developed certain interview protocols for witnesses (such as the ABE Guidelines and the NICHD protocol when interviewing children) and the PEACE model of interviewing suspects, other countries continue to use physical coercion and other questionable tactics to elicit information.

Until now, there has been very little empirical information about the overall interview and interrogation practices in non-western countries, especially the Middle and Far East. This book addresses this gap, bringing together international experts from over 25 countries and providing in-depth coverage of the various interview and interrogation techniques used across the globe. Volume 1 focuses on the interviewing of victims and witnesses, aiming to provide the necessary information for an understanding of how law enforcement agencies around the world gain valuable information from victims and witnesses in criminal cases. Together, the chapters that make up this volume and the accompanying volume on interviewing suspects, draw on specific national case studies and practices, examine contemporary challenges and identify best practice to enable readers to develop an international, as well as a comparative, perspective of developments worldwide in this important area of criminal investigation.

This book will be an essential resource for academics and students engaged in the study of policing, criminal investigation, forensic psychology and criminal law. It will also be of great interest to practitioners, legal professionals and policy-makers around the world.

David Walsh is an Applied Criminologist and a Fellow of the UK's Higher Education Academy. He has published several articles and book chapters and co-authored a book on corruption. Prior to joining academia he was an investigation professional in government departments in the UK for over 20 years. Dr Walsh has presented his work at many national and international academic and practitioner conferences.

Gavin E. Oxburgh is a registered Forensic Psychologist with the UK Health and Care Professions Council, a Chartered Psychologist and Scientist, and a Fellow of the UK Higher Education Academy. Dr Oxburgh is an expert witness and has provided psychological advice in legal cases in the UK and overseas. Prior to academia, he had a highly successful 22-year career with the Royal Air Force Police where he was a senior detective specialising in crime management, child protection and sexual offences, serving throughout the UK and across Europe.

Allison D. Redlich, PhD, is an internationally-known researcher on police interrogation who began her career studying child victim/witnesses. She has published many peer-reviewed articles on these and related topics and is often asked to provide expert testimony in court and to educate law enforcement and court professionals. She has served on the Executive Committee of the American Psychology-Law Society and co-chaired their 2014 conference.

Trond Myklebust gained his Bachelor degree from the University of Oslo and an MSc in Investigative Psychology from the University of Liverpool while serving as a police officer. In 2009 he became the first police officer in Norway to obtain a PhD (Department of Psychology, University of Oslo). He holds a position as Assistant Chief of Police at the Norwegian Police University College and a Visiting Lectureship at Newcastle University in the UK. He is a Chartered Psychologist in the British Psychological Society and Co-Founder and Co-Director of the International Investigative Interviewing Research Group (iIIRG).

Routledge Frontiers of Criminal Justice

1. **Sex Offenders: Punish, Help, Change or Control?**
   Theory, policy and practice explored
   Edited by Jo Brayford, Francis Cowe and John Deering

2. **Building Justice in Post-Transition Europe**
   Processes of criminalisation within Central and Eastern European societies
   Edited by Kay Goodall, Margaret Malloch and Bill Munro

3. **Technocrime, Policing and Surveillance**
   Edited by Stéphane Leman-Langlois

4. **Youth Justice in Context**
   Community, compliance and young people
   Mairead Seymour

5. **Women, Punishment and Social Justice**
   Human rights and penal practices
   Margaret Malloch and Gill McIvor

6. **Handbook of Policing, Ethics and Professional Standards**
   Edited by Allyson MacVean, Peter Spindler and Charlotte Solf

7. **Contrasts in Punishment**
   An explanation of Anglophone excess and Nordic exceptionalism
   John Pratt and Anna Eriksson

8. **Victims of Environmental Harm**
   Rights, recognition and redress under National and International Law
   Matthew Hall

9. **Doing Probation Work**
   Identity in a criminal justice occupation
   Rob C. Mawby and Anne Worrall

10. **Justice Reinvestment**
    Can the criminal justice system deliver more for less?
    Chris Fox, Kevin Albertson and Kevin Wong

11. **Epidemiological Criminology**
    Theory to practice
    Edited by Eve Waltermaurer and Timothy A. Akers

12. **Policing Cities**
    Urban securitization and regulation in a twenty-first century world
    Edited by Randy K. Lippert and Kevin Walby

13. **Restorative Justice in Transition**
    Kerry Clamp

14. **International Perspectives on Police Education and Training**
    Edited by Perry Stanislas

15. **Understanding Penal Practice**
    Edited by Ioan Durnescu and Fergus McNeill

16. **Perceptions of Criminal Justice**
Vicky De Mesmaecker

17. **Transforming Criminal Justice?**
Problem-solving and court specialization
Jane Donoghue

18. **Policing in Taiwan**
From authoritarianism to democracy
Liqun Cao, Lanying Huang and Ivan Y. Sun

19. **Reparation for Victims of Crimes against Humanity**
The healing role of reparation
Edited by Jo-Anne M. Wemmers

20. **Victims of Violence and Restorative Practices**
Finding a voice
Tinneke Van Camp

21. **Long-Term Imprisonment and Human Rights**
Edited by Kirstin Drenkhahn, Manuela Dudeck and Frieder Dünkel

22. **Working within the Forensic Paradigm**
Cross-discipline approaches for policy and practice
Edited by Rosemary Sheehan and James Ogloff

23. **Positive Criminology**
Edited by Natti Ronel and Dana Segev

24. **Inmates' Narratives and Discursive Discipline in Prison**
Rewriting personal histories through cognitive behavioral programs in prison
Jennifer A. Schlosser

25. **Municipal Corporate Security in International Context**
Kevin Walby and Randy K. Lippert

26. **Victims and Restorative Justice**
Edited by Ivo Aertsen, Inge Vanfraechem and Daniela Bolivar

27. **The Role of Community in Restorative Justice**
Fernanda Fonseca Ronseblatt

28. **Pre-crime**
Pre-emption, precaution and the future
Jude McCulloch and Dean Wilson

29. **Punishing the Other**
The social production of immorality revisited
Anna Eriksson

30. **International Developments and Practices in Investigative Interviewing and Interrogation**
Volume 1: Victims and witnesses
Edited by David Walsh, Gavin Oxburgh, Allison Redlich and Trond Myklebust

31. **International Developments and Practices in Investigative Interviewing and Interrogation**
Volume 2: Suspects
Edited by David Walsh, Gavin E. Oxburgh, Allison D. Redlich and Trond Myklebust

International Developments and Practices in Investigative Interviewing and Interrogation

Volume 1: Victims and witnesses

Edited by David Walsh, Gavin E. Oxburgh, Alison D. Redlich and Trond Myklebust

Routledge
Taylor & Francis Group
LONDON AND NEW YORK

First published 2016
by Routledge
2 Park Square, Milton Park, Abingdon, Oxfordshire OX14 4RN
and by Routledge
711 Third Avenue, New York, NY 10017

First issued in paperback 2017

Routledge is an imprint of the Taylor & Francis Group, an informa business

British Library Cataloguing in Publication Data
A catalogue record for this book is available from the British Library

Library of Congress Cataloging-in-Publication Data
A catalog record for this book has been requested

ISBN 13: 978-1-138-06599-4 (pbk)
ISBN 13: 978-1-138-78174-0 (hbk)

Typeset in Times New Roman
by Deer Park Productions

Dedications

DW: For Joanna and Sue for such wonderful memories, and my love to Fiona, Emma and the newly arrived Jenson. To all those who have supported me in this and all my other endeavours.

GO: The journey from being a police officer in the Royal Air Force to entering academia has been enormously fulfilling. Many people along the way have greatly inspired me, not least my late father, Eric Oxburgh, my mother Hope Oxburgh, my devoted wife Laura and my daughter Susan. Your inspiration and belief in my ability has been unwavering and greatly appreciated. Thank you.

AR: My journey into researching the most effective and efficient methods to interview individuals in criminal contexts began with my first 'real' job. After college, I was fortunate enough to secure a position working with Michael Lamb at the National Institute of Child Health and Human Development (NICHD). While there, I assisted with his (and several others') research on interviewing alleged child sexual abuse victims – research that laid the foundation for the NICHD Interview Protocol. From there, I went on to graduate school where I (again fortunately) worked with the 'founding mother' of child victim-witness research, Gail Goodman. Gail is an exemplar mentor in all respects and much of what I know about interviewing I learned from her. During graduate school, I read an article by Saul Kassin on interrogating suspects. I was fascinated and the rest, as they say, is history. Thus I dedicate these volumes to Michael, Gail and Saul. All three have been wonderful mentors to me over the years and each played an important role in this never-ending journey in determining how and how not to interview and interrogate persons involved in the criminal justice systems as victims, witnesses and suspects.

TM: To Siren and Mathilde – for your never ending love, joy and support in my endeavours.

Contents

Figures and tables

Figures

Tables

Contributors

Kamiar Alaei, MD, DrPH, MPH, MS, is a Public Service Professor in the Department of Public Administration and Policy and the founding Director of the Global Institute for Health and Human Rights. He and his brother Arash co-founded the first 'Triangular Clinic' for three target groups in Iran (drug users, HIV patients and STD cases), which was documented by the World Health Organisation as a 'Best Practice Model' for HIV/AIDS and injecting drug users' prevention and care. Dr Alaei's extensive experience in both global health policy and international human rights law allows him to focus on the intersections between international health and international law, while remaining sensitive to the needs and realities of vulnerable target groups, including the rights of prisoners. Kamiar Alaei received his Medical Doctorate (MD) from Isfahan Medical University and his Master of Public Health (MPH) in Epidemiology from Tehran Medical University, two of the most prestigious universities in Iran. He received his Master of Science in International Health from Harvard University and his doctoral degree on Health Policy and Management from the State University of New York at Albany. He is currently completing his degree in International Human Rights Law at the University of Oxford.

Telma Sousa Almeida finished her Master's Degree in the Psychology of Justice and Deviant Behaviour in Portugal in 2010, and since then has completed a higher degree in Legal Medicine and another in the Psychopathology and Psychotherapy of Children and Adolescents. She first worked as a forensic psychologist intern and after that as a clinical psychologist. Simultaneously, Telma has been collaborating in scientific research in the fields of forensic psychology and juvenile delinquency as well as peace psychology and human rights since 2010. At present she is a PhD candidate in the Department of Psychology at the University of Cambridge and her doctoral research interests focus on episodic memory, suggestibility and the interviewing of individuals with autistic spectrum disorders and individuals with intellectual disabilities. She also collaborates with the Portuguese National Institute of Legal Medicine and Forensic Sciences in a research project concerning the implementation of a forensic interview protocol for child victims, witnesses and perpetrators.

E. Aminudin Aziz is Professor of Linguistics at the Department of English Education, Indonesia University of Education (Universitas Pendidikan Indonesia/UPI). Upon completing his diplomas and undergraduate degree at UPI, he continued his study at the Department of Linguistics, Monash University, Australia, where he earned his Master's (1994–6) and PhD (1997–2000). His main research interests include pragmatics, forensic linguistics, philosophy of language and intercultural communication. He has extensively conducted research and widely published mainly on topics related to concepts of face and politeness phenomena, speech act realisations and culture core values. He is currently leading two research projects funded by the Ministry of Education and Culture, the Republic of Indonesia, namely Police Report vs Suspect Confessions During Police Investigations and the Cultural Core Values of Sundanese People in West Java and the Challenges for Sundanese Language Maintenance. He has been active in the training programmes for Indonesian police officers in regard to the improvement of police competencies particularly in investigative interviewing as well as acting as the expert working with police officers in analysing linguistic data. Since 2010, he has been appointed as Vice Rector for Institutional Planning, Research and Development at the UPI.

Igor Areh is a Senior Lecturer in Forensic Psychology at the Faculty of Criminal Justice and Security, University of Maribor, Slovenia. His lectures and research work focus mainly on interviews of crime victims and suspects. Having majored in psychology, he accepted a teaching position at the Faculty and narrowed his research work to the issues related to eyewitness testimony. In his successfully defended 2008 PhD thesis in psychology, he researched gender differences in eyewitness memory recall. In recent years, his research interests have moved towards suspect interrogation focusing on two main themes: detecting deceit with the polygraph (concealed information test) and the investigative interview. He has published over 70 articles and three books on forensic and investigative psychology issues. He also works as a criminal investigation advisor, mainly by evaluating the veracity of suspects' statements, as well as an expert witness in court.

Gustavo Noronha de Ávila is a criminal lawyer holding a PhD in Criminal Sciences from the Pontifical Catholic University of Rio Grande do Sul, Brazil, and is a member of the Faculty at the Law School of the State University of Maringá (UEM), Paraná, Brazil. He is also a member of the research team responsible for the national study on interviewing practices and identification procedures in Brazil (2014–15), supported by the Ministry of Justice and the Institute of Applied Economic Research (IPEA).

Bianca Baker is a PhD student at the University of Derby in the United Kingdom where she is currently examining the employment of therapeutic methods during investigative interviewing settings across cultures. Her aim is to find methods of obtaining information that may culturally vary. Simultaneously, she is pursuing education in psychotherapy. Bianca Baker obtained her BA in Psychology at the University of Southern Maine, USA and her MS in Forensic and Legal Psychology at Leicester University in the United Kingdom. The focus of her research is largely on empathy, suggestibility, rapport-building methods and cultural differences in these areas.

Nicholas C. Bala has been a Professor at the Faculty of Law at Queen's University in Canada since 1980. His primary area of teaching and research is Family and Children's Law. Much of his research work is interdisciplinary and he has undertaken collaborative projects with psychologists, social workers and health professionals. He has published extensively on a range of topics, including separation and divorce, parental alienation, spousal violence, child witnesses and youth justice. His work is regularly cited by all levels of court in Canada, including the Supreme Court, as well as by courts in Australia, Britain and the USA.

Luis Roberto Benia is a psychiatrist with a Master's degree in Psychology. He is also a PhD student in the Psychology Postgraduate Department of the Pontifical Catholic University of Rio Grande do Sul, Porto Alegre, Brazil, as well as a criminal expert of the Forensic Medical-Legal Institute of Rio Grande do Sul, Porto Alegre, Brazil.

Deirdre A. Brown is a Senior Lecturer in the School of Psychology at the Victoria University of Wellington, New Zealand. Her research interests include children's memory development, narrative ability and interviewing strategies that facilitate their ability to communicate their knowledge and experiences. She has a particular interest in the abilities and vulnerabilities of children with developmental disorders. Dr Brown works closely with Child, Youth and Family, and with the New Zealand Police to train and evaluate the practice of specialist child witness interviewers.

Sonja P. Brubacher is a researcher and Lecturer in Psychology at Deakin University. Her PhD research, defended in 2011, focused on developing and modifying techniques for interviewing children about events they had experienced repeatedly, and helping them to accurately describe specific occurrences of these events. Her postdoctoral research continued to focus on child-witness interviewing and revived her interest in understanding the effects of interview preparatory phases. Dr Brubacher is also a researcher and industry trainer with the Centre for Investigative Interviewing and a member of the executive committee of the International Investigative Interviewing Research Group.

Ray Bull is Professor of Criminal Investigation at the University of Derby and Visiting Professor at the Universities of Portsmouth and London South Bank. In 2012 he was elected President-Elect of the European Association of Psychology and Law. In 2010 he was 'Elected by acclaim' an Honorary Fellow of the British Psychological Society 'for the contribution made to the discipline of psychology' (this honour is restricted to 40 living psychologists).

In 2009 he was made a Fellow of the Association of Psychological Sciences for 'sustained and outstanding distinguished contribution to psychological science' (FAPS) and received from the International Investigative Interviewing Research Group the Senior Academic Award for his 'significant lifetime contribution to the field of investigative interviewing'. In 2008 Ray received from the European Association of Psychology and Law the Award for Life-time Contribution to Psychology and Law. He has testified as an expert witness in many trials.

Michel Carmans graduated in social issues at the Institut Supérieur de Formation Sociale in Brussels. He has also graduated in family and sexuality sciences at the University of Louvain and has several degrees in educational sciences. Since 2002, he has been a member of the Behavioural Sciences department within the Federal Judiciary Police, where he has been coordinating the project Interviewing Minors. A lecturer at the national criminal investigation school of the Federal Police, he participates as an expert at the request of national or international bodies in meetings, programmes of instruction and projects regarding the issue of interviewing minors in terms of its methodological and organisational aspects.

Kyndra C. Cleveland is a doctoral candidate and National Science Foundation Graduate Research Fellow at the University of California, Irvine, where she is pursuing a PhD in Developmental Psychology specialising in Psychology and Law and Quantitative Methods. Her work focuses on children and families' experiences with the juvenile justice system. She has received fellowships and grants supporting her work from the American Psychology-Law Society, the Society for the Psychological Study of Social Issues and the Department of Health and Human Services. Kyndra was also awarded the UCI Social Ecology Dean's Award for Community Engagement in recognition of the public impact of her research with children. She has presented her research at national conferences including those held by the American Psychology-Law Society and the Society for Research in Child Development.

Julie Courvoisier completed her academic career at the University of Lausanne in Switzerland. She earned a Bachelor's in Psychology in 2007 and then a Master's of Law (MLaw) in Criminal Justice (with Criminology and Security) in 2009. She then became an assistant at the Institute of Criminology and Criminal Law of the School of Criminal Sciences at the university where she is now studying for her PhD regarding police interrogation in Switzerland. In addition, she has also worked as research manager on a preventative project regarding child sexual abuse.

Mireille Cyr gained a doctorate in psychology in 1984 and for 25 years has been a full Professor in the Psychology Department at the University of Montreal. She is the scientific director of the Centre for Interdisciplinary Research on Domestic Violence and Sexual Abuse and the co-holder of the Marie-Vincent Inter-university Research Chair for the sexual abuse of children. For 15 years, her primary focus of research was on child sexual abuse. She is particularly interested in the effects of sexual abuse on children and adolescents, parental support as a determinant of child's adaptation, and investigative interviews of alleged young victims of child sexual abuse.

Samuel Demarchi, PhD, is an Associate Professor at the Université Paris 8. His research interests deal with some of the main factors in criminal investigation (description and identification of criminals, lie detection, witness interviewing). His current research studies concern the detection of criminals according to their description and the improvement of lie detection by the use of uncontrolled cues (e.g. pupil diameters). He is also interested in the strength of evidence in the trial process (line-up fairness, DNA vs line-ups, sequential vs simultaneous line-ups, etc.).

Stephanie Denzel received an MEd in Special Education from George Mason University and an MA in Social Ecology from the University of California, Irvine. She also received a JD from the University of Michigan Law School, where she represented children and parents in child maltreatment cases as a student attorney. Her research interests include the development of maltreated children and the application of that research in legal settings. She is currently a practising attorney in Washington, DC.

Hervé Fabrizi is a forensic doctor in the Forensic Department of the Hospices Civils de Lyon. He is an expert to the Court of Appeal of Lyon, the Administrative Court of Appeal of Lyon and the International Criminal Court in The Hague. He has extensive experience in the field of care for victims of violence and also ballistics. For several years he has taught forensic medicine at the Lyon Est medical school.

Ivar A. Fahsing is a Detective Superintendent and Assistant Professor at the Norwegian Police University College. He has earlier published in the fields of investigative interviewing, eyewitness testimony, detective skills, detectives' decision-making, knowledge management and organised crime. He has appeared as an expert witness in courts and has for several years conducted training of law-enforcement personnel throughout Europe and Asia. He has 15 years of experience as a homicide detective in the Oslo Police department and at the National Criminal Investigation Service of Norway.

Laurent Fanton is a forensic doctor in the Forensic Department of the Hospices Civils de Lyon. He is an expert to the Court of Appeal and the Administrative Court of Appeal of Lyon. He has extensive experience in the field of care for victims of violence and also forensic toxicology. He is also Professor of Forensic Medicine at the Lyon Est medical school and is attached to the biomedical imaging research laboratory CREATIS.

Raquel Veludo Fernandes completed her Master's in Psychology of Justice and Deviant Behaviour at the Catholic University of Portugal, Porto. Raquel is a graduate in the Psychopathology and Psychotherapy of Children and Adolescents by the Portuguese Institute of Psychology. She has previous professional experience in the field of forensic psychology and in the psychological counselling of children, adolescents and adults. Since 2013 Raquel has been a researcher at the National Institute of Legal Medicine and Forensic Sciences, North Branch, on a research project on the implementation of a forensic interview protocol for children who are victims, witnesses and offenders, supported by the Portuguese Science and Technology Foundation (FCT) and by the Operational Programme for Competitive Factors (COMPETE). She is a co-author of book chapters (published or in press) in the field of forensic psychology.

Francisco García recently graduated Summa Cum Laude in Psychology from the University of Chile in 2014 and has been working in the research team of Professor Carolina Navarro since 2011. During his time as Professor Navarro's research assistant, Francisco developed a strong interest in the area of investigative interviewing with child victims, and in particular investigative interview protocols and their components. Francisco is now working along with other professionals in developing an investigative interview model based on research, good practices and specific Chilean requirements.

Stuart Houston is a Detective Chief Inspector with the Police Service of Scotland, based within the Edinburgh Division. He has been a police officer since 1996 and has been involved in various criminal investigation roles including senior investigating officer for a number of homicides. Between 2008 and 2010, he also worked within the Detective Training Unit.

Nakissa Jahanbani received her Bachelor's degree in International Relations from American University, Washington DC, with a specialisation in international development and the Middle East. She gained extensive experience with US national security issues, human rights and international detainee policies and practices while working at Physicians for Human Rights' Anti-Torture Program. Prior to that, Ms Jahanbani researched and worked on issues concerning community development, poverty eradication and ethnic minorities in the Middle East. She is currently pursuing a PhD in Political Science at the State University of New York at Albany.

Kristina Kepinska Jakobsen is a Psychologist and Assistant Professor at the Norwegian Police University College with responsibility for developing and conducting postgraduate studies in investigative interviewing. In addition, she is a PhD student at the Faculty of Law doing research on the investigative interviewing of traumatised witnesses. She has previously worked at the Danish National Police Board as a researcher and teacher.

Eunkyung Jo is Professor of Psychology at Hallym University in South Korea. Her research focuses on investigative interviewing and the detection of deception. As the current president of the Korean Association of Psychology and Law, she is leading developments in the application of research findings to criminal justice practices in South Korea.

Kristjan Kask has a PhD in Forensic Psychology from the University of Leicester, UK, and is currently a researcher at the Institute of Public Law at the University of Tartu as well as Associate Professor in Psychology in the Institute of Psychology at Tallinn University, Estonia. He is an accredited clinical psychologist specialising in cognitive-behavioural therapy. His research interests are the investigative interviewing of child and adult victims and witnesses, factors influencing eyewitness issues, adolescents' use of alcohol and issues regarding military psychology. He has conducted several training programmes with police investigators, prosecutors, judges and child protection workers about the principles of investigative interviewing of child victims and witnesses. He has published papers in several international peer-reviewed journals.

Carmit Katz is an Assistant Professor at the Bob Shapell School of Social Work at Tel Aviv University, Israel. She received her PhD in 2007 and continued to work as a research associate at Cambridge University, UK. Her studies have been published in leading journals, and she co-edited the updated version of the important book *Children's Testimony: A Handbook of Psychological Research and Forensic Practice* (2nd edn) by Wiley. Katz is intensively developing and disseminating practices and training for child forensic interviewers in Israel as well as practitioners within the forensic context (such as lawyers and judges).

David La Rooy received his BA, MSc and PhD degrees from the University of Otago in New Zealand. In 2004 he accepted a Post-Doctoral Research Fellowship at the National Institutes of Health (NIH) in Maryland, USA, and received specialist police training on child forensic interviewing, as well as training in the assessment of the quality of investigative interviews conducted with children alleging abuse. Dr La Rooy provides specialist training to police, social workers, solicitors, lawyers, advocates, sheriffs and judges. He was awarded a Scottish Institute for Policing Research Lectureship at the University of Abertay, Dundee, Scotland, in 2008, and in 2014 received the Academic Excellence Award from the iIIRG. He has co-edited two volumes for the Wiley Series in the Psychology of Crime, Policing and Law.

Michael E. Lamb is Professor of Psychology at the University of Cambridge and editor-in-chief of *Psychology, Public Policy and Law*. His current research focuses on forensic interviewing and the factors affecting children's adjustment. He and his colleagues have shown how developmentally sensitive interviewing improves the amount and quality of information obtained from young victims, witnesses and offenders in investigative settings.

Decio Mettifogo, PhD, is a highly experienced Professor of Social Psychology at the University of Chile. He has over 30 years of experience in the design, evaluation and implementation of public policies in the areas of drugs and crime prevention and youth justice. Decio has been part of interdisciplinary and multicultural teams in Latin America implementing management skills and communication and planning programmes for the social reintegration of young offenders.

R. Dian D. Muniroh is a Lecturer at the Department of English Education, Indonesia University of Education (Universitas Pendidikan Indonesia/UPI). She earned her undergraduate and Master of Humanities (Linguistics) degrees from UPI. Her main research interests are pragmatics, socio-linguistics, critical discourse analysis and forensic linguistics. She has focused her recent research projects on deception detection and investigative interviewing. In 2012, she received a Visiting Fellowship from UPI to work with Dr Georgina Heydon, a Senior Lecturer and Director of the Criminal Justice Postgraduate Program, RMIT University on a special project for detecting deception. She is currently involved in two forensic linguistics projects funded by the Ministry of Education and Culture, the Republic of Indonesia, i.e. Police Report vs Suspect Confessions During Police Investigations and Detecting Deception in Interviews in Indonesian Contexts. She has presented papers and published articles on pragmatics, critical discourse analysis and forensic linguistics. She is also an instructor in the training programme for Indonesian police officers to improve police competencies, particularly in deception detection.

Makiko Naka PhD is Professor of Psychology at Hokkaido University in Sapporo, Japan. She has conducted research on developmental and cognitive psychology, including language acquisition, indirect speech acts, everyday memory, eyewitness testimony and investigative interviews. Since 1992, she has been asked to appear as an expert witness on the credibility of eyewitness testimony and interviews of children. In 2008, she started a project to develop a training programme on investigative interviews and has trained more than 2,000 professionals. She is currently a director of Psychology and Human Science, a project supported by Grant-in-Aid for Scientific Research on Innovative Areas by the Japanese Ministry of Education, Culture, Sports, Science and Technology.

Carolina Navarro is a Professor at the University of Chile, teaching on juridical psychology, victimology and sexual violence. As a researcher her work has been focused on the clinical consequences of sexual abuse and the psychodiagnostic and credibility assessment of sexually abused children. Nowadays, her interests are in best techniques for interviewing child victims and the prevention of secondary victimisation. Carolina is also the Director of the Childhood and Justice Research Group, an interdisciplinary research team that studies the situation of Chilean children in the legal system. In addition, she has participated as an expert advisor in public policy of childhood and victims in Chile.

Annabelle Nicol is a PhD student at the University of Abertay, Dundee, Scotland. Her research focuses on the training of investigative interviewers of children and assessing the quality of role-play training interviews with adult actors as well as field interviews. She has been trained to analyse, code and assess the quality of forensic interviews. She works closely with a number of police jurisdictions in Scotland delivering inputs to their child forensic interviewing courses and participating in their practical role-play interviewing exercises.

Mahnaz Parakand attended Tehran University Law School, one of the most prestigious universities in Iran. While attending the school in 1980, she was arrested in a demonstration. During her interrogation, she did not have access to a lawyer and was severely tortured. Two years after her release, she returned to school and finished her law degree. In 2001, immediately after being awarded her licence, Ms Parakand began as a human rights lawyer in defence of prisoners of consciousness and human rights activists in Iran. In the aftermath of the 2009 elections, she was forced to leave the country. Since then, Ms Parakand has continued her activities in defence of human rights and establishing the order of law in Iran. During her presence in Norway, Ms Parakand has written several books as both principal and co-author, including *The Accused Rights in the Iranian Criminal Justice System* and *Women's Rights in Iran*. In addition, her articles addressing the labour law, the criminal law and the criminal procedure law have been published on various Iranian websites and journals. Ms Parakand works with the United Nations Special Rapporteur for Human Rights in Iran, Ahmad Shahid, regarding the human rights violations in Iran.

Pierre Patiny is a Superintendent of Police in Belgium. He began as a policeman in 1972 and he has been a criminal investigator since 1980. He has always been interested in the issue 'interviewing'. In 1997 he attended an intensive programme of instruction in Québec regarding the non-suggestive interviewing of minors and is still using this technique. Since 2001, he has been an instructor in the techniques of investigative interviews at the National Criminal Investigation School as well as in the technique of audio-visual interviewing of minors. As an expert at the Council of Europe in 2003, he gave classes at the magistrates' school in Albany. In 2010 and 2011, he worked at the national magistrates' school in Paris. He regularly participates in meetings and conferences and provides teaching as an expert and instructor in the field of recording the words of minors in a criminal framework.

Tinkara Pavšič Mrevlje, PhD, is a Lecturer in Forensic Psychology at the Faculty of Criminal Justice and Security, University of Maribor, Slovenia. She started her teaching work at the Faculty in 2009 as an assistant lecturer. In 2013 she successfully defended her PhD thesis in clinical psychology in which she studied post-traumatic symptomatology in crime scene investigators. Her main focus of research remains police trauma, but she is additionally interested in the topics of elderly victims of crime and teenage violence towards parents.

Carlos E. Peixoto has a PhD in Psychology from the University of Porto, Portugal. He is a Forensic Psychologist in the Northern Branch of the Portuguese National Legal Medicine and Forensic Sciences Institute (INMLCF, IP) with extensive experience on forensic psychological assessment of criminal, family, civil and labour law cases. He is also the lead researcher on a research project on the implementation of a forensic interview protocol for children who are victims, witnesses and offenders, supported by the Portuguese Science and Technology Foundation (FCT) and the Operational Programme for Competitive Factors (COMPETE) and conducted in the INMLCF and in the Faculty of Medicine of the University of Porto. Carlos is also a Researcher at the Centre for Studies in Human Development (CEDH) of the Catholic University of Portugal (Oporto Regional Centre), an Invited Auxiliary Professor at the Health Sciences High Institute – North/CESPU, and a trainer and consultant on investigative interviewing in the public and private sector in organisations such as the police, the judiciary and insurance companies.

Francesco Pompedda, MSc, graduated from the University of Turin, Italy, having specialised in forensic psychology and is currently pursuing his PhD in psychology at the Åbo Akademi University, Turku, Finland. He is also employed by the psychology department at the Åbo Akademi University as a research assistant. He is a member of LEPÅ: Legal Psychology Research Group at Åbo Akademi University, and is responsible for designing EIT software in the intensive professional training programme 'Interviewing Alleged CSA Victims with EIT (Empowering Interviewer Training)' at SSF Rebaudengo in Turin, Italy.

Heather Price is an Associate Professor of Psychology at the University of Regina, Canada. Her research on children's memory development is funded by the Natural Sciences and Engineering Research Council of Canada, the Social Sciences and Humanities Research Council of Canada and the Canada Foundation for Innovation. Dr Price is an instructor for the Saskatchewan Police College's Child Abuse Investigator's Course and has consulted on cases involving allegations of child physical and sexual abuse. Dr Price has published more than 30 articles in the areas of children's memory and credibility, investigative interviewing, eyewitness testimony and cognitive biases in investigations.

Jodi A. Quas is Professor of Psychology and Social Behaviour at the University of California, Irvine. She received her PhD in 1998 from the University of California, Davis, and completed postdoctoral training at the University of California, Berkeley. Much of her work focuses on memory development in high-risk children, particularly those who have suffered maltreatment. She has addressed important questions regarding the effects of stress on children's memory and suggestibility and on optimal methods of interviewing suspected victims to elicit complete and accurate accounts. In other work, she has examined the effects of stress and adversity on children's socio-emotional functioning and the consequences of legal involvement and testifying in court on child victims. She has received numerous awards for her contributions to science and policy regarding treatment of suspected child victims and for her efforts mentoring students.

Hossein Raeesi is an attorney and an expert on Iran's justice system. Born and raised in Iran, Raeesi has experience in criminal and civil law, but his main focus is on human rights. For over 20 years he has defended hundreds of clients, with more than 50 on death row. He was part of the Board of Directors of the Bar Association and was active in training young lawyers. He founded the Nedayeh Edalat Association (Voice of Justice) and worked with numerous other NGOs in conducting workshops for the community in partnership with domestic and international organisations. His private practice in Shiraz, Iran, was a safe haven for the political, religious and LGBs, children, women and ethnic minorities who were at risk of prison sentences. Due to persecution from the Iranian government, Raeesi was forced to leave Iran in 2012. Since relocating to Toronto, Canada, he has advocated for judicial reform in Iran in over 30 articles, legal commentaries and a book on justice for children. He has also created online Iranian law courses, made appearances in the media and lent his expertise in Iranian law and culture to organisations like the United Nations, Amnesty International and the Iran Human Rights Documentation Center. For more information visit http://www.hosseinraeesi.com.

Catarina Ribeiro has a degree in Psychology from the Faculty of Psychology and Educational Sciences at the University of Porto, Portugal (1999) and a Master's in the Psychology of Deviant Behaviour: Violence and Victims (2007) from the same university. She is finishing her PhD dissertation in psychology under the title 'Judicial Decision Making in Child Abuse Cases: Psychological Processes and Judges' Experiences'. Since 2007 she has been a Lecturer at the Catholic University of Porto (Faculty of Education and Psychology and Faculty of Law) and at the Institute for Biomedical Sciences Abel Salazar – University of Porto. She is a Forensic Psychologist Expert at the Portuguese National Institute of Legal Medicine and Forensic Sciences, where she performs psychological forensic assessments on criminal, family, civil and labour cases. Catarina has a wide experience as a trainer of professionals who work in the context of justice (e.g. judges, lawyers, public prosecutors, police, doctors and child protection system professionals). She is author and co-author of several scientific publications related to child abuse, psychological forensic assessment, forensic interview and other forensic psychology issues.

Anne Ridley, PhD, is a co-editor of *Suggestibility in Legal Contexts: Psychological Research and Forensic Implications* (2013). In addition to research on suggestibility in adults and children, she conducts research on vulnerable witnesses including juror perceptions, initial interview methods and cross examination. Anne Ridley is a Principal Lecturer at London South Bank University.

Imke Rispens is a psychologist and works as a behavioural scientist and investigative psychologist at the Police Academy in the Netherlands. She studied clinical psychology and neuropsychology and graduated in the field of the reliability of eyewitness statements and person recognition. At the Police Academy Imke teaches detectives about topics concerning psychology and law and investigation: witness and suspect interview techniques (children and adults), cold cases, missing persons, eyewitness identification procedures, false allegations, false confessions and sexual abuse cases. She coordinates training courses in interviewing techniques for vulnerable persons and supervises interviews of vulnerable persons in police practice. Her expertise is in how to deal with interviews that involve vulnerable witnesses and suspects. She is a guest lecturer at the Training and Study Centre for the Judiciary and teaches public prosecutors and judges about eyewitness statements and interviewing vulnerable witnesses.

Kim Roberts is a Professor at Wilfrid Laurier University, Canada. Dr Roberts worked at the National Institute of Health with Dr Michael Lamb while the NICHD interviewing protocol was being developed. Dr Roberts has received grants from the Natural Sciences and Engineering Research Council, the Social Sciences and Humanities Research Council, the Canadian Foundation for Innovation, the Department of Justice and the Australian Research Council. She works with police and social workers in many countries, and taught on the Interviewing Offences Against Children course at the Ontario Police College for eight years. She was awarded the Premier's Research Excellence Award.

Emma Roos af Hjelmsäter, PhD, is a Senior Lecturer at the University of Gothenburg, Sweden. She conducts research within the field of legal psychology, with a particular focus on eyewitness psychology, memory and children in the legal system. She teaches psychology at Bachelor's, Master's and PhD levels, and regularly gives lectures to Swedish prosecutors, judges and police investigators.

Vittorio Maria Rossini holds a degree in Law and has been a lawyer of the Turin Bar since 2002, practising criminal law. In addition to his legal practice, he is an active participant of the Scientific Commission of the Turin Bar Association. He has experience in teaching for many organisations throughout the legal community. He works as a consultant and an instructor for UNICRI (the United Nations Interregional Crime and Justice Research Institute). He also teaches courses for the School of Professional and Legal Ethics Training of the Turin Bar Association and the 'Camera Penale' of Piedmont.

Massimo Scarabello is currently a Judge at the Court of Cuneo, dealing with civil law matters, from real estate law to contract law. Up until December 2014 Massimo served as a Judge for Preliminary Investigations at the Court of Turin. The author is involved in a collaboration with the intergovernmental institution Eurocontrol, which provides various services to air traffic management. He is counsel for the Just Culture policy and coordination between criminal investigations and safety investigations carried out when incidents or accidents occur. He offers a judiciary point of view and expertise on the matter of interactions between the two fields. Twice a year the author is invited to the Brussels headquarters of Eurocontrol to present seminars and courses covering this topic.

Aurélien Schaller completed his academic career at the University of Lausanne in Switzerland. He first obtained a Master's in Psychology in 2006 and then a Master's of Law (MLaw) in Criminal Justice (with Criminology and Security) in 2008. After that, he became a probation assistant/psychologist at the Probation Service of Neuchâtel, before joining the judicial police as a scientific investigator/psycho-criminologist in the same canton. In addition to this work, he is completing his PhD research into risk assessment and management.

Adrian J. Scott is an Associate Director of the Sellenger Centre for Research in Law, Justice and Social Change, and a Lecturer in the School of Law and Justice at Edith Cowan University, Perth, Australia. His research interests include investigative interviewing and eyewitness testimony.

Lilian Milnitsky Stein is a Professor in the Psychology Postgraduate Department, Pontifical Catholic University of Rio Grande do Sul, Porto Alegre, Brazil. She is an Accredited Investigator (Grantee of Research Productivity level 1) by the Brazilian National Council for Scientific and Technological Development (CNPq). Lilian obtained her PhD at the University of Arizona in the USA in 1998, having first taken her Master's degree a the University of Toronto, Canada, in 1989. Her laboratory in Brazil has pioneered both research on eyewitness testimony as well as investigative interviewing training with police officers and forensic professionals.

Anaïs Taddeï is a PhD candidate in the CHArt Lab in Paris. Her field of interest concerns social cognition (stereotypes) and cognitive (visual attention) processing in criminal detection and identification, using eyetracking tools. Focusing on description methods (obtained by eyewitnesses) in natural and complex situations, her approach is based on signal detection theory in criminal detection tasks.

Stefania Tamasan is a Master's graduate student in Social Psychology at the Université Paris 8. Stefania's diploma paper focused on the study of the quantitative efficacy of an interviewing method for person description (Person Description Interview). Partial results of her paper were presented at the 7th Annual Conference and Masterclass 2014 of iIIRG, Lausanne.

Jane Tudor-Owen is a PhD student at Edith Cowan University, Perth, Australia, and works as the project manager for the Criminal Justice Review Project in the Sellenger Centre for Research in Law, Justice and Social Change. Outside of her PhD research analysing recruitment interviewing practices she is also interested in research examining wrongful conviction.

Jannie van der Sleen is an investigative and legal psychologist. She owns Kinterview, a consulting agency on investigative interviewing, and has done so for the past 13 years. Before that she worked at the Police Academy of the Netherlands for 15 years. She trains, coaches and supervises detectives on the investigative interviewing of witnesses and suspects. She is an expert in the field of vulnerable witnesses and suspects (minors, learning disabled, mentally disordered). She also works as an expert court witness in cases in which (most often vulnerable) witnesses or suspects are involved. She reports on the value of the statements of the witnesses or suspects in these cases.

Renate Volbert is a Research Fellow at the Institute of Forensic Psychiatry, Charité Berlin, Germany, and a Professor in the Department of Psychology at the Free University Berlin, Germany. She got her diploma in psychology from the University of Bielefeld, her PhD from the Technical University of Berlin and the Venia legendi from the Free University of Berlin. She is licensed as a Specialist in Legal Psychology. Professor Volbert has been a member of the Executive Committee (1999–2009) and chair (2007–9) of the Psychology and Law Division of the German Psychological Association and is currently (since 2014) president elect of the European Association of Psychology and Law. Her main research interests are credibility assessment, suggestibility, secondary victimisation and false confessions. She often appears as a court-appointed expert witness on credibility assessment.

Genevieve Waterhouse is a PhD researcher at London South Bank University. Having completed her MSc at the University of Leicester with a dissertation examining the use of support in child interviews, she is continuing to research this topic during her PhD. Genevieve is the International Investigative Interviewing Research Group's student representative.

Nina J. Westera is a Research Fellow whose research examines how understandings in psychology can be used to improve criminal justice practice. Her area of expertise is investigative interviewing and criminal investigation, with a particular interest in the investigative and evidential interviewing of adult complainants in cases of sexual and violent offending. Nina's career began as an officer in the New Zealand Police, where she investigated serious crime and implemented evidence-based policy and practice for the interviewing of witnesses and suspects. She has educated and advised police officers, lawyers and judges about investigative interviewing.

Rachel Wilcock is a Lecturer in Psychology at the University of Winchester, UK. Eliciting accurate eyewitness evidence is her major research interest, in particular investigating methods to improve the performance of vulnerable witnesses (children, those with intellectual disability and adults aged 60 and over). She is co-investigator on a grant of over £400,000 to develop methods to help child witnesses with autistic spectrum disorder give their best evidence. She has published widely in international peer-reviewed journals on the subject of identification and interviewing procedures.

Misun Yi, PhD, studied at the Department of Psychology at the University of Cambridge. Her research interests focus on investigative interviewing with sexually abused child victims in South Korea.

Rachel Zajac is a Senior Lecturer in the Psychology Department at the University of Otago, New Zealand. Her research interests encompass children's and adults' eyewitness testimony, social influences on memory and psychological factors in the interpretation of forensic evidence. Dr Zajac is frequently called on to advise New Zealand police officers, legal practitioners, forensic scientists and policy-makers on the psychological science behind criminal investigations. She is closely involved with the New Zealand Police, where she contributes to benchmarking practice, procedural review and training.

Angelo Zappalà is a psychologist, clinical criminologist, cognitive behavioural therapist and Honorary Judge Tribunal for Minors of Turin. He is also Professor of Criminal Psychology, CRIMELAB, SSF Rebaudengo, Torino, Italy, and Professor of Investigative Criminology, Università di Alessandria, Italy. In addition Angelo is a member of LEPÅ: Legal Psychology Research Group at Åbo Akademi University, and a co-founder and member of HYPOTHESES (Forensic Psychology Consulting).

Sabina Zgaga, PhD, graduated from the Faculty of Law, University of Ljubljana, Slovenia, in 2006 with the thesis 'The Relation Between the Constitution and the Theoretical Model of the Criminal Procedure'. In her doctoral study of criminal law at the same faculty she focused on international criminal law, especially its general aspect. For this she has been granted two Max Planck Institute for Foreign and International Criminal Law fellowships. Her doctoral thesis from April 2011 ('Necessity and Duress in International Criminal Law'), for which she received the United Nations Association for Slovenia award, focused on the regulation of necessity and duress (and other related issues such as self-defence, military necessity and superior order) in international, comparative and Slovenian criminal law. Currently she is working at the Faculty of Criminal Justice and Security, University of Maribor, Slovenia, as a Senior Lecturer. Her research work is focused on international criminal law and criminal substantive and procedural law.

Acknowledgements

The editors would like to thank Anna Day, University of Derby, UK, for all her hard work from the start of this project in helping the editors and chapter authors to keep to deadlines and towards the final completion of the two volumes. In addition, special thanks must go to Millie Fuller, Newcastle University, UK, for helping to bring the project to completion. Thanks also to Kaneko Shobo for their permission to reproduce previously published material in Chapter 4 of this book. Finally, many thanks go to Heidi Lee at Routledge for all her work in ensuring that the editors were on course to complete this volume.

Abbreviations

ABE	Achieving Best Evidence
ACPO	Association of Chief Police Officers
ACT	Australian Capital Territory
AFP	Australian Federal Police
aIAT	autobiographical Implicit Association Test
ANZCoPP	Australia New Zealand Council of Police Professionalisation
ANZPAA	Australia New Zealand Policing Advisory Agency
APAV	Associação de Apoio à Vítima
APSAC	American Professional Society on the Abuse of Children
AVR	Audio and Visual Recording
BAI	Behavioral Analysis Interview
BARS	Behaviourally Anchored Rating Scale
BOQ	Behaviour Observation Questions
CAC	Child Advocacy Centres
CBCA	Criteria-based Content Analysis
CCP	Chinese Communist Party
CCP	Code of Criminal Procedure
CCTV	Closed-Circuit Television
CFIP	CornerHouse Forensic Interview Protocol
CGC	Child Guidance Centers
CGF	Concept Général de Formation
CI	Cognitive Interview
CIA	Central Intelligence Agency
CIB	Criminal Investigation Branch
CID	Criminal Investigation Department
CIDE	Center for Economic Research and Teaching (Mexico)
CLPS	Sri Lanka Police Service
CM	Conversation Management
CNJ	Conselho Nacional de Justiça
CNPCJR	Comissão Nacional de Protecção de Crianças e Jovens em Risco
COI	Case-oriented Interview
CoP	College of Policing
CPA	Criminal Procedure Act

CPC	Canadian Police College
CPC	Criminal Procedure Code
CPL	Criminal Procedure Law
CPPS	Code de Procédure Pénale Suisse
CPS	Code Pénal Suisse
CPT	Committee for the Prevention of Torture
CPTU	Central Police Training Unit (UK)
CR	Cued Recall
CRC	Convention on the Rights of the Child
CREAS	Center for Referral of Social Services
CRIME	Custody, Rights, Investigation, Management and Evidence
CSA	Child Sexual Abuse
DCI	Detective Chief Inspector
DCM	Dialogical Communication Method
DFS	Direccion Federal de Seguridad
DIPD	Dirección de Investigaciones para la Prevención de la Delincuencia
DMF	Declarações para Memória Futura
DNA	Deoxyribonucleic Acid
DNE	Developmental Narrative Elaboration
DPER	Death Penalty Evidence Rules
DSER	National Research School (Belgium)
ECHR	European Court of Human Rights
ECI	Enhanced Cognitive Interview
ECTS	European Credit Transfer and Accumulation System
FACV	Federal Act on Assistance to Crime Victims
FBI	Federal Bureau of Investigation
FCT	Science and Technology Foundation (Portuguese)
FLETC	Federal Law Enforcement Training Center
FNPP	First Nations Policing Program
GC	Guardianship Council
GIS	General Interviewing Strategy
GSS	Gudjonsson Suggestibility Scale
GVG	Gerichtsverfassunggesetz
GWSC	Behavioural Science Section (of the Belgian Police)
HIG	High-value Detainee Interrogation Group
HMA	Her Majesty's Advocate (Scotland)
HO	Home Office (UK)
HUMINT	Human Intelligence
IBGE	Instituto Brasileiro de Geografia e Estatística
ICCT	International Centre for Counter Terrorism
ICITAP	International Criminal Investigative Training Assistance Program
ICPC	Indonesian Criminal Procedure Code
iIIRG	International Investigative Interviewing Research Group
INP	Indonesian National Police
IPC	Islamic Penal Code

IPEA	National Institute for Applied Economic Research
IQ	Intelligence Quotient
IRGC	Iranian Islamic Evolutionary Guard Corps
IRI	Investigation Relevant Information
IRRD	Interrogation-related Regulatory Decline
ISP	Institut Suisse de Police
IVS	Interviewing Vulnerable Suspects
KNPA	Korean National Police Agency
KREATIV	K – communication; R – due process; E – ethical and empathetic; A – active awareness; T – trust through transparency; I – information access; V – based on science (Norway)
KRIPOS	National Criminal Investigation Service (Norway)
LAVI	Loi fédérale sur l'aide aux victimes d'infractions
LCP	Law of Criminal Proceedings
LPI	La Police Intégrée
LTE	Education Custody Law (Portugal)
MAI	Ministry of Home Affairs (Portugal)
MGEF	Ministry of Gender Equality and Family
MP	Ministerio Público
NAO	National Audit Office
NBI	National Bureau of Investigations
NCANDS	National Child Abuse and Neglect Data System
NCF	National Crime Faculty
NCO	Non-commissioned Officer
NEO PI-R	Neuroticism, Extraversion, Openness to experience, Personality, Inventory – Revised
NIAVE	Specific Victims Intervention and Support Team (Portugal)
NICA	National Intelligence Coordinating Agency
NICHD	National Institute of Child Health and Human Development
NP	National Police
NPA	National Police Agency
NPIA	National Policing Improvement Agency
NSW	New South Wales
NT	Northern Territory
NZ	New Zealand
NZMoJ	New Zealand Ministry of Justice
OD	Open Depth
OPD	Office of the Public Defender
OPP	Office of the Public Prosecutor
PACE	Police and Criminal Evidence Act
PADR	Personne appelée à donner des renseignements
PC	Penal Code
PCFQCE	Preparation, Contact and orientation, Free report, Questioning, Conclusion, Evaluation
PCPC	Portuguese Criminal Procedure Code

PCPI	Person Called to Provide Information
PEACE	Planning and preparation, Engage and explain, Account, clarify and challenge, Closure, Evaluation
PIP	Professionalising the Investigation Programme
PM	Pubblico Ministero (public prosecutor)
PNP	Philippine National Police
PNS	National Security Plan (Belgium)
POI	Person-oriented Interview
POLRI	Indonesian Republic National Police
POPP	Police Officers and Public Prosecutors
PP	Public Prosecutor
PPC-GRT	Procedure for Penal Codes in General and Revolutionary Trials
PPS	Prison Population Survey
PRC	People's Republic of China
PRI	Partido Revolucionario Institucional
PRICE	Preparation, Rapport, Information gathering, Confirming the content, Evaluation and action
ProGREAI	Processus General de Recueil des Entretiens, Auditions et Interrogatoires
PSB	Public Safety Bureau
PTI	Professional Training in Interviewing
Qld	Queensland
RATAC	Rapport, Anatomy identification, Touch inquiry, Abuse scenario, and Closure
RCMP	Royal Canadian Mounted Police
RNC	Royal Newfoundland Constabulary
SA	South Australia
SAI	Self-administered Interview
SARCS	Sexual Assault Referral Centres
SCA	Statute of the Child and Adolescent
SCAN	Scientific Content Analysis
SCPC	Swiss Criminal Procedure Code
SINPIA	Società italiana di neuropsichiatria dell'infanzia, and dell'adolescenza
SIP	Swiss Institute of Police
SISF	Società Italiana di Science Forensi
SLPS	Sri Lanka Police Service
SNS	Social Networking Services
SOCIT	Sexual Offences and Child Abuse Investigation Team
SOP	Standard Operating Procedures
SPC	Supreme People's Court
STD	Sexually Transmitted Disease
STI	Sexually Transmitted Infection
StPO	Strafprozessordnung
SUE	Strategic Use of Evidence

SVA	Statement Validity Analysis
TAM	Techniques for Interviewing Minors
Tas	Tasmania
TID	Terrorist Investigation Department
TMR	Tactical Method of Reasoning
TUE	Tactical Use of Evidence
UDP	Universidad Diego Portales
UK	United Kingdom of Great Britain and Northern Ireland
UN	United Nations
UNICEF	United Nations Children's (Emergency) Fund
USA	United States of America
VAJA	Vezarat-e Ettela'at Jomhuri-ye Eslami-ye Iran (Ministry of Intelligence of the Islamic Republic of Iran)
Vic	Victoria
ViCLAS	Violent Crime Linkage Analysis System
VKGZ	Interviewing Vulnerable Witnesses in Sexual Abuse Cases (Netherlands)
VRI	Video Recorded Interview
VWA	Victim/Witness Assistant
WA	Western Australia
WPL	Witness Protection Law
ZeG	Zelfrapportage voor getuigen

Introduction

International developments in practice for victim and witness interviews

Gavin E. Oxburgh, Trond Myklebust, Allison D. Redlich and David Walsh

Investigative interviewing is a key feature both in the investigation of crime as well as in the way that it can enable justice. Given how essential interviewing and interrogation is to law enforcement agencies internationally, it is surprising how little we know of the techniques and practices used across the world. Policing has, without doubt, changed over the past century, but the majority of our general understanding is primarily stereotypical presentations from television shows or movies, many of which are unreliable as a means of understanding what actually happens when victims, witnesses and suspects are interviewed by law enforcement investigators. Those of us within the police and academic fields of police science, psychology, criminology, law and others see an urgent need for providing balanced information on the various techniques used in law enforcement.

In interviewing victims, witnesses and suspects, law enforcement are faced with a challenging task. It is beyond dispute that memory fades over time, that crimes often occur under conditions that impede accurate and complete recollection of events and that there are numerous reasons for people to be less than forthcoming (especially suspects) and reluctant to speak with law enforcement. However, the need for victims, witnesses and suspects to share their experiences – that is, be interviewed and/or interrogated – has always been and will remain essential. Despite advancements in forensic science and technology, the need to rely on humans to both ask and answer questions is unlikely to diminish. Thus the ability to obtain accurate, comprehensive and up-to-date information about criminal happenings remains of great import.

In this volume, concerned with the interviewing of victims of and witnesses to crime, the importance of effective questioning techniques was brought to the forefront in the 1980s and 1990s with a spate of unfounded child sexual abuse allegations, often originating in daycare settings and involving multiple children. For example, in Norway, the *Bjugn* case began with pre-school children alleging abuse by the daycare staff but then spread to allegations against others in the community, including the sheriff. This case, now labelled a ‘witch hunt’, resulted in financial compensation to the children and the alleged abusers (who were never prosecuted but rather believed to be innocent). Although this case now epitomises inappropriate and ineffective interviewing, another outcome was to create standardised and regularised methods of interviewing victims/witnesses and the training of law enforcement agencies. Several other countries, including the USA, South Korea and Denmark, went through similar experiences. That is, they experienced high-profile and often embarrassing cases of false allegations (or witch hunts), which in turn led to proposed reforms which sometimes were not adopted into practice. In contrast, some countries' methods of questioning alleged victims and witnesses of any age remain unchanged.

The editors and contributing authors of these volumes aim to provide you with the necessary information for an understanding of how law enforcement agencies around the world gain valuable information from victims, witnesses and suspects in criminal cases. To this end, we have gathered a distinguished collection of authors from over 25 countries around the world (including Asia, Australia, Europe, North America and South America), culminating in many years of specialist knowledge and practice. We believe these volumes provide readers with an in-depth coverage of the various interview and interrogation techniques used across the world, taking into account the two major types of legal system: adversarial and inquisitorial.

Adversarial versus inquisitorial legal systems

Between countries, there are many, and sometimes extensive, legal differences in the process of gathering forensically robust information. An inquisitorial system is where the court is actively involved in investigating the facts of the case. France is one country with an inquisitorial or non-adversarial[1] system. The main feature of the inquisitorial system is the function of the 'examining or investigating judge', who investigates serious crimes or complex inquiries in an inquisition or investigation of the crime. Judges can question victims, witnesses and suspects, order searches for evidence, declare the final verdict and decide on the punishment. Their role is not to prosecute the accused but to gather facts to reach the correct verdict, and as such their duty is to look for any and all evidence, incriminating or exculpatory.

In contrast, in adversarial systems, judges focus on the issue of the law and procedure and act as a referee in the arguments presented by the defence and prosecutor. Sometimes, juries decide on the matter of the presented facts according to the requirements in law. The prosecution services will be in charge of the cases presented for the court. However, the function of the prosecution services differs between countries. For most countries, the prosecution service is organised outside the police, such as in England and Wales, the USA, and South Africa. In England and Wales, the police will initiate the investigation and when the case is completed, it is sent to the Crown Prosecution Service for a decision to be made regarding whether there is a realistic chance of conviction and if it is in the public interest to proceed with a prosecution. In Sweden, the police initiate the investigation and make preliminary inquiries before sending it to the prosecutor who decides if there will be further investigation. In the Norwegian system, the police initiate the investigation with a representative of the prosecution authority as a formal leader in charge of the case. The present volumes do not intend to suggest whether an adversarial system is in some way 'better' than an inquisitorial system, but at this stage it is important to highlight to readers that a country's approach may well affect the interviewing practice found in that country.

The legal framework of the investigation will be one of the variables underlying differences in how investigative interviews or interrogations are conducted around the world. Other differences between practices in countries can be explained by a range of factors which may include economic, political, cultural, religious, socio-philosophical and historical traditions, which individually or collectively combine to shape the practices of investigators in any particular domain. Further, scientific advancements in our understanding of how victims, witnesses and suspects remember, discuss and choose to disclose events has played a large role in redefining interviewing and interrogation methods. However, as will become clear in these two volumes, countries, are aware of differing extents of scientific advancements; whereas some countries' policies are seemingly unaware of the research literature, other countries' policies are developed from and entrenched in the literature.

The editors wish to thank the many contributors for their efforts in shining a light on contemporary interviewing and interrogation practices throughout the world. Many of the chapters have not been extensively covered before (and some chapters not covered at all). Their contributions enable readers to develop both an international as well as a comparative perspective of developments worldwide in this important area of criminal investigation and its contribution to attaining justice.

Note

1. Some legal scholars consider inquisitorial misleading and prefer the word non-adversarial (M. A. Glendon, P. G. Carozza and C. B. Picker (2008) *Comparative Legal Traditions*. St Paul, MN: Thomson-West, p. 101).

Asia

1 The contemporary practices of Indonesian police interviewing of witnesses

R. Dian Dia-an Muniroh and
E. Aminudin Aziz

Interviewing witnesses is the cornerstone of the process of examination in the police office. The information from witnesses becomes so important that it may help investigators to establish a clear picture of a case being investigated and to reveal the truth behind it. It is also essential because it constitutes the basis for the investigators to write a police investigation report, which will be further used by prosecutors to officially accuse the alleged perpetrators of committing a crime. According to Indonesian Laws No. 8/1981 and No. 13/2006, witnesses are, 'People who can testify for the purposes of investigation, prosecution, and adjudication on a criminal case which they have heard, seen, or experienced themselves.'

A number of factors are believed to influence the success of information elicited from witnesses, including internal and external factors (e.g. Gudjonsson and Pearse, 2011). Internal factors include witnesses' willingness to share any relevant information, their motivation, age, memory, psychological condition and personalities (Hope *et al.*, 2011; Griffiths *et al.*, 2011). External factors relate to the investigators' beliefs and questioning practices. The main purpose of the police questioning witnesses is to extract details from them about what they saw, heard or experienced in conjunction with the crime under investigation. How the police interview witnesses can determine the accuracy and quality of the information given (see Dixon, 2010; Heydon, 2005; Wright and Alison, 2004; Vrij *et al.*, 2006). However, it is undeniable that, in practice, investigators are often not able to elicit facts or details from the witnesses. This is more likely due to their inability to formulate various types of questions intended to obtain such facts or details, or their misconduct in the treatment of witnesses, for instance by applying techniques involving force. Thus, the suspect of the crime could escape criminal charges.

The important role of witnesses in the world of justice is unquestionable and therefore the elicitation of information from them becomes critical. This chapter will address two main issues in conjunction with the practices of interviewing witnesses in Indonesia. On the one hand, this will look at the interviews as ascribed in legal documents, and on the other it will show how interviews have been practised by police investigators. Issues in the training for interviewing in the context of the Indonesian police will also be shown. In addition to using information from legal documents such as the Indonesian Criminal Procedure Code (ICPC) and the Article Re Indonesian National Police (INP), we also use interview data obtained from five senior police investigators.

Ascriptions from the laws

In Indonesia, the examination of witnesses by investigators is undertaken mainly by reference to Laws No. 8/1981 Re Indonesian Criminal Procedure Code (ICPC) and No. 2/2002 Re Indonesian National Police, Chapter V regarding the professional development of the police. The assessment of witnesses is regulated in more operational detail in the Regulations of Chief of Indonesian National Police No. 14/2012 Re Management of Criminal Investigation, No. 7/2006 Re Professional Codes of Conduct of the Indonesian National Police and No. 8/2009 Re Implementation of Human Rights Principles and Standards in the Task Performance of the Indonesian National Police. More technically, it is outlined in the Decree of Chief of Indonesian National Police No. 1205/IX/2000 regarding the Guidelines for Examination.

According to the above mentioned laws and regulations, the examination of case and expert witnesses can only be held in the investigators' office after they receive an official letter of summons. However, in a situation where the witnesses cannot comply with the summons twice due to strong reasons such as serious illness, the investigators may conduct the examination, either in the witness's residence or in hospital. During the examination, the witness shall provide information without fear of others or of receiving any kind of intimidation. In the Indonesian police setting, witness interviews are not video/audio-recorded but are typed. The investigators and the witnesses create the report together (cf. van Charldorp, 2011). Having posed a question to a witness, the investigator simultaneously listens to the participant and take some time to type the response. Once endorsed by the witness the report becomes part of the legal documentation which will be used and referred to by lawyers, prosecutors and judges in the courtroom. To this day, the Indonesian criminal justice system still relies heavily on this particular type of written report (cf. Westera *et al.*, 2011).

Historically, the practice of witness interviewing mentioned in the ICPC was greatly influenced by the criminal justice system operated by the Dutch during the colonial period. The *Inlandsch Reglement* codified in 1848 was in use up to its revision in 1941 and was known as the *Herzien Inlandsch Reglement*. Further, during the Japanese occupation, the *Herzien Inlandsch Reglement* was renamed the *Herzien Indonesisch Reglement*. Later, following the Indonesian independence, the *Herzien Indonesisch Reglement* was officially adopted and translated into Indonesian without changing or modifying the essence (Strang, 2008). It is clear at this stage that in terms of practice, Indonesia follows the civil law tradition and extends the Dutch legacy of criminal procedure.

The ICPC divides the procedures of justice into four distinct stages: (1) investigation; (2) prosecution; (3) (cross) examination in the court hearing; and (4) the implementation of the final court decision. Investigation is a sequential process, beginning with a preliminary investigation, submission of the notice of the commencement of the investigation, investigative activity and enquiries, examination, case conference, compilation of the investigation dossier, submission of the dossier to prosecutors, surrendering the suspect and evidence, and termination of the investigation. More specifically to the examination, it is conducted when the case concerned is formally declared a criminal action after preliminary investigations and a notice of commencement of investigation is submitted to prosecutors. This examination is aimed at gathering information from witnesses, expert witnesses and suspects so that the role of those accused and proof of a criminal action become obvious.

Essentially, present methods of investigation have changed significantly from the practices of the past, particularly since the separation of the police as one of the powers constituting the Indonesian National Armed Forces in April 1999. This followed the downfall of the Suharto New Order Era regime marking the beginning of the Reform Era. At that period of time, as part of the Armed Forces, the police were mandated to guard the state and nation. In so doing, the police used to be more militaristic. This greatly affected the process of investigations conducted by police officers when they were assigned to investigate criminal cases involving non-military suspects. Psychological oppression such as the use of offensive language, mockery and derisory comments or physical oppression such as torture, slaps while blindfolded, lashes, punches, scorches and burns from cigarette butts were often used by police investigators, especially when interrogating uncooperative suspects or witnesses and they wanted to draw the investigation session to an immediate conclusion. Nevertheless, as our informants have revealed, it cannot be denied that such oppressive investigatory practices still occur today, although they were also quick to say that such practices are only found in a very few locations and are only carried out by lower-rank assistant police investigators.

Following the separation, the Education and Training Institute as one of the supporting bodies of the Indonesian National Police was restructured and changed its name to the Police Education Institute. The Education Centre of Criminal Investigation is one of the service branches of the Institute, which arranges the development of police investigators' technical abilities in investigating criminal activities and identifying crime. Recently, to improve police investigators' performance, the headquarters of the Indonesian Police Force established a School of Police Inspectors for Criminal Investigation.

Following the Reform Era, legal reforms have been widely demanded, especially revision of the ICPC, to accommodate international human rights conventions. To achieve this purpose, in 2000, the government of Indonesia formed a Working Group consisting of government officials, practitioners and academics. Removal of the preliminary investigation stage and improvements in police/prosecutor cooperation are among the points proposed for consideration. These proposals have been submitted mainly to reduce redundancy in the criminal justice system so that the main business of tackling crime might not be delayed (Strang, 2008). Unfortunately, the proposed revision of the ICPC, to date, has not been ratified by the House of Representatives.

The ICPC does not explicitly mention the procedures to secure witnesses' rights. In response to these needs, the government of Indonesia issued Law No. 13/2006 Re Witnesses' Rights, Security and Protection. This regulation is intended to protect witnesses and victims so that they feel safe when giving evidence. The document spells out that the Protection of Witness and Victim Agency will decide which cases require protection. There are various types of protection which may be given to a witness, from the investigatory procedures to the implementation of the final court decision.

The rights of vulnerable witnesses are observed in Government Regulation No. 3/2008 Re the Provision of Special Service Room and Examination Procedures of Witnesses or Victims of a Crime. This service room protects vulnerable witnesses from the traumatic effects resulting from sexual abuse, human trafficking or domestic violence. Therefore the presence of this kind of room is expected to enhance the quality of information sought because it is anticipated that the witnesses will be (medically, psychologically, socially) put at ease. However, unlike the judicial system of England and Wales, the judicial process in Indonesia does not allow for the use of video interviews as evidence (Westera *et al.*, 2011).

Relevant literature

The practices of interviewing witnesses have garnered much attention not only from academics and researchers but also from practitioners in legal studies, psychology and linguistics (see, for example, Griffiths *et al.*, 2011; Hope *et al.*, 2011; Snook *et al.*, 2010; Vallano and Compo, 2011; Vrij *et al.* 2006; Wright and Alison, 2004). Two major issues always become of concern: miscarriages of justice and lack of interview training courses. The former deals with poor interviewing practices while the latter deals with inadequate supervision or evaluation.

Given that the interviewing of witnesses is intended to collect as much information as a witness can share, poor interviewing practices will only bring undesirable results, e.g. a decline in the amount of information the witnesses provide, an increase in inaccurate responses and a disruptive influence on the witnesses' psychological health. These unsalutary practices are marked by an absence of the development of rapport, talk dominated by the investigators and a high occurrence of closed questions including those that are leading or suggestive (Cederborg *et al.*, 2000; Fisher and Geiselman, 2010; Griffiths *et al.*, 2011; cf. Vallano and Compo, 2011). It is more likely that the interview begins with a set of formal questions about the witness's personal details (e.g. name, address). Following this, open-ended type questions are posed to reveal what happened (e.g. 'Tell me what happened'). Unfortunately, at this stage the witness is often unable to complete his/her narrative response because the investigator quickly moves on to a set of closed type questions addressing specific facts the investigator wants to confirm. The interview finally ends when the predetermined lists of question have all been addressed and no new information is added by the witness. Such practices have been prototypical among police investigators in many countries, for instance the UK (George and Clifford, 1992), Canada (Snook and Keating, 2011), Finland (Korkman *et al.*, 2006) and Sweden (Cederborg *et al.*, 2000).

The literature on witness interviewing has highlighted some measures that can be taken to improve the quality of witness interviewing practices: (1) promoting a humanitarian interviewing style instead of one based on domination (see Madsen, 2010); (2) developing interview protocols (see Fisher and Gieselman, 2010) and tools (see Hope *et al.*, 2011); and (3) intensifying formal training in interviewing witnesses (see Hill and Moston, 2010).

Madsen (2010) has conducted experimental research to investigate whether humanitarian and dominating interviewing styles have different effects on the search for information through the memory and psychological health of the witness. The amount of information retrieved by applying a humanitarian style is shown to be larger than that from a dominating style and the psychological well-being of the witness is better supported. This humanitarian style was in fact employed by Geiselman and his cohorts as the ideology behind developing protocols for interviewing witnesses. In 1984, they coined the term Cognitive Interview (CI) to encompass cognitive, social and communicative techniques to elicit information from witnesses (Geiselman *et al.*, 1984). The CI requires both the witness and the police investigator to have a shared feeling that the witness is not merely the provider of information for the investigator and the investigator is not purely the question producer; thus establishing rapport is essential to building a social bond between them. It also maintains accuracy of recall by encouraging the investigator to use open-ended question formats and reinstate contexts of an event cognitively, to ask the witness to report everything, to recount events in different orders and to change perspectives. This witness-centred procedure has been empirically proven as an effective interviewing method because it fully engages the witness in a detailed memory recall of the event.

Furthermore, drawing on the working principles of the CI, Hope *et al.* (2011) designed a tool to elicit a comprehensive account from witnesses, especially in a situation where the interview is delayed: the so-called Self-Administered Interview (SAI). As the quality of information from witnesses decreases while the waiting time for recall increases, the SAI functions to counteract the deleterious effects of the delay. Taking the form of a paper booklet, the SAI guides the witness through reporting the details of any incident witnessed through the seven sections provided, namely free recall, descriptions of people, sketches, other witnesses, vehicle details, witnessing conditions and other information.

The last measure identified to improve the police force's skills in questioning witnesses is improving the training for witness interviewing. The need for increased formal witness interviewing has been echoed by numerous researchers from such countries as the UK (Griffiths *et al.*, 2011), Canada (Snook and Keating, 2011) and Australia (Hill and Moston, 2011). They highlight the poor performance of the police investigators in interviewing witnesses. For instance, investigators apply a similar approach to interviewing witnesses as they do to interviewing suspects. That is, investigators, by exerting too much control in the interview – for example interrupting frequently and asking closed questions – inhibit the quality and completeness of the information witnesses are able to give. Another major issue related to the training for witness interviewing is the absence of supervision after the training. Even when training is available, it has not significantly affected interview performance (cf. Snook *et al.*, 2012). Griffiths and Milne (2006) insist that as a skill, interviewing absolutely needs regular maintenance, supervision and feedback.

Current practices

In interviewing witnesses, for the success of the practice, Indonesian police have to meet the standardised requirements and work with examinations published by the INP Headquarters. This section will address best practice in the three stages of the witness interview (i.e. pre-, during and post-interview), the emerging practice of involving academics during training and the unsupported practice in the interviews.

Current regulations require that investigations be conducted by police officers whose ranks are not lower than Second Police Inspector (equivalent to Second Lieutenant). This suggests that seniority and experience become so important that investigations will be thorough. These investigators can be assisted by a number of assistant investigators whose ranks must not be lower than Second Police Brigadier (equivalent to Second Sergeant). Appointments of these investigators are to be made by the District or Provincial Police Commanders. Nevertheless, the geography of the country and the limited number of senior investigators have always been critical issues. This has resulted in the investigation being carried out by inexperienced junior officers, making the overarching goals of the investigation only partly achieved.

Prior to the investigation, all investigators are required to prepare questions that conform with the content/material requirements of an investigation report, i.e. the report must demonstrate the answers to the *wh-* and *how* questions. In addition, the investigators have to decide which witnesses are to be categorised as primary, secondary and tertiary, according to their level of involvement or the facts they know. During the interview, to reveal facts objectively, the witnesses must be examined individually. To prove that the information from one witness is connected to another, the investigator can invite them to a confrontation session. The interview is valid when, in giving witness, the witnesses are healthy, free from threats and legally summonsed. The investigators are not allowed to intimidate or make threats physically, psychologically or sexually; torture the witnesses or suspects to obtain information from them; instruct or incite others to carry out torture; manipulate or falsify the information written in the investigation report; engineer the report to loosen or distort the facts; or elicit payments from anyone involved in the crime.

The Regulation of Indonesian Chief of Police (No. 8/2009) Article 27 outlines the conduct of police interviews. While some types of misconduct are often found, this regulation seems to have considered the rights of the examinees fully. The Article states, for example, that any police officer examining witnesses or suspects is obliged to allow opportunities for them to call and be accompanied by a lawyer before the interview commences. The investigators will also have to begin the examination by asking about the examinee's state of health and their readiness, and mention the status of the interviewee and the objectives of the interview. Questions to the interviewee have to made clearly, politely, understandably and relevant to the objectives of the interview. They also have to consider and value witnesses' rights to give information without restraint as well as to respect witnesses' rights to refuse to giving information related to their private lives as well as their job titles. Examinees are given the opportunity to rest, perform prayers or carry out other personal needs in accordance with the regulation.

Basically, the foci and sequences of questions during interviews are divided into three parts: (1) initial; (2) substantial and additional; and (3) final. The initial part focuses on the witness's personal details or identity. Substantial questions seek answers to the *wh-* and *how* questions of the criminal event, while additional questions are those developed from the substantial questions but are more concerned with eliciting answers on the background or factors triggering the criminal action. The final part concludes the questioning session with the opportunity for the witness to review the report prepared by the investigators during the interview, whether they wish to change, add or omit some information, and whether they are willing to sign the report. In so signing, the outcome of the witness's examination is as shown in the investigation report as approved by the witness.

When interviewing vulnerable witnesses, including children, an investigator must comply with Regulation No. 3/2008. The regulation requires that investigators should not wear formal uniforms and should use simple and understandable language (or even provide an interpreter if necessary), should not ask sensitive questions, should not force the witnesses to confess or answer questions and should listen carefully to everything the witness says. In some cases, witnesses might have uncorroborated evidence. This can happen in cases involving vulnerable witnesses or victims. This non-cooperative measure is often made when they find themselves at risk of disclosing the evidence. A case of organised crime involving prominent figures or other 'external powers', for instance, might put witnesses under pressure. Many witnesses choose not to explicitly mention the facts they actually do know due to intimidation from outside the investigation room. A rape experienced by a witness is another example where a witness may feel uncomfortable disclosing the evidence. Not only is s/he a witness, but s/he is also the victim. Being shamed and losing face are the main reasons for not wanting to disclose evidence: the social sanctions s/he will receive later will be so severe that s/he will prefer to remain silent. Thus, if such a case is taken to investigation, the investigator has to rely on the willingness of this vulnerable victim-witness to share the evidence in the investigation room.

There seems to be some difficulty obtaining full descriptions of a case in investigations involving children. Sometimes children feel oppressed and uncomfortable by the presence of strangers, and may be less forthcoming in disclosing the evidence they might have been exposed to. The linguistic and communicative competence of such witnesses becomes the main factor of difficulty with the potential of making a witness reluctant or decline when asked to witness before an investigator.

In some criminal cases, a witness can later become a suspect if police investigators are confident about the suspect's involvement in a case after obtaining at least two kinds of convincing evidence through the interviews they have conducted. It is this possibility that has made some witnesses hesitant to give witness before the investigators. However, they cannot escape such interviews as police investigators have the right in law to compel anyone to appear in the investigation room for interviews. Thus, in a case in which investigators have to interview a hesitant/reluctant case witness and they are fully confident that the witness has evidence regarding the case, they will find a way to collect as much information from the case witness as possible.

For example, when an investigator asked a hesitant janitor to explain the criminal incident he had witnessed, the janitor told the investigator that he could not explain the details because he was very nervous and felt insecure in doing so in the belief of receiving intimidation afterwards. The investigator explained repeatedly that as a witness he is protected by the law. Having understood the details about the protection that he might receive from the Witness and Victim Protection Agency, the janitor agreed to share his experience. However, rather than giving an oral explanation of the case, the janitor then provided a sketch plan about the place and the people involved in the incident.

The illustrations made by the janitor especially helped the investigators to locate the setting for the events which was used to determine the roles of each participant involved. This strategy seemed to be a successful attempt by the investigators to reduce the tension experienced by the witnesses. Many of them mumbled while drawing the sketches, though the investigators took notes on what the witnesses were explaining about the illustrations. What is not clear is the kind of reports made by the investigators if illustrations are used as the medium for giving witness to an incident. Nor is it clear whether sketches made by a witness are attached to the report prepared by the investigators.

As far as the language used during an investigation is concerned, our observations in the investigation rooms in West Java Police Office have revealed that many investigators used Sundanese, i.e. the local language in West Java province, mostly to suspects and witnesses of petty crimes who are usually from the lower social classes. Having this information about suspects in mind, the investigators often used a coarse/rude variety of the language instead of the refined forms. The investigators were also reluctant to use *Bahasa Indonesia*, the national language. They claimed that the use of the national language with such criminals was too indulgent and less emotive. They thought that if *Bahasa Indonesia* was to be used, they could hardly express their emotions in their language. When a local language is to be used with a witness, they would use a more refined form. With regard to suspects and witnesses from the higher social classes, the national language *Bahasa Indonesia* is mostly used, although on some occasions, such as when making jokes, changing the topic of conversation or trying to be more persuasive, the investigators reverted to the local language.

With regard to where examinations should be conducted, the regulations require that such locations have to be safe, quiet, clean, clear and comfortable. In this context, the investigator's office or desk is always a choice. However, we found that such places are far from being conducive for conducting investigations but instead are overcrowded and noisy and the desks littered with used cigarette ends.

In many cases, suspects might have hidden the information. The questions addressed to witnesses in such circumstance will therefore be oriented to measuring the level of confidence to be had in the witnesses so that the case can be proven in the courtroom. However, it appears that many investigators are more interested in unearthing information regarding the direct involvement of a witness by means of plain speaking than in trying to work out the implied statements made by the witnesses. This results in a shallow report in a case in conjunction with the confessions from the witnesses. When this happens, the case will be examined less critically.

Training of investigators

To become an investigator, a police officer has to attend and pass a series of training courses ascribed by the Indonesian National Police Headquarters. Appointment to attend a training course is made by the Provincial Police Commander, whose nomination is submitted by the District Police Commanders or Directors of the Directorate of Detectives/Investigation at the Provincial Police Office. We have found that training courses for witness interviewing seem inadequate (cf. Snook *et al.*, 2010) and the practical impact on the interviewers' practice is little (cf. Freeman and Morris, 1999). Our informants claimed that training often seems so bureacratic that they feel bored and dissatisfied. On return from training courses, structured/regular supervision sessions or provision for feedback from the supervisors of the training are rarely given (cf. Snook *et al.*, 2012).

Training courses administered by the Police Education Institute, are at bottom of two types: basic and advanced. While basic level training courses are required to be attended by all detective police officers, the advanced level is only intended for more senior detectives who will later be assigned to investigate special cases. In addition to these two levels of training, there are also refresher training programmes to update (senior) detectives on contemporary criminal cases.

Courses given in the basic level training include the foundations of investigations, the administration of investigations, codes of conduct and the practice of investigations. However, as shared in the interviews with some detectives, even at this basic level, no special topics on investigations using linguistic tools are taught. It seems that this topic has not attracted or become of concern to the Police Education Institute so it has not yet been integrated into the training curriculum. Yet these interviewees realised that investigators should be equipped with the capability of investigating criminal cases from/by using linguistic perspectives. In a workshop for police investigators where linguists were involved, the participants confirmed the need to have linguistic perspectives in their curriculum. Introduction to the formulation of different types of questions, understanding responses containing hedges and boosters and the use of indirect speech acts are among the topics of interest that need to be given to the trainees. It needs to be mentioned here that it is only recently that police investigators, prosecutors and/or judges involved in the Indonesian legal system have requested linguists to become expert witnesses, especially during hearing sessions in the courtroom.

At the advanced level, trainees are given courses, the contents of which address prevailing serious criminal cases in society. Such cases include, for example, illegal logging, human trafficking, narcotics and drugs, money laundering, (transnational) terrorism and so on. Very often, training of this kind is administered in collaboration with institutions that have more competency in explaining the nature of the issues. More often, these institutions are outside the police. Training on illegal logging, for instance, will be conducted in collaboration with the Ministry of Forestry, training on money laundering with financial institutions, narcotics and drugs with the Ministry of Health. During the training, the nature of the issues are explained to participants and they are often exposed to cases that are mostly not yet covered by the existing laws and regulations that investigators can use to associate them with crime. Such advanced training is intended to familiarise investigators with the issues prevailing in society so that they can deal with contemporary crime.

Implications for research, policy and practice

This chapter has presented the practices of criminal investigation of witnesses by the Indonesian police organisation. From the discussion throughout the chapter, several implications for research, policy and practice are evident. The fact that little research has been conducted in this area has resulted in the need to carry out research on the quality or best practices of witness interviewing, and this has to be done in collaboration with academics and scholars from various related disciplines. The Indonesian Police Headquarters needs to set out policies that will support improvements in investigator performance, the provision of adequate and specific witness interviewing training through extensive supervision, and the establishment of more comfortable and standardised locations for interviews to take place. At the practical level, investigators are recommended to apply different interviewing techniques to witnesses and suspects in order to obtain accurate and truthful information.

Acknowledgement

The authors would like to extend their thanks to five senior investigators from the Police Office of West Java Province, who were willing to be interviewed.

References

Cederborg, A., Orbach, Y., Sternberg, K. and Lamb, M. (2000) 'Investigative interviews of child witnesses in Sweden', *Child Abuse and Neglect*, 24: 1355–61.

Dixon, D. (2010) 'Questioning suspects: a comparative perspective', *Journal of Contemporary Criminal Justice*, 26 (4): 426–40.

Fisher, R. P. and Geiselman, R. E. (2010) 'The cognitive interview method of conducting police interviews: eliciting extensive information and promoting therapeutic jurisprudence', *International Journal of Law and Psychiatry*, 33: 321–8.

Freeman, K. and Morris, T. (1999) 'Investigative interviewing with children: evaluation of the effectiveness of a training program for child protective service workers', *Child Abuse and Neglect*, 23: 701–13.

Geiselman, R.E., Fisher, R.P., Firstenberg, I., Hutton, L.A., Sullivan, S., Avetissian, I. and Prosk, A. (1984) 'Enhancement of eyewitness memory: an empirical evaluation of the cognitive interview', *Journal of Police Science and Administration*, 12: 74–80.

George, R. C. and Clifford, B. (1992) 'Making the most of witnesses', *Policing*, 8: 185–98.

Griffiths, A. and Milne, R. (2006) 'Will it all end in tiers? Police interviews with suspects in Britain', in T. Williamson (ed.), *Investigative interviewing: Rights, Research and Regulation*. Cullompton: Willan, pp. 167–89.

Griffiths, A., Milne, B. and Cherryman, J. (2011) 'A question of control? The formulation of suspect and witness interview question strategies by advanced interviewers', *International Journal of Police Science and Management*, 13 (3): 255–67.

Gudjonsson, G. H. and Pearse, J. (2011) 'Suspect interviews and false confession', *Current Directions in Psychological Science*, 20 (1): 33–7.

Hendradi, T. (2010) 'Securing protection and cooperation of witnesses and whistle-blowers', *UNAFEI*, pp. 68–75.

Heydon, G. (2005) *The Language of police interviewing: a critical analysis*. New York: Palgrave Macmillan.

Hill, J. A. and Moston, S. (2011) 'Police perceptions of investigative interviewing: training needs and operational practices in Australia', *British Journal of Forensic Practice*, 13 (2): 72–83.

Hope, L., Gabbert, F. and Fisher, R. P. (2011) 'From laboratory to the street: capturing witness memory using the Self-Administered Interview', *Legal and Criminological Psychology*, 16: 211–26.

Korkman, J., Santilla, P. and Sandnabba, N. K. (2006) 'Dynamics of verbal interaction between interviewer and child in interviews with alleged victims of child sexual abuse', *Scandinavian Journal of Psychology*, 47: 109–19.

Madsen, K. (2010) 'Humanity and Dominance in Police Interviews: Causes and Effects'. Masters thesis, Kristianstad University. Retrieved from http://www.diva-portal.org/smash/get/diva2:391525/FULLTEXT01.pdf.

Snook, B. and Keating, K. (2011) 'A field study of adult witness interviewing practices in a Canadian police organization', *Legal and Criminal Psychology*, 16: 160–72.

Snook, B., Eastwood, J., Stinson, M. and Tedeschini, J. (2010) 'Reforming investigative interviewing in Canada', *Canadian Journal of Criminology and Criminal Justice*, 52 (2): 215–29.

Snook, B., House, J., MacDonald, S. and Eastwood, J. (2012) 'Police witness interview training supervision, and feedback: a survey of Canadian police officers', *Canadian Journal of Criminology and Criminal Justice*, 54 (3): 363–72.

Strang, R. R. (2008) '"More adversarial, but not completely adversarial": reformasi of the Indonesian Criminal Procedure Code', *Fordham International Law Journal*, 32 (1): 188–231.

Vallano, J. P. and Compo, N. S. (2011) 'A comfortable witness is a good witness: rapport-building and susceptibility tomisinformation in an investigative mock-crime interview', *Applied Cognitive Psychology*, 25: 960–70.

van Charldorp, T. (2011) 'The coordination of talk and typing in police interrogations', *Crossroads of Language, Interaction and Culture*, 8 (1): 61–92.

Vrij, A., Mann, S. and Fisher, P. R. (2006) 'Information gathering vs. accusatory interview style: individual differences in respondent's experiences', *Personality and Individual Differences*, 42: 589–99.

Westera, N. J., Kebbell, M. R. and Milne, B. (2011) 'Interviewing witnesses: do investigative and evidential requirements concur?', *British Journal of Forensic Practice*, 13 (2): 103–13.

Wright, A. M. and Alison, L. (2004) 'Questioning sequences in Canadian police interviews: constructing and confirming the course of events', *Psychology, Crime and Law*, 10 (2): 137–54.

Legal materials

Chief of Indonesian National Police Decree, 2000/1205-IX
Chief of Indonesian National Police Regulations, 2006/7
Chief of Indonesian National Police Regulations, 2009/8
Chief of Indonesian National Police Regulations, 2012/14
Government Regulation, 2008/3
Indonesian Law, 1981/8
Indonesian Law, 2006/13
Indonesian National Police Code, 2002/2, c.5

2 Interviewing victims and witnesses in Iran

Hossein Raeesi, Mahnaz Parakand, Kamiar Alaei and Nakissa Jahanbani

Introduction

Victims and witnesses form two essential yet easily overlooked and vulnerable communities within the criminal law apparatus of any legal system throughout the world. From those countries who are most developed to those that are beginning the process of development and the concomitant assumption of international law responsibilities, victims and witnesses exist in parallel of recognition and a lack of protection. This trend rings true in the Islamic Republic of Iran (Iran), where statutory law and religious law exist together to form the core legal structures within which victims and witnesses exist and must seek protection and validation.

In Iran, these issues are made further complex by the existence of both civil and common law systems that manifest themselves in differences between accusatory and inquisitive criminal laws and court structures. Islamic canonical law (*Shari'a*) dominates the civil law structure in Iran. Within the court systems existing in Iran, victims find themselves subject to dual identities as potential prosecutors of many claims and also as subjects of questions of value, as in the case of "blood money" determinations.[1] As part of the numerous responsibilities that victims shoulder, bringing complaints to the court has been their responsibility, while nearly always the public prosecutor will go after only the felonies. Criminal prosecution has mostly been the struggle between the litigants, the plaintiff (i.e. victim), and the defendant (i.e. accused), in initiating the judicial process. Other court components, the prosecutor and the judge, perform subsidiary functions.

Simultaneously, witnesses find themselves subject to valuation in terms of the credibility of their testimony based on personal beliefs and practices as well as on gender and religious identity. Further, both victims and witnesses are in somewhat precarious situations since a finding against either of them can result in their own prosecution for criminal conduct. For example, in rape cases both the victim and the witness should testify that the rape was forced in order for there to be a finding that rape in fact occurred. If the rape was forced in nature, it would be a sexual assault. If it cannot be proven that the crime was a forcible rape, the victim might be sentenced to corporal punishment. This issue is intensified for male victims of rape, because a finding that forcible rape did not occur makes it possible the act may be treated as sodomy instead of rape. These, then, form conflicting yet vital distinctions in Iranian law and court practice. By examining Iranian practices, this chapter provides insights into attempts to balance religious and civil laws regarding the valuing of witness testimony.

Historical background[2]

Before the Constitutional Revolution (*Enghelab-e Mashrute*), which took place between 1905 and 1907, Iran lacked legal processes and justice courts for filing criminal cases and preliminary investigations. During the *Qajar* dynasty in Iran, some justice courts were established. These courts were where people brought any kind of disputes and conflicts, including non-juridical, legal, and criminal conflicts. The king, or *shah*, appointed the head of these justice courts. Lawsuits and criminal complaints that arose were referred to religious leaders and scholars or to government officials by the heads of courts based on their legal or non-legal nature. Legal proceedings, including criminal proceedings and legal proceedings that required defensive investigation, were referred to religious leaders for dispute resolution. By contrast, non-legal complaints were referred to government departments for resolution and dispute settlement.

Handling these disputes was not subject to any approved rule or statute by the Legislative Assembly. For dispute resolution, one person carried out the tasks of the official in charge of investigation as well as the authority in charge. The value of evidence was determined and evaluated by the ruler or religious expert that was in charge of handling the dispute. Rulers and religious leaders counted the confession of the defendant as proof of the occurrence of a legal event or a crime and sworn or other testimony were regarded as acceptable methods of proof.

After the Constitutional Revolution, justice courts were established and specific structures were designed for them. A criminal court was created and renamed justice (*Dadgostari*) after Reza Pahlavi became king. However, this institution resolved criminal and legal problems without the guidance of any statutory provisions or specific customary law until 1920. In that year, which was concurrent with the initiation of Iran's legislative parliament, a series of criminal laws were approved by the parliament and referred to as the "Provisional Laws of Criminal Trials." Since then, Iran has had a series of criminal laws for the interrogation and investigation of criminal complaints. These regulations were modified significantly in some periods in accordance with social and political conditions at the time.

Governing systems on criminal procedures in Iran

From 1911 to the present, the judicial system of Iran has experienced several models of criminal procedure systems. One model, heavily dependent on criminal procedure law, placed the public under prosecutorial and official supervision. In another model, the constitution established criminal courts in two categories depending on the crimes involved, and then established a system of prosecutorial appointment for handling these crimes. In this system, the criminal court judge was allowed, in all crimes, to immediately and directly start the defendant's trial after taking into consideration the issue and subject matter involved. If the trial required preliminary investigation, the judge would be able to start the research or command the judicial officer or court to conduct the research at a very early point in the trial process.

A third model related to the law of forming public and revolutionary courts in criminal matters. In this system, the judge assumed the position of both the examiner and the prosecutor. It should be noted that this system still presides in matters of litigation relating to the armed forces through the current Criminal Procedure Code (2014).[3] Finally, the fourth model has modified the law regarding the formation of public and revolutionary courts. Within this structure, the public prosecutor controls the court and affiliated entities. For example, the magistrate (i.e. judicial officer) and investigator (i.e. detective), who are under the management of the district prosecutor, are responsible for preliminary investigation. In this system, the investigator, the prosecutor, and the district prosecutor can request the execution of part of the preliminary research from any judicial officer (i.e. magistrate). In certain cases, the judge is directly and personally responsible for investigation.

Prosecution and its regulation under the criminal laws of Iran

Prior to the enactment of the first Criminal Procedure Code in 1982,[4] the official in charge of investigating crimes was a religious leader or appointed government officer. The procedure for implementing the required methods of interrogation and punishment for crime was based on the principles derived from their attitudes or from the interests of political powers. Following the approval of the Criminal Procedure Code, interrogation was conducted under explicit regulations and rules.

The Criminal Procedure Code covers the regulations and procedures for investigating crimes (in turn, crimes are divided into three categories: minor and major misdemeanors and general). In the first article of the Criminal Procedure Code, the principle of "criminal procedure" is defined as procedures and rules that are formulated for the detection and investigation of crime and determining the liability of criminals based on legal provisions. Under the Code, the public prosecutor is in charge of prosecution and litigation and the cross-examiner is responsible for inspection and investigation of the crime. Among the matters for consideration are both the public and private reputations of those involved in the investigation.

Over the years, with new iterations of the Criminal Procedure Code, some structural changes have occurred regarding the roles assigned to the investigator and prosecutor. Currently, the investigator operates independently, and the prosecutor operates under the direction of the district attorney in charge of preliminary investigation in criminal matters.[5] Despite these changes, the core principles in the Iranian criminal procedures have been maintained, namely regarding types of crimes and the punitive consequences based on *Shari'a*.[6] However, changes regarding speedy investigations and trials are among the most significant modifications.

In any court, there are several branches of investigation, headed by one person who is assigned to the office of head investigator. Thus in Iran's judicial system there is a difference between the investigation and the investigator. Investigating is one of the relevant institutions of the court and, the investigator is employed to carry out this function.

The preliminary investigation is under the direction of the investigatory arm of the Ministry of Justice, and any appointed investigators may be as well. The preliminary investigation can be briefly defined as those set of actions directed by the judiciary to prove either the crime or innocence, with the main goal of preparing the case for court, and expediting the investigative process (Ashouri, 2004: 10). Considering this definition, preliminary investigation is simply a process to discover the crime before the case is sent to the court, and it is completed before trial.

In the Criminal Procedure Code, there is a position for the head of the inquest, although no definition is offered. Therefore, in cases where the investigation is deemed to have failed, the judge can personally start the investigation. Thus we can define the inquest as a series of investigations that are conducted before and during the trial.

The "Provisional Laws of Criminal Trials," adopted over a hundred years ago from the French legal system, included 506 articles and was ratified by the Iranian Parliament. These laws included a position called "interrogator," along with its duties (Arts. 43–52), such as neutrality in seeking and collecting evidence (Art. 44), prohibiting delay in carrying out this process (Art. 45), and preventing the suspension of the investigation due to the absence of the accused or offender (Art. 52). These laws remained effective in the Iranian legal system for over 83 years until the Iranian Islamic revolution in 1979. After the Islamic revolution, a new constitutional law was developed and approved in 1980 and amended a decade later. In 1995, new laws established general and revolutionary trials and replaced the "Provisional Laws of Criminal Trials."

Literature review

This review of the current literature regarding interviewing practices for victims and witnesses is limited to the context of the criminal justice system in Iran. While the focus is on procedures in the penal process that relate to criminal law, which is separate from the Islamic law (*Shari'a*),[7] the latter widely influences criminal law-making in Iran (Rahami, 2005: 587). Literature on this subject in Persian is highly specialized as well as tailored to academic audiences in institutions of higher education and government officials in criminal justice and legal studies.

There are a handful of peer-reviewed academic journal articles in English that provide an overview of discussions, overlaps, and distinctions between *Shari'a* law and Iranian customary law (Rahami, 2005; Osanloo, 2012; Sadeghi, 2014; Maftei, 2010). These few sources, however, are informative and provide some important insights into the interviewing practices of victims and witnesses. It should be noted that many of the English language sources are somewhat historical in nature in that they refer to situations and practices under previous codes that have occurred within recent years rather than the situation as it is under the newest iteration of the Criminal Procedure Code. While in some ways this can be limiting, in other ways it is actually quite useful in that it allows a better picture of these practices to be provided as they are ingrained in law and society across time and political regimes.

Currently, there are no specifications for the appropriate treatment of and respect for victims and witnesses in the Iranian criminal justice system (Asli, 2006: 192). Khaleghi (2013) in his book *Regulations of Penal Prosecution* described the procedure for interviewing victims. As police officers are the first to interact with victims, their initial interaction with the latter group is significant. In the Iranian criminal justice system, police officers are regarded as justice officers, and their duties are delineated in the First Chapter of Book One in the 1999 Procedure Act of General and Revolutionary Courts in Penal Matters (Asli, 2006: 192). However, the police are not instructed specifically in the proper treatment of victims (Asli, 2006: 192). Judges are mediators, arbitrators, and decision-makers in legal trials, much like the Anglo-Saxon legal systems. Unlike the aforementioned Western systems, judges, in certain situations, may also act as investigators.[8]

Victims

Victimology, the study of victims' rights and concentration on their multilateral protection (Asli, 2006: 198), became an academic focus in Iranian universities in the 1990s, which led to greater awareness of these issues for Iranian policy-makers. As a result, Iranian policy-makers incorporated such issues and concerns into new laws, with special attention to women, children, and the elderly (Asli, 2006: 199, 205). Regarding protection of and sensitivity to victims' issues, little is stipulated specifically in penal codes and those provisions that are included relate not to victims in general, but rather to particularly vulnerable groups. For example, Arts. 88 and 204 of 1999 Procedure Act of General and Revolutionary Courts in Penal Matters respectively provided for medical assistance to victims and legal protections for victims who are disabled (Asli, 2006: 200). Under Iranian penal law, victims have the right to be informed of matters regarding their case.

Witnesses

There is some literature regarding witnesses' place and rights in criminal proceedings in Iran within the literature in English. Existing literature describes the place of witnesses in criminal proceedings within the context of Islamic law, yet it does not describe protocols or actual practices in terms of how witnesses are interviewed and, consequently, how witness testimony is acquired in the context of the Iranian criminal justice system.

Witnesses are classified in the Iranian criminal justice process in terms of the weight and value of their testimony. Those that are deemed "just" are given the most weight, while all other witness testimonies are of secondary weight and value (Reza, 2013; Tellenbach, 2009). These stipulations are enumerated in *Shari'a*, and they have particular bearing on *hudud* crimes (i.e. crimes against God) (Reza, 2013: 5). Witnesses are urged to testify as soon as possible, lest the validity of the testimony, and therefore the alleged crime, comes under speculation (Tellenbach, 2009: 695). In court, judges have the ability to reject witness testimony if they think that the witness is providing false information or lying; however, this has seldom been reported (Sadeghi, 2014: 3; Reza, 2013: 22). As witness testimonies are entered as evidence, they are classified into two types: *Shari'a* evidence and legal evidence. For example, *hudud* crimes require *Shari'a* evidence (i.e. testimonies of the appropriate number of just witnesses). Regardless of the legal evidence presented, a *hudud* crime cannot be proven without *Shari'a* evidence.

Current interviewing practices in Iran

The current criminal system in Iran is a hybrid system, a combination of the inquisitorial and adversarial systems. This hybrid system has existed for the last century with only minor changes. Practices and procedures in criminal trials in Iran have several essential characteristics that set them apart from their global counterparts.

Dual inquisitorial and adversarial system

One of the main characteristics of the adversarial system is the lesser amount of power given to the prosecutor and the imposition of the duties of the prosecutor on the plaintiff or victim. In this system, the victim accuses a person (or persons), prepares, and provides the evidence. In no case may the victim play the role of a witness, which can be trying when one is making a case against an accused party.[9] The victim is solely responsible for managing the claim or the complaint (i.e. plea) and the case. He/she further designates and introduces witnesses during a trial. This system is characterized as defensive, meaning that the plaintiff asserts the crime, and the accused has to defend himself/herself. This method is particularly common with regard to some crimes, such as murder (i.e. *hudud*). Although a prosecution proceeding may also commence without a complaint by the victim, investigation is not possible without the involvement of the victim's family.

An important point about the Iranian criminal system is that it is a combination of the adversarial and inquisitorial systems with Islamic methods and ideology. The Iranian trial system is based on *Shari'a* law, in which penal laws are defined as well as the pronouncements of high-ranking politicians of the Islamic Republic of Iran, especially those in the judiciary who are of the status of *Mojtahed*, as recognized by the government. At the Head of the Judiciary branch is the Chief Justice, who is a delegate of the Supreme Leader, and the heads of the Supreme Court, the Court of Administrative Justice, and the Public Prosecutor's office are all Mullahs who have reached the degree of *Mojtahed*. This status and practice reflects one of the theories of the Iranian government that requires a competent jurist over the people.

Pre-trial criminal justice process

During the criminal justice process, victims and witnesses are questioned twice – once in a pre-trial interview and again in front of a judge in court. Victims and witnesses are first brought in for interviewing during the pre-trial phase. The pre-trial phase is initiated with the victim filing an official complaint against the accused. To file a complaint, victims may do one of two things. First, they may call or go to the police station in the cases of an emergency to request help from the police. Conversely, if it is not an immediate event, the victim must go to the prosecutor's office in the town court building to file a formal complaint against the accused. The victim has his/her statement taken by either the local police or a city prosecutor. At this point, victims are asked certain information regarding their identity and background, such as their religion and their criminal record (if any). Victims who are deemed as just are taken most seriously. In other words, they must be Muslim and not have a criminal record.

The interviewing process with victims and witnesses almost always occurs in the Criminal Investigation Department (CID Police) in Iranian Law Enforcement (*Niroy-e Entezami*). However, there are specific circumstances in which officers from other law enforcement agencies may interview victims and witnesses. In national security issues, all those involved in the case are questioned by the security forces of the Ministry of Intelligence of the Islamic Republic of Iran (*Vezarat-e Ettela'at Jomhuri-ye Eslami-ye Iran* (VAJA)), and also other parallel security agencies in the Islamic Revolutionary Guard Corps (IRGC), the police department, and the intelligence office of the judiciary branch. Also, all the interviewing and interrogation, if any, in a military prosecution occurs inside the military court of the Iranian National Army (*Artesh*), the IRGC, the Basiji Forces (that are now affiliated with the IRGC), and the Iranian Law Enforcement. Regarding offenses against chastity, such as adultery and prostitution, as well as crimes against the national security, there are more restrictions in the entire process, and, as a result, there is much more possibility for a violation of the rights of the accused.

After the victim's statement is taken, either the city prosecutor or the assistant prosecutor[10] confirms that the complaint is classified as a crime. If it is deemed a crime, then an investigator opens an official file. The victim must be there every step of the way and follow up to ensure that the file is progressing and changing hands accordingly. After the complaint has been filed, the police are asked to collect evidence at the scene of the crime. Much of this process is relegated to the city prosecutor, who enlists the help of the appropriate classification of detectives. Policemen are directed to carry out requests of the prosecutor or judge, such as delivering arrest warrants and bringing in the accused, among other activities. According to previous and the most recent iterations of the Criminal Procedure Code, during any point in the investigation and/or the trial, the judge may reject any police reports and order a new investigation to be conducted.

At this time, the victim must enumerate the witnesses, who are then brought to a police station and questioned about the events of the crime in the complaint. Witnesses are urged to testify as soon as possible to maintain the validity of the testimony and subsequently the crime (Tellenbach, 2009: 695). In cases where the victim is not the one initially reporting the crime, witnesses are urged to provide police with a statement. This has been incorporated into the last two iterations of the Criminal Procedure Code. In such cases, victims can later be brought in for questioning regarding the crime.

Police are very seldom witnesses. Witnesses may be brought in by the police for further questioning by detectives or the city prosecutor prior to the trial. The victim must be present for the questioning of witnesses. Victims are allowed to be in the room with the witnesses or remain in the vicinity as the interviewing is occurring. In the cases of juvenile criminals (i.e. those under 15 years) and sexual crimes, police and detectives may not interrogate. Instead, this task must be left to the judge or prosecutor.

The types of questions that are asked during an interrogation are previously stipulated in the standard operating procedures (SOP) of detectives. Police may also interview the victims and witnesses; however, they do not have standard procedures like detectives. During this process, both victims and witnesses are asked similar questions. First, they are asked about their qualifications, faith, and character. This entails questions such as if they have a previous criminal record. If so, it must be stated at this point. Then, they have to state if they are single or married, as well as, if they are Muslim, whether they are Sunni or Shi'a. Their home address is also requested and recorded, and they submit a guarantee that the court will be notified of a change of address. These types of questions have implications for both plaintiffs as well as witnesses, and the weight of their respective testimonies.

Witness qualifications

In this system, the position of witness has a specific definition and must meet particular qualifications (Art. 177, Criminal Procedure Code). First and foremost, the victim is not considered a witness in the complaint they have filed against the accused, even though they are permitted to give their testimony in court. In addition, not everyone can qualify as a witness in Islam since legitimacy of birth, faith, and justice are some of the requirements of a witness.[11]

Witnesses are questioned multiple times – in the pre-trial phase as well as in public during the trial – regarding their morality in order to overturn incongruities or character flaws that could potentially void their testimony. Should the witness's character come into question after a *hudud* punishment has or is being administered, the investigator who conducted the interview and "declared the witness qualified is liable to the defendant for damages" (Reza, 2013: 22).

Faith and justice are assessed based on the individual's practice of Islam and religious devotion. In such circumstances, according to the previous version of the Criminal Procedure Code (2000), the testimony of all religious minorities and those not devoted to Islam cannot be accepted as religious evidence against an accused Muslim; however, specific and valuable information might be considered as circumstantial evidence (Art. 155). Otherwise, conventionally, witnesses must be deemed as legitimate and just (*adel*; Arabic: '*adl*), meaning they must be Muslim, and they must not have a criminal record. Witnesses who are just men are given preference. In *hudud* crimes, Islamic law stipulates that the witness testimonies of just women are two to one of a just man.

Confidentiality for victims and witnesses

According to Art. 154 of the Procedure for Penal Codes in General and Revolutionary Trials (herein PPC-GRT) ratified in 2000, the identities of witnesses and victims need to be revealed and documented. However, nothing is mentioned in this article regarding the protection of their identities. Only in Art. 151 is it mentioned that the prosecutor can interview a witness without the presence of the accused person; however, this does not imply that the accused person has no access to the content of the file and cannot identify the witness.

Given this challenge, the new Criminal Procedure Code (2014) tries to address this issue of confidentiality in Arts. 125–47: "if there is any life, financial or reputational threat to the witness or his/her family, the prosecutor can protect the witness ...". In this article, it was emphasized that "this procedure should not violate any right of the accused to defend himself/herself in a fair trial." Therefore, according to this article, it seems that there is a conflict between the right to the protection of the identity of the witness and the right of the accused to defend himself by asking the witness questions. In practice, the latter has been prioritized. Furthermore, unlike an accused person, a witness has no right to free access to an attorney to assist him/her. It is up to him/her to consult with an attorney; however, s/he is responsible for any related cost.

Training of personnel involved in interviewing victims and witnesses

The police department, as the first domestic law enforcement agency in Iran, has been under the direction of the Home Secretary (*Vezarat-e Keshvar*). Although the revolutionary organizations, such as the Basiji militia, have had considerable authority regarding internal security as well as providing a law enforcement auxiliary, they are not under the control of the Home Secretary. Entering the police force in Iran does have some similarities to and differences from Western counterparts. Officers are recruited from either a vocational setting (i.e. recruited into a police academy) or an academic one (i.e. recruited from an institution of higher education and trained as an investigator). For the former, cadets may enter police academies directly from high school. For investigators, as well as high-ranking positions, officers first complete college and graduate education before entering the police force. Since 2003, female officers have once again been recruited, following a hiatus in recruitment after the 1979 Islamic Revolution. As a prerequisite for recruitment, police candidates must demonstrate belief in the Islamic ideology.

Implications for research, policy, and practice

Given the background and practices provided in this chapter regarding the treatment and issues surrounding victims and witnesses in Iranian law and the Iranian criminal justice system, there are significant implications for academic research, law, and policy-making. Two essential areas of research involve the need for the establishment of mechanisms that review the application of laws and rules. The first area relates to the overall application of procedure and criminal law across the various stages of the criminal justice system in Iran. The second area relates to the equality of application of procedure and criminal law throughout the geographical confines of Iran itself, examining whether the practices in urban areas are the same as those in rural areas. Through this research, a clearer understanding of the even nature of the criminal justice system would emerge. Further, it will be essential to study how procedure and criminal law are applied to vulnerable populations, including women, seniors, the disabled, and minorities. Immigrants are also a highly vulnerable group that would benefit from further research and study.

In conclusion, there are some deficits to the guaranty of rights of victims and witnesses during a fair trial procedure based on human rights and justice that need further study and improvements. Looking forward, Iranian policy-makers should take measures to enable and support local, state, and federal law enforcement agencies in developing appropriate training for such protections, particularly for incoming personnel. Separately, academic institutions should again pick up the torch for studying and investigating trends in these protections. Given this legal and policy-making landscape, as well as improvements in the iterations of the Criminal Procedure Code and other relevant legislation, we may be optimistic that protections for victims and witnesses in criminal proceedings will continue to improve in Iran.

Acknowledgements

This chapter could not have been completed without the authorship of Mahnaz Parakand, Hossein Raeesi, Kamiar Alaei, and Nakissa Jahanbani. Each offered their decades of collective academic and professional experiences to explain and contextualize the background and current practices of the Iranian criminal justice system with respect to the treatment of victims and witnesses. Alexandra

Harrington, Mehrnoosh Karimi Andu, Reza Raeesi, and Mohamad Shamei each also contributed to the writing of this chapter in providing a review of the appropriate literature and research provided in other areas. Finally, this chapter benefited from the tremendous translation skills of Samaneh Hassanli and Tahereh Saheb, who both painstakingly labored over the translation of the structures of criminal investigations.

Notes

1. Blood money – or *diyya* – delineates a form of compensation (i.e. reparation) rather than a category of punishment. In lieu of *qisas* (i.e. retribution), the victim's family may elect to seek reparations from the perpetrator. The Iranian penal code has codified *diyya* allocations for numerous crimes (Entessar, 1988: 98).
2. This introduction has been written with reference to the "Report on Iranian Judiciary from the Beginning until Today" by the Young Journalists Club (see References).
3. This legislation is formally titled as the "Criminal Code of Procedure in Public and Revolutionary Courts." Different authors and academic traditions refer to it in slightly different terms. For instance, Asli (2006), cited in this chapter, refers to it as the "Procedure Act of General and Revolutionary Courts in Penal Matters," shortened to "Criminal Procedure Act." Herein, this legislation will be referred to as the "Criminal Procedure Code" and will be regarded in its most recent iteration that was enacted and later enforced in 2014. If a previous version of the Code is referred to, it will be cited to include the year of its enforcement.
4. Immediately after the 1979 Revolution, there was no Islamic criminal law. The Islamic Penal Code (IPC) is an important component of Islamic criminal law, as are the procedures enumerated in the Criminal Procedure Code. The first IPC was passed on 22 May 1982, and was implemented on 15 December 1982. The second IPC was passed in 1991. A new section on *ta'zir* crimes was added to that code in 1996. The newest version of the IPC was enacted and later enforced in 2013.
5. This process is discussed in greater depth in the practices section of this chapter.
6. The Iranian penal code upholds the four major categories of crime of Islamic law: *hudud*, *qisas*, *ta'zir*, and *diyya*. *Hudud* crimes include theft, robbery, adultery, drinking alcohol, and rebellion. In Islamic law, adultery is classified as intercourse that could result in the creation of offspring (Reza, 2013: 21). Punishments for *hudud* crimes are enumerated in *Shari'a*, and range from stoning to bodily mutilation to execution. *Qisas* crimes include murder, manslaughter, and mutilation. These offenses are regarded as acts against the victim. It is left to the discretion of the victim's family whether retributive injury should be inflicted on the perpetrator that is exactly equal to that inflicted on the victim (Entessar, 1988: 98). Despite the legalization of retribution and vendettas, the Quran and Iranian penal code recommend forgiveness as it is deemed pleasing to God (Entessar, 1988: 98). *Ta'zir* crimes are not otherwise specified in *Shari'a*. Punishments for these crimes range from fines to seizure of property and public flogging. The judge is burdened with determining an appropriate punishment considering the temporal culture and public interest of the community (Entessar 1988: 98). *Diyya*, or blood money, delineates a form of compensation (i.e. reparation) rather than a category of punishment. In lieu of *qisas* (i.e. retribution), the victim's family may elect to seek reparations from the perpetrator. The Iranian penal code has codified *diyya* allocations for numerous crimes (Entessar, 1988: 98).
7. Islamic law is known as the law of God or the *Shari'a*. Classically, Islam draws no distinction between religious and secular life. Hence, *Shari'a* covers not only religious rituals, but also many aspects of day-to-day life, politics, economics, banking, business or contract law, and social issues. The term *Shari'a* itself derives from the

verb *Shara'a*, which connects to the idea of spiritual law and the system of divine law. *Shari'a* has certain laws that are regarded as divinely ordained, concrete, and timeless for all relevant situations (i.e. the ban against drinking liquor as an intoxicant). *Shari'a* is based on four primary sources: (1) the Quran; (2) the *hadith*, or tradition; (3) *ijma'*, or consensus of jurists; and 4) *'aql*, or reasoning (Entessar, 1988: 94). The Quran is the foundational source of law for all *Shari'a*; however, Shi'a *Shari'a* also places a great deal of weight on the considerations and views of the Imams in the formation of its legal system (Entessar, 1988: 94). *Hadith* refers to the statements, deeds, and sayings of the Prophet and the Imams recorded and codified by their companions (Entessar, 1988: 94). Both *ijma'* and *'aql* are considered as secondary sources of Shi'a law, with the former delineating the views of the Shi'a scholars who were close companions of the Imams and the latter describing judgments based on pure and practical reason from which religious law can be inferred (Entessar, 1988: 94). Certain laws are extracted based on principles established by Islamic lawyers and judges (*Mujtahed*; pl. *Mujtahedun*). In deriving *Shari'a* law, Islamic law-makers attempt to interpret divine principles. An Islamic lawyer or judge's attempt to rule according to Islamic law can be described as ruling by *Shari'a*; it can concurrently be heavily influenced by local customs (*urf*). Islamic jurisprudence is called *figh* (meaning understanding of details) and refers to the inferences about Islamic rules drawn by scholars from the principles divined from *Shari'a*. *Figh* is divided into two parts: the study of the sources and methodology (*usul figh* – roots of the law) and the practical rules (*furu figh* – branches of the law). Legal scholars hope that *Shari'a* and *figh* are in harmony at all times, but in any given case cannot be sure.

8. This will be described more fully later in this chapter.
9. This is unlike Anglo-Saxon or Western legal systems where the victim may hire or be appointed an attorney to handle matters related to the plea in their stead.
10. The city prosecutor and assistant prosecutor are comparable to the American district attorney or assistant district attorney, respectively.
11. Reza (2013: 22) refers to this as "moral probity" (see also Tellenbach, 2009: 695).

References

Ashouri, M. (2004) *Criminal Procedure Law. Vol. 2*. Tehran: Samt Publishing.

Asli, M. R. (2006) "Iranian criminal justice system in light of international standards relating to victims?" *European Journal of Crime, Criminal Law and Criminal Justice*, 14: 185–207.

Criminal Code of Procedure for Public and Revolutionary Courts [Islamic Republic of Iran], 1999. Available at: http://www.ghavanin.ir/detail.asp?id=11610.

Criminal Code of Procedure for Public and Revolutionary Courts [Islamic Republic of Iran], 2014. Available at: http://www.shenasname.ir/didgah/2329-aeen.html.

Entessar, N. (1988) "Criminal law and the legal system in revolutionary Iran," *Third World Law Journal*, 8: 91–102.

Islamic Republic of Iran (2013) *Islamic Penal Code of the Islamic Republic of Iran*. A translation is available from: http://www.iranhrdc.org/english/http://www.iranhrdc.org/english/human-rights-documents/iranian-codes/1000000455-english-translation-of-books-1-and-2-of-the-new-islamic-penal-code.html?gclid=CN_TsbOPyMUCFaMewwodqgkATQ.

Khaleghi, A. (2013) *Regulations of Penal Prosecution*. Tehran: Shahr Danesh Publishing.

Maftei, C. V. (2010) "The sanctions of the Islamic criminal law: aspects regarding penalties of the criminal law of the Islamic Republic of Iran. Religion and tradition vs. observing human rights," *Juridical Current*, pp. 139–48. Available at: http://revcurentjur.ro/arhiva/attachments_201003/recjurid103_13F.pdf.

Osanloo, A. (2012) "When blood has spilled: gender, honor, and compensation in Iranian criminal sanctioning," *Political and Legal Anthropology Review*, 35: 308–26.

Rahami, M. (2005) "Development of criminal punishment in the Iranian post- revolutionary Penal Code," *European Journal of Crime, Criminal Law and Criminal Justice*, 13: 585–602.

Reza, S. (2013) "Due process in Islamic criminal law," *George Washington International Law Review*, 46: 1–27.

Sadeghi, H. (2014) "The Catania Papers: filling the gap in favour of the accused: the approach of Islamic criminal law in light of the rule No Punishment in case of doubt," *Tulane European and Civil Law Forum*, 29: 147–56.

Tellenbach, S. (2009) "Aspects of the Iranian code of Islamic punishment: the principle of legality and the temporal, spatial and personal applicability of the law," *International Criminal Law Review*, 9: 689–705.

Young Journalists Club (n.d.) "Report on Iranian Judiciary from Beginning until Today." Available online at: http://www.yjc.ir.

3 Investigative interviews with alleged victims and witnesses in Israel

Consequences of the 1955 law for practice

Carmit Katz

Introduction

Exploring the issue of interviewing victims or witnesses in Israel reveals a considerable gap between different groups of victims and witnesses, resulting mainly from legislative and organisational differences. The relevant legislation and organisations differ depending on the ages of the victims or witnesses. Based on the notion that children can be adversely harmed by repeated interviews and cross-examination, the Israeli legislature initiated the Law of Evidence Revision Protection of Children, which was passed by the Israel Knesset in 1955. This law prioritises children's well-being over the basic rights of a suspect, and it was initiated to ensure that children would not be further traumatised in the forensic process. This law requires all children who were victims or witnesses of violence to be interviewed by a special practitioner ('a child forensic interviewer'). The child forensic interviewer is a social worker who works within the welfare office, in the Service of Investigative Interviews. The child forensic interviewers have extensive powers in the investigation process and play a major role in any trials that follow. A recent law in Israel (2010) recognised another vulnerable group of victims and witnesses: young people and adults with developmental disabilities, such as autism spectrum disorder. This law granted to the Service of Investigative Interviews with Children the duty of interviewing them.

This unique law is not applicable to children above the age of 14 years, who are interviewed by a special unit in the police, the unit for alleged victims of abuse. It is important to stress that there is no documentation of these interviews. Moreover, no published research was conducted in this area and therefore interview practices of youth cannot be elaborated. Above the age of 18, young people and adults are interviewed by police officers, among this group there is also no standardised documentation and no published research on interviewing practices.

These differences in legislation have resulted in different organisations being responsible for forensic investigation in Israel: the welfare office and the police. Whereas the main aim of the welfare office in Israel is the promotion of its clients' welfare, the main aim of the police is to enforce the law. These basic differences might influence the practices that practitioners within these organisations are instructed to adopt. However, as was mentioned before, no published information exists in relation to forensic investigation practices with children above the age of 14 and adults. Therefore most of the information that will be explored in the current chapter will address interviewing practices of children and people (of all ages) with disabilities in Israel.

The development of interview practices for alleged victims and witnesses in Israel

The differences in the laws, relevant organisations and practitioners (social workers versus police officers) created different interview practices and training programmes. Whereas interviewing children within the Service of Investigative Interviews has received considerable public and research attention, resulting in the emergence and development of refined techniques, the interview practices of the police have not received much (or any) attention or resources, resulting in no documented research in that area. Information from the field reveals that practitioners within the police are highly committed to forensic investigations with victims and witnesses. However, to date, no best practices or standardisation of interview practices and no training programmes have been documented. Furthermore, unlike the interviews conducted by the Service of Investigative Interviews with children and people with special needs, which are all mandatorily video-recorded, the police are not unambiguously instructed to document interviews.

In the Service of Investigative Interviews with children and people with special needs, rapid changes have emerged in interview practices. The NICHD (National Institute of Child Health and Human Development) Protocol became mandatory in 1998 and all forensic interviewers in the service have been conducting interviews according to it. In 2007, certain changes were integrated into the NICHD Protocol related to the Updated NICHD Protocol, including the use of drawings in forensic contexts and repeated interviews.

Current practice: developmental attribution

The current practice in the Service for Investigative Interviews in Israel is the use of the NICHD Protocol. The NICHD Investigative Interview Protocol is a set of structured guidelines for interviewing children about experiences or witnessed events (Lamb *et al.*, 2011). The NICHD protocol was developed to translate professional recommendations into operational guidelines and to guide interviewers through all phases of investigative interviews (Lamb *et al.*, 2008; Lamb *et al.*, 2011).

In the introductory/pre-substantive phase, the interviewer introduces him/herself, clarifies the child's task and explains the ground rules and expectations. Several questions designed to establish that the child understands the difference between true and false statements are asked in this phase. The rapport-building phase that follows the introductory phase comprises two sections. The first is designed to create a safe and relaxed environment for the child and to establish trust between the child and interviewer (Lamb *et al.*, 2008; Lamb *et al.*, 2011).

In the second phase, children are prompted to describe a recently experienced neutral event in detail. This task familiarises the child with open-ended investigative interview strategies while also demonstrating the specific level of detail expected of them. In the transitional part between the pre-substantive and the substantive phase, a series of prompts are used to non-suggestively identify the target event(s) under investigation with prompts that are as open as possible. If the child makes an allegation, the free-recall phase begins with an invitation ('Tell me everything …') and other free-recall prompts. As soon as the first narrative is completed, the interviewer prompts the child to state whether the incident happened one or more times and secures incident-specific information. Only after free-recall prompting do interviewers proceed to directive questions mentioned by the child and request information within specific categories (Lamb *et al.*, 2008; Lamb *et al.*, 2011).

Lamb and his colleagues (2007) reviewed research concerning the protocol and found that controlled studies repeatedly show that the quality of interviewing reliably and dramatically improves when interviewers employ the protocol. Interviewers following the protocol use at least three times more open-ended and approximately half as many option-posing and suggestive prompts as they do when exploring comparable incidents involving children of the same age without the protocol. The protocol has been shown to elicit more information from children of all ages in response to free-recall prompts (Orbach *et al.*, 2000). The protocol has been implemented, and these results have been replicated in the USA, Israel, Sweden, the UK and Canada (Lamb *et al.*, 2007; Orbach *et al.*, 2000).

The development of the NICHD Protocol led to considerable improvements in interviews with children; however, several factors contributed to the eventual revision of the NICHD Protocol into the Revised NICHD Protocol. The first was the feedback that the forensic interviewers received from the legal system in Israel. In several discussions in courts, judges criticised the forensic interviewers and said that the legislators' intention in 1955 when creating the special role of child forensic interviewer was that children, alleged victims of abuse, would receive not only cognitive-based best practices but also emotional-based best practices. In addition to this feedback, the child forensic interviewers also felt that the NICHD Protocol did not address the children's emotional difficulties. As a result, the interviewers often struggled when interviewing reluctant children who refused to disclose any allegation despite external evidence suggesting a high probability of abuse (Hershkowitz *et al.*, 2006; Katz *et al.*, 2012). All of this feedback from the field was accompanied by research developments, especially those obtained from a laboratory context (e.g. Davis and Bottoms, 2002; Goodman *et al.*, 1991), that indicate a positive contribution of non-suggestive support during interviews with children.

All of these sources led to the development of the Updated NICHD Protocol (Katz, 2013; Hershkowitz *et al.*, 2013), which aimed to integrate best practices within developmental psychology with best practices with clinical relevancy, integrating non-suggestive support intervention to:

- enhance the rapport-building between the forensic interviewer and the child;
- provide the child appropriate, non-suggestive support in the pre-substantive and the substantive parts of the interview;
- provide the child with alternative interview techniques, such as repeated interviews or drawing, when needed.

The key non-suggestive interventions that were identified and disseminated were as follows (Katz, 2013; Hershkowitz *et al.*, 2013):

- Reinforcement of the child's behavior during the interview. For example, interviewers were encouraged to thank the child for sharing the information that they had revealed, and express how that information had helped them understand what had happened.

  The interviewers are instructed to avoid providing children with any 'grades' of their performance, such as 'excellent' or 'good job', to prevent social desirability bias.

- Establishment of the rapport between the interviewer and child:

  - '*How are you feeling?*'
  - '*Are you cold?*'

  Such neutral prompts are encouraged throughout the interview to signal to the child that the forensic interviewer sees him/her and cares about him/her.

- Emotional support when the child displays verbal or non-verbal difficulties:

  - '*I see that you are crying. Could you please tell me what you are feeling right now?*'
  - '*You are saying you were scared. Tell me more about being scared.*'

  The interviewers' training includes practical knowledge that helps them assess the children's verbal and non-verbal behaviour, which can indicate reluctance in the early stages of the interview (Katz *et al.*, 2012). When identifying these signals, the interviewers are instructed to approach the child with both verbal and non-verbal support, such as maintaining eye contact.

- Empowerment of the child, by, for example, providing him/her the opportunity to choose the way s/he expresses themselves. For example, if the child was viewed as having difficulty saying a particular word the interviewer would invite the child either to draw or write the word down.

  This strategy, which aims to empower the children and to provide them with control in the interview after control has been taken away from them, was developed based on the notion that the forensic investigation with the child can be not only a significant phase within the legal process but also an opportunity to facilitate the child's recovery process (Katz, 2015; Katz *et al.*, 2014).

The pilot study of the Updated NICHD Protocol (Hershkowitz *et al.*, 2013) pointed to higher disclosure rates in forensic investigations with the revised versus the standard NICHD Protocol. Furthermore, children who were interviewed with the revised protocol were less reluctant and provided more details in response to open-ended prompts. The Updated Protocol is now being disseminated to child forensic interviewers all over Israel.

An additional improvement in the NICHD Protocol was the integration of drawing, which was first evaluated in a field study conducted in Israel in 2007 (Katz and Hershkowitz, 2010; Katz *et al.*, 2014). Many researchers have attempted to understand the effect of drawing on children's narratives (Butler *et al.*, 1995; Gross and Hayne, 1998; Katz and Hershkowitz, 2010; Salmon *et al.*, 2003; Wesson and Salmon, 2001). Although there are many ways to use drawing, integrating drawing in a forensic context also brings about some risk given the basic notion that victimised children occasionally suffer from dissociative disorders that can hamper their performance within the legal context and their testimonies (Lev-Wiesel and Liraz, 2007). Perhaps that is why the preferred way for integrating drawing into the forensic context is the 'draw and talk' method, which provides children with the opportunity to draw while recounting their experiences. Only their verbal responses are of interest (i.e. the content of the drawing is not evaluated). The facilitative effects of allowing children to draw while talking are thought to derive from a number of possible mechanisms. One possible explanation is that drawing allows children to generate their own retrieval cues by reminding them of additional event-related details as they construct their drawings. Drawing may also serve to make the interview context more comfortable by giving children a focus other than the interviewer (Brown, 2011).

The 'draw and tell' technique has mainly been studied in laboratories, where drawing is integrated into interviews with children concerning personally experienced events. The results clearly demonstrate that, under ideal circumstances (non-suggestive interventions), drawing yields an increase in the amount of information recalled without compromising accuracy (Butler *et al.*, 1995; Gross and Hayne, 1998; Salmon *et al.*, 2003; Wesson and Salmon, 2001).

A recent field study was designed to explore the effects of drawing in investigative interviews with children who were alleged victims of abuse (see Katz and Hershkowitz, 2010). The sample included 125 children aged 4–14 years who were alleged victims of sexual abuse. The children were first interviewed with open-ended invitations before being randomly assigned to one of two interview conditions, with (n = 69) or without (n = 56) event drawing. They were then re-interviewed. The children in the drawing group disclosed more free-recall information about the abusive events than the children in the comparison group, including forensically relevant information about people, actions and the time and location of the incidents. The effect of drawing was evident for young children as young as four as well as for older children aged 14 years. It was also found to be beneficial for both boys and girls and enhanced the children's testimonies regardless of the type of the abuse or the time delay between the alleged incidents and the investigations. This strategy of 'draw and tell' is being employed in investigative interviews to allow interviewers to assess its necessity and is being subjected to additional field studies to assess its contribution to forensic investigations with pre-schoolers.

Another strategy that was employed in the drawing field study and is now integrated into the Updated Protocol is a set of free-recall prompts at the end of each interview, as follows:

- Tell me how you felt before the interview.
- Tell me how you felt during the interview.
- Tell me how you are feeling now that the interview is finished.

The interviewers are instructed to try to help the children elaborate their narratives using cue invitations, for example 'Tell me more about feeling scared'. Past studies have focused mainly on the legal outcomes of the investigative interviews with children in terms of the quality of investigations and then the quality of the children's testimonies. However, the focus of a recent study (Katz *et al.*, 2014) was the children's perceptions and experiences before, during and after the interview, including a comparison of children who were interviewed with and without drawing.

When exploring the children's experiences before the investigations, it was found that children displayed more negative feelings towards the investigation than positive feelings. For example, in Katz's study children reported that they were scared, believing they were taken to jail and that they had done something wrong.

Katz also found that during the interview, children in both research conditions reported more positive experiences with respect to the interview than negative emotions. Nonetheless, the children in the drawing condition provided more words indicating positive experiences during the interview than the children in the comparison group. This finding stresses the contribution of drawing to the investigation. Apparently, during the investigation, drawing gave the children control and strength during the process, as some of the children reported that beginning to draw was the only way that they could be understood and explain what had happened, while feeling positive about how helpful they were being.

Following the interview, in response to free-recall invitations, the children used three main words to describe their experiences following the investigation: relief, hope and success. The children in both research conditions reported experiences of relief and hope following the investigation. While relief and hope were evident regardless of the research condition, success was more prevalent among children in the drawing group than children in the comparison group. A feeling of success can be seen as part of an empowering process that the children experienced during and following the investigations. The children's narratives emphasise this process:

> *'After drawing I felt ok. Now I can talk to you. Now I can tell you everything that had happened to me and I am proud of myself for succeeding.'*

Another interview technique that was supported in the Katz and Hershkowitz study was the contribution of repeated interviews to the children's testimonies (Katz and Hershkowitz, 2010; Katz and Hershkowitz, 2013; La Rooy *et al.*, 2010). When the first interview was based solely on open-ended prompts and a second interview was conducted following a short break, children provided twice as much information as in the first investigation, information that was provided mainly in response to open-ended prompts. The strategy of repeated interviews is now being integrated into the Updated NICHD Protocol, offering the interviewer the possibility of meeting with the child again when detecting reluctance.

Regardless of the improvements in interview practices following the development of the Updated NICHD Protocol, additional challenges were identified among practitioners as well as researchers, and the following developments are a focus for research and development in Israel. The first is related to the development and dissemination of practical guidelines based on the NICHD Protocol that are better suited to interviews with pre-schoolers. Similar to the development of the Updated NICHD Protocol, several factors led to this effort: forensic interviewers reported a set of challenges when interviewing pre-schoolers according to the NICHD Protocol related to the children's limited attention skills, difficulties in retrieval and poor narratives. In addition, several judges criticised the application of the NICHD Protocol to pre-schoolers, commenting on the gap it creates between the interviewers and the children, which results in discrimination towards pre-schoolers by the legal process. To better address pre-schoolers, alleged victims and witnesses, a research group integrating senior forensic interviewers, together with Katz and her research team, are working on the development of practical guidelines for interviews with pre-schoolers.

An additional challenge that needs to be addressed is the cultural adaptation of the NICHD Protocol. Although practitioners worldwide contend with cultural diversities, little research effort has focused on this issue. Fontes (1993) found that certain cultural groups might disclose less often and recant more often than others due to cultural taboos about sexual abuse (Elliott and Briere, 1994; Fontes, 1993; Shaw *et al.*, 2001). Many theorists have posited that such cultural and ethnic differences exist (Futa *et al.*, 2001; Rao *et al.*, 1992; Tang, 2002; Toukmanian and Brouwers (1998); Wong, 1987). These findings strengthened claims about the cultural impacts on reporting abuse, revealing these groups' significant difficulties with disclosure and their vulnerability to recantation.

Currently, intensive efforts are underway (by Katz and her research team) to explore cultural issues by interviewing Israeli Arab children and Jewish Orthodox children who are alleged victims of abuse to identify both possible challenges for interviewers and special considerations for the children. In Israel, these two groups are considered to be highly conservative, collectivist societies that value family cohesion at any price (Ben-Arieh and Haj-Yahia, 2006; Leshem and Roer-Strier, 2003). Furthermore, the relationship between the government and its institutions and these groups is characterised by mutual mistrust, which creates even greater difficulties in the forensic process.

Additional efforts are being made to adapt the NICHD Protocol to the interviewing of children, young people and adults who are diagnosed with developmental disabilities. It has often been reported in the literature that this vulnerable group of victims and witnesses is at greater risk of abuse largely due to their increased dependence on caregivers and intervention services (Henry *et al.*, 2011). They are seen as 'easy targets' because they have difficulty defending themselves or reporting abuse (Sobsey and Doe, 1991) and because their accounts are frequently dismissed by the professionals conducting criminal investigations (Groce, 1999) and rarely result in a conviction (Mishra, 2001).

Due to the challenges of eliciting testimonial evidence from children with developmental disorders, the establishment of clear rules and specific guidelines for the professionals who collect children's testimonies is urgent (Ribeiro, 2009). Currently, the Haruv Institute, a leading organisation in the prevention and care of children who are alleged victims of abuse in Israel, is supporting a study to develop a system to interview children, young people and adults without verbal abilities.

Considerable developments concerning investigative interview practices in Israel are being considered (including the training of interviewers). One of the key issues that must be addressed in this respect is that the Israeli government each year dedicates considerable amounts of money for such training. Currently, child forensic interviewers undergo three types of training:

- *Emotional support system*. Each group of six child forensic interviewers is provided with a social worker who specialises in secondary trauma. Her main goal is to provide the participants with a relaxing and safe environment and a place to share their experiences. This emotional support system has three main aims:
  - preventing secondary trauma among child forensic interviewers;
  - preventing burnout;
  - stressing the emotional aspect of interview and forensic practices to promote and model it.
- *Ongoing supervision sessions with a mentor*. Each child forensic interviewer is assigned a senior forensic child interviewer as his/her mentor. They are supposed to meet on weekly basis so that the mentor can provide the interviewer with feedback on his/her interview practices and on credibility assessment issues. It is important to note that there is currently no standardisation of this process, which means that the structure and content of these weekly supervision sessions mainly depend on the mentor (e.g. the mentor's personality, experience and values).
- *Organised courses targeted to specific stages in the forensic interviewers' professional lives*. The first course is an orientation, which usually takes place at the beginning of an interviewer's employment. This course, which lasts 20 intensive days, includes the basic components of forensic interviews with children and practical guidance on the use of the NICHD Protocol. In the interviewer's first year, a mentor is paired with him to help with the

dissemination of the interview practices. The second course is taken after two years in the position, where up to 20 forensic interviewers from all districts in Israel are invited to an advanced course in forensic practices, mainly practices with respect to involvement in court in providing expert testimony and assessing a child's credibility. These courses are developed and disseminated by Katz and the national inspector of the service. Forensic interviewers who have completed these courses consistently report considerable improvement in their practical knowledge. Additional courses are being planned and developed to address more of the needs of forensic interviewers.

Implications for research, policy and practice

This chapter emphasises the unique situation in Israel, whereby children are protected by special law until the age of 14 years and are interviewed by child forensic interviewers from the Service of Investigative Interviews in Israel, while other children (above the age of 14 years), young people and adults are interviewed by the police with no evidence-based practices or standardised interviews.

This difference, first and foremost, is the result of legislative and organisational differences, but its origin is at the cultural, perhaps religious, level based on the perception of children in Israeli society. Israel decided to place children as its top priority, which is reflected in the innovative law of 1955. It is important to note that the authority of the child forensic interviewers goes beyond conducting the interviews. These interviewers also decide how the child is allowed to participate within the legal process based on an assessment of the effect of any proceedings on the child's welfare and risk for trauma. An example of the forensic interviewers' far-reaching authority is that if the child forensic interviewer decides that the child cannot testify in court, s/he then presents that child's evidence in the child's place. The child forensic interviewer also assesses the child's reliability as a witness and then determines the child's role in the investigation and, if applicable, the trial. The court cannot overrule any of his decisions (for example, whether the child is subjected to a medical examination or even cross-examination).

This law has created a situation in which children under the age of 14 years are subject to evidence-based interview practices with forensic interviewers who receive a variety of intensive training. However, children over the age of 14 years, young people and adults work with practitioners who may be highly dedicated to their work but who, however, lack evidence-based interview practices, standardised practical guidelines and relevant training. This situation clearly highlights the important challenge of promoting best practice and standardisation for interviews with children over the age of 14, young people and adults.

References

Ben-Arieh, A. and Haj-Yahia, M. M. (2006) 'The geography of child maltreatment in Israel: findings from a national data set of cases reported to the social services', *Child Abuse and Neglect*, 30: 991–1003.

Brown, D. A. (2011) 'The use of supplementary techniques in forensic interviews with children', in M. E. Lamb, D. La Rooy, L. C. Malloy and C. Katz (eds), *Children's Testimonies: A Handbook of Psychological Research and Forensic Practice*, 2nd edn. Cichester: Wiley, pp. 217–50.

Butler, S., Gross, J. and Hayne, H. (1995) 'The effect of drawing on memory performance in young children', *Developmental Psychology*, 31: 597–608.

Davis, S. L. and Bottoms, B. L. (2002) 'Effects of social support on children's eyewitness reports: a test of the underlying mechanism', *Law and Human Behavior*, 26: 185–215.

Elliott, D. M. and Briere, J. (1994) 'Forensic sexual abuse evaluations of older children: disclosures and symptomatology', *Behavioral Sciences and the Law*, 12: 261–77.

Fontes, L. A. (1993) 'Disclosures of sexual abuse by Puerto Rican children: oppression and cultural barriers', *Journal of Child Sexual Abuse*, 2: 21–35.

Futa, K. T., Hsu, E. and Hansen, D. J. (2001) 'Child sexual abuse in Asian American families: an examination of cultural factors that influence prevalence, identification, and treatment', *Clinical Psychology: Science and Practice*, 8: 189–209.

Goodman, G. S., Bottoms, B. L., Schwartz-Kenney, B. and Rudy, L. (1991) 'Children's memory for a stressful event: improving children's reports', *Journal of Narrative and Life History*, 1: 69–99.

Groce, N. (1999) *An Overview of Young People Living with Disabilities*. New York: UNICEF.

Gross, J. and Hayne, H. (1998) 'Drawing facilitates children's verbal reports of emotionally laden events', *Journal of Experimental Psychology*, 4: 163–79.

Henry, L. A., Bettenay, C. and Carney, D. P. J. (2011) 'Children with intellectual disabilities and developmental disorders', in M. E. Lamb, D. J. La Rooy, L. C. Malloy and C. Katz (eds), *Children's Testimony: A Handbook of Psychological Research and Forensic Practice*, 2nd edn. Chichester: Wiley-Blackwell, pp. 251–83.

Hershkowitz, I., Lamb, M. E., Katz, C. and Malloy, L. C. (2013) 'Does enhanced rapport building alter the dynamics of investigative interviews with suspected victims of intra familial abuse?', *Journal of Police and Criminal Psychology*, 30: 6–14.

Hershkowitz, I., Orbach, Y., Lamb, M. E., Sternberg, K. J. and Horowitz, D. (2006) 'Dynamics of forensic interviews with suspected abuse victims who do not disclose', *Child Abuse and Neglect*, 30: 753–69.

Katz, C. (2015) 'Stand by me: the effect of emotional support on children's testimonies', *British Journal of Social Work*, 45: 349–62.

Katz, C. and Hamama, L. (2013) 'Draw me everything that happened to you: the effect of drawing on children's testimonies', *Children and Youth Services Review*, 35 (5): 877–82.

Katz, C. and Hershkowitz, I. (2010) 'The effect of drawing on the richness of accounts provided by alleged victims of child sexual abuse', *Child Maltreatment*, 15 (2): 171–9.

Katz, C. and Hershkowitz, I. (2013) 'Repeated open questions and its effect on children's testimonies', *Research on Social Work Practice*, 23: 210–18.

Katz, C., Barnetz, Z. and Hershkowitz, I. (2014) 'The effect of drawing on children's experiences of investigations following child abuse', *Child Abuse and Neglect*, 38 (5): 858–67.

Katz, C., Hershkowitz, I., Malloy, L. C., Lamb, M. E., Atabaki, A. and Spindler, S. (2012) 'Non-verbal behavior of children who disclose or do not disclose child abuse in investigative interviews', *Child Abuse and Neglect*, 36 (1): 12–20.

La Rooy, D., Katz, C., Malloy, L.C. and Lamb, M. E. (2010) Do we need to update our policy on repeated interviews?', *Journal of Policy, Psychology and the Law*, 16: 373–92.

Lamb, M. E., Hershkowitz, I., Orbach, Y. and Esplin, P. W. (2008) *Tell Me What Happened: Structured Investigative Interviews of Child Victims and Witness*. Chichester: Wiley.

Lamb, M. E., La Rooy, D., Malloy, L. C. and Katz, C. (2011) *Children's Testimony: A Handbook of Psychological Research and Forensic Practice*, 2nd edn. Chichester: Wiley.

Lamb, M. E., Orbach, Y., Hershkowitz, I., Esplin, P. W. and Horowitz, D. (2007) 'Structured forensic interview protocols improve the quality and informativeness of investigative interviews with children', *Child Abuse and Neglect*, 31: 1201–31.

Leshem, E. and Roer-Strier, D. (eds) (2003) *Cultural Difference as a Challenge for Human Services*. Jerusalem: Magnes Press (in Hebrew).

Lev-Wiesel, R. and Liraz, R. (2007) 'Drawings vs. narratives: drawing as a tool to encourage verbalization in children whose fathers are drug abusers', *Clinical Child Psychology and Psychiatry*, 12 (1): 65–75.

Mishra, R. (2001) 'In attacks on disabled, few verdicts despite evidence, law enforcement drops most cases', *Boston Globe*. Boston, MA. Retrieved from: http://libsta28.lib.cam.ac.uk:2166/hp/printsavews.aspx?pp=Save&hc=Publication.

Orbach, Y., Hershkowitz, I., Lamb, M. E., Sternberg, K. J., Esplin, P. W. and Horowitz, D. (2000) 'Assessing the value of structured protocols for forensic interviews of alleged child abuse victims', *Child Abuse and Neglect*, 24: 733–52.

Rao, K., DiClemente, R. and Ponton, L. E. (1992) 'Child sexual abuse of Asians compared with other populations', *Journal of the American Academy of Child and Adolescent Psychiatry*, 31: 880–6.

Ribeiro, C. (2009) *A Criança na Justiça – Trajectórias e significados do processo judicial de crianças vítimas de abuso sexual intrafamiliar*. Coimbra: Almedina.

Salmon, K., Roncolato, W. and Gleitzman, M. (2003) 'Children's reports of emotionally laden events: adapting the interview to the child', *Applied Cognitive Psychology*, 17: 65–79.

Shaw, J. A., Lewis, J. E., Loeb, A., Rosado, J. and Rodriguez, R. A. (2001) 'A comparison of Hispanic and African-American sexually abused girls and their families', *Child Abuse and Neglect*, 25: 1363–79.

Sobsey, D. and Doe, T. (1991) 'Patterns of sexual abuse and assault', *Sexuality and Disability*, 9: 243–59.

Tang, C. S. (2002) 'Childhood experience of sexual abuse among Hong Kong Chinese college students', *Child Abuse and Neglect*, 26: 23–37.

Toukmanian, S. G. and Brouwers, M. C. (1998) 'Cultural aspects of self-disclosure and psychotherapy', in S. S. Kazarian and D. R. Evans (eds), *Cultural Clinical Psychology: Theory, Research, and Practice*. New York: Oxford University Press, pp. 106–26.

Wesson, M. and Salmon, K. (2001) 'Drawing and showing: helping children to report emotionally laden events', *Applied Cognitive Psychology*, 15: 301–20.

Wong, D. (1987) 'Preventing child sexual assault among Southeast Asian refugee families', *Child Today*, 16: 18–22.

4 Interviews with victims and witnesses of crime in Japan

Research and practice

Makiko Naka

Introduction

In Japan, not much attention has been paid to investigative interviews with victims and eyewitnesses in general. During the last decade, victim's rights have become acknowledged and the use of screens and closed-circuit television (CCTV) in court has become popular. In 2008, Higaisha Sanka Seido (victim participation system) was passed into legislation so that victims of crime can put questions to a defendant in court. However, how to put questions to or elicit information from victims was not studied until interviewing methods for child victims/witnesses were developed. The situation was the same for eyewitnesses. We suffered from many miscarriages of justice due to eyewitnesses' misidentification, as in the case of the murder of the Hirosaki University professor's wife. This was a case in which a woman was stabbed to death at night, and her mother, who was sleeping next to her, identified someone male. This person was subsequently convicted of the crime but was later proven to be innocent. There were also a series of burglaries at three post offices, in which five clerks were highly confident of identifying two men as burglars but who were later found to be innocent (see Watanabe, 1992, for a review). In a number of other studies, real cases were analyzed to establish factors that might affect the accuracy of identification, and the effects of such factors were examined under experimental conditions (Naka *et al.*, 1996; Naka *et al.*, 2002). Other studies have analyzed the effect of mnemonics on the Cognitive Interview (Fisher and Geiselman, 1992), including context reinstatement and report everything, on the quantity and quality of eyewitness memory (see Kasahara and Ochi, 2006; Shiraishi *et al.*, 2006). However, results from these studies were not applied to real-life interviews with eyewitnesses before child investigative interviews became popular.

Therefore, in this chapter, there will be a particular focus on investigative interviews with children who are alleged victims or witnesses. Their vulnerability made researchers and practitioners realize how important the development of interviewing methods and training were. In the rest of this chapter, the background and problems with child interviews in Japan will be discussed, together with research related to interviewing, the training of interviewers, and the current situation and future directions. To conclude, there will be a description of how interviewing methods with child victims are applied to others, such as children in custody cases, vulnerable suspects, and less vulnerable adult victims and eyewitnesses.

Background and problems

Similar to Western countries, the testimony of Japanese children has often not been received well in court. Asada (1998) studied 12 criminal cases in which children were involved. He argued that although children are usually admitted as competent to testify in court (i.e. they are acknowledged to have the ability to perceive, remember, and communicate the incident), the credibility of their testimony is frequently dismissed.

Reading through old Japanese legal journals, we find quite a few cases in which children's testimony was not believed. I will give two examples. In one case, a ten-year-old girl was allegedly molested by a man in the apartment building where she lived. She did not discuss the incident with her parents, but rather with her classmates at school. During the conversation with her peers, one classmate confessed that she had also been followed by a man who looked like a foreigner. Another classmate said that a foreigner lived in the apartment building where the child (the alleged victim) lived. After this conversation, the child came to believe that she had been molested by the foreigner who lived in her apartment building. However, the defendant was acquitted because he had an alibi, plus the clothes that he was wearing, and the items in his possession on the day in question, did not match the child's testimony.[1]

In another case, a sexual offender already in custody confessed that he had committed another crime in a specific school district. He described the victim, and when a police officer showed him a group photo of the school children in the district, he pointed to one girl. Based on the photo, the police officer located and interviewed the girl. She initially denied that any crime had occurred, but in her fourth interview she admitted having been molested by the defendant. However, when the suspect saw her in person, he denied that she was his victim. The court decided that the child might have been molested by someone else previously but was misled by the police officer into believing that the defendant had been her perpetrator.[2]

These cases highlight the problem of inappropriate communication and how it can harm children's testimony. If the children had been interviewed earlier and in a more appropriate manner, inaccurate charges or misidentification may not have occurred. Instead, the real perpetrator might have been apprehended. Furthermore, the second case suggests that even a professional investigator is not free from such problems. In fact, the United Nations (UN) recommended that Japan should train professionals so that they can communicate more effectively with children (Committee on the Rights of the Child, 2010).

Research and a sample case

Relevant research

Previous scientific research has shown that interviews with inadequate questions affect eyewitness memory in children and adults (e.g. Ackil and Zaragoza, 1998; Brady *et al.*, 1999; Bruck *et al.*, 2002; Cassel *et al.*, 1996; Leichtman and

Ceci, 1995; Kikuno, 1993; Mori *et al.*, 1996; Naka, 2012; Uematsu, 1958). In the following, we will describe the Japanese research on suggestive questions, which may be difficult for non-Japanese readers to access – for additional research, please refer to Naka (2013).

Tadasu Uematsu was a pioneering forensic psychologist in Japan. He majored in psychology, then studied law and became a judge and later a law professor. During his career as a judge, he conducted many research studies that are relevant even today. One of his studies examined the effect of questions on children's testimony (Uematsu, 1958). In this experiment, conducted in 1939, he showed 51 pre-school children a picture for one minute. In the picture, a man was riding a motorcycle with a sidecar in which there were three children. A research assistant then asked the children many questions about the picture they had seen. These included questions on objects that were actually depicted (e.g. "Was the man wearing a pair of glasses?" when there was actually a pair of glasses), and questions on objects that were not actually depicted (e.g. "Was a flag that the boy was holding a Japanese flag?" when actually no flag was depicted). Although the children performed fairly well on the questions regarding objects that were depicted, they answered incorrectly, or fabricated the answers on objects that were not actually depicted. Only one child correctly answered "No, he wasn't holding a flag" to the question above. Forty-eight children stated that the boy had a *Japanese flag* and the other two said that he had *an army flag*.

Such questions as "Was a flag that the boy was holding a Japanese flag?", when actually no flag was depicted, are now known as suggestive or misleading questions. They affect the accuracy of answers, alter the original memory of events, and even create false memories (e.g. Ackil and Zaragoza, 1998; Bruck *et al.*, 2002; Cassel *et al.*, 1996; Leichtman and Ceci, 1995; Kikuno, 1993; Mori *et al.*, 1996; Naka, 2012). In Japan, Mori *et al.* (1996) demonstrated the effect of misleading questions. They presented 129 four- and five-year-old children with a story in which a thief stole objects from a house. Children were then asked questions about typical objects of robberies that were actually stolen (e.g. a necklace), typical objects that were not stolen (e.g. a pendant), atypical objects that were actually stolen (e.g. slippers), and atypical objects that were not stolen (e.g. a broom). At one- and ten-week intervals, they were given a recognition test on these objects. Results showed that false recognition was greater for typical objects that were not stolen, especially among young children.

Kikuno (1993) conducted a similar experiment with 284 second- and fifth-grade children, who were shown a picture and then asked questions on objects that were depicted and objects that were not. Later, children were given a recognition test and a source-monitoring test[3] asking whether they had seen the object in the picture or were only asked about it in the questions. The results showed that a considerable misinformation effect occurred even among the fifth-grade children. That is, these children became to say they saw some items in the picture which were actually presented only in the questions.

These results corroborate the many research studies from all over the world on the ability to elucidate fallibility in children. Indeed, it is said that episodic memory, the memory of specific events, emerges around four years old, together with other aspects of cognitive ability, such as linguistic skills, self-awareness, source monitoring, and meta-control (Harley and Reese, 1999; Nelson, 2000; Shing *et al.*, 2010). Young children are more susceptible to suggestive questions because they do not have auto-noetic (self-knowing) awareness, and thus easily confuse what they have experienced with what others have told them (Perner and Ruffman, 1995; Schacter *et al.*, 1995). Furthermore, even schoolchildren can also confuse what they experienced and what they imagined or are forced to tell (Ackil and Zaragoza, 1998; Naka, 2012). To demonstrate this point, Naka (2012) showed a film to second- and fifth-grade children and then asked them either to recall events from the film on their own (recall condition), to draw an image for one minute and then recall events on their own (imaging condition), to answer questions that included both accurate and inaccurate information (questioning condition), or to participate in an interview including open-ended questions and then specific questions. After this reminiscing, the children were given a recognition test about scenes depicted or not depicted in the film. Results showed that false recognition was greater for the younger children and especially so in the imaging and questioning conditions. Those in the imaging condition incorrectly recognized the items that contained visual information (e.g. wrong color) more often than those in other conditions, whereas children in the questioning condition incorrectly recognized the items that contained misinformation provided by the questions (e.g. a hat). The results suggest that young children were affected by internal information from their own imaging and by external information from questions.

These studies demonstrate children's fallibility but also help us to know how to override it. By using open-ended questions that do not contain external information, we can elicit more accurate information from children. In addition, we can improve accuracy not by asking children to make images but by encouraging them to explain what really happened as accurately as possible. For instance, having a truth/lie discussion before talking about the incident helps children to be more accurate in their responses (Huffman *et al.*, 1999; London and Nunez, 2002). Ochi (2011) studied the effect of having children say "It is wrong" if an interviewer says something about the incident that is misleading, finding that this technique also helps children to report more accurately. Such research helps us to develop better interviewing methods, as we will see below. However, before proceeding on to that topic, let us look at another case illustrating that the accuracy of a report is not a matter of all or nothing. Rather, each utterance and question can contribute to the degree of accuracy of a report.

A sample case[4]

In the following case, the situation and names have been changed to ensure anonymity, but the original wordings have been retained. Note that grammatical subjects can be omitted in Japanese therefore parentheses are used to show words that were not stated but would be understood by native speakers.

In this case, a man named Taro, whose IQ was estimated to be equivalent to that of a pre-school child, lived in an institution. He confided in a director of the institution, Ms Sato, that one of the institution's staff had done something wrong to him. Ms Sato conducted an interview with a voice recorder.

S: I am sorry but, Taro, (you) told Ms Sato (i.e. the interviewer herself) about the incident. Um, tell me about that time again. From Taro, um, Taro, don't hide, but tell me what (you) think. Um, it's okay, okay. It's okay to tell anything.
T: Yes.
S: Okay?
T: Yes.
S: Can you talk about that time? The one you mentioned in the resting room today.
T: Yes.
S: Will you talk? What did (the alleged suspect) do? (Two seconds of silence.)
T: (My) pants, taken off. (Six seconds of silence.)
S: Where?
T: Stock room.
S: Stock room. (Three seconds of silence.) You said "taken off," did you? Was there anything else? (Four seconds of silence.)
T: Taken off.
S: Taro, whatever (you) said in the resting room. You may tell that. Okay?
T: Hit.
S: Then?
T: Took off all.
S: Taken off all. Then (the alleged suspect) did something. Hit. What else?
T: Laid down.
S: Laid down, and then?
T: Took (my) underwear off.
S: Um.

So far, the interview seems fairly appropriate. Ms Sato gave some instructions before starting the interview, used open-ended prompts with pauses, and elicited Taro's utterances. However, later in the interview, she began to ask closed-ended questions.

S: Did he close the curtain and put on the light?
C: Didn't put on the light.
S: Didn't put on the light. (Four seconds of silence.)
S: Did he *close* the entrance door?
C: *Closed* the door.
S: *Closed* the door, oh …
C: *Closed.*

S: *Closed*. (Nine seconds of silence.)
S: Were you told to *take off* the clothes?
C: Yes.
S: Yes? You didn't take off the clothes by yourself, er … did (you) *take off* by yourself, or were (your clothes) *taken off*?
C: Taken off.
S: Taken off, weren't they? Taro felt bad, weren't you? At that time, Taro, were (you) *scared*?
C: *Scared*.
S: *Scared*. Is that so?

The first question of this section is a multifaceted question that asks two things in one sentence (i.e. "Did he close the curtain?" and "Did he put on the light?"). Taro answered only the second question. In the subsequent conversation on closing the door, it is as if Ms Sato and Taro are performing a duet; Taro could simply be echoing her words. In the next exchange, the interviewer inadvertently asked whether Taro took off his clothes by himself. It is notable that Taro answered "Yes" to this question. Ms Sato realized that the answer contradicted what Taro had said previously (that his clothes were taken off by another person). Then she asked again, "Did (you) *take off* by yourself, or were (your clothes) *taken off*?" to which question Taro replied "Taken off." Finally, when Ms Sato asked "Scared?," Taro replied "Scared." He might have just been repeating what Ms. Sato said.

As we can assume that information elicited by open-ended questions is more accurate (Brown *et al.*, 2013; Lamb and Fauchier, 2001; Orbach and Lamb, 2001), some pieces of information produced by open-ended prompts (clothes being taken off, in the stock room, laid down) may be more reliable in this instance than other pieces of information (such as closed, scared). If we can elicit information without asking specific questions, then the accuracy of the testimony will be maximized.

Interviewing method and training

Investigative interviews

Such difficulties in listening to children and obtaining accurate information have raised awareness of the importance of interviewing methods. Research on episodic memory, misinformation effects, suggestibility, and pragmatics of communication have enabled the development of guides for investigative interviews such as the Cognitive Interview (Fisher and Guiselman, 1992), Achieving Best Evidence (Ministry of Justice, 2011), Narrative Elaboration (Saywitz and Snyder, 1996), Stepwise Interview (Yuille *et al.*, 1993), and the National Institute of Child Health and Human Development (NICHD) protocol (Lamb *et al.*, 2007).

To elicit free narratives from child witnesses, these methods share two features. First, the use of open-ended prompts (e.g. "Tell me what happened") is strongly emphasized (e.g. Lamb *et al.*, 2008). Second, in order to motivate a child to talk accurately as well as to maximize the child's ability to talk, the methods involve ground rules such as having a "truth/lie discussion" to encourage the child to tell the truth (Huffman *et al.*, 1996; London and Nunez, 2002); asking the child to say "I don't know" if she/he does not know the answer (Fisico and Scoboria, 2010); and rapport-building and training of episodic memory (Roberts *et al.*, 2004; Sternberg *et al.*, 1997) before the interviewer transitions into the substantive questioning phase. In addition, to make the most of one interview and avoid repetition, a multidisciplinary approach is recommended so that relevant agencies (e.g. prosecutors, police officers, social workers, and medical staff) can obtain the information all at once.

Training

The process of developing an interviewing method and its implementation are not the same. Research has shown that, although training makes professionals more knowledgeable, it does not necessarily improve their skills. For instance, Aldridge and Cameron (1999) studied the effect of one week of training and found that it did not affect the use of questions or the quality of elicited information. Lamb *et al.* (2002) also studied a one-week training program and obtained similar results. Westcott *et al.* (2006) examined the effect of a nine-months' training including follow-up, determining that the improvement was still limited.

Based on these findings, Lamb *et al.* (2007) developed a scripted guideline, the NICHD Protocol (http://nichdprotocol.com). The protocol provides exact wordings that an interviewer should use for the introduction, to explain the ground rules, to build rapport, to train the child to talk about past events, and to transition to the substantive topic. It also presents effective open-ended prompts that elicit free narratives: "Tell me what happened" (invitation), "Tell me from time point A to time point B" (time segmentation), "Tell me more about [what the child said previously]" (cued recall), and "Then what happened?" (follow-up). By following this script, an interviewer can achieve good practice.

In 2008, after encountering many inadequate interviews with children, we applied for a research grant to develop and train professionals in investigative interviewing. After some modifications, the training now consists of an introductory lecture on problems in interviews with child witnesses, cognitive development in children, the difference between investigative interviews and counseling, as well as the traumatic influence of repeated interviews (Fulcher, 2004). Next, we familiarize trainees with four types of open-ended prompts. After they have practiced the use of these prompts, we introduce the simplified structure of the NICHD Protocol. This simplified structure consists of:

1. introduction (greetings and explanation of the interview);
2. ground rules;
3. rapport-building;
4. episodic memory training;

5. transferring to the substantive topic;
6. separation of incidents ("Did it happen one time or more than one time?");
7. open-ended questions;
8. *wh*-questions;
9. a break (when the interviewer can review the interview with *back staff* (prosecutor, police officer, social worker, psychologist, and so on);
10. follow-up questions;
11. additional questions, if necessary, about conversations with the perpetrator if any, other witnesses, previous disclosures, and the suspected incident; and
12. closure.

After becoming familiar with the NICHD Protocol structure, the trainees receive lectures on planning an interview as well as on corroborative evidence, and they then participate in role playing.

Obstacles in training

The first evaluation of the training was not so impressive. Although the amount of information covered in interviewees' free narratives increased after the training, on the whole, interviewers still talked more than interviewees, and the total amount of speech by the interviewees did not change much. However, by revising the training program, we were eventually able to obtain better results. For instance, some trainees could not distinguish open-ended prompts from *wh*-questions. Thus we rearranged the training so as first to make trainees familiar with these prompts and then to introduce the protocol. Also, some trainees thought that investigative interviews were akin to clinical counseling. To highlight the difference, we contrasted an investigative interview with counseling, pointing out that the former seeks to learn about the *past*, whereas the latter aims to help an alleged victim for the *future*. We also concluded that, at least in our collective society, working as a team produces better outcomes. That is, trainees form teams in which each member takes a role (i.e. as interviewer, interviewee, or back staff) and they then work together. They role play as a team, and the review of role plays is team-based, rather than focusing on individuals (see Naka, 2014a). These modifications apparently worked. In one study, we analyzed interviews conducted before and after the training of 32 professionals (Naka, 2011). We found that trainees used more open-ended prompts after the training, and that interviewees' utterances increased accordingly.

Many problems have been solved. Nevertheless, some aspects of training may still need to be strengthened. On one occasion we had an opportunity to conduct a quiz immediately after the introductory lecture. Out of the 42 professionals, 89 to 100 percent correctly answered questions on the purpose of interviewing, the differences between semantic and episodic memory, the differences between investigative interviews and counseling, the types of open-ended questions, suggestibility, the importance of eliciting free narratives, and the recommendation not to repeat interviews. However, it was striking that only 38 percent of participants correctly answered "No" to "The purpose of ground rules is to build a trusting relationship" (actually, ground rules are to motivate children to provide more information accurately) and only 69 percent correctly responded "No" to "If there is not enough time, it is okay to omit the training on episodic memory" (this training should *not* be omitted). After seeing these results, we began to spend more time explaining why these components are important.

Another point on which we focus is whether interviewers are aware of what information they have to collect for establishing a case. We notice that trainees sometimes collect information that is important for social work but not necessarily related to establishing a case, i.e. everyday routines of abuse, the child's feelings, or the child's needs, rather than the specific details of a unique event of abuse. To understand interviewers' perceptions as to what information to collect in an investigative interview, and as to whether it changes after training, we conducted a questionnaire study. The 98 participating professionals were given a brief case in which a child said "Daddy hit me," and they were asked to choose seven items that they considered most important to collect from the following list: Daddy's age, Daddy's occupation, Daddy's name, Daddy's personality, Daddy's motivation to hit, the last incident of hitting, everyday routines of hitting, temporal information about the incident, the place of the incident, the child's feelings toward Daddy, the body part that was hit, the child's needs, etc. Overall, items such as the last incident of hitting, the body part that was hit, temporal information, and place of the incident were chosen more frequently than other items, suggesting that most trainees already know that they should collect factual information to establish the incident. However, the training had an effect. After the training, the last incident of hitting and temporal information were more likely to be chosen, and everyday routines of hitting, and the child's feelings toward Daddy were less likely to be chosen. The training therefore raised trainees' awareness of what information to collect (Naka, 2014b).

The current situation and future directions

The use of forensic interviews and challenges

Since we began our training, we have trained 1,726 professionals, of whom 1,141 were social workers and psychologists from Child Guidance Centers (CGCs). According to Yamamoto (2013), out of the 206 CGCs in Japan, the number of CGCs using the method of investigative interviewing increased from 12 in 2007 to 160 in 2011. Yamamoto also showed that the existence of abuse was confirmed in 84 percent of the cases when forensic interviews were conducted, whereas 74 percent of the cases were confirmed when ordinary interviews were conducted; the difference was statistically significant at the .01 level.

However, the number of cases that proceed to court still seems low. There is no official report that documents how many referrals to CGCs are provided in court, but according to the Ministry of Health, Labor and Welfare, the number of sexual abuse cases reported to CGCs was 1,460 in 2011, whereas, according to the National Police Agency, the number of cases handled by police officers was only 112. A simple comparison of these figures suggests that fewer than 10 percent of reported cases are treated in a criminal context.

One obstacle that may hinder the process by which referrals are provided in court is the hearsay rule, which stipulates that statements given outside the court are not admissible as evidence. Although there are exceptions to this rule, they are limited to statements taken by prosecutors and police officers, the conditions to override the hearsay rule being more stringent for police officers than for prosecutors (Japanese Criminal Procedure Law, sections 321.1.2 and 321.1.3). Thus, even if good interviews are conducted at CGCs, the children must be interviewed by police officers. Furthermore, if a police officer has conducted a good interview, the child must also be heard by a prosecutor, who decides whether the case should go to court. During the process, children's memory may decay or be contaminated. To solve this problem, a multidisciplinary approach is necessary.

Recently, police officers and prosecutors have shown some interest in improving their methods of investigative interviewing. From 2008 to 2010, no police officers or prosecutors took our training, but the number has gradually increased since then from 41 (11 percent of total trainees) in 2011 to 158 (27 percent) in 2012, and 227 (45 percent) in 2013. This training now enables professionals from different agencies to work together, sometimes with exceptional results. In one such case, both the social workers and police officers involved underwent training. When a suspected victim was referred to a CGC, the social worker reported the situation to the police. The police officer bypassed the normal procedure of repeated interviews and instead took the girl to the prosecutor's office. The idea of investigative interviewing was new to the prosecutor, but she underwent a brief training and then interviewed the child with police officers and a psychologist serving as back staff. In this case, the number of interviews was held to a minimum because the case was forwarded to court immediately by the prosecutor's decision.

In another case, a suspected victim of physical abuse was sent to a hospital. A medical doctor familiar with the investigative interviewing process contacted us. We contacted medical staff, prosecutors, police officers, and social workers so that the interview could be conducted in a multidisciplinary setting. The prosecutor served as the interviewer, for the reason mentioned above. The police officers looked for evidence, social workers supported the child's coping, and doctors treated the child medically.

As far as I know, the number of such cases of multidisciplinary cooperation is still fewer than ten. However, we are striving to connect agencies. Conducting training with professionals from different agencies together seems to be one way of encouraging the multidisciplinary approach.

Further development

Although the investigative interview protocol was developed for children who are alleged victims of sexual abuse and witnesses, the structure and open-ended questions are useful for other settings, such as interviews with children in custody cases (Saywitz *et al.*, 2010) and suspect interviews (Hershkowitz *et al.*, 2004; Shepherd, 2007).

In Japan, one such application has been implemented by family court investigators. Following the structure of investigative interviews, they created a set of introductory instructions with some illustrations. These cover initial greetings, the role of family court investigators, an explanation that the child should state their own recollections and thoughts (and not, for example, those of his/her parents), and ground rules. Messages to be communicated to the children include "Your parents won't ask you what you told us in this interview"; "Tell me what *you* think"; "If you don't know the answer, tell me that you don't know"; "If you don't understand the question, tell me that you don't understand"; and "If the interviewer says something wrong, say that it is wrong" (Miyazaki *et al.*, 2013).

Miyazaki *et al.* (2013) used these instructions in nine custody cases, in which the children involved were 4 to 12 years old. In comparison to traditional interviews in which investigators play with a child for a while to build rapport and then gradually transition to substantive questions, investigators found that the instructions helped not only children (in eight out of nine cases) but also parents (in three cases) to understand the purpose of the interview, making it easier to transfer to the substantial topic (four cases); helped children to speak more spontaneously (two cases); and reduced anxiety (one case), suggesting that these instructions are promising.

Another application relates to interviews of suspects. Miscarriage of justice is one of the most urgent issues in Japan's criminal justice system. In a well-known Ashikaga case, for example, DNA testing proved that a man convicted for rape and murder was innocent. He had made a false confession. In a Himi case, a man confessed (falsely) to a rape and was convicted. He served his sentence, after which the real perpetrator was found. In a Shibushi case, 13 people were accused of violations of election law based on false confessions without objective evidence; they were acquitted due to the coercive interrogations that had occurred, including long detentions of more than one year accompanied by verbal and psychological harassment. Due to these cases, along with the initiation of the lay judge system in 2009, video-recording of suspect interviews is now being used on a trial basis. If an interview is videotaped there is the opportunity to view how well it has been conducted. In 2011, the National Police Agency issued a document, *Torishirabe (Kiso Hen)* [*Interviewing (The Basics)*], which encourages interviewers to make use of open-ended questions, utilizing the techniques of cognitive interviewing. Furthermore, in May 2013, Torishirabe Gijutsu Sogo Kenkyu-Kenshu Center (the Integrated Research and Training Center for Interviewing Skills) was set up within the National Police Academy. This center now provides training in interviewing skills based on "scientific findings in psychology" (National Police Academy, 2013).

The Public Prosecutor's Office has also started to videotape interviews with suspects who have learning difficulties and/or in cases that may be forwarded to Saibanin-saiban (lay judge court). In a few districts, psychologists have been asked to offer training to prosecutors. Moreover, some psychologists are asked to attend suspect interviews to assist with the communication between the prosecutor and the suspect, and to ensure that the interview is conducted properly. In such practices, the interview structure and the use of open-ended prompts are emphasized.

Such applications appear not to be limited to interviews of suspects. Very recently, the prosecutors and police in certain districts have started to videotape interviews with vulnerable victims and witnesses. This reform may promote the use of forensic interviews of a wider range of interviewees, including adult victims and eyewitnesses in general.

In 1999, we visited a constabulary in the UK en route to the Psychology and Law International Conference held at Trinity College, Dublin. They showed us the Memorandum of Good Practice (Home Office/Department of Health, 1992), a guideline for child witnesses/victims, and the PEACE model for the interviewing of suspects. We were surprised at how advanced they were, thinking that we were 20 years behind. After 15 years, we are still behind. However, our methods of interviewing are gradually changing toward procedures based on scientific evidence. It would never have been possible for us to improve our interviewing methods without knowing the practices in other parts of the world and sharing scientific findings internationally. I do hope that such communication will continue to flourish even more in the future.

Notes

1. Shogakko 4 nensei no shojo ni taisuru kyosei waisetsu jiken nitsuki hikokunin ga hannin dearu to suru migi shojo no kyoujutsu tou no shinyosei wo kouteisita genshin no yuzai hanketsu ga hakisare dai 1 shin no muzaihanketsu ga iji sareta jirei: Itabashi kyosei waisetsu jiken jokokushin hanketsu (1990) Hanreijiho, 1331, 145–161. [A case that dismissed the credibility of a fourth-grade girl and maintained the decision of not guilty in the first trial: Decision of appellant trial in the Itabashi molestation case.]
2. Yojo ni taisuru kyosei waisetsu tou no kosojijitsu ni tsuki higaisha no higijijitsu no sonzai wo mitometa monono hikokunin no hanko to dantei suruniha gouriteki na utagai ga nokorutoshite muzai ga iiwatasareta jirei (1989) Yokohama chisai, 1989. 12.21. [A case in which the decision of not guilty was made regarding molestation of a young girl, by admitting that the girl was molested but with a reasonable doubt as to whether the defendant committed the crime.]
3. Source-monitoring test is a test where children are asked to identify the source of information they recalled or recognized. In this study, they were asked whether the information they recognized was originally presented in the picture or in the post-event questions.
4. Cited in Naka (2007), reproduced with kind permission from the publishers Kaneko Shobo.

References

Ackil, J. K. and Zaragoza, M. S. (1998) “Memorial consequences of forced confabulation: age differences in susceptibility to false memories,” *Developmental Psychology*, 34: 1358–72.

Aldridge, J. and Cameron, S. (1999) Interviewing child witnesses: questioning techniques and the role of training. *Applied Developmental Science*, 3: 136–47.

Asada, K. (1998) "Nenshosha no shogen to kantei" ["Child testimony and expert testimony"], in A. Idota, H. Niwayama, K. Mitsudo, T. Odanaka, and Y. Ode (eds), *Gohan no boshi to kyusai* [*Prevention of Miscarriage and Its Relief*]. Tokyo: Gendai Jinbun Sha, pp. 341–70.

Brady, M. S., Poole, D. A., Warren, A. R., and Jones, H. R. (1999) "Young children's responses to yes–no questions: patterns and problems," *Applied Developmental Science*, 3: 47–57.

Brown, D. A., Lamb, M. E., Lewis, C., Pipe, M.-E., Orbach, Y., and Wolfman, M. (2013) "The NICHD Investigative Interview Protocol: an analogue study," *Journal of Experimental Psychology: Applied*, 19: 367–82.

Bruck, M., Ceci, S. J., and Hembrooke, H. (2002) "The nature of children's true and false narratives," *Developmental Review*, 22: 520–54.

Cassel, W. S., Roebers, C. E. M., and Bjorklund, D. F. (1996) "Developmental patterns of eyewitness responses to repeated and increasingly suggestive questions," *Journal of Experimental Child Psychology*, 61: 116–33.

Committee on the Rights of the Child (2010) *Consideration of Reports Submitted by States Parties Under Article 12(1) of the Optional Protocol to the Convention on the Rights of the Child on the Sale of Children, Child Prostitution and Child Pornography*. United Nations Convention on the Rights of the Child, 11 June 2010.

Fisher, R. P. and Geiselman, R. E. (1992) *Memory-Enhancing Techniques for Investigative Interviewing: the Cognitive Interview*. Springfield, IL: Charles Thomas.

Fisico, S. and Scoboria, A. (2010) *Instructions from Interviewers Regarding "Don't Know" Responses Increase Response Accuracy*. Paper presented at the 3rd Annual Conference of the International Investigative Interviewing Research Group (iIIRG) "Program and Abstract." Norway, 22–24 June, p. 40.

Fulcher, G. (2004) "Litigation-induced Trauma Sensitisation (LITS): a potential negative outcome of the process of litigation," *Psychiatry, Psychology and Law*, 11: 79–86.

Harley, K. and Reese, E. (1999) "Origins of autobiographical memory," *Developmental Psychology*, 35: 1338–48.

Hershkowitz, I., Horowitz, D., Lamb, M. E., Orbach, Y., and Sternberg, K. J. (2004) "Interviewing youthful suspects in alleged sex crimes: a descriptive analysis," *Child Abuse and Neglect*, 28: 423–38.

Home Office/Department of Health (1992) *Memorandum of Good Practice on Video Recorded Interviews with Child Witnesses for Criminal Proceedings*. London: The Stationery Office.

Huffman, M. L., Warren, A. R., and Larson, S. M. (1999) 'Discussing truth and lies in interviews with children: whether, why, and how?' *Applied Developmental Science*, 3: 6–15.

Kasahara, H. and Ochi, K. (2006) "The effect of enhanced imagination strategy on eyewitness memory recollection," *Japanese Journal of Criminal Psychology*, 44: 9–17.

Kikuno, H. (1993) 'Effects of verbal questions on visual memory of children," *Japanese Journal of Educational Psychology*, 41: 99–105.

Lamb, M. E. and Fauchier, A. (2001) "The effects of question type on self-contradictions by children in the course of forensic interviews," *Applied Cognitive Psychology*, 15: 483–91.

Lamb, M. E., Orbach, Y., Hershkowitz, I., Esplin, P. W., and Horowitz, D. (2007) "A structured forensic interview protocol improves the quality and informativeness of investigative interviews with children: a review of research using the NICHD Investigative Interview Protocol," *Child Abuse and Neglect*, 31: 1201–31.

Lamb, M. E., Sternberg, K. J., Orbach, Y., Hershkowitz, I., Horowitz, D., and Esplin, P. W. (2002) "The effects of intensive training and ongoing supervision on the quality of investigative interviews with alleged sex abuse victims," *Applied Developmental Science*, 6: 114–25.

Leichtman, M. D. and Ceci, S. J. (1995) "The effects of stereotypes and suggestions on preschoolers' reports," *Developmental Psychology*, 31: 568–78.

London, K. and Nunez, N. (2002) "Examining the efficacy of truth/lie discussions in predicting and increasing the veracity of children's reports," *Journal of Experimental Child Psychology*, 83: 131–47.

Ministry of Justice (2011) *Achieving the Best Evidence in Criminal Proceedings: Guidance for Vulnerable and Intimidated Witnesses, Including Children*. London: Ministry of Justice.

Miyazaki, H., Yokoshima, K., Nishida, H., Shiga, Y., Kondo, K., Satoh, K., and Echigo, N. (2013) "Kodomo to mukiau: Hubo no hunso no kachu niaru kodomo no shinjo haaku ni tsuite" ["Meeting with a child: on understanding the feelings of a child who is in the dispute of parents"], *Kasai Chosakan Kenkyu Tenbo* [*Kachokyo Journal*], 40: 58–74.

Mori, T., Sugimura, M., and Minami, M. (1996) "Effects of prior knowledge and response bias upon recognition memory for a story: implications for children's eyewitness testimony," *Japanese Psychological Research*, 38: 39–46.

Naka, M. (2007) "Kyojutsu to iu kaiwa no tokushitsu: yocho wo minogasanai jijo choshu" ["Characteristics of utterances in testimony: investigative interviews not to miss signs"], in N. Uchida and A. Sakamoto (eds), *Risuku Shakai wo Ikinuku Komunikeshon Ryoku* [*Communication Ability to Survive in Insecure Society*]. Tokyo: Kaneko Shobo, pp. 149–69

Naka, M. (2011) "The effect of forensic interview training based on the NICHD structured protocol," *Japanese Journal of Child Abuse and Neglect*, 13: 316–25.

Naka, M. (2012) "Effect of interview techniques on children's eyewitness reports and subsequent memories of a viewed event," *Japanese Journal of Psychology*, 83: 303–13.

Naka, M. (2013) "Psychology and law in Japan: recent developments," *Annual Report of Educational Psychology in Japan*, 52: 115–27.

Naka, M. (2014a) "A training program for investigative interviewing of children," in R. Bull (ed.), *Investigative Interviewing*. New York: Springer, pp. 103–22.

Naka, M. (2014b) *Information to Deal with in Forensic Interviews: Practitioner's View Before and After the Training*, International Congress of Applied Psychology, CAP14-ABS1975, Paris, 8–13 July.

Naka, M., Itsukushima, Y., and Itoh, Y. (1996) "Eyewitness testimony after three months: a field study on memory for an incident in everyday life," *Japanese Psychological Research*, 38: 14–24.

Naka, M., Itsukushima, Y., Itoh, Y., and Hara, H. (2002) "The effect of repeated photo identification and time delay on the accuracy of the final photographic identification and the rating of memory," *International Journal of Police Science and Management*, 4: 53–61.

National Police Agency (2012) *Torishirabe (Kiso Hen)* [*Interviewing (The Basics)*].

National Police Academy (2013) Available at: https://www.npa.go.jp/keidai/keidai.html.

Nelson, K. (2000) "Memory and belief in development," in Daniel L. Schacter and Elaine Scarry (eds), *Memory, Brain, and Belief*. Cambridge, MA: Harvard University Press, pp. 259–89.

Ochi, K. (2011) "Forensic interview and the training for reduction of children's suggestibility," *Japanese Journal of Child Abuse and Neglect*, 13: 326–30.

Orbach, Y. and Lamb, M. E. (2001) "The relationship between within-interview contradictions and eliciting interviewer utterances," *Child Abuse and Neglect*, 25: 323–33.

Perner, J. and Ruffman, T. (1995) "Episodic memory and autonoetic consciousness: developmental evidence and a theory of childhood amnesia," *Journal of Experimental Child Psychology*, 59: 516–48.

Roberts, K. P., Lamb, M. E., and Sternberg, K. J. (2004) "The effects of rapport-building style on children's reports of a staged event," *Applied Cognitive Psychology*, 18: 189–202.

Saywitz, K. J. and Snyder, L. (1996) "Narrative elaboration: test of a new procedure for interviewing children," *Journal of Consulting and Clinical Psychology*, 64: 1347–57.

Saywitz, K., Camparo, L. B., and Romanoff, A. (2010) "Interviewing children in custody cases: implications of research and policy for practice," *Behavioral Sciences and the Law*, 28: 542–62.

Schacter, D. L., Kagan, J., and Leichtman, M. D. (1995) "True and false memories in children and adults: a cognitive neuroscience perspective," *Psychology, Public Policy, and Law*, 1: 411–28.

Shepherd, E. (2007) *Investigative Interviewing: The Conversation Management Approach*. New York: Oxford University Press.

Shing, Y. L., Werkle-Bergner, M., Brehmer, Y., Muller, V., Li, S. C., and Lindenberger, U. (2010) "Episodic memory across the lifespan: the contributions of associative and strategic components," *Neuroscience and Biobehavioral Reviews*, 34, 1080–91.

Shiraishi, H., Naka, M., and Ebihara, N. (2006) "The cognitive interview and a modified cognitive interview: recall for a witnessed event and source recognition of repeated misinformation," *Japanese Journal of Cognitive Psychology*, 4: 33–42.

Sternberg, K. J., Lamb, M. E., Hershkowitz, I., Yudilevitch, L., Orbach, Y., Esplin, P. W., and Hovav, M. (1997) "Effects of introductory style on children's abilities to describe experiences of sexual abuse," *Child Abuse and Neglect*, 21: 1133–46.

Uematsu, T. (1958) *Shinban Saiban Shinrigaku no Shoso* [*Forensic Psychology: A New Version*]. Tokyo: Yushindo.

Watanabe, Y. (1992) *Muzai no Hakken: Shoko no Bunseki to Handan Kijun* [*Finding the Innocence: Analysis of Evidence and Criteria of Judgment*]. Tokyo: Keiso Shobo.

Westcott, H. L., Kynan, S., and Few, C. (2006) "Improving the quality of investigative interviews for suspected child abuse: a case study," *Psychology, Crime and Law*, 12: 77–96.

Yamamoto, T. (2013) *Kodomo kara no higai no uttae wo kiku: Seido to shiteno shihou mensetsu wo jitsugen suru tameni* [*Listening to Child Victims: To Establish a System for Forensic Interviews*]. Paper presented at 19th Annual Meeting of the Japanese Society for the Prevention of Child Abuse and Neglect, Matsumoto, Nagano, Japan, 13–14 December.

Yuille, J. C., Hunter, R., Joffe, R., and Zaparniuk, J. (1993) "Interviewing children in sexual abuse cases," in G. S. Goodman and B. L. Bottoms (eds), *Child Victims, Child Witnesses: Understanding and Improving Children's Testimony*. New York: Guilford Press, pp. 95–115.

5 Investigative interviewing of child victims in South Korea

Misun Yi, Eunkyung Jo and Michael E. Lamb

Introduction

Investigative interviewing of child victims in South Korea has changed dramatically over the last few decades. Several high-profile cases involving miscarriages of justice, directly linked to misconduct by investigative interviewers, have led to changes in legislation and police policies. Moreover, the National Institute of Child Health and Human Development (NICHD) investigative interview protocol was recently chosen as an appropriate guideline for interviewing child victims in South Korea (Ministry of Gender Equality and Family (MGEF), 2010). In this chapter, although this volume focuses on interviewing victims and witnesses in general, our attention is drawn only to sexually abused child victims rather than other types of incidents or victims such as adults or the disabled due to the absence of the related research and known practice. Therefore, firstly, we describe the child sexual assault cases, which prompted legislative changes and the introduction of new interviewing procedures. Then, the systems and processes of investigation for child victims are explained. Lastly, we focus on police officers' practices and training by summarising a recent field study (Yi *et al.*, under review) showing the applicability of the NICHD Protocol in South Korea.

Two cases leading to changes in legal proceedings associated with child sexual abuse cases

Miryang gang rape case[1]

In December 2004, the gang rape of five teenage girls by 44 high-school boys in Miryang region shocked the nation. A 14-year-old girl who lived in Ulsan (about 25 miles away from Miryang) had been repeatedly kidnapped, robbed and raped by a group of boys over the course of about a year. The girl was threatened to keep the rapes secret and was ordered to come to Miryang whenever they commanded. She was then ordered to bring her younger sister and cousins to Miryang, who became further victims as well. She could not disclose the abuse for a year because the boys blackmailed her by threatening to publish pictures of her rape on the Internet if she told anyone.

The brutal crime only became worse when the police became involved. When the girls came to Miryang to be interviewed, police officers blamed the victims by saying that they had 'embarrassed their hometown' and ignored the teenage girls' requests to be interviewed by female officers. Instead, the girls had to publicly see and identify dozens of offenders. Further, when the victims were interviewed at the police station, the parents of the boys besieged the victims, threatening them with additional attacks. The girls had to visit the police station nine times and endured seven- to eight-hour-long interviews each time.

Of the 44 boys accused, only 20 boys were charged in court while the others were freed. Four boys were sentenced to three to four years in juvenile prison while 16 of them received probation with mandatory social and sex education services because the boys' families paid compensation to the principal girl's father without her consent or that of her mother. After the case was closed, the girls were left struggling with the aftermath of the horrific incidents. The girls could not return to school after personal information – including photos, SNS (social networking services), email addresses and phone numbers – were published on the Internet due to the police officers' carelessness.

The Cho Doo-Soon case

Nayoung (an alias) was eight years old when she suffered irreparable damage to her genital organs and colon that meant she would be dependent on a colostomy bag for the rest of her life after being beaten, tortured and violently raped by a 57-year-old man named Doo-Soon Cho. In December 2008, while on her way to school, Cho lured Nayoung into a public toilet and repeatedly penetrated her genital organs, anus and an ear after which the girl was beaten and then strangled. In an attempt to remove his semen from Nayoung's anus, Cho forcibly extracted it with a toilet pump, thereby rupturing her large intestine and causing permanent damage to her genital organs. Finally, Cho washed and left her lying in cold water.

Although Cho was arrested several days after the attack, the poor girl's tragedies were not over. While she was suffering from deep physical and psychological injuries in hospital, she was subjected to unnecessary, insensitive and repeated investigative interviews. Prosecutorial investigators summoned her four times to be asked the same questions on the inexcusable grounds that 'the previous interview was not video-recorded' or 'the sound was too faint', etc. Unbelievably, Cho was sentenced to only 12 years in prison because the court accepted the argument that alcohol had diminished his capacity.

Lessons from these two tragic cases

When these sexual assault cases were revealed to the public in December 2004 and 2008, the entire Korean society was outraged, not only because the cases were so horrific but also because the government, investigative officers and courts had behaved so irresponsibly. Under pressure from social and child welfare advocates, the National Assembly agreed to change the procedures governing the treatment of criminal victims thereby ensuring that these two tragic cases led to important changes in the legal system and laws concerning child sexual abuse in South Korea.

The *Miryang* case led to the enactment of the Crime Victim Protection Act in 2005 and the Protection of Children and Juveniles from Sexual Abuse Act in 2006 which together provide a framework for the protection and support of crime victims. In response to criticisms of police officers for conducting improper investigations that included practices such as the face-to-face confrontations between victims and suspects, unprofessional interview techniques and procedures, as well as police officers' secondary victimisation of rape victims by defamation, blaming and assaultive behaviour the Korean National Police Agency introduced a 'Sexual Assault Investigators System', placing female police officers in charge of cases that involved the sexual abuse of women, children and the disabled (Korean National Police Agency (KNPA), 2013). They also accelerated the establishment of One-stop Support Centres, which ensured that medical examinations, investigative interviews and the provision of social welfare and legal support were provided to adult and child victims of sexual and domestic violence at a single location.

As a result of the *Cho Doo-Soon* case, Nayoung and her family sued the government, claiming damages for the harmful experiences associated with the inadequate investigation. The court ruled in favour of Nayoung and her family. The prosecutor's office officially apologised to Nayoung and her family for interviewing her several times because they had not prepared properly to record their interviews. In addition, the *Cho Doo-Soon* case led to the revision of the act on the Prevention of Sexual Violence and Protection of Victims in 2010, increasing possible penalties for child sexual abuse and removing the statute of limitations which previously ranged from one to 15 years depending on the seriousness of the crime. As a result, courts are no longer allowed to reduce the sentences of sex offenders who claim leniency because they were under the influence of alcohol.

Investigation of child sexual abuse cases

One-stop Support Centres

Given criticisms of the ineffective and traumatic investigative and interviewing procedures, One-stop Support Centres were established to provide integrated services for adult, child and vulnerable victims of sexual and domestic physical abuse at a single location. Like Children's Advocacy Centers (CACs) in the USA (National Children's Alliance, 2014; National Children's Advocacy Center, 2014) and Sexual Assault Referral Centres (SARCs) in the UK (Department of Health, 2005), One-stop Support Centres facilitate coordination of the diverse services, including medical, social, legal and psychological support and investigation, offered to alleged victims. After the first One-stop Support Centre was established in the National Police Hospital in 2005, a further 14 centres were established in 2006 and 25 centres were operating nationwide in 2013 (KNPA, 2013). While 4,764 cases were reported to the centres in 2006, the number of reported cases increased rapidly to 13,625 in 2011(KNPA, 2013).

The centres are located within hospitals to increase the accessibility to medical experts and facilities thereby facilitating the timely collection of uncontaminated evidence of sexual abuse while ensuring that immediate medical attention is provided to treat physical and psychological injuries. While the accessibility of services has thus increased, they remain confidential and alleged perpetrators and other unrelated people are not allowed access. A waiting room and a reception area have child-friendly decorations with playthings and children's books. There is a medical testing room where medical evidence is collected. Interview rooms have video-recording systems so that, while police officers conduct investigative interviews, other related professionals such as psychologists, public defenders for the victim and intermediaries can observe the interviews from monitoring rooms.

The One-stop Support Centres operate with multidisciplinary personnel including investigative, medical, social, legal and psychological support teams. Police officers, social workers and nurses work at the centres 24 hours a day in three shifts while psychologists and public defenders for the victim attend as needed. All services are provided to the alleged victims free of charge. The desired practices are summarised in Figure 5.1.

Investigative support teams

The investigative support teams are led by female police officers who direct the investigative interviews of child victims as well as the general investigative proceedings. Victims and their families (or support persons) are notified of the victims' rights and told about the investigative process and possible trial procedures early in the investigation. To prepare for investigative interviews, police officers arrange for the presence of stenographers as well as intermediaries to help vulnerable witnesses to communicate with the police. When necessary, they give advice during the interview and later write a report regarding the appropriateness of the interview and the victim's credibility (KNPA, 2013).[2] Since the enactment of the Punishment of Sexual Crimes and Protection of Victims Act (Clause 3 of Article 21), which covers interviews with victims who are under 19 years of age or disabled, video-recording has been mandated in order (1) to prevent unnecessary repetition; (2) to prevent possible secondary victimisation of victims of sexual violence; and (3) to make the recordings and transcripts available to courts and interested parties.

While police officers interview child victims, support people can sit in the interview room to ease the associated psychological stress, while stenographers, intermediaries and public defenders observe the interviews from monitoring rooms via CCTV links. Another responsibility of the police officers is to cooperate and coordinate with the police station investigating the case and interrogating suspects, as well as with the prosecutor's office.

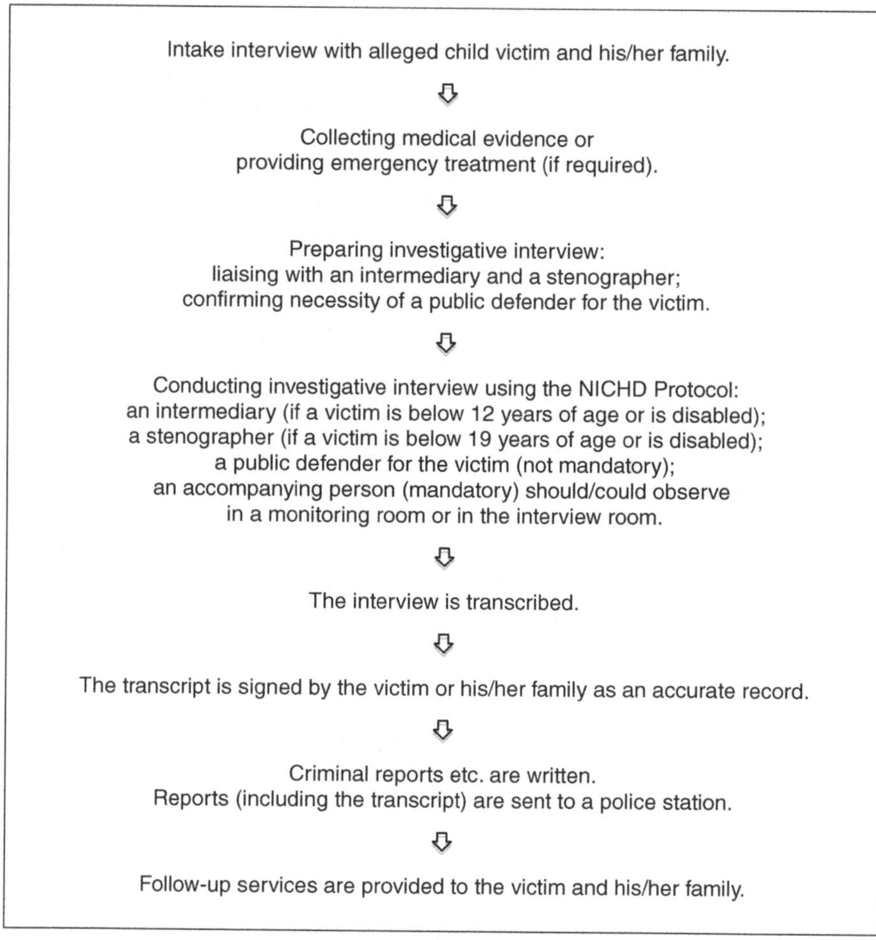

Figure 5.1 Process of investigation at One-stop Support Centres.

Medical support teams

Frequently, urgent medical interventions are needed both to collect forensic medical evidence, which must be carefully gathered by experts, and to treat physical and psychological injuries promptly. Generally, one or two nurses work at each centre and collect the medical evidence using an 'emergency rape evidence collection kit', developed and distributed by the Ministry of Gender Equality and Family (MGEF) (MGEF, 2002).[3] When victims need treatment for physical, obstetric, gynaecological or psychological injuries, they are transferred to the adjacent hospitals. Victims and their families can receive assistance with the expenses associated with treating physical and psychological injuries, tests and treatment for sexually transmitted infections (STIs) or diseases (STDs), emergency contraception, abortion, etc.

Social work teams

When victims and their families visit the centres or are transferred from police stations or related agencies, social workers conduct brief intake interviews in order to obtain general information. Once the case is accepted, the social worker manages the case and coordinates with other necessary social services such as shelters or 'Crime Victim Support Centers'[4] (which provide financial support to victims and their families with living, housing and educational expenses) or 'Sunflower Children Centers'[5] where sexually abused children can obtain long-term psychological treatment and counselling.

Legal support teams

Legal services are provided to child and juvenile victims of sexual abuse under the age of 19 throughout the legal proceedings, from the early stages of the investigation up to the trial. When victims ask for legal support, prosecutors appoint public defenders. The services cover the entire length of the process and include counselling about legal proceedings and forensic interviews, attending investigative interviews and trials, etc. (Ministry of Justice, 2012).

Psychological support teams

Psychological assessments and treatment for victims and their families are provided through Sunflower Children's Centres or by liaising with local hospitals. The Sunflower Children's Centres were established for victims under 19 years of age to provide psychological assessments, evaluations and treatments. Recently, the functions of the Sunflower Children's Centres have been integrated within the One-stop Support Centres. Thus far, seven of 25 One-stop Support Centres have combined with Sunflower Children's Centres while eight Sunflower Children Centres remain independent (KNPA, 2013).

Investigative interviewing of child victims in South Korea

The revision of the act on the Punishment of Sexual Crimes and Protection led to the video-recording of investigative interviews in 2003, allowing victims' evidence-in-chief to be presented to court via CCTV from a separate room or via video-recorded interviews earlier conducted in police stations. Whereas the quality of earlier investigative interviews could not be assessed, those conducted after enactment of the law have to be properly conducted in order to be admissible in court. Guidelines for interviewing child victims (Ministry of Justice, 2003; KNPA, 2008) were produced to promote evidence-based best practice. Previous guidelines had placed more emphasis on video-recording procedures than interview strategies, and despite changes in the guidelines, police officers remained unable to apply the guidance in their everyday interviewing practice (MGEF, 2010). Moreover, because Korean police officers were not systematically trained to conduct interviews in accordance with the new best-practice guidelines, they often failed to obtain accurate and abundant information from child victims. Investigative interviewers clearly needed operational guidance, and these needs were met by the introduction of the NICHD Protocol.

The NICHD Protocol

The NICHD Protocol is a structured evidence-based investigative interview procedure prepared for interviews with allegedly abused children (Lamb *et al.*, 2008; Orbach *et al.*, 2000). All phases of the protocol are designed to maximise the amount of information elicited from the free-recall memory of child witnesses by taking advantage of relevant research findings (Lamb *et al.*, 2008; Orbach *et al.*, 2000). Using the protocol, interviewers introduce themselves and clarify the ground rules (i.e. describing events in as much detail as possible, telling only the truth, saying 'I don't know', 'I don't remember' and correcting the interviewer when applicable). Interviewers then establish rapport and practise episodic memory retrieval to show children how to describe past experiences in response to open-ended prompts. During the substantive part of the interviews, police officers ask about incidents using open-ended prompts as much as possible. A break allows the children a rest while the interviewer reviews missing information and plans the rest of the interview. Finally, the interview closes with an opportunity for children to disclose additional information before they are thanked and the focus of discussion shifts to a neutral topic. Empirical research in several different countries has shown that use of the Protocol enhances the quality and quantity of information elicited from alleged victims (Cyr and Lamb, 2009; Lamb *et al.*, 2009; Orbach *et al.*, 2000; Sternberg *et al.*, 2001).

In South Korea, the NICHD Protocol was first introduced by the third author of this chapter in 2010 by way of a master class and workshops. The protocol was also translated into Korean and distributed to police officers in One-stop Support Centres (MGEF, 2010). The first training programmes focused on the utility of the protocol were hosted by KNPA and conducted in April 2011, right after the police had been advised to start using the protocol in their interviews. Recently, the first field study designed to determine whether training in use of the protocol improved the quality of child investigative interviews was conducted (Yi *et al.*, under review). In the following sections, we describe the police training procedures and their interview practices by summarising the results of the study conducted by Yi and her colleagues (under review).

The police training programmes

In April 2011, two-day training courses were given to all One-stop Support Centre police officers by the first and second authors of this chapter (see Figure 5.2).

	Day 1	Day 2
9:00 – 9:15	Registration	Practice interview 1 and feedback
9:15 – 10:30	Reviews: strengths and limitations of child witnesses	
10:30 – 10:45	Break	Break
10:45 – 12:00	Open questions and question type practice	Child interview video review
12:00 – 13:00	Lunch	Lunch
13:00 – 14:30	NICHD Protocol	Practice interview 2 and feedback
14:30 – 14:45	Break	Break
14:45 – 16:45	Rapport building and episodic memory training	Practice interview 3 and feedback
16:45 – 17:00	Discussion	Discussion

Figure 5.2 The protocol training schedules.

The training programmes were designed to explain the conceptual background and show the practical utility of the protocol to police officers. The programmes were informed by published recommendations for the investigative interviewing of child victims (see Lamb *et al.*, 2008: 253–66), with emphasis on providing very detailed and specific explanations of the protocol, opportunities to exercise and practise each phase of the protocol, and many actual cases as examples. Feedback during and after the training were also included. On the first day, police officers were informed of psychological research on aspects of child development which could affect children's memory and reports. The importance of using proper types of questions was stressed in all the training sessions by describing the conceptual justification for recommendations, showing examples of proper and improper question usage, and providing guided practice analysing the types of questions used in some of their own prior interviews. The conceptual and empirical foundations for each phase of the protocol were also explained in detail. The second day primarily comprised opportunities to practise using the protocol by interviewing instructors and colleagues, who then provided immediate feedback. Video-recorded interviews were also presented to illustrate how the protocol was used in practice.

As part of the training, police officers received written feedback on their interviews. At the beginning of the training, they were asked to submit one transcript of an interview with a child less than 14 years of age. Detailed feedback on those interviews was provided by the first and second authors of this chapter as well as

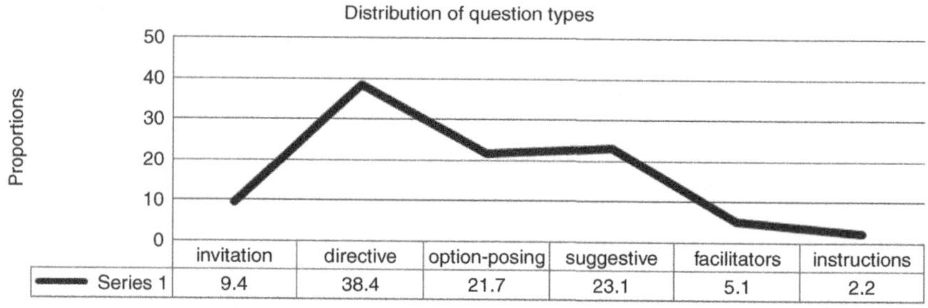

This graph shows the types of questions used during the interview. It shows that invitations comprised approximately 10%, directive questions 38%, option-posing 22%, suggestive questions 23% and facilitators and instructions 5% and 2% respectively of all the questions asked. Fairly typical proportions of invitations and directive questions were used but the proportion of suggestive questions was very high. Since younger children are more vulnerable to such suggestive questions than older children and adults, you should be very careful when you ask more focused questions. I recommend that you use cued-invitations instead of many of your option-posing and suggestive questions.

Figure 5.3 An example of feedback: distribution of question types and comments on the profile.

by postgraduate students who had been trained to use the NICHD Protocol and to analyse question types. The feedback included graphical comparisons of the question types used, comments on each proper and improper question used by the interviewers and suggestions about better alternatives (see Figure 5.3). Further recommendations for future interviews were also given to them. A total of 77 female police officers attended one of the three identical trainings. All police officers submitted pre-training transcripts and received written feedback within three months of the session.

Korean police officers' interview behaviour

After the training sessions, we conducted a study to determine how effective the NICHD Protocol training had been (Yi *et al.*, under review). A total of 36 transcribed interviews conducted before and after training by 18 police officers were compared. To assess the police officers' interview behaviour, the types of questions used during the substantive part of interviews were categorised using the coding system and definitions introduced by Lamb and his colleagues (Lamb *et al.*, 2007). This showed that, after training, police officers use invitations and facilitators more and suggestive prompts less often than before the training. Specifically, while these Korean police officers mostly depended on directive ($M = 39.06$, $SD = 13.37$) and option-posing ($M = 30.81$, $SD = 11.59$) prompts while using few invitations ($M = 3.54$, $SD = 4.73$) and facilitators ($M = 1.86$, $SD = 2.69$) before the training, the mean frequencies changed significantly after training. The use of invitations increased to 10.65 per cent ($SD = 6.54$) while use of suggestive prompts decreased to 18.89 per cent ($SD = 10.39$) on average (see Table 5.1).

Table 5.1 Mean proportions of prompts used by interviewers

M (SD)	*Pre-training*	*Post-training*	*t*
Invitation	3.54 (4.73)	10.65 (6.54)	–3.47**
Facilitator	1.86 (2.69)	4.38 (4.48)	–2.10*
Directive	39.06 (13.37)	36.62 (7.85)	0.82
Option-posing	30.81 (11.59)	35.42 (26.14)	–0.92
Suggestive	24.73 (8.87)	18.89 (10.39)	1.99+

**P < 0.01,
*p = 0.05,
+p = 0.06
(Yi *et al.*, under review)

This result is consistent with findings obtained in previous studies (Lamb, Orbach *et al.*, 2002; Lamb *et al.*, 2000; Orbach *et al.*, 2000; Price and Roberts, 2011), although this was the first study to show that use of the protocol changed the behaviour of interviewers and alleged victims with non-Western ethnic and cultural backgrounds.

Current situations and the way forward

Training and use of the NICHD Protocol by Korean police officers is now being adopted nationwide. Since the first training programmes were provided in 2011, training courses focused on how to conduct investigative interviews of child sexual abuse have been established as regular programmes provided annually to the police at the Korean Police Investigation Academy.[6] Recently, KNPA (2013) surveyed all police officers based in One-stop Support Centres to better understand their actual situations. Eighty-nine questionnaires were distributed and 70 (74.4 per cent) were completed. According to the survey, 87.1 per cent of the police officers in One-stop Support Centres had attended NICHD Protocol training sessions. Moreover, 60 (85.7 per cent) of the respondents reported using the protocol when interviewing child victims, while only one (1.4 per cent) stated she did not use the protocol and 9 (12.9 per cent) failed to answer the question (KNPA, 2013).

However, although the training has been provided annually, the curricula remain unstandardised and the instructors unknown so the quality of training provided cannot be ascertained. Moreover, although most police officers reported that they used the protocol, their actual practices may be aligned poorly with recommended practices. Previous research has shown that police officers underutilise recommended investigative interviewing practices even when they believe they were adhering to them. Therefore supervision and feedback designed to raise awareness about actual practices is needed to promote adherence to the protocol. The recent survey (KNPA, 2013) also revealed that 41 (41 per cent) of the respondents had received some feedback with approximately 80 per cent stating that feedback was useful because (1) it helped them recognise problems of which they were not aware when conducting the interviews; (2) they understood the risks associated with the use of improper types of questions (e.g. suggestive questions); and (3) it allowed them to correct improper interview behaviour. Although these responses suggested that the feedback was useful, no systematic feedback system currently exists. Feedback is costly but indispensable. Because it is possible to effect major improvements in the quality of forensic interviews only when interviewers are given continuing supervision and feedback (Lamb, Sternberg *et al.*, 2002; Lamb *et al.*, 2000; Orbach *et al.*, 2000; Sternberg *et al.*, 2001), such feedback and supervision should be provided to police officers in South Korea.

There has been only a little research directly focused on the investigative interviews conducted with alleged child victims in South Korea. This could be due mainly to the lack of Korean academic experts in this field and the lack of support from related institutes. With well-established training and feedback systems, academic research directly focused on effective investigative interviewing strategies and developmental factors which affect children's memories and accounts would have the additional benefit of establishing strong investigative and interview systems in South Korea. Recently, data has been collected in the next wave of workshops and several projects on investigative interviewing have been planned and run by researchers in cooperation with the Police Agency.

In addition, while there has been some progress concerning interviews with children as victims and witnesses, it still remains the case that other potentially vulnerable groups of witnesses have not benefited from similar advances in law and practice. South Korea is still in the process of implementing radical changes in legal proceedings. We hope that the future for both the research into and practice of investigative interviewing will be bright.

Notes

1. More information regarding the case can be found at: http://koreajoongangdaily.joins.com/news/article/article.aspx?aid=2503972.
2. http://kcvc.or.kr/new/05_sub/5c_sub01.php?mode=view&number=1750&page=1
3. http://www.mogef.go.kr/korea/view/news/news03_01.jsp?func=view&currentPage=285&key_type=&key=&search_start_date=&search_end_date=&class_id=0&idx=163666
4. http://kcvc.or.kr/new/05_sub/5c_sub01.php?mode=view&number=1733&page=1&b_name=data
5. http://www.womannchild.or.kr/en/sub01_1.asp
6. Training programmes are presented at http://www.kpia.go.kr/.

References

Cyr, M. and Lamb, M. E. (2009) 'Assessing the effectiveness of the NICHD investigative interview protocol when interviewing French-speaking alleged victims of child sexual abuse in Quebec', *Child Abuse and Neglect*, 33: 257–68.

Department of Health (2005) *National Service Guidelines for Developing Sexual Assault Referral Centres (SARCs)*, Department of Health Publication 270788.

Korean National Police Agency (2008) *A Manual for Investigative Interviews of Alleged Sexual Abuse Child Victims*. National Police Agency, Republic of Korea.

Korean National Police Agency (2013) *Improving Ways to Prevent Sexual Assault*. Korean National Police Agency, Republic of Korea.

Lamb, M. E., Hershkowitz, I., Orbach, Y. and Esplin, P. W. (2008) *Tell Me What Happened: Structured Investigative Interviews of Child Victims and Witnesses*. Hoboken, NJ and Chichester: Wiley.

Lamb, M. E., Orbach, Y., Hershkowitz, I., Esplin, P. W. and Horowitz, D. (2007) 'A structured forensic interview protocols improves the quality and informativeness of investigative interviews with children: a review of research using the NICHD Investigative Interview Protocol', *Child Abuse and Neglect*, 31: 1201–31.

Lamb, M. E., Orbach, Y., Sternberg, K. J., Aldridge, J., Pearson, S., Stewart, H. L., Esplin, P. W. and Bowler, L. (2009) 'Use of a structured investigative protocol enhances the quality of investigative interviews with alleged victims of child sexual abuse in Britain', *Applied Cognitive Psychology*, 23: 449–67.

Lamb, M. E., Orbach, Y., Sternberg, K. J., Esplin, P. W. and Hershkowitz, I. (2002) 'The effects of forensic interview practices on the quality of information provided of information by alleged victims of child abuse', in L. Westcott, G. M. Davies and R. Bull (eds), *Children's Testimony*. Chichester: John Wiley & Sons, pp. 131–45.

Lamb, M. E., Sternberg, K. J., Orbach, Y., Esplin, P. W. and Mitchell, S. (2002) 'Is ongoing feedback necessary to maintain the quality of investigative interviews with allegedly abused children?', *Applied Developmental Science*, 6: 35–41.

Lamb, M. E., Sternberg, K. J., Orbach, Y., Hershkowitz, I., Horowitz, D. and Esplin, P. W. (2000) 'The effects of intensive training and ongoing supervision on the quality of investigative interviews with alleged sex abuse victims', *Applied Developmental Science*, 6: 114–25.

Ministry of Gender Equality and Family (2010) *Guidelines on Investigative Interviewing of Child Victims*. Ministry of Gender Equality and Family, Republic of Korea.

Ministry of Justice (2003) *Understanding Child Investigation*. Ministry of Justice, Republic of Korea.

Ministry of Justice (2012) *Guide to Public Defenders*. Ministry of Justice. Republic of Korea.

National Children's Advocacy Center (2014) Accessed April 2014 at: http://www.nationalcac.org/history/history.html.

National Children's Alliance (2014) Accessed April, 2014 at: http://www.nationalchildrensalliance.org/index.php?s=6.

Orbach, Y., Hershkowitz, I., Lamb, M. E., Sternberg, K. J., Esplin, P. W. and Horowitz, D. (2000) 'Assessing the value of structured protocols for forensic interviews of alleged child abuse victims', *Child Abuse and Neglect*, 24: 733–52.

Price, H. L. and Roberts, K. P. (2011) 'The effects of an intensive training and feedback program on police and social workers' investigative interviews of children', *Canadian Journal of Behavioral Science*, 43: 335–44.

Sternberg, K. L., Lamb, M. E., Orbach, Y., Esplin, P. W. and Mitchell, S. (2001) 'Use of a structured investigative protocol enhances young children's response to free-recall prompts in the course of forensic interviews', *Journal of Applied Psychology*, 86: 997–1005.

Yi, M., Jo, E., Lamb, E. M. and Kim, A. (under review) 'Effects of the NICHD Protocol training on child investigative interview quality in Korean police officers', *Journal of Police and Criminal Psychology*.

Australia

6 Interviewing witnesses in Australia

Jane Tudor-Owen and Adrian J. Scott

Introduction

Much has been written internationally since the early 1990s concerning the development, implementation and evaluation of investigative interviewing models. In Australia, however, what is known as investigative interviewing was not adopted in most jurisdictions until a decade later and in some jurisdictions almost 20 years later. While investigative interviewing in the context of interviews with adults was imported to Australia from England and Wales, the various Australian jurisdictions have adapted the approach to suit local needs. The impetus for the development of investigative interviewing in England and Wales has been attributed, at least in part, to a number of widely publicised miscarriages of justice. In Australia, by comparison, the motivation to introduce investigative interviewing models has largely been attributed to individual jurisdictions observing improvements in practice internationally and pursuing change locally as a result.

The importance of interviewing witnesses[1] cannot be overstated, and while anecdotal evidence suggests witness interviews are considered less important than interviews with persons of interest, it is acknowledged that poor witness statements can weaken the prosecution's case. As Fisher (1995) states, complete and accurate witness statements maximise the likelihood of a perpetrator being successfully prosecuted and subsequently minimise the likelihood of a wrongful conviction. Recognition of the importance of witness interviews and the corresponding statements in achieving just outcomes in court has resulted in increased efforts to improve the quality of interviews with witnesses.

Within Australia there are eight policing jurisdictions, seven of which comprise police services in New South Wales (NSW), the Northern Territory (NT), Queensland (Qld), South Australia (SA), Tasmania (Tas), Victoria (Vic) and Western Australia (WA). In addition, Commonwealth matters are dealt with by the Australian Federal Police (AFP) which incorporates police services in the Australian Capital Territory (ACT). This chapter will initially discuss the governance of interviewing practices in Australia, including the statutory provisions pertaining to the interviewing of witnesses. It will then discuss the development of investigative interviewing practices in Australia, with specific reference to training. Best practice and relevant literature will be incorporated throughout the chapter to provide context for these discussions. Finally, the chapter will consider some of the challenges associated with implementing investigative interviewing practices in Australia and the ways in which jurisdictions are attempting to overcome these challenges.

Governance of interviewing practices

The Australia New Zealand Policing Advisory Agency (ANZPAA), established in 2007, serves to provide policy advice to policing jurisdictions in Australia and New Zealand (ANZPAA, 2010). In recognition of the need for uniformity in policing practices across Australia, ANZPAA and the Australia New Zealand Council of Police Professionalisation (ANZCoPP) are developing a Police Practice Standards Model which promotes professional development, and will consolidate and further build the evidence base for policing practices (ANZPAA, 2013). Despite these advances, there are still issues of jurisdictional discretion with regard to the adoption of any agreed upon best practice and limited relevant statutory provisions in the context of witness interviews. Although there is legislation governing the conditions under which persons of interest can be detained and interviewed (e.g. Criminal Investigation Act 2006 (WA)), there is no equivalent legislation governing the interviewing of witnesses.

There is, however, statutory provision in each Australian jurisdiction allowing the use of pre-recorded statements as evidence in certain cases involving vulnerable witnesses. The use of pre-recorded statements as evidence means that a vulnerable witness may only be required to be interviewed once, and this interview may be used in court if it satisfies the relevant rules of evidence. Repeated interviewing may increase the number of details recalled by witnesses (Ceci and Bruck, 1995; Martin and Thomson, 1994), but there is concern that this practice may cause additional trauma and contaminate the witness's recollection. Given the suggestibility of vulnerable witnesses, there is an increased risk that officer bias and the unintentional use of leading questions will contaminate the details recalled (Melnyk *et al.*, 2007). Although there are still instances where vulnerable witnesses are interviewed on more than one occasion, it is important that police officers are skilled in conducting dual-purpose interviews in order to capture information relevant to the investigation and prosecution of an offence as efficiently as possible (Westera *et al.*, 2011). To this end, it has been recommended that interviewers are provided with training around the investigative and evidential purposes of the interview, with the potential for input from stakeholders involved in court proceedings, for example from the prosecution and defence counsel, and the judiciary (Powell, 2002).

There are no government-based bodies providing documentation and advice regarding best practice in investigative interviewing in Australia (Green, 2012), although ANZPAA are currently developing relevant practice standards for police. It is appropriate, therefore, given the adoption of similar investigative interviewing practices in Australia and England and Wales, to consult the *Achieving Best Evidence for Criminal Proceedings* guidelines (ABE – Ministry of Justice, 2011). Given the scope and detail of the ABE, not every aspect will be covered in detail. Instead, key areas of similarity and difference between what is contained in the ABE and what is known of practice in Australian jurisdictions will be highlighted.

The ABE defines vulnerable witnesses as people under 18 years of age and/or with mental disorders, learning and/or physical disabilities, and intimidated witnesses (people whose evidence is likely to be diminished because of fear or distress). It is recommended that these witnesses are afforded Special Measures including the pre-recording of statements for use as evidence. The fundamental concern of the ABE is that the most suitable Special Measures are employed such that the quality of the resulting evidence is maximised (Ministry of Justice, 2011).

Consistent with the recommendations of the ABE, the Australian Law Reform Commission's (1997) report entitled *Seen and Heard: Priority for Children in the Legal Process* proposed that all jurisdictions make provisions for the video-recording of interviews with children to be admissible in court proceedings. While all states and territories now provide for the pre-recorded statements of children to be admitted as evidence, the definition of child varies between jurisdictions. A child may be defined as 16 years or less or 18 years or less and, in certain jurisdictions, there are additional conditions that the person needs to satisfy before they are eligible for their pre-recorded statement to be admitted as evidence. For example, in Tasmania, a child's pre-recorded statement can be admitted if the child is 18 years or less and the witness to specified crimes, including sexual and serious violent offences (Evidence (Children and Special Witnesses) Act 2001 (Tas)).

With regard to mental disorder, learning and/or physical disability, there is again variation between jurisdictions. There are provisions allowing for the admittance of a pre-recorded statement where the witness has a cognitive or mental impairment likened to learning disability but, similar to a child's evidence, there are additional conditions that need to be satisfied in certain jurisdictions before they are eligible for their pre-recorded statement to be admitted as evidence. For example, in Victoria, a person's pre-recorded statement may be admitted as evidence where the person has a mental impairment and is the witness of a sexual or assault offence (Criminal Procedure Act 2009 (Vic)). However, Queensland is the only jurisdiction to have made specific provision for the admittance of a pre-recorded statement as evidence when the witness has a physical impairment, where this impairment would likely disadvantage the witness (Evidence Act 1977 (Qld)). Finally, the provisions for intimidated witnesses are generally more broadly characterised with provisions for witnesses who are likely to experience a particular disadvantage or emotional trauma (e.g. Evidence Act 1939 (NT)), or in relation to specific offences such as organised crime (e.g. Evidence Act 1929 (SA)) or sexual and/or violent crimes (e.g. Evidence (Miscellaneous Provisions) Act 1991 (ACT)).

It is apparent that statutory provisions relating to the interviewing of vulnerable witnesses in Australia vary across the jurisdictions. However, the principle that vulnerable witnesses should be given special provisions to facilitate their participation in the criminal justice system remains the same Australia-wide. The varying definitions of 'vulnerable witness' (or equivalent) are important to note because they determine which witnesses need to be interviewed for both investigative and evidential purposes. This distinction also becomes relevant when considering the specialised training offered to interviewers of vulnerable witnesses and where these specialised interviewers are posted. In Queensland, there are 'child-friendly' interview rooms for use within each region and in WA there are designated child interview facilities staffed by specialised interviewers. It is important, however, to consider where other vulnerable witnesses are interviewed (e.g. adults who are mentally impaired). For example whether there are specialised interviewers posted at additional locations or whether vulnerable adult witnesses are interviewed at designated child interview facilities. In order to make decisions regarding the appropriate interviewing of vulnerable witnesses, officers must be able to identify vulnerable witnesses as early as possible (O'Mahony *et al.*, 2011). Although it is possible to identify particular vulnerabilities through the course of an interview (Cooke and Davies, 2001), it is important that identification occur prior to the interview in order for it to be recorded for later use as evidence.

The introduction and development of investigative interviewing

The introduction and development of investigative interviewing in the context of interviews with adults in Australia was similar in a number of jurisdictions. For example, in Queensland and Victoria, individual members of the respective police services spent time training in England and Wales so they were able to implement training courses in their respective states. Following the initial implementation of the model, supplementary training for Australian police services has been provided at regular intervals by visiting international experts.

In Queensland, the principles of investigative interviewing were initially introduced in 1993, whereas in Victoria and Tasmania the principles were not introduced until the late 1990s and early 2000s. In WA it was not until 2009 that investigative interviewing was formally implemented as part of Project Anticus, a state-wide programme to improve investigative outcomes (Western Australia Police, 2009). In 2007, Queensland Police undertook a review of their interview training and updated their curriculum in line with developments in investigative interviewing in England and Wales. Similarly, Victoria Police have updated their curriculum since the introduction of investigative interviewing practices, with an increased emphasis on interviews with witnesses and the use of online learning. The curriculum in WA has also continued to develop since its introduction in 2009 with a specific training précis for interviews with witnesses issued in 2012.

Broadly speaking, what has been adopted (and adapted) for use in Australian jurisdictions in interviews with adults is what is referred to in England and Wales as the PEACE model. PEACE (Preparation and planning; Engage and explain;

Account, clarification and challenge; Closure; and Evaluation) is the nationally endorsed model of interviewing in England and Wales, and is suitable for interviews with witnesses and persons of interest (Association of Chief Police Officers, 2012). Importantly, the phased model of interviewing independently proposed in the ABE contains a similar framework for interviewing to that outlined in the PEACE model (Association of Chief Police Officers, 2009; Milne *et al.*, 2007).

Relevant to this discussion, NSW, Queensland, Tasmania, Victoria and WA have each introduced the PEACE model as the overarching model informing investigative interviewing. In the NSW, Queensland and WA police literature, the PEACE model is clearly used to inform the structure of the interview, with the Free Recall, Enhanced Cognitive Interview and Conversation Management models being used within the Account phase of the interview. The use of these three models is dependent upon the circumstances of the interview and the interviewee. The interviewee-led Free Recall and Enhanced Cognitive Interview models are encouraged for use with victims and cooperative witnesses, the latter also being used with persons of interest in complex cases or cases involving serious offences. The Conversation Management model, by comparison, is an interviewer-led model used in interviews with uncooperative witnesses and persons of interest.

Aside from vulnerable witnesses, there is limited recognition for other populations requiring a tailored approach to interviewing. Within interview training there are cultural awareness components that highlight specific issues of which to be mindful when interviewing Aboriginal and Torres Strait Islander people and people from non-English-speaking backgrounds. In Queensland, for example, Aboriginal and Torres Strait Islander people are considered to have a 'special need' in an interviewing context due to socio-cultural considerations (Queensland Police Service, 1995). Furthermore, across Australia, policy regarding the interviewing of Aboriginal and Torres Strait Islander people recognises the Anunga Rules (*R.* v. *Anunga*, 1976). Of relevance for interviews with witnesses, these guidelines suggest the presence of an interpreter and/or an interview friend, as well as the use of non-suggestive questioning techniques. In the first paper to propose interviewing guidelines for Aboriginal and Torres Strait Islander people, Powell (2000) outlined the PRIDE model. PRIDE stands for *P*rior knowledge about the interviewee and the wider context; *R*apport with the interviewee; *I*nterpretative assistance; a *D*iverse array of hypotheses about the event; and *E*ffective questioning techniques for eliciting a free narrative. PRIDE emphasises the importance of identifying language and cultural differences before the interview and subsequently making appropriate arrangements; for example, procuring an interpreter. Given the vast number of Aboriginal and Torres Strait Islander language groups, it is important that police are aware of differences between groups and are conscious of identifying sufficiently independent parties to provide translation services. In NSW, officers are provided with detailed guidelines as to when an interpreter is required and how to conduct an interview when an interpreter has been engaged (New South Wales Police Force, 2012).

Furthermore, in NSW and Queensland, it is a requirement that every effort is made to engage 'official professional interpreters' and caution is advised where multilingual family, friends or staff are unavoidably utilised in this role (New South Wales Police Force, 2012; Queensland Police Service, 1995).

The ABE suggests the use of specialised training for interviewing with additional parties present; for example, interpreters and/or support people. The use of interpreters in interviews has received increasing attention in the Australian interviewing literature, perhaps as a result of the growing number of people in Australia with a non-English-speaking background (Wakefield *et al.*, 2014). This awareness has highlighted the need to utilise interpreters effectively; that is, taking into account the change in dynamic caused by having an additional party present. In particular, it is noted that there is residual concern by police that interviews where interpreters are present take longer, require a modified interviewing strategy and involve additional cost. With regard to the guidelines of the ABE, Queensland officers surveyed in the study by Wakefield *et al.* (2014) expressed support for further training for interviewing with an interpreter present. It is suggested that this support may be due in part to the perceived difficulty of interviewing victims requiring an interpreter as there is the potential for a more emotive and lengthy narrative in the interview. Queensland officers currently receive specific instruction concerning the engagement of interpreters during their level two interview training and in WA, experienced interviewers supervise the engagement of interpreters in the interview context.

The operationalisation of research findings into a practical interviewing model for vulnerable witnesses has posed particular difficulty in this area of interviewing (Bull, 2010). However, the adoption of a specialised approach to working with vulnerable witnesses is consistent with the recommendations outlined in the ABE, namely that interviewers need to give particular consideration to the needs of these populations. Unlike the staggered adoption of investigative interviewing in Australia, developments in interviewing vulnerable witnesses have been adopted in a number of jurisdictions within a short period of time. A centralised model for training interviewers of vulnerable witnesses has now been developed for use in Australian jurisdictions, making standardised practices across Australia a possibility in this specialised area of interviewing.

The National Institute of Child Health and Human Development (NICHD) Investigative Interview Protocol has been adopted internationally for use with vulnerable witnesses (Lamb *et al.*, 2007; Pipe *et al.*, 2013). In Australia, the approach to interviewing vulnerable witnesses has been informed by previous research in this area, particularly that originating in the United States, and emphasises the mastery of combining basic interviewing skills with an understanding of the evidential requirements of the interview. The aim of training interviewers in psychological and legal principles is to enable them to efficiently elicit sufficient information required for investigative and evidential purposes. Of note, interviewers are encouraged to gain enough information to enable particularisation, where relevant, but not to focus on identifying dates and times to the detriment of interview quality. This approach reflects research findings suggesting that legal professionals themselves differ on requirements of particularisation; that is, the information required in order to differentiate between repeated incidents of abuse (Guadagno *et al.*, 2006).

Training

The ABE recommends an agreed-upon protocol with policies in place to ensure continued improvement in both the skill of interviewers and the quality of interviews. As with the implementation of investigative interviewing as a practice, interview training varies across Australia. In many respects, each jurisdiction operates independently of the others. There is, however, some information sharing that occurs cross-jurisdictionally. For example, Tasmania Police credit their Conversation Management materials to Victoria Police and WA Police credit the New Zealand and Queensland police services for providing some of the material used as the basis for their investigative interview training manuals. Furthermore, in 2011, an inaugural collaborative research meeting brought together police representatives from a number of Australian and international jurisdictions, in addition to representatives from Australian Customs, Border Protection, the Australian Crime Commission and the Australian Federal Police.

Across NSW, Queensland, Tasmania, Victoria and WA, the interview training provided by the various police services is generally in-house, with external providers invited to present guest lectures and workshops. The setup of training varies across the jurisdictions, with WA, for example, offering all interview training through the Detective Training School, with the exception of training for the Child Assessment and Interview Team. The setup in other jurisdictions is more fragmented. For example, in Queensland, recruits receive their level one interview training through the Recruit Training Unit and other level one training is offered by regional Education and Training Offices. All other interview training, including the specialist child interview training, is coordinated and delivered by the Specialist Investigations and Intelligence Development Unit. In Tasmania, recruits receive their training through Recruit Training Services and officers receive their training through Professional Development Services. In Victoria, the majority of interview training for both recruits and officers is offered through the Centre for Investigator Training, although specialist child interview training is provided by the Sexual Offences and Child Abuse Investigation Teams (SOCIT). In NSW, the approach to training officers in interviewing vulnerable witnesses differs to that of other jurisdictions as officers outside specialised Child Abuse and Sex Crimes squads are selected to attend a workshop relating to the interviewing of child witnesses conducted by Local Area Command.

Interview training is primarily delivered in the form of workshops that include practice interviews. For witness interview training, these workshops may include time designated to developing witness statements after the practice interviews. In some jurisdictions there is also a requirement for in-field assessment. For example, in Queensland, Victoria and WA, recruits and officers complete assigned tasks and receive feedback from their supervisors before submitting the work to the relevant training body. In an attempt to encourage continued improvement in a convenient setting, as well as to mitigate de-training, some substantive and refresher training is provided in Queensland and Tasmania. Furthermore, some jurisdictions, including Victoria and WA, are currently developing materials for online interview training which will facilitate training across geographically large jurisdictions. These strategies aim to maximise the learning and retention of skills by participating officers. They are also consistent with recommendations that investigative interview training include clearly operationalised research-based practices; opportunities to practise skills and receive feedback during training; and follow-up training; for example, refresher courses and/or additional tasks to complete in the field (Clarke and Milne, 2001; Powell, 2002). As recruits have been trained in the use of investigative interviewing for a number of years in most jurisdictions, subsequent training needs to recognise the prior skills of officers and target skill deficits (Hill and Moston, 2011; Scott *et al.*, 2014).

In a development reflecting the growing professionalism of policing in Australia, the training provided for recruits and officers in Queensland, Tasmania and Victoria contributes to satisfying the requirements for a tertiary qualification. The Public Safety Training Package provides standardised training for emergency service professionals across Australia. Of particular relevance is the Diploma of Public Safety (Policing) and Advanced Diploma of Public Safety (Police Investigation). Both of these qualifications contain units relating to interviewing. In Queensland, officers who successfully complete the detective training programme are awarded the Advanced Diploma of Public Safety (Police Investigation). This qualification is a prerequisite for officers wishing to gain detective classification. In Victoria, recruits graduate with a Diploma of Public Safety (Policing) upon completion of their probation, and similar to practices in Queensland, officers graduate with an Advanced Diploma of Public Safety (Police Investigation) upon completion of detective training school. In Tasmania, the recruit training satisfies partial requirements for the Bachelor of Social Science (Police Studies). Additional studies offered as part of in-service promotional pathways also contribute to satisfying the requirements for this degree. Although currently under review, NSW recruits graduate with an Associate Degree in Policing Practice. Having investigative interview training embedded in broader courses is ideal in that it enables recruits and officers to understand the importance of quality interviewing in the context of policing in general. In particular, some of the resistance associated with emphasising the importance of witness interviews, in comparison to interviews with persons of interest, is mitigated when discussing the role of witness statements in the investigation and prosecution of the case.

With regard to the five-tier interview training that originated in England and Wales, since condensed to three/four tiers (Green, 2012), various jurisdictions have adapted it for use in the Australian context. In WA, for example, the revised model consists of four levels: interviews for volume and simple crimes; interviews for serious and complex crimes; specialist interviews; and interview advisors. Level one training is offered to recruits in NSW, Queensland, Tasmania,

Victoria and WA, with more specialised training offered to officers on particular promotional pathways. Level one training includes instruction in the use of the Free Recall or Free Narrative model, basic memory retrieval techniques and generic communication skills. In Queensland, Victoria and WA, officers have additional requirements in order to successfully complete their probation. In Queensland and WA, officers are required to complete an additional assessment based on an interview conducted in the field. In Victoria, officers are required to attend a one-day refresher course at the conclusion of their probation.

Depending on the jurisdiction, level two training can be offered as part of a 'stand-alone' investigator course or as part of detective and/or sergeant promotional pathways. The interview training offered at level two varies across jurisdictions. For example, in Queensland, the interview techniques learnt in level one are extended and applied specifically to the context of serious and complex investigations. In Victoria, by comparison, training includes instruction in using the Cognitive Interview and more advanced memory retrieval techniques. In addition to teaching advanced memory retrieval techniques, level three training in Queensland introduces the Enhanced Cognitive Interview and develops specialist knowledge, including skills relevant to the interviewing of vulnerable adult witnesses. The structure for level three interview training in Victoria is currently under review, with the proposed course increasing in duration. In WA, specialist level three training is offered to the Child Assessment and Interview Team. The level four training offered in Victoria and WA (and proposed in Queensland) equips officers as interview advisors for their particular areas of work and appears to be a hybrid of the original tier four and tier five PEACE training incorporating supervision and advisory roles (Green, 2012).

With regard to interviewing vulnerable witnesses, relevant interview training has been made available online. This approach to training is unique in Australia, in that training is centralised and officers in multiple jurisdictions are able to access training simultaneously. The training is designed to be collaborative, with the sharing of information and resources an essential component. This approach is an example of the strength of collaborations between police (and other legal professionals) and academics. A number of jurisdictions have consulted with academic and industry experts in order to revise policy and procedures. In addition to the example of the development with regard to interviewing vulnerable witnesses, NSW Police sought advice from a forensic linguist, social workers, legal professionals and the Ethnic Affairs Commission when developing their Code of Practice for Custody, Rights, Investigation, Management and Evidence (CRIME) in 1998 (Gibbons, 2001). As a result, the interviewing of witnesses in Australia is informed by psychological principles, an awareness and knowledge of the relevant law and an understanding of the needs of unique populations.

When questioned about the challenges faced in implementing interviewing protocol and developing training, jurisdictions commented on the limited resources at their disposal. A number of jurisdictions were concerned about the need to centralise training within their respective police services and to develop highly skilled personnel to deliver interview training in an informed and engaging manner. The movement of staff was also cited as a concern in the ongoing development and delivery of the interview training curriculum. The loss of expertise through the systematic rotation of officers is one of the key issues that potentially inhibits the gains made thus far in investigative interviewing practices in Australia. Officers involved in designing and implementing training are moved on to other areas of service and, despite comprehensive handover procedures, some level of expertise is lost. Policy reasons for the rotation of officers, including the prevention of corruption (McCusker, 2006), are valid but it would assist the development of interview training if exceptions were made for this particular area of service.

Changing the culture towards interviewing was also raised as a challenge for jurisdictions. The techniques used previously, including the more confrontational approach to interviewing, have not been entirely eliminated from practice. In Queensland, one strategy has been to deliver training to key experienced officers in order to facilitate the elimination of out-of-date practices and the adoption of current interviewing practices. In addition, interview trainers are challenged by recruits and newer officers who comment that the investigative approach to interviewing takes too much time. In particular, it would seem that memory retrieval techniques are seen as using time that could be better utilised elsewhere. While the benefits of such techniques can be explained in training, it is unlikely that officers will understand the rationale behind the techniques until they conduct interviews. What is essential in developing a new culture of interviewing, therefore, is that senior officers are practising and promoting investigative interviewing in the field.

Finally, it is important to acknowledge that interviewing protocols do not provide complete safeguards against poor interviewing practices. While the adoption of standardised practices is a positive step, it is their integration into sound investigative practices that is the key to excellence in interviewing. For example, officers may adhere to the interviewing protocol in their interviews but only probe the witness about particular aspects of the recollection that confirm any possible biases. Therefore, emphasis must be placed on the broader investigative purpose of the interview and officers must engage in critical analysis of their performance. This process requires officers to be aware of any bias prior to the interview and to focus on eliciting all available facts, whether incriminating or exculpatory, as opposed to simply adhering to a protocol. The issue of questioning is particularly important in the context of interviews with victims of alleged child abuse as they are likely to have made multiple disclosures prior to being interviewed by the police. It is essential the police gather as much information about any pre-interview disclosures, so the motives and/or preconceptions of caregivers can be addressed during the interview (Korkman *et al.*, 2014). The inclusion of these details in recorded interviews with vulnerable witnesses will also allow any concerns around contamination to be raised by the defence counsel.

Conclusion

The absence of legislation governing the practice of interviewing witnesses in any jurisdiction has created difficulty with regard to the development of uniform practices across Australia. It has been suggested that greater collaboration and a centralised approach to developing interviewing protocol and administering training would assist the improvement of interviewing practices (Powell, 2008). To this end, the establishment of ANZPAA and ANZCoPP provides an opportunity for the development of standardised practice, although there may be some merit in jurisdictions retaining a degree of autonomy. Given the ever-increasing diversity of the Australian population, it may be that a hybrid approach would be best suited, where an overarching framework is developed at a national level but jurisdictions are given autonomy in adapting and implementing any recommendations.

Having established investigative interviewing as standard practice across Australia, it is clear that jurisdictions are now developing their own unique approaches to training and development. As evidenced by the adoption of Australian-based centralised interview training for interviews with vulnerable witnesses, Australian policing jurisdictions are keen to make use of internationally- and locally-based resources. While there is concern regarding the loss of skills following training, even with regard to the provision of intensive programmes (Powell, 2002), there is considerable innovation in the development of training practices across the jurisdictions. As the move towards shared knowledge and resources among the jurisdictions gains momentum, there will be more room for improved quality and delivery of training.

The statutory provisions allowing for the admissibility of pre-recorded statements with vulnerable witnesses is a strong indication of the priority of vulnerable witnesses' participation in the criminal justice system in Australia. It would, however, be beneficial to have uniform provisions across the jurisdictions, if only to demonstrate equity with regard to the treatment of vulnerable witnesses. The ABE recommends the recording of police interviews with key witnesses for the purposes of increasing the 'amount and quality of information gained from the witness' (Ministry of Justice, 2011: 9). Following the now mandatory recording of police interviews with persons of interest, it is open for jurisdictions to consider the mandatory recording of interviews with witnesses. To date, there are no statutory provisions allowing the recording of police interviews with key witnesses (who do not satisfy the criteria of being vulnerable in the particular jurisdiction) as being admissible as evidence. In Queensland, interviews with witnesses who are not considered vulnerable may be recorded in instances where it is considered beneficial to the investigation although these recordings cannot be admitted as evidence (Queensland Police Service, 1995). The benefit of recording police interviews with witnesses as a matter of course would be to improve the quality of the resulting witness statements and to eliminate uncertainty around identifying vulnerable witnesses prior to interview. Mandatory recording of all interviews with witnesses would also provide transparency in the court process and provide the defence counsel with an opportunity to assess the questioning of witnesses in the pursuit of particular lines of enquiry.

Anecdotal comments from a number of Australian jurisdictions suggest that there needs to be marked improvement in the quality of witness statements provided in briefs of evidence. As an interview trainer from one jurisdiction commented, guilty pleas sometimes 'hide' the poor quality of witness statements as they are not exposed to the scrutiny of defence counsel or the judiciary. It has further been suggested that the single most influential development in the change from a confrontational approach to interviewing towards an investigative approach has been the installation of video-recording devices in interview rooms. Notwithstanding logistical concerns, if accountability is considered a key motivator in implementing change at the micro-level, the mandatory recording of interviews with witnesses is the next logical step to further improve the quality of investigative interviews with witnesses in Australia.

Acknowledgements

The Australia and New Zealand Policing Advisory Agency (ANZPAA) and all policing jurisdictions in Australia were contacted for information pertaining to the practice of interviewing witnesses and the associated training of interviewers. The authors would like to thank ANZPAA and the police services in New South Wales, Queensland, Tasmania, Victoria and Western Australia for the information and materials they provided, and highlight that the views expressed in this chapter are those of the authors and do not necessarily represent the views of the respective agency or police services. The authors would also like to thank Professor Donald Thomson, from Deakin University, for providing a critical review of an earlier version of the chapter.

Note

1. In the context of this chapter, the term 'witness' includes both witnesses and victims, and the term 'vulnerable witness' includes vulnerable adults and children.

References

Association of Chief Police Officers (2009) *National Investigative Interviewing Strategy*, Briefing Paper. London: Association of Chief Police Officers.

Association of Chief Police Officers (2012) *Practice Advice on Core Investigative Doctrine*, 2nd edn. London: Association of Chief Police Officers.

Australia New Zealand Policing Advisory Agency (2010) *About Us*. Retrieved from: https://www.anzpaa.org.au/.

Australia New Zealand Policing Advisory Agency (2013) *Australia New Zealand Police Professionalisation Strategy 2013–2018*. Retrieved from: https://www.anzpaa.org.au.

Australian Law Reform Commission. (1997) *Seen and Heard: Priority for Children in the Legal Process*, Report 84. Retrieved from: https://www.alrc.gov.au.

Bull, R. (2010) 'The investigative interviewing of children and other vulnerable witnesses: psychological research and working/professional practice', *Legal and Criminological Psychology*, 15: 5–23.

Ceci, S. J. and Bruck, M. (1995) 'The effects of repeated questioning', in S. J. Ceci and M. Bruck (eds), *In Jeopardy in the Courtroom: A Scientific Analysis of Children's Testimony*. Washington, DC: American Psychological Association, pp. 107–25.

Clarke, C. and Milne, B. (2001) *National Evaluation of the PEACE Investigative Interviewing Course*, Police Research Award Scheme, Report No. PRAS/149. London: Home Office.

Commonwealth of Australia (2014) *Information Publication Scheme*. Retrieved from http://www.afp.gov.au.

Cooke, P. and Davies, G. (2001) 'Achieving best evidence from witnesses with learning disabilities: new guidance', *British Journal of Learning Disabilities*, 29: 84–7.

Criminal Investigation Act, Western Australia (2006).

Criminal Procedure Act, New South Wales (1986).

Criminal Procedure Act, Victoria (2009).

Evidence (Children and Special Witnesses) Act, Tasmania (2001).

Evidence (Miscellaneous Provisions) Act, Australian Capital Territory (1991).

Evidence Act, Northern Territory (1939)

Evidence Act, Queensland (1977).

Evidence Act, South Australia (1929).

Evidence Act, Western Australia (1906).

Fisher, R. P. (1995) 'Interviewing victims and witnesses of crime', *Psychology, Public Policy, and Law*, 4: 732–64.

Freedom of Information Act, Commonwealth (1982).

Gibbons, J. (2001) 'Revising the language of New South Wales police procedures: applied linguistics in action', *Applied Linguistics*, 22: 439–69.

Green, T. (2012) 'The future of investigative interviewing: lessons for Australia', *Australian Journal of Forensic Sciences*, 44: 31–43.

Guadagno, B. L., Powell, M. B. and Wright, R. (2006) 'Police officers' and legal professionals' perceptions regarding how children are, and should be, questioned about repeated abuse', *Psychiatry, Psychology and Law*, 13: 251–60.

Hill, J. A. and Moston, S. (2011) 'Police perceptions of investigative interviewing: training needs and operational practices in Australia', *British Journal of Forensic Practice*, 13: 72–83.

Korkman, J., Juusola, A. and Santtila, P. (2014) 'Who made the disclosure? Recorded discussions between children and caretakers suspecting child abuse', *Psychology, Crime and Law*, 20: 994–1004.

Lamb, M. E., Orbach, Y., Hershkowitz, I., Esplin, P. W. and Horowitz, D. (2007) 'Structured forensic interview protocols improve the quality and informativeness of investigative interviews with children: a review of research using the NICHD Investigative Interview Protocol', *Child Abuse and Neglect*, 31: 1201–31.

Legislation Act, Australian Capital Territory (2001).

McCusker, R. (2006) *Review of Anti-corruption Strategies*, Technical and Background Paper No. 23. Australian institute of Criminology. Retrieved from: http://www.aic.gov.au.

Martin, S. E. and Thomson, D. M. (1994) 'Videotapes and multiple interviews: the effects on the child witness', *Psychiatry, Psychology and Law*, 1: 119–28.

Melnyk, L., Crossman, A. M. and Scullin, M. H. (2007) 'The suggestibility of children's memory', in M. P. Toglia, J. D. Read, D. F. Ross and R. C. L. Lindsay (eds), *The Handbook of Eyewitness Psychology. Volume I. Memory for Events*. London: Lawrence Erlbaum Associates, pp. 401–27.

Milne, B., Shaw, G. and Bull, R. (2007) 'Investigative interviewing: the role of research', in D. Carson, B. Milne, F. Pakes, K. Shalev and A. Shawyer (eds), *Applying Psychology to Criminal Justice*. Chichester: John Wiley & Sons, pp. 65–80.

Ministry of Justice (2011) *Achieving Best Evidence in Criminal Proceedings: Guidance on Interviewing Victims and Witnesses, and Guidance on Using Special Measures*. London: Home Office.

New South Wales Police Force (2012) *Code of Practice for CRIME (Custody, Rights, Investigation, Management and Evidence)*. Sydney: New South Wales Police Force.

O'Mahony, B. M., Smith, K. and Milne, B. (2011) 'The early identification of vulnerable witnesses prior to an investigative interview', *British Journal of Forensic Practice*, 13: 114–23.

Pipe, M.-E., Orbach, Y., Lamb, M. E., Abbott, C. B. and Stewart, H. (2013) 'Do case outcomes change when investigative interviewing practices change?', *Psychology, Public Policy, and Law*, 19: 179–90.

Powell, M. B. (2000) 'PRIDE: The essential elements of a forensic interview with an Aboriginal person', *Australian Psychologist*, 35: 186–92.

Powell, M. B. (2002) 'Specialist training in investigative and evidential interviewing: is it having any effect on the behaviour of professionals in the field?', *Psychiatry, Psychology and Law*, 9: 44–55.

Powell, M. B. (2008) 'Designing effective training programs for investigative interviewers of children', *Current Issues in Criminal Justice*, 20: 189–208. Retrieved from: http://heinonline.org.

Queensland Police Service (1995) *The Operational Procedures Manual*. Brisbane: Queensland Police Service.

R. v. *Anunga*, 11 ALR 412 (1972).

Scott, A. J., Tudor-Owen, J., Pedretti, P. and Bull, R. (2014) 'How intuitive is PEACE? Newly recruited police officers' plans, interviews and self-evaluations', *Psychiatry, Psychology and Law*. Advance online publication.

Wakefield, S. J., Kebbell, M. R., Moston, S. and Westera, N. (2014) 'Perceptions and profiles of interviews with interpreters: a police survey', *Australian and New Zealand Journal of Criminology*. Advance online publication.

Westera, N. J., Kebbell, M. R. and Milne, B. (2011) 'Interviewing witnesses: do investigative and evidential requirements concur?', *British Journal of Forensic Practice*, 13: 103–13.

Western Australia Police (2009) *Annual Report '09*. Retrieved from: http://www.police.wa.gov.au.

7 Witness interviewing practices in New Zealand

Nina J. Westera, Rachel Zajac and Deirdre A. Brown

Introduction

New Zealand is a small island chain, similar in physical size to Japan or Great Britain but with far fewer inhabitants (4.4 million). The New Zealand Police is a national organisation operating under a single governance structure. The service has nearly 12,000 members, of whom approximately 75 per cent are sworn (New Zealand Police, 2012). It is divided into 12 geographical districts which are administered from the Police National Headquarters in Wellington. Each district has a District Commander and a team of Area Commanders who manage day-to-day operations. The chief executive of police is known as the Commissioner of Police, who is appointed by New Zealand's representative of the Queen, the Governor General. The Commissioner is accountable to the Minister of Police for the administration of police services, but the New Zealand Police act as an independent body in terms of law enforcement decisions.

Since 2007, the New Zealand Police have undergone substantial reforms to investigative interviewing policy and practice. The reforms borrowed much from the developments in England and Wales associated with the introduction of the PEACE model (PEACE refers to the phases of all investigative interviews: Planning and preparation, Engage and explain, Account, Closure, and Evaluation; see Clarke and Milne, 2001). New Zealand, however, is distinct from these other countries by virtue of its one police service, which enabled national organisational change. Consequently, interviewing in New Zealand has become governed and resourced at a national level, with the development of national interviewing policy and standards. The reforms have also resulted in the implementation of a competency programme that includes supervision, training and assessment in an attempt to address the difficulties associated with developing and retaining interviewing skills (see Powell *et al*., 2005).

Here, we discuss the review of police practice that led to the reforms, the resulting changes to police interviewing practice and the implications of these changes for research, policy and practice.

Witness interviewing in New Zealand

New Zealand Police carry out upwards of 1.8 million investigative interviews per year. If we add to this around 274,000 suspect interviews, the annual cost of investigative interviewing in New Zealand sits at around $135 million. Interviewing accounts for roughly one-fifth of the average officer's time (Schollum, 2006a).

Until recently, however, police officers in New Zealand received minimal interview training. Approximately 23 hours (2.8 per cent) of recruit training was devoted to interviewing, and most of this time was spent dealing with operational requirements rather than specific techniques that would allow officers to maximise completeness and accuracy.

In late 2004, New Zealand's Police Executive Committee commissioned a nationwide review of investigative interviewing. The impetus for the review came from various avenues, including the recognition of recent developments in scientific research around interviewing, identified deficiencies in officers' practice and knowledge, and unfavourable comparisons made by former UK officers now working in New Zealand (Schollum, 2006b).

The Executive Committee initially commissioned a comprehensive review of the international investigative interviewing literature – completed in September 2005. The report singled out the commitment of all police forces in England and Wales to ethical, reliable and effective interviewing through the Association of Chief Police Officers' (ACPO) investigative interviewing strategy and subsequent widespread adoption of the PEACE model (Schollum, 2005). On the basis of this literature review, the Committee ordered a systematic appraisal of investigative interviewing in New Zealand. Specifically, the Committee requested:

> (i) identification of gaps in police policy, practice, training, technology, and management;
> (ii) comparisons with international best practice; and
> (iii) recommendations to ensure that interviewing was of a sufficient standard to maximize opportunities for the presentation of best evidence.
>
> (Schollum, 2006b)

A Project Team comprising both constabulary and civilians was established in anticipation of the work that would be required to achieve these goals and to bring New Zealand into line with international best practice. As well as a comprehensive search of existing statistics, case law and other relevant policies and documentation related to investigative interviewing, the team collected contemporary data on both perceptions of interviewing and interviewing performance (see Schollum, 2006a). This process was wide-ranging, involving multiple sources of information and diverse data collection methods.

The data demonstrated considerable variation in attitudes towards interviewing, both within and across information sources. One common misperception held by officers was that interviewing is really only important for detectives, and that front-line uniform staff do not have the time or the need to conduct full interviews with witnesses. Others saw witness interviewing as crucial, looking at the longer-term implications of competent interviewing when it came time to make decisions about prosecutions.

Just over 91 per cent of the 279 sworn officers who took part in a nationwide survey described themselves as 'skilled' or 'highly skilled' interviewers; only 9 per cent felt they needed more interview training. Despite these glowing self-evaluations, officers did not rate the same abilities in their colleagues nearly as highly. For example, while 90 per cent of officers said that they 'usually' displayed good listening skills, their rating for other officers was only 30 per cent. There were, however, some contexts in which staff noted a lack of support (e.g. interviewing vulnerable witnesses). Officers also noted a lack of supervision of – and feedback on – interview performance. In fact, 46 per cent said that they had never received constructive feedback on their interviews from their peers or superiors.

Notably, there was a distinct perception among many officers that interviewing is not something that can be taught. In line with this attitude, officers showed a poor appreciation of the foundations of good interviewing. Critically, only 30 per cent of officers saw knowledge of how memory works as 'very important' in conducting a good interview compared to 68 per cent for knowledge of body language.

To benchmark current practice, officers selected at random from five districts were each asked to submit a video-taped witness interview for analysis. A project team (comprising one non-sworn police researcher, five experienced detectives and two psychological scientists, including one of the authors, RZ), rated each interview on a number of dimensions using the UK PEACE model as a yardstick. While the interviews were typically conducted in a professional manner, it was clear that officers' interview methods – dictated largely by those they had been taught or developed on the job – did not meet best-practice standards. Overall, 64 per cent of interviews were rated as 'poor', mainly due to insufficient planning, inadequate probing or topic development, inflexibility, interruptions of witnesses' reports and poor questioning style.

Having identified considerable weaknesses in officers' interviewing skills, the scoping phase of the review culminated in a pilot study of the PEACE interviewing approach (Schollum *et al.*, 2006). A UK trainer was brought out to train six staff from one police station as PEACE trainers, and these new trainers then delivered week-long courses (two trainers and a maximum of ten trainees) to all staff at that station with a rank of senior sergeant or below (approximately 110 staff). The training was very well received by participants and their superiors, with much of the feedback from participants taking the form of 'why hasn't anyone told us this before?'

The recommendations

> Action is needed now, and it should be decisive and far-reaching. (Schollum, 2006b: 32)

In the final step of the review, Schollum (2006b) recommended an organisational overhaul of investigative interviewing to bring the New Zealand Police towards evidence-based practice. Twenty-four recommendations were made, touching on nearly every aspect of policing – governance, resourcing, policy, standards, supervision, training and assessment. The recommendations were largely modelled on the lessons learnt from the PEACE approach in England and Wales (e.g. Clarke and Milne, 2001). The first recommendations were implemented in late 2007 with the establishment of a three-person Investigative Interviewing Unit (including one of the authors (NW) who was responsible for guidance, policy, standards and training). Reporting to the National Crime Manager, this team was responsible for the governance and implementation of a national investigative interviewing strategy.

From 2007 to 2012, the team implemented nearly all of the recommendations. For the first time, practices for interviewing witnesses were clearly defined and resourced. The police adopted the PEACE interviewing framework for all interviews and implemented an ethical framework to underpin this practice. The interview models endorsed for interviewing witnesses were evidence-based protocols. The *Investigative Interviewing Doctrine* and *Investigative Interviewing Witness Guide* were developed, peer-reviewed and published to provide official guidance for investigators (New Zealand Police, 2007, 2008a). Despite a recommendation to video record all witness interviews, the use of written statements remained the norm due to resourcing constraints. However, a Commission of Inquiry into Police Conduct including how police investigate adult sexual assault cases (Bazley, 2007) led to the immediate introduction of video recording in adult interviews where the witness was vulnerable or investigatively important (New Zealand Police, 2008a).[1] Police stations without physical spaces to interview witnesses were funded to build specially designed interviewing suites with recording equipment (Penney, 2010).[2]

From this foundation, the New Zealand Police gradually implemented the first three levels of a four-level hierarchical training framework for interviewers (Level 1: Foundation; Level 2: Advanced; Level 3: Specialist Child or Adult Witness or Suspect; Level 4: Advisory[3]). Each level is underpinned by national standards and involves both foundation learning and a face-to-face training programme incorporating skills practice with expert feedback (New Zealand Police, 2008b). To aid in programme delivery, three full-time national investigative interviewing trainer positions were established.

On completing the training, participants enter into an ongoing learning and workplace assessment programme to become accredited at that level. This process involves submitting evidence of field interviews – and self-reflective evaluation thereof – to designated assessors. The purpose of this process is twofold: (1) to create national consistency in standards; and (2) to provide interviewers with expert feedback for skill development. Assessors evaluate each interview and the self-reflection document against national standards, and then provide an assessment of competency along with constructive feedback. Interviewers deemed to be 'not yet competent' develop a plan with the trainer to address issues arising and must then submit a further recording for evaluation. Although the broad structure of the programme is the same at each level, the specifics vary, with increased intensity at higher levels.

Competency programme

Level 1: Foundation witness interviewing

Level 1 equips all officers with the skills to conduct interviews with witnesses (including victims) and suspects of priority and volume crime (New Zealand Police, 2008b). The interviewing model used is free recall, a simplified version of the cognitive interview (CI). This model omits some of the more complex CI mnemonics such as imagery and the change of order (see Dando *et al.*, 2009). The free recall model includes building rapport, explaining the interview process, the report everything and context reinstatement instructions, obtaining a free report, questioning, using sketch plans and covering any investigatively important topics. Extensive testing of the CI has found that it increases the completeness of recall without compromising accuracy (see Memon *et al.*, 2010).

The perceived benefits of the pilot training programme created the impetus to provide the Level 1 training to all sworn officers below the rank of inspector from 2007 to 2011. Trainers were contracted from England to train 24 New Zealand trainers from across all police districts. In this initial implementation, most officers who conduct investigative interviews as part of their role received the Level 1 training. Over half of the training course was dedicated to knowledge about memory and communication and to learning witness interview skills. Officers also learned to record interviews via a written statement. The scenario-based training course was typically held over five days, with 12 participants and two trainers. Subsequent workplace assessment involved the participant submitting two written statements to an assessor (usually the participant's supervisor) within 12 months of training.

From 2009, the Level 1 programme was embedded in recruit training and delivered by the national trainers at the Royal New Zealand Police College. As a result, all new recruits are now trained. There has been no outcome evaluation of the effectiveness of the Level 1 learning programme.

Level 2: Advanced witness interviewing

In 2009, Level 2 was implemented to provide those in an investigator role with the skills to conduct interviews with witnesses and suspects of serious crime. Interviews are still recorded in writing but participants advance their skills in eliciting free recall and learn more about the use of two CI mnemonics: report everything and context reinstatement. Trainees also learn to apply interviewing skills across more complex scenarios, such as dealing with reticent witnesses and using interpreters. The training is typically delivered by two national trainers over five days with ten participants and is followed by workplace assessment similar to Level 1 but conducted by Level 2 trainers. The Level 2 programme has not become part of the detective training programme as originally intended but many districts have implemented the training to up-skill all officers from the Criminal Investigation Branch. The Level 2 programme is yet to be formally evaluated.

Level 3: Specialist adult witness interviewing

In 2007, Level 3 was implemented to develop a specialist interviewing capability for witnesses to major crime, especially sexual assault. Over the next five years, a national pool of 130 specialist interviewers were trained in the CI (Fisher and Geiselman, 1992). This eight-phase interview process is described by Milne (2004); it is modelled around the 'PEACE' framework and includes all CI mnemonics combined with communication skills. All interviews are video recorded and the introduction of the Evidence Act 2006 means these recordings can now be used as the basis for an adult's courtroom evidence (see Westera *et al.*, 2013). Each region selected participants (often also detective trained) to attend a five-day residential national interview training course. This training was originally delivered by two trainers who were contractors from England (including the academic Dr Becky Milne), and later by one of the authors (NW) and another trainer who was an accredited Level 3 interviewer. More recently, the national interview trainers – who are all also Level 3 adult witness interviewers – have performed this role.

During the residential training course, the ten participants learn about memory and the scientific basis for the CI from an academic expert in this field (currently one of the authors, RZ), and practise the skills and receive feedback from the trainers. A unique feature of this and the child specialist interviewing programmes (see the next section) is the attempt to overcome the difficulty in developing and retaining interview skills. Consistent with evidence-based practice in learning skills (e.g. Ericsson *et al.*, 1993; Powell *et al.*, 2005), expert feedback is provided to the interviewers through an ongoing development and assessment process (Ericsson *et al.*, 1993).

After the training, all interviewers must complete a yearly accreditation process allowing them to continue interviewing adults on video. This process involves submitting recordings of two interviews (within six months of training), alongside a completed self-reflective evaluation of the interviews, to the national assessors. The original assessors were one of the authors (NW) and the other Level 3 trainer. More recently, the national trainers have taken over this intensive role with support from a small number of operational Level 3 interviewers selected by the national trainer. The assessors undergo moderation at least once a year. Interviewers who do not meet competency standards are removed from the interviewing pool. All interviewers are also required to attend a peer review workshop each year, which includes professional development and education sessions as well as group supervision on interview practice.

Two of the authors (RZ and NW) are currently conducting a formal evaluation of the effectiveness of the Level 3 programme.

Level 4: Specialist child witness interviewing

In New Zealand, investigative interviews with children and adolescents are conducted by either Child, Youth and Family Services social workers or New Zealand Police officers. Because this was the only interviewing programme in New Zealand that already reflected evidence-based principles of learning and practice, it was the last area to be reformed. Prior to 2010, training and professional development consisted of attendance at a two-week residential training course and optional attendance at an annual peer review meeting; locally arranged professional development and supervision opportunities occurred on an ad hoc basis. Investigative interviewing with child witnesses was reviewed between 2010 and 2013 by a team including all of the authors. This review led to a revision of the training curriculum to reflect recent research evidence, a radical overhaul of training delivery and the implementation of an accreditation process.

The New Zealand child interview model follows the PEACE framework (New Zealand Police, 2007). It includes a pre-substantive phase that establishes the ground rules of the interview, promotes rapport building, and gives children an opportunity to practise providing a narrative account of a recent past event. The substantive part of the interview is aligned with international best-practice guidelines (e.g. American Professional Society on the Abuse of Children (APSAC), 2012; Ministry of Justice, 2011) as well as empirically validated interviewing protocols such as the National Institute of Child Health and Human Development Investigative Interview Protocol (Brown *et al.*, 2013; Orbach *et al.*, 2000). Verbal prompts that may cue additional recall by assisting children to mentally reinstate the context of the event (Dietze *et al.*, 2012) are also included. Aligned with empirical evidence to date, these prompts are restricted to prompting children to think about what they could see and what they could hear during their experience (Brown and Pipe, 2003; Poole and Lindsay, 1995).

The child interviewing model allows interviewers to employ a range of non-verbal aids to elicit further detail or clarify ambiguous responses from children, although the evidence base for these strategies varies (Brown and Zajac, 2015). Human body diagrams and non-anatomically detailed dolls can be used, for example, but only to clarify reports of touch. Interviewers may also choose to provide children with drawing materials, either to provide an alternate focus when children recount difficult information or to help them communicate specific details about their experience (e.g. spatial layouts).

In 2013, a training model was introduced for specialist child witness interviewers. Participants now complete four e-learning modules, written primarily by two of the authors (DB and NW):

1. Interviewing children for the criminal justice process, and care and protection
2. Sexual and violent offending
3. Child development and memory
4. From interviewing theory to practice.

Each module comprises reading material, review questions and assessment tasks, together with relevant legislation, protocols and policies, and the research base for the presented material. Modules are complemented by two practical tasks – participants observe an interviewer completing an entire interview and also role-play an 'engage and explain' phase. A video recording of the latter is submitted to the Child Interviewing National Coordinator for feedback. Once participants have successfully completed the modules and practical tasks, they attend a 4½-day residential training programme. Trainers (including one of the authors (DB)) review each phase of the interview model in the first two days, and participants then have 2½ days of practice, culminating in a final assessment (a recorded interview with a child actor).

From the end of 2013, specialist child witness interviewers must complete a yearly accreditation procedure – assessed by the National Coordinator (or designated alternative) – to be able to continue interviewing children. Interviewers who trained under the previous curriculum and model completed the new e-learning modules and then attended a two-day workshop (delivered by one of the authors (DB) and the National Coordinator) to prepare for accreditation.

The content of the curriculum was informed by an evaluation study that assessed the presence of key components of the child interview model and interview practice during the 'account' phase of the interview (Wolfman *et al.*, 2014). While some aspects of the model were consistently implemented, even some of the more scripted components (e.g. advising the child that the interviewer knows nothing about the alleged events) were frequently absent. While predominantly using open-ended questions, interviews relied heavily on 'wh-' type directive questions rather than narrative-based, input-free prompts (e.g. 'tell me everything about that'). Commonly used interview aids were sketch plans (66 per cent), body diagrams (21 per cent) and dolls (10 per cent). Consistent with previous research (La Rooy *et al.*, 2011; Powell and Hughes-Scholes, 2009; Smith *et al.*, 2009), interviewing quality was not associated with years of experience or time since training.

At this early stage, it remains to be seen how the accreditation programme influences the quality of interviews conducted. Further evaluation will be necessary.

Implications for research, policy and practice

A number of research, policy and practice implications arise from the reforms described above. First, the learning programme will need to be systematically evaluated. In addition to examining the efficacy of the initial training at each level in imparting foundation skills, it is crucial to understand how the varying degrees of skill-based supervision in the new workplace assessment and accreditation process affect the well-documented problems with skill development and retention (see Powell *et al.*, 2005). In particular, we need to ascertain whether the more intensive Level 3 programmes – which go beyond most programmes by having an ongoing professional development regime – are adequate. The importance of regular supervision and feedback for maintenance of interviewing standards has been clearly established, even when interviewers have extensive experience, are following an evidence-based interviewing model and have completed intensive training (e.g. Lamb *et al.*, 2002). Indeed, research shows that experience is not a substitute for interviewing quality (La Rooy *et al.*, 2011; Powell and Hughes-Scholes, 2009; Smith *et al.*, 2009).

If the current Level 3 programme is inadequate, there would be several challenges for police. Accessing appropriate supervisors is a challenge within a small country like New Zealand, and interviewers have expressed that managers are not always supportive of the resources, time and workload implications of engaging in supervision and other skill maintenance activities. An important direction for future research will therefore be to examine alternative forms of supervision activity (e.g. group supervision, self-evaluation tools) and their impact on interviewing practice. As such, a further challenge for the future of witness interviewing in New Zealand may be for policy-level and top-down support to be implemented for the provision of – and access to – supervision and other forms of professional development for all interviewers working with vulnerable witnesses. This may require even more financial commitment and a long-term strategy for developing expertise within New Zealand or using communication technology to access off-shore expertise.

Second, testing of the efficacy of current interview training and practice is required. In child interviewing at least, interviewers are using a range of interviewing techniques, some of which have a limited – or no – evidence base. Without formal evaluation, it is difficult to know whether similar practices are occurring in adult interviews. Examining how techniques used in practice but not tested for efficacy (e.g. using sketch plans with children) affect the accuracy and completeness of witnesses' accounts is an important issue – while some methods may be detrimental to eliciting best evidence, others may be effective innovations developed by interviewers to cope with the complexities of interviewing (e.g. especially reluctant children or distressed witnesses).

Third, the majority of interviews are still recorded on a written statement. Not only is this method unreliable (e.g. Lamb *et al.*, 2000; Köhnken, 1995), it also makes effective review of interviewer practice impossible because it does not capture the types of questions asked. Notably, the need to prepare the statement prolongs the interview process and can encourage interviewers to manage the flow of information by reverting to poor interview practices (e.g. interrupting the witness, asking leading questions: Clarke and Milne, 2001; Köhnken, 1995). Witnesses are therefore subjected to a drawn-out interviewing process and can be cross-examined against this unreliable written record. The New Zealand Police's recent adoption of smart devices that can video-record witness interviews provides an opportunity to make a policy decision to eliminate the written statement.

Finally, police and scholars need to work together to ensure that the interview methods available to police – and the learning of those methods – continually adapt to the complex needs of policing. In the child interviewing programme, for example, a series of topics has been flagged as content for an 'advanced' programme to meet the needs of the more challenging cases that police officers deal with. These advanced topics include working with children and adults with intellectual impairments, where there is an emerging evidence base for ways in which government agencies can develop sound interviewing practice.

Conclusion

New Zealand Police have shown a strong commitment to invest in the new programme and to work with investigative interviewing scholars. This commitment has provided a foundation for the move towards evidence-based practice. As in any police organisation, the complexity of learning interview skills makes it unlikely that the New Zealand Police will ever have sufficient resources to enable all employees to conduct all witness interviews to the highest level. The challenge for the police is therefore how best to use their limited resources. This creates a reciprocal challenge for scholars: to increase the utility of interview methods to meet the evolving needs of policing and to understand the best ways to support interviewers to learn those methods effectively and to implement them consistently in their practice.

Notes

1. Child complainant interviews have been video-recorded since 1989.
2. In NZ, suspect interviews have been video-recorded since 1992.
3. Level 4 has not yet been implemented.

References

American Professional Society on the Abuse of Children (2012) *Practice Guidelines: Investigative Interviewing in Cases of Alleged Child Abuse*. Chicago: APSAC.

Bazley, M. (2007) *Report of the Commission of Inquiry into Police Conduct*. Retrieved from: http://www.cipc.govt.nz/cipc.nsf/.

Brown, D. and Pipe, M.-E. (2003) 'Individual differences in children's event memory reports and the narrative elaboration technique', *Journal of Applied Psychology*, 88: 195.

Brown, D. A. and Zajac, R. (2015) 'The Impact of Visual Aids on Children's Responsiveness in Forensic Interviews: A Review'. Manuscript under review.

Brown, D. A., Lamb, M. E., Lewis, C., Pipe, M.-E., Orbach, Y. and Wolfman, M. (2013) 'Evaluating the NICHD Investigative Interview Protocol: a laboratory study', *Journal of Experimental Psychology: Applied*, 19: 367–82.

Clarke, C. and Milne, R. (2001) *National Evaluation of the PEACE Investigative Interviewing Course*, Police Research Award Scheme, Report No. PRAS/149. Institute of Criminal Justice Studies, University of Portsmouth.

Dando, C., Wilcock, R. and Milne, R. (2009) 'The cognitive interview: novice police officers' witness/victim interviewing practices', *Psychology, Crime* and *Law*, 15: 679–96.

Dietze, P. M., Powell, M. B. and Thomson, D. M. (2012) 'Examination of the effect of mental reinstatement of context across developmental level, retention interval and type of mnemonic instruction', *Psychiatry, Psychology and Law*, 19: 89–103.

Ericsson, K. A., Krampe, R. T. and Tesch-Römer, C. (1993) 'The role of deliberate practice in the acquisition of expert performance', *Psychological Review*, 100: 363–406.

Fisher, R. P. and Geiselman, R. E. (1992) *Memory Enhancing Techniques for Investigative Interviewing: The Cognitive Interview*. Springfield, IL: Thomas.

Köhnken, G. (1995) 'Interviewing adults', in R. Bull, and D. Carson (ed.), *Handbook of Psychology in Legal Contexts*. New York: John Wiley & Sons, pp. 215–33.

La Rooy, D., Lamb, M. E. and Memon, A. (2011) 'Forensic interviews with children in Scotland: a survey of interview practices among people', *Journal of Police and Criminal Psychology*, 26: 26–34.

Lamb, M. E., Orbach, Y., Sternberg, K. J., Hershkowitz, I. and Horowitz, D. (2000) 'Accuracy of investigators' verbatim notes of their forensic interviews with alleged child abuse victims', *Law* and *Human Behavior*, 24: 699–708.

Lamb, M. E., Sternberg, K., J., Orbach, Y., Esplin, P. W. and Mitchell, S. (2002) 'Is ongoing feedback necessary to maintain the quality of investigative interviews with allegedly abused children?', *Applied Developmental Sciene*, 6: 35–41.

Memon, A., Meissner, C. A. and Fraser, J. (2010) 'The Cognitive Interview: a meta-analytic analysis and study space analysis of the past 25 years', *Psychology, Public Policy and Law*, 16: 340–72.

Milne, R. (2004) *The Enhanced Cognitive Interview: A Step-by-step Guide*. Portsmouth: University of Portsmouth.

Ministry of Justice (2011) *Achieving Best Evidence in Criminal Proceedings: Guidance on Interviewing Victims and Witnesses, and Guidance on Using Special Measures*. London.

New Zealand Police (2007) *Investigative Interviewing Doctrine*. Wellington: NZ Police.

New Zealand Police (2008a) *Investigative Interviewing Witness Guide*. Wellington: NZ Police.

New Zealand Police (2008b) *Investigative Interviewing: Accreditation Policy*. Wellington: NZ Police.

New Zealand Police (2012) *Annual Report: NZ Police 2011–2012*. Wellington: NZ Police.

Orbach, Y., Hershkowitz, I., Lamb, M. E., Sternberg, K. J., Esplin, P. W. and Horowitz, D. (2000) 'Assessing the value of structured protocols for forensic interviews of alleged abuse victims', *Child Abuse and Neglect*, 24: 733–52.

Penney, J. (2010) *Investigative Interviewing: Witness Interview Room and Equipment Set-up Guide*. Wellington: NZ Police.

Poole, D. A. and Lindsay, D. S. (1995) 'Interviewing preschoolers: effects of nonsuggestive techniques, parental coaching, and leading questions on reports of non-experienced events', *Journal of Experimental Child Psychology*, 60: 129–54.

Powell, M. B. and Hughes-Scholes, C. H. (2009) 'Evaluation of the questions used to elicit evidence about abuse from child witnesses: Australian study', *Psychiatry, Psychology and Law*, 16: 369–78.

Powell, M. B., Fisher, R. P. and Wright, R. (2005) 'Investigative interviewing', in N. Brewer and K. Williams (eds), *Psychology and Law: An Empirical Perspective*. New York: Guilford, pp. 11–42.

Schollum, M. (2005) *Investigative Interviewing: The Literature*. Wellington: NZ Police.

Schollum, M. (2006a) *Investigative Interviewing: The Current Situation*. Wellington: NZ Police.

Schollum, M. (2006b) *Investigative Interviewing: The Recommendations*. Wellington: NZ Police.

Schollum, M., Westera, N., Grantham, R. and Chartres, M. (2006) *Investigative Interviewing: Evaluation of the Manurewa Trial*. Wellington: NZ Police.

Smith, R. M., Powell, M. B. and Lum, J. (2009) 'The relationship between job status, interviewing experience, gender, and police officers' adherence to open-ended questions', *Legal and Criminological Psychology*, 14: 51–63.

Westera, N., Kebbell, M. and Milne, B. (2013) 'Losing two thirds of the story: a comparison of the video recorded police interview and live evidence of rape complainants', *Criminal Law Review*, issue 3 [online].

Wolfman, M., Jose, P. and Brown, D. A. (2014) 'Evaluation of specialist child witness interviewing in New Zealand', Final Report to New Zealand Police and Child, Youth and Family.

Europe

8 Interviewing victims and witnesses in Belgium

Michel Carmans and Pierre Patiny

Introduction

As a victim or witness, the Belgian citizen is generally speaking in rapid contact with a police unit. Consequently, a statement is taken allowing the collection of as much information as possible relating to facts, places and clues in order to identify and interview a suspect.

Interviewing within judicial procedure is one of the essential elements of the investigation process conducted by the public prosecutor or examining magistrate. The procedure is inquisitorial and written. Each person interviewed within the framework of an investigation, whether a victim, witness or suspect, should be briefly informed about the facts for which he/she will be heard. The interview should be subject to a written record, which is dated and signed by a police officer.

Interviewing implies knowledge, know-how and life skills. The interviewer knows basic verbal and non-verbal communication, applies non-selective listening and shows at all times a respectful attitude through both verbal and non-verbal communication; he also shows empathy. Further, he masters the aptitudes of selective listening and formulates open and non-suggestive questions. He paraphrases, reformulates, synthesises and uses emotional reformulations. These skills are applicable to the framework of judicial interviews of victims, witnesses and suspects.

Definition and practice

A police interview is an officially recorded conversation between a police officer and a person who could be involved directly or indirectly in events likely to concern judicial authorities, in order to gather all relevant clues for finding the truth, within all provisions prescribed by the law (Bockstaele, 2011). The technique of judicial interview is not fixed by the law.

However, general principles exist regarding legality, loyalty and the right to silence. The principle of legality checks for judicial correctness and the principle of loyalty is related to handling evidence with honesty and objectivity. Non-compliance with these principles could lead to the nullifying of the interview when not observing the rights concerning the assistance of a lawyer during the interview (Judgement by the Constitutional Court, 2013), the use of language

(German, French and Dutch), making different attempts to put pressure on the interviewee or having a biasing or biased attitude, or when observing threats of any form, tricks, lies, promises or staging.

For the trial judge, the police interview has a demonstrative value for intelligence. The materiality is established until proved otherwise or challenged. The judge is not bound to admit the truthfulness of the interview and a suspect can retract his/her confession or change it.

When interviewing a person, victim or witness, the following rules (see Section 47b of the Rules of the Criminal Procedure) should be respected:

1. At the beginning of the interview, the person interviewed is briefly informed concerning the facts about which he/she will be heard. Practical example: *We inform you that you are interviewed as a victim of an assault that you encountered last Monday. We inform you:*

   (a) *that you can ask that all our questions and all your answers should be recorded in the used terminology;*
   (b) *that you can ask for a specific inquiry or interview;*
   (c) *that your declarations can be used as evidence in justice;*
   (d) *that you cannot be forced to accuse yourself.*

   These items are accurately set down in the interview record.
2. The interviewee can use all the documents in their possession, although this cannot result in the postponing of the interview. At that time or later, they can require that these documents are attached to the interview report or deposited at the court registry.
3. The police report notes when the interview starts, resumes and ends and whether it is interrupted. It accurately mentions the identity of the persons who intervene in the interview or intervene in a part of it by mentioning the moment of their arrival and departure. It also mentions particular circumstances that can throw new light on the declaration and the circumstances under which it was made.
4. At the end of the interview, the police report is handed over to the interviewee for reading, unless he/she requests it being read aloud. He/she will be asked if the statement has to be corrected or completed.
5. The interviewed person, victim or witness is informed about his/her status as an 'injured party'. A declaration of such allows him/her to be informed about further procedures in which he/she is involved.
6. If the interviewed person wishes to use another language, a sworn interpreter can be called, or his/her statements are recorded in his/her language, or he/she is asked to record him-/herself his/her own statements. When the interview takes place with the assistance of an interpreter, his/her identity and status are mentioned.

If during the interview of a person who is initially not considered as a suspect, some elements suggest that facts can be attributed to him/her, that person is informed about his/her rights as a suspect and another procedure is initiated in order to respect the defence rights.

The information obtained by the prosecutor is secret. Any person who is asked to provide assistance is bound by professional secrecy. Anyone who violates this secret is punishable by the stipulated penalties (Section 458 of the Rules of Criminal Procedure).

Without prejudice to the stipulations of the particular laws, the interviewed person should be informed of the fact that he/she may request a copy of the interview, which is delivered free of charge. This copy is issued immediately or sent to him/her within a month. However, under exceptional circumstances, the prosecutor or the examining magistrate can decide in a reasoned decision recorded in the file to defer communication for a delay of a maximum of three months which can be renewed once. When a person under 18 years of age is involved and there is apparently a risk of him/her of being deprived of the copy or of not being able to protect the personal aspects, the prosecutor or the examining magistrate may decide, in a reasoned decision recorded on file, to refuse communication. In that situation, the minor can consult a copy of the text of the interview when accompanied by a lawyer or a judicial assistant from the victims' department of the prosecution service. However, in grave and exceptional circumstances, the moment of consultation can be deferred for a maximum of three months which can be renewed once. Decisions can be made to deliver a free copy of the minor's interview text to his/her lawyer.

For reasons of public interest, the prosecutor can communicate information to the press. He ensures compliance with the presumption of innocence, with the defence rights of suspects, victims or third parties and with the privacy and dignity of individuals. Insofar as possible, the identity of individuals listed in the records is not communicated. Similarly, when required for the interests of the client, the lawyer also can communicate information to the press under the same conditions.

Current practices: written interview of an adult victim or witness

With the exceptions noted above, an interview by a police officer of an adult (a person 18 years or older), victim or witness is generally written. His statement is recorded and the record is sent to the prosecutor or the examining magistrate. For offences against decency (e.g. indecent assault, rape, etc.), the victim may be accompanied by an adult of his/her choice during the interview. The decision always belongs to the examining magistrate to take a reasoned order contrary to this provision when, for example, physical integrity may be put at risk. We note that the 'Salduz' Act (13.08.2011, referring to the decision of the European Court of Human Rights (ECHR) concerning the Salduz case against Turkey, request no. 36391 of 27.11.2008) did not provide the presence of a lawyer of a victim or a witness during his/her interview. If there is a request for it, the police officer refers to the prosecutor or to the examining magistrate who required the inquiries.

The interviewing technique, as taught, follows the classic blueprint (i.e. PEACE) based upon a maximum of free story followed by a questionnaire which is largely composed of open and non-leading questions:

- The introduction containing the legal part and the rights of the interviewed person. We call it *establishing the relationship.*
- The *free story* phase: *'Tell us exactly and in chronological order how your last Monday was, starting at …'*
- The questioning phase during which we seek clarification for certain excerpts from the *free story* phase: *'Give a description of the person who assaulted you'* … *'Talk to us about the car used by your assaulter'* … *'Specify the time of the facts'*, etc.
- The closing of the interview with information concerning further procedures: *'Tell us about what topics you want to talk about and about which we haven't talked about yet'* … *''Do you want to give us documents to be attached to your interview?'* … *'Do you wish that certain persons should be interviewed?'* … *'Do you wish to modify your interview or add anything?'*

Current practices: the audiovisual interview of an adult victim or witness

When a person is in a vulnerable position (shock, post-traumatic syndrome, mental disability), the prosecutor or the examining magistrate may order an audiovisual interview (Section 112*ter* of the Rules of the Criminal Procedure (§1 to §7)).

No definition of this way of interviewing is given by the legislator. Nevertheless a written statement has to be made after the interview. The recorded medium can be viewed as part of the evidence. Whenever he considers it necessary, the prosecutor or the examining magistrate may carry out or order the interview of victims and witnesses on serious facts. The scope for application is unlimited.

The Rules of Criminal Procedure ((Section II Audiovisual and Audio Recording of the Interview), modified by 07.07.2002 Act, section 5) provide the prosecutor or the examining magistrate with the power to order the audiovisual or audio recording of an interview (Section 112*ter* of the Rules of Criminal Procedure). This decision is communicated before the start of the interview. The magistrate himself carries out the interview or appoints a police officer (in practice, it is mostly always a police officer who does the interview) to do so.

A report must be drawn up containing, without prejudice to the laid down rights (Section 47*bis* of the Rules of Criminal Procedure), the main elements of the interview and, possibly, a transcription of the most significant passages. The reasons for which the audiovisual or audio recording was ordered should also be mentioned in the report.

The prosecutor, the examining magistrate, the interviewed person or other parties of the process can request a literal transcript of the interview. It will be added to the file as soon as possible.

Two copies of the interview are made, both valid as originals. Both have the status of originals. They are deposited at the court registry office as forensic evidence.

The recordings can be viewed or listened to by persons who professionally participated in the preliminary investigation (under the direction of the prosecutor), the investigation (under the direction of the examining magistrate) or the judgement related to the judicial file, as well as the parties of the process and the interviewed person. The convicted person who is not under detention and the civil party (possibly the victim) can submit a request to that end to the examining magistrate (Section 61*ter* of the Rules of Criminal Procedure).

All parties are entitled to view or, as the case might be, to listen to the record after the requirements for procedural regulations (Section 61*ter* of the Rules of Criminal Procedure) have been undertaken.

The polygraph test is an accepted and regulated (Circular Letter from the College of General Prosecutors, col. 3, 05.06.2003) police technique. An audiovisual interview is mainly used for suspects.

The National Security Plan 2012–2015 (Section 4 of the 7 December 1998 Act) organised an integrated police service which was structured on two levels (LPI). The Ministers of Home Affairs and of Justice agreed on the National Security Plan (PNS), 'Ensuring together a safe and sustainable society'. The plan specified that particular attention must be paid to violations of physical integrity, particularly where women are concerned. The enumeration of priority criminal phenomena mentions in particular intra-familial violence and violence against women. Necessary initiatives are taken in order to act in a qualitative way: police officers have an interviewing framework allowing them to optimise the quality of received information.

Police officers are obliged to inform the victims of the offence and to redirect them to a victim support service (Adriaensens *et al.*, 1997).

Training of police officers

During their general training, police applicants attend a 20-hour course on interview techniques. After initial training, applicant officers attend a 36-hour course about interview techniques. All the instructors are police officers.

A functional judicial training, available for all police constables, enables them to acquire a certificate allowing them to practise in a local inquiry section or at the Federal judicial police. During this training, the students attend a 16-hour training session based on the theory and the practice of inquiry interview. The instructors are lecturers recognised by the National Research School (DSER) of the Federal Police. They are police officers or external to the school (e.g. magistrates, judicial experts).

The audiovisual interview of a minor victim or witnesses

In Belgium, the purpose of interviewing a minor (victim, witness or suspect) is to gather as much complete and accurate information as possible. In order to achieve this goal, the Behavioural Science Section (GWSC) of the Federal Belgian Police (National Research School), has developed an integrated approach by means of interviews, education and organisational implementation of the project in the different judicial districts in the country.

Over the past several decades, Belgium did not effectively promote new practices to gather what a child had to say. A first pilot project was initiated in 1996 by the Minister of Justice: in four judicial districts, audiovisual premises were equipped for the interviewing of minors. The National Commission on Child Sexual Abuse (instituted by a decision of the Ministers Council dated 30.08.1996) encouraged in its final report (National Commission on Child Sexual Abuse, Final Report, 23.10.1997) the use of video for interviewing children. The so-called 'Dutroux' affair (1996) was an accelerator for the use of video in order to gather the words of a child. The Penal Protection of Minors 2000 Act through the Rules of Criminal Procedure and the Circular Letter about the audiovisual recording of the interview of minors who are victims or witnesses of offences (2001 – see above) regulated the use of this technique. The creation of GWSC in 2001, within the framework of the General Direction of the Judicial Police, enabled the operational implementation of the legal principles and the methodology of the interview of minors who are victims or witnesses of offences. More recent developments in Belgium are believed to have led to improved legislation in 2011 relating to sexual abuse and paedophilia within a power relationship. Such initiatives have further reinforced the usage of video and the particular approaches to the interviewing of minors who allege to be victims of, or witnesses to, certain offences (such as indecent assault and rape, suborning of minors and procuring, mutilation of female sexual organs).

Definition and practices

Beyond the common law, the legislator provides particular provisions for the interview of minors who are victims or witnesses of offences. According to these provisions, any minor who is the victim or witness of an offence has the right to be accompanied by a person of his choice during the interview: this person is called 'a confidential advisor' (Section 9*bis* of the Rules of Criminal Procedure). The minor must be clearly informed of this right and his/her choice has to be written down in the record of the interview. Nevertheless, if the presence of the confidential advisor is likely to damage the interests of the minor (e.g. the advisor is a person whose testimony has to be collected later), to disturb the functioning of the interview (e.g. the advisor is afraid of speaking) or to be harmful to the disclosure of the truth (e.g. the advisor has a conflict of loyalty), the interviewer informs the public prosecutor or the examining magistrate judge who will decide if it is necessary to exclude the confidential advisor by means of a reasoned decision.

The interviewer also has to explain to the minor the reasons for the audiovisual recording and that she can at any moment ask for an interruption of the recording (Section 95 of the Rules of Criminal Procedure). The minor will also be informed in a language suited to his/her age and cognitive development that his/her statements can be used as evidence in court (Section 47*bis* of the Rules of Criminal Procedure). The interviewer cannot make false promises by ensuring the strict confidentiality of the facts exposed. S/he informs the minor that the recording can be viewed by third parties within the framework of the inquiry or during the trial. The agreement of the parents is not required when interviewing the minor. Nevertheless, the minor has to give his/her explicit agreement to this recording (Section 92 of the Rules of the Criminal Procedure). If the minor is under the age of 12, the interviewer informs him/her that his/her statement will be recorded. Finally, the minor may at any moment ask to interrupt the recording (Section 95, paragraph 2 of the Rules of the Criminal Procedure). The request is written down and the recording has to be stopped immediately.

Current practices: the audiovisual interview of a minor victim or witness

The recording of the interview starts with a global view of the interview room after the interviewer, the minor and possibly the confidential advisor have sat down in the room. During the recording, the date and time are continuously displayed on the video so that the relationship between the interviewer and the minor and the attitude of the confidential advisor during the interview can be fully controlled. The recording stops when the interviewer and the minor finish the interview and leave the interview room. In case of a possible break, any communication between the minor and other persons concerned with the interview should be avoided (for instance: 'When I am in the monitoring room, I will ask you not to talk to the person that you have chosen as confidential advisor').

The Circular Related to the Audiovisual Recording of the Interview of Minors Who Are Victims or Witnesses of an Offence (2001) recommends that the structure of the interview be organised in four steps (phases): the introduction, the free story phase, the questioning and the closing. During the questioning and according to the phase, the interviewer uses general and open questions, followed by specific closed questions. The principles of this interview are still used today, called a 'Respectful, Non-Suggestive and Step-by-Step Interview Protocol' (Yuille *et al.*, 1992). Several studies (Cederborg *et al.*, 2000; Lamb *et al.*, 2007) showed the limits of this protocol due to the important number of closed, directive or choice-minded questions (Cyr *et al.*, 2003).

Since 2010, and in accordance with the principles better defined in the guide NICHD (Lamb *et al.*, 2000; French translation Cyr *et al.*, 2002), many changes have been implemented to the interview structure and to the questioning. The present interview protocol is structured in five phases: 'Salduz', introduction, free story, questioning and closing.

The so-called 'Salduz' phase is meant to check the identity of the minor, his/her age and place of residence, and also to provide the same information as for an adult, i.e. brief information on the facts (Section 47*bis*, paragraph 1 of the C.I.cr.) for which he/she is being interviewed.

The aim of the first part of the introduction phase is to familiarise the minor with the equipment, the people and the legal provisions. All persons present are mentioned (the interviewer, the police officer in the monitoring room, the judicial expert, the interpreter, the confidential advisor) and an explanation is given about the motivation for carrying out an audiovisual interview (for instance, as a rule, the minor has to attend on only one occasion to discuss the matters or incident). The minor is reminded that he/she has the right to have a confidential advisor whose mission is also explained (to support the minor in his/her emotional feelings): the minor has to confirm if the confidential advisor will be present or not during the interview. The minor will be informed of his/her right to interrupt the interview and that his/her statement can be used as evidence in justice (for instance, 'Everything you tell me will be written down in my statement and the public prosecutor can use it to make decisions'). The interviewer will inform the minor about the persons who have the right to view his/her interview, and that he/she has the right not to accuse him/herself (for instance, 'The police officers are present to listen to everybody and everybody has their own version. Tell me everything about the things everyone did/ about everyone's role. You decide what you tell me or what you don't want to tell me'). The interviewer must have the consent of a minor aged 12 or older to be filmed and recorded (for instance, 'Do you agree to be filmed and recorded. I will ask you to answer by yes or no'). In the second part of this introductory phase, the interviewer establishes a working alliance with the minor (Hébert *et al*., 2011).

The interviewer presents the basic rules which are:

- that the minor is not compelled to answer (e.g. 'If you don't want to answer, you say "sir, I don't want to answer"');
- in order to ensure understanding (e.g. 'If you don't understand the question, you say "sir, I don't understand the question" and I will formulate the question in other words');
- in order to avoid guessing (e.g. 'If you cannot answer the question, you say "sir, I don't know the answer"');
- that the minor has the right to correct or complete these statements.

After having presented these basic rules, the interviewer directs the interview to neutral subjects (e.g. 'Tell me about your favourite hobby', 'Tell me everything about …') in order to decrease stress level for the minor and allow for the interview to become more relaxed. The interviewer should also attempt to stimulate the recall of the event or events by using open and inviting questions (e.g. 'Tell me everything about …'), thus helping build rapport with the minor.

The free story phase reminds the minor of the reason for the interview as described in the phase 'Salduz', followed by an invitation (for instance, 'Tell me about that'). The free story of the minor is stimulated by the interviewer using non-selective, non-verbal hearing skills (for instance, silence, 'hmm') or verbal skills (for instance, 'and', 'afterwards', 'later', etc.). At the end of this statement phase, the interviewer gives a summary of the statement and gives the minor the opportunity to complete, modify or correct the statement.

During the questioning phase, the interviewer clarifies and goes deeper into the statement obtained. As a priority, he/she uses open questioning, by segmentation and clues (Hébert *et al.*, 2011), and ends, if necessary, with directive, even suggestive questions.

During the closing phase, the interviewer offers the minor the chance to add new elements to his/her initial statement and to make possible corrections. Finally, the interviewer thanks the minor for coming to the police and informs him/her about further judicial proceedings and possible assistance.

The training of police officers

The training related to the 'Techniques for Interviewing Minors (TAM)' is the responsibility of the DSER for the organisation and the department of behavioural sciences for the content. The initial training, called functional training, can accommodate 16 volunteer police officers. The training consists of two parts: theory and practice. In the theoretical part (57 hours), different aspects are approached (methodological, judicial, psychological and sexual) which can be useful for interviewing children. At the end of this first part, a certified evaluation focused on the knowledge is organised. It is necessary to succeed in the evaluation to be admitted to the practical part (47 hours), where the student is able to develop skills through several practical situations. At the end of this second part, a second and final certified evaluation follows. If the officer successfully passes this stage he/she can undertake audio-visual interviews with those minors who are victims or witnesses of suspected offences.

When the certificate is obtained, the interviewer is obligated to attend three days of continued training annually, allowing him/her to keep up, improve or further develop skills. Parallel to this system and with the assistance of an experienced TAM trainer, the interviewer is offered personalised coaching in which he/she can exchange experiences and express any difficulties in order to optimise his/her interviewing practice.

Finally, for those who where not able to practise during the previous year, refresher training is offered on a voluntary basis. This training, in groups of 12 interviewers, offers a theoretical and practical quality upgrading in order to optimise previously acquired skills.

Conclusion

The interviewing of victims and witnesses, minors or adults, is of particular importance in the process of the judicial inquiry. The quality of the first statement can be decisive for the following investigation. Knowledge of the legal procedures and protocols, of the mission of an intervening third person and of the task enables everyone to feel respected and avoid confusion in their roles. The international research on the subject forces interviewers to constantly review practices and improve. Nothing can ever be taken for granted, everything can be improved.

Acknowledgement

The authors would like to thank J. Demelenne and P. Sempels for translation into English under authorisation of Laurent Coucke, Director of the Technical and Scientific Police of the Belgian Judiciary Police.

References

Adriaensens, P., Cappelaere, G., Hasevoets, Y.-H., Swartele, F., Tulkens, F. and Vandermeersch, D. (1997) *Rapport final de la Commission nationale contre l'exploitation sexuelle des enfants* (*Final Report from the National Commission against Child Sexual Abuse*). Brussels: Inbel

Bockstaele, M. (2011) *Processen-verbaal*. Antwerp: Maklu, p. 335.

Cederborg, A.-C., Orbach, Y., Sternberg, K. J. and Lamb, M. E. (2000) ‚Child witnesses in Sweden', *Child Abuse and Neglect*, 24: 1355–61.

Circulaire 12/2011, du 23 novembre 2011, du Collège des procureurs généraux près les Cours d'appel, relative à l'organisation de l'assistance d'un avocat à partir de la première audition dans le cadre de la procédure pénale belge – Situation des mineurs d'âge et des personnes suspectées d'avoir commis un fait qualifié infraction avant l'âge de dix-huit ans.

Circulaire 8/2011 du Collège des procureurs généraux près les Cours d'appel (version révisée 13.06.2013) relative à l'organisation de l'assistance d'un avocat à partir de la première audition dans le cadre de la procédure pénale Belge.

Circulaire ministérielle du 16 juillet 2001 relative à l'enregistrement audiovisuel de l'audition des mineurs victimes ou témoins d'infractions (2001) Ministère de la Justice, M. Verwilghen, du 16 juillet 2001.

Cyr, M., Bruneau, G., Perron, A. and Vignola, V. (2003) 'Application d'un guide d'entrevue d'investigation auprès de jeunes victimes d'agression sexuelle: résultats d'une expérience québécoise', in M. Tardif (ed.), *L'agression sexuelle: Coopérer au-delà des frontières*. Ebook from CIFAS (2005) available at: http://www3.unil.ch/wpmu/cifas2011/cifas-precedents/gatineau-2005/.

Cyr, M., Dion, J., Perreault, R. and Richard, N. (2002) *Guide NICHD d'entrevue d'investigation en matière d'agression sexuelle envers les enfants*. Montréal: Centre de Recherche Interdisciplinaire sur les Problèmes conjugaux et les Agressions sexuelles (CRIPCAS).

De Valkeneer, Ch. (2005) *Manuel de l'enquête pénale*. Brussels: De Boeck and Larcier, 143-174.

Hébert, M., Cyr, M. and Tourigny, M. (2011) *L'agression sexuelle envers les enfants*. Québec: Presses de l'Université du Québec.

Judgment by Constitutional Court (2013) Affecting the Belgian Bulletin of Acts (2011) and modifying the Criminal Code and the 07.20.1990 Act about Preventive Custody in Order to Confer Rights of Assistance and Consultation of a Lawyer, to Every Interviewed and Arrested Person.

Lamb, M. E., Orbach, Y., Hershkowitz, I., Esplin, P. W. and Horowitz, D. (2007) 'A structured forensic interview protocol improves the quality and informativeness of investigative interviews with children: a review of research using the NICHD Investigative Interview Protocol', *Child Abuse and Neglect*, 31: 1201–31.

Loi du 28 novembre 2000 relative à la protection pénale des mineurs (2000) Moniteur belge, du 17 mars 2001, p. 8503.

Loi du 30 novembre 2011 modifiant la législation en ce qui concerne l'amélioration de l'approche des abus sexuels et des faits de pédophilie dans une relation d'autorité. Moniteur belge, du 20 janvier 2012, p. 4386.

Plan National de Sécurité 2012–2015.

St-Yves, M. and Tanguay, M. (2007) *Psychologie de l'enquêter criminelle: la recherche de la vérité (Partie I Les entrevues d'enquête)*. Cowansville, Québec: Édition Yvon Blais.

Yuille, J. C., Hunter, R., Joffe, R. and Zaparnuik, J. (1992) 'Interviewing children in sexual abuse cases', in J. Van Gijseghem (1993), *L'enfant mis à nu, L'allégation d'abus sexuel: la recherché de la vérité*. Montréal: Méridien, pp. 69–113.

9 Investigative interviewing in England and Wales

Adults, children and the provision of support for child witnesses

Genevieve Waterhouse, Anne Ridley, Rachel Wilcock and Ray Bull

Introduction

This chapter will outline the current guidelines used in England and Wales for police interviews of victims and witnesses of crime (henceforth both referred to as witnesses). This will include sections on current best practice for interviewing 'typical' adult witnesses as well as the more specific guidelines in place for interviewing and providing social support to child witnesses. We will also review research into the effectiveness of social support measures.

This focus has been chosen because child interviews are particularly important in England and Wales, not only as a source of evidence for investigations, but also because (unlike typical adult interviews) children's investigative interviews are video-recorded and frequently used as evidence-in-chief during criminal trials. Although this reduces the need for in-depth interviewing by the prosecution in court, children are nevertheless likely to be cross-examined by the defence on the evidence provided in this interview. As a result, these interviews, and the support provided to children while they are conducted, may also have a direct influence on jurors' decision-making and verdicts.

Although an increasing number of cases involving child victims and witnesses make it to court, many do not. In 2012/13, 73,900 children under 16 years old reported being the victim of sexual abuse (National Society for the Prevention of Cruelty to Children, 2014). However, only 18,700 offences of child sexual abuse were recorded by the police in the same time period, which in turn led to 3,600 defendants being brought to court on charges of child sexual abuse and 2,100 guilty verdicts being returned. This begs the question of whether there are issues related to investigations involving child witnesses and victims, such as the quality of the interview and support provided, that need to be addressed. This review will explore some of these issues.

Investigative interviewing of victims and witnesses in England and Wales

PEACE is the current investigative interview model used in England and Wales (College of Policing (CoP), 2013). Introduced in 1992, PEACE is based in conversation management techniques (Shepherd and Milne, 2006) and is an acronym of the mnemonic stages of an investigative interview. *Planning and preparation* refers to organising the interview itself, obtaining information regarding the interviewee and creating an interview plan. The interview plan identifies the aims and objectives of the interview as well as any points to prove. When appropriate, an intermediary's pre-interview assessment would also be included in the *planning and preparation* phase ('intermediary' is defined in Table 9.1 and described in greater detail below). The officer should then conduct the interview. This begins with the *engage and explain* phase, consisting of explaining the purpose and main aims of the interview and describing how it will be conducted (e.g. free recall followed by questions). The interviewee is then encouraged to give an *account*. This involves free recall, during which the interviewer should make no interruptions and use active listening and judicious use of simple prompters (such as nodding) to incite the interviewee to give as much detail as possible. As part of the *account* phase, following free recall the interviewer has the opportunity for 'clarification and challenge', during which the interviewer asks questions. Interviewers are encouraged to use particular types of questions (see Table 9.2) to obtain further details of the interviewee's account. The interview comes to an end with *closure*, in which the interviewee is given an opportunity to expand upon their account and the interviewer summarises what information the witness has provided. If a witness statement is appropriate, this will be written and signed during the *closure* phase. The final phase for the interviewer is *evaluation*. Interviewers should consider both the witnesses' and their own performance during the interview, and put the account into the context of the rest of the investigation. They should also make decisions as to what should happen next in the investigation (CoP, 2013).

The intention behind the introduction of PEACE was to discourage the widespread use of directive questioning (i.e. questioning that tightly confines the direction of the interview and thus the responses of the interviewee) and use empirically evidenced techniques to obtain the most accurate and rich detail from witnesses (Shepherd and Milne, 2006). Thus during the *account* phase of a PEACE interview with witnesses the Enhanced Cognitive Interview (ECI) is employed. This interview protocol uses a number of empirically supported

Table 9.1 Definitions

Social support	'Social interaction or communication that fosters a feeling of well-being in the target' (Davis and Bottoms, 2002: 186).
Cognitive support	Forms of support that help children to verbalise and recall details of an event.
Intermediary	Expert in a relevant field present in the interview to improve communication between the interviewer and a vulnerable witness such as those with learning disabilities and children.
Interview supporter	Individual known to the interviewee who is present in the interview to provide emotional support.

Table 9.2 Description of question types

Question type	*Description*	*Example*	*Use in investigative interviews*
Open-ended	Allows interviewee to give free recall and control what information they disclose.	'Tell me everything that happened.'	✓
Specific-closed	Asks for a more narrow account of a specific aspect of the event.	'Who was in the room?'	✓
Forced-choice	Includes a number of choices from which the interviewee should select their answer.	'Would you like tea or coffee?'	×
Multiple	Asking a number of questions in one utterance, or for information about more than one subject.	'Did you see him? Where was he? What was he wearing?' 'What did they look like?'	×
Leading	Questions that suggest one answer is correct (regardless of whether it is or not), or include information that has not previously been mentioned by the interviewee.	'You did see the gun, didn't you?' 'Where was the gun?' (when the interviewee has not mentioned a gun)	×

Source: Ministry of Justice (2011).

psychological techniques to encourage extensive recall from cooperative witnesses (La Rooy *et al.*, 2013; Milne and Bull, 1999).

There are four cognitive components:

1. *Report everything* – where prior to the initial recall, the interviewee is instructed explicitly to recall anything and everything they remember, no matter how unimportant they perceive it to be.
2. *Mental reinstatement of context* – where prior to the initial recall the interviewer encourages the witness to mentally reinstate the context of the crime by asking the interviewee to think back to the event and all the sensory aspects of it, including what they saw.
3. *Change perspective* – during an additional retrieval attempt the interviewee is asked to describe the crime from a different person's perspective.
4. *Change the temporal order* – in which, during a further retrieval attempt, interviewees are asked to recall the event in a different order, such as from the end of the crime to the beginning.

In addition, the ECI contains a number of additional techniques such as: building rapport (see discussion of this below), transferring control of the interview from the interviewer to the interviewee by explaining that the interviewee has all of the information and therefore should be providing the majority of input into the interview, and ensuring that questions are asked in a manner which is compatible with the interviewee's memory trace by asking questions in the same order as the interviewee's initial recall. Research has demonstrated that the ECI leads to a large statistically significant increase in correct recall as compared with a control interview (Memon *et al.*, 2010).

Training of all police interviewers in England and Wales is done in accordance with the tiered Professionalising Investigation Programme (PIP) (Association of Chief Police Officers, 2009) which includes the PEACE model and elements of the ECI depending upon which tier of training is completed. All interviewers must be trained to at least PIP level one which allows them to conduct interviews with witnesses of less serious crime (volume crime). Level two PIP training is for officers conducting interviews for serious and complex crime and specialist interviews such as those with children, and level three PIP training addresses the supervision and management of interviewing. Most witness interviews in England and Wales are conducted by these trained police officers, although in particular circumstances, other trained professionals (such as social workers) may jointly lead the interview. The interviewing technique used with the witness varies according to the seriousness of the crime. For volume and relatively minor crimes, a formal written statement may be taken there and then whereas with more serious crime (such as child sexual abuse or murder), investigating officers are likely to conduct a full interview that includes the ECI and extensive planning.

Despite the success of the cognitive interview (Memon *et al.*, 2010) research has shown interviewers use certain aspects of the ECI, such as the 'report everything' instruction, more regularly than others, such as the 'mental reinstatement of context' (Dando *et al.*, 2009). This may be due to perceiving some techniques as more effective and/or less time-consuming (Dando *et al.*, 2008) and so, despite the training, some techniques in the ECI may not be used in practice as often as they could be. However, for child interviews, research has suggested that not all ECI techniques are appropriate (for a review, see Memon *et al.*, 2010). For example, the instructions for 'change perspective' and 'change temporal order' may be too difficult for young child witnesses to fully understand.

There are, however, additional things that can be done to support child witnesses during an investigative interview to ensure that they obtain access to justice. The Achieving Best Evidence (ABE) guidelines currently in use across England and Wales (Ministry of Justice, 2011) explain in detail how witness interviews should be conducted, in particular the *special measures* that are available for vulnerable witnesses, which includes children, who will be the focus for the remainder of this chapter.[1] Along with ways of cognitively supporting children, the ABE addresses the interviewer–interviewee relationship, interviewer demeanour and within-interview social support in a number of ways (see Table 9.1 for definitions of support types). It advises that interviewers:

- build rapport at the beginning of all interviews;
- avoid an authoritative demeanour but appear confident and competent;

- communicate sympathy, respect and, where necessary, reassurance;
- use a 'warm demeanour' (p. 177) in interviews with very young and psychologically disturbed children;
- include an intermediary or interview supporter in the interview, when appropriate.

These suggestions are made in order for interviewers to avoid witnesses becoming overly compliant, acquiescent or feeling daunted by the experience, and to help reduce the power imbalance between the interviewer and interviewee which, of course, is further evident when the interviewee is a child.

Interview support for child witnesses

Investigative interviews are, for many, a traumatic experience. They often involve recounting memories to a complete stranger of experiences that may have been distressing and confusing. Such an interview has the potential to cause the witness to feel embarrassed and anxious and, if carried out in an unsympathetic manner, re-victimised by the experience. This can be particularly true for witnesses who do not understand legal proceedings, for example due to their age. Leander *et al.* (2007) found law enforcement professionals often perceived children's emotional barriers (such as feelings of discomfort, fears of being misunderstood or not believed) to disclosing sexual abuse as greater than their cognitive barriers. Thus there appears to be awareness of the need to support child witnesses emotionally during investigative interviews. However, empirical evidence into the effects of social support in child witness interviews is as yet somewhat limited.

In the psychological literature, social support has usually been examined as an interviewer-provided characteristic of the interview, and therefore verbal and non-verbal supportive interviewer behaviours, including rapport-building, will be examined. However, for the purpose of this review, the abilities of other interview participants to provide social support (i.e. intermediaries and interview supporters) will also be examined. Although the mental well-being of the witness is important, so is the accuracy and extensiveness of their recall for the investigation, so interview support options will be discussed in regard to both their effects on witnesses' emotions and on their event recall. The rest of the chapter will examine research relating to these different types of support – rapport, verbal and non-verbal support, intermediaries and interview supporters – in relation to child witnesses.

Rapport-building

Rapport-building is a form of verbal support encouraged by ABE (Ministry of Justice, 2011). It is thought of as leading to a more comfortable interviewer–interviewee relationship, improving the interview's atmosphere (Collins *et al.*, 2002). Tickle-Degnen and Rosenthal (1990) describe rapport as consisting of three components: mutual attentiveness (paying attention to and being involved in what the other person is saying), positivity (mutual friendliness) and coordination (both parties should be able to work together). They argue that although coordination is less important for meetings that occur early in the relationship, as forensic child interviews regularly do, all three components must be present. ABE (Ministry of Justice, 2011) includes concepts of positivity and mutual attentiveness in its guidelines by suggesting that rapport-building should include discussion of positive or neutral subjects and the use of active listening. However, studies of real investigative interviews have found that this training is not being translated effectively into practice. Using a sample of children's interview transcripts, Westcott and Kynan (2006) found rapport was often carried out in a 'list-like' manner and not used as an opportunity for the interviewer and interviewee to bond. Furthermore, in child protection agency interviews with suspected victims of child sexual abuse, Wood *et al*., (1996) frequently found interviewers were 'mechanical' in their rapport-building, resorting to questions with brief answers (e.g. What's your favourite subject?) and responding in a lukewarm fashion. Without proper rapport, interviewees may feel the interviewer is not genuinely interested in what they have to say and thus may report less crucial information.

There exists very little research comparing interviews with and without rapport-building in children. To our knowledge, the only research that has included this necessary control condition is Collins' (2012) doctoral thesis. In her research, she found that a rapport-building phase consisting of open questions about a neutral subject (as recommended in ABE (Ministry of Justice, 2011)) had no significant effects on children's recall or their suggestibility compared to a no-rapport condition. In contrast, a play rapport-building phase, in which the child and interviewer together completed a play task, such as a jigsaw, was found to lead to children providing more detailed and accurate information in a subsequent mock forensic interview, and also responding correctly to misleading questions (questions that imply an incorrect response) more often. This suggests that alternative rapport-building procedures may have more beneficial effects on children's recall than the procedures currently encouraged by ABE (Ministry of Justice, 2011). Collins (2012) also examined children's self-reported state anxiety and their heart rate variability and did not find these to differ significantly between rapport conditions, suggesting that rapport may not affect children's anxiety.

A recent field study has looked at enhanced rapport-building behaviours during child interviews and compared them with those advocated in the NICHD interview protocol (Hershkowitz *et al*., 2013).[2] It is important to note here that the NICHD protocol is itself more extensive in its rapport-building than ABE-recommended procedures. The NICHD protocol includes encouraging children to talk about their likes and dislikes as well as recalling a past neutral event during the rapport-building phase, whereas ABE merely suggests a brief discussion of neutral topics. In addition to the standard NICHD recommendations, enhanced rapport-building involved more reference to and empathy with children's emotions, greater interest in their experiences and positive reinforcement of their efforts. Hershkowitz *et al*. (2013) found this enhancement resulted in less reluctance to disclose by suspected child victims of sexual abuse than the NICHD standard rapport building, although there was no difference in the total amount of information recalled in the interview. Thus it may be that the ABE (Ministry of Justice, 2011) rapport-building techniques are simply not sufficient to support children adequately. However, the more extensive procedures are likely to take longer than the average ABE rapport-building, and lengthy rapport-building has been found to have negative consequences for children's recall, being associated with shorter and less detailed answers from children (Davies *et al.*, 2000; Hershkowitz, 2009). Thus it would be interesting to conduct a comparative study between both forms of rapport-building used in Hershkowitz *et al.* (2013), no rapport-building and the standard ABE rapport-building in order to determine whether using these rapport-enhancing techniques would be more effective or whether the increased time they take would have negative consequences on children's recall.

The rapport-enhanced protocol in Hershkowitz *et al.* (2013), however, advocated not only greater support during the rapport-building phase, but also throughout the interview. Hershkowitz *et al.* (2013) argue that this is important for encouraging children to give as much detail as possible during the interview and suggest that the reason that children who experienced enhanced rapport-building did not give significantly more information overall when compared to the standard NICHD rapport-building interviews was because the interviewers were no more supportive during the substantive phase. This again is a possible improvement that could be included in ABE interviews guidelines: after rapport-building the interviewer could provide support throughout the interview via their verbal and non-verbal behaviours.

Interviewer verbal and non-verbal supportive behaviours in the substantive phase

Interviewer support during the substantive phase can have a significant effect on child interviewee well-being. For example, Almerigogna *et al.* (2008) found children rated interviewers who smiled and did not fidget as more friendly and less strict, bored or stressed than those who did not smile or fidget. Other studies have manipulated different behaviours to vary how supportive interviews are. These are presented in Table 9.3 which focuses on experimental studies since 2001, as the findings of older studies are thought to have been incorporated in the earlier (2002) version of ABE.

The majority of studies in Table 9.3 have found positive, or at worst neutral, effects of supportive behaviours on children's recall. This is particularly the case for responses to misleading questions and reductions in anxiety levels. The only study that showed some possibly undesirable effects is that of Bull and Corran (2003) who included *correctly* leading questions (i.e. questions that implied the correct response). In their study, 36 7–14 year olds viewed a short video clip which was followed by 12 standardised specific recall questions (four misleading, four leading and four neutral) asked in an authoritative or non-authoritative manner.

Table 9.3 Results of experimental studies since 2001 on the effects of interviewer-provided supportive behaviours on children's recall

Study	*Sample ages*	*Supportive behaviours*									*Effect of support (+ / 0 / – : positive / neutral / negative)*					
		Body posture	*Close proximity*	*Casual dress*	*Eye contact*	*'Friendly'*	*Introduction/ rapport*	*Indiscriminate praise/ verbal encouragement*	*Smiles*	*Vocal warmth*	*Free recall*	*Misleading questions*	*Leading questions*	*Specific questions*	*Direct (misleading and specific) questions*	*Reduced anxiety*
Almerigogna *et al.* (2007)	8–10	✓		✓	✓	✓	✓		✓			+		0		+
Bull and Corran (2003)	7–14	✓							✓	✓		+	–[1] 0[2]	–[3] 0[4]		
Davis and Bottoms (2002)	6–7	✓	✓		✓		✓		✓	✓	0	+		0		+
Peter-Hagene *et al.* (2014)	7–8	✓	✓		✓		✓		✓	✓		+				
*Davis and Bottoms (2002) sample one year on																
Quas *et al.* (2004)	4–6	✓		✓	✓		✓	✓	✓	✓					+[5] –[6]	
Quas and Lench (2007)	5–6	✓	✓		✓		✓	✓	✓		0				+	

1. 7–11 year olds
2. 12–14 year olds
3. 7–8 year olds
4. 10–14 year olds
5. Children with high autonomic reactivity
6. Children with low autonomic reactivity

For the younger participants, the authoritative manner increased the number of correct responses they gave to correctly leading questions and neutral specific questions about the video. However, this study did not manipulate the introduction or rapport-building of the interviewer (unlike the other studies) which may explain these different findings. Thus it could be that the other non-verbal supportive behaviours are only as effective in combination with a supportive introduction to the interview.

Although the currently available experimental research largely endorses the use of supportive behaviours in child interviewing, basing practice solely on laboratory results that frequently use video-recorded crimes or live non-crime events which lack the emotional impact of being a victim is less ecologically valid. The anxiety related to recalling a clip from a movie to a researcher within a known, safe environment is in no way comparable to the anxiety caused by recounting experiences as a victim of abuse or neglect to a police officer within an unknown environment such as an interviewing suite. Therefore applying conclusions about social support from such experiments alone to actual interviews with children about alleged sexual abuse is not ideal. Thus field studies are invaluable and so it is unfortunate that very few address support in child investigative interviews. Those that have done so report positive effects. Teoh and Lamb (2013) found that children were more informative (e.g. gave more information of probative value) when interviewed by supportive interviewers than non-supportive interviewers, irrespective of age. However, they also found that police officers were inconsistent in the support they provided, being more supportive to older children than younger ones. Hershkowitz *et al.* (2006) also found that children who experienced more verbally supportive interviews gave more informative responses than those that had less support. However, interviewers in this sample were also found to be more supportive in the substantive phase of the interview to children who disclosed than to those who did not. Possibly, in response to this lack of support, non-disclosing children were increasingly uninformative and resistant to interviewers' questions in this phase. Additionally, Ahern *et al.* (2014) found that when interviewers used an enhanced rapport-building protocol (as in Hershkowitz *et al.*, 2013, discussed above) and were supportive in response to children's reluctance during the substantive phase of the interview, children displayed significantly less reluctance than when interviewers used the same protocol but were not supportive in response to children's reluctance. In contrast, when interviewers used the standard NICHD protocol (as in Hershkowitz *et al.*, 2013), support in the substantive phase had no effect on children's continued reluctance (Ahern *et al.*, 2014). Thus consistent and continued support from the beginning and throughout investigative interviews may well be beneficial for children's testimony.

Although all of the interviews used in Hershkowitz *et al.* (2006) and Ahern *et al.* (2014) were regarding credible allegations, the veracity of the children's testimony cannot be ascertained. Thus these children may not have been providing extra accurate information in the interviews but giving more information to please their friendly interviewer and fill in the spaces in the conversation.

Furthermore, none of the field studies measured children's emotional well-being, instead they only examined verbal support. The interviewers' non-verbal behaviours may not have been consistent with their verbal ones and so their overall level of supportiveness may not have been accurately assessed. Indeed, interviewer support may be equally (or more) strongly indicated by non-verbal than verbal behaviour. However, these real-life findings in conjunction with the experimental studies (in Table 9.3) do indicate the possible efficacy of using friendly and unintimidating verbal and non-verbal behaviours in child interviews. Interviewers themselves clearly have the opportunity to support a child via rapport-building and supportive verbal and non-verbal behaviours. However, additional people can be present during an interview to support a child and it is to this that we now turn.

The role of intermediaries and interview supporters

All vulnerable witnesses are eligible for interview supporters and intermediaries. The decision as to whether these *special measures* are implemented lies with the police officers conducting the interviews and running the investigation.

The interview supporter's role is solely to provide emotional support for the interviewee. They should not interrupt the interview in any way other than to provide them emotional comfort (ABE: Ministry of Justice, 2011). Interview supporters can be anyone that the interviewee feels comfortable with who is not personally involved in the investigation. Interview supporters may not receive any training, although professional bodies (such as Victim Support) can provide volunteers to act as interview supporters who will have received general training on supporting witnesses and victims.[3]

Intermediaries, on the other hand, are present to aid communication between the interviewer and interviewee during both police interviews and court appearances. According to Cooper (2012), the majority of the 144 registered intermediaries in England and Wales are speech and language therapists but some are also from psychology, teaching or other relevant backgrounds. Their role in the interview setting is:

1. to conduct pre-interview assessments of an interviewee and advise as to whether they are able to communicate their evidence;
2. to give guidance on how to best interview the victim; and
3. to be present during the investigative interview to monitor and facilitate interviewer–interviewee communication.

Intermediaries should limit their interventions during questioning to when they feel the interviewee could not or did not understand the question and/or when they feel they should take action to settle the interviewee in order to help him/her focus (Ministry of Justice, 2012). Thus, although the intermediary's role does not explicitly include the emotional support of the witness, their work during the interview arguably serves a similar purpose. This view is supported by Plotnikoff and Woolfson's (2007) evaluation of the work of intermediaries during criminal trials (where they continue to aid communication). They found that many carers of vulnerable witnesses reported that the intermediary's presence decreased the stress of the vulnerable witness in court and thus it is likely the intermediary's presence will have this beneficial effect in the investigative interview also. Additionally, both lawyers and intermediaries believed asking developmentally inappropriate questions to be likely to affect children's emotional well-being by decreasing their confidence (Krähenbühl, 2011). Thus intermediaries may be aware that their work has the unintended consequence of affecting children's well-being positively.

In contrast to England and Wales, many countries do not offer child witnesses intermediaries at all. These include Western Australia (despite there being legislative provisions for them) (Henderson, 2010) and New Zealand (although they are considering implementation) (Hanna *et al.*, 2013). Even in those countries that currently use intermediaries, they are often limited to working within the court room (e.g. Austria (NZMoJ, 2010), South Africa and the USA (Henderson, 2012)). Some countries, on the other hand, use specialists to conduct their child interviews. These are often specially trained police officers (e.g. Austria (NZMoJ, 2010), Norway and France (Henderson, 2010)), but can also have social work backgrounds (e.g. Israel's 'youth interrogators' (Hershkowitz, 2009)). The intermediary's role within England and Wales is, therefore, currently unique.

Although the inclusion of these theoretically supportive options in the ABE makes moral sense (the witness may have been through a traumatic experience and disclosure of such trauma should be made as easy and comfortable as possible), the research supporting these techniques is scarce and not always consistent in its findings. We review this evidence in the following sections.

Registered intermediaries

Intermediaries were introduced to law in the Youth Justice and Criminal Evidence Act 1999 as one of a number of 'Special Measures' in an endeavour to improve communication between the interviewee and the criminal justice system, be that within the court or interview setting. The literature suggests this improvement is much needed: many studies have shown children have difficulty understanding the questions asked in investigative interviews (e.g. Carter *et al.*, 1996; Korkman *et al.*, 2008) and give more accurate answers when questions are reworded to be developmentally appropriate (Imhoff and Baker-Ward, 1999).

Krähenbühl (2011) found that intermediaries identified twice as many inappropriate statements or questions in a mock transcript of a child interview and cross-examination than did lawyers. However, her study did not look at intermediaries' actual behaviours and so it is unknown whether they would have intervened after every inappropriate question (as their role suggests they should). In a survey of 25 registered intermediaries who had been involved in investigative interviews with vulnerable witnesses (Plotnikoff and Woolfson, 2007), 72 per cent of intermediaries said that they intervened very little or not at all in interviews and 56 per cent of these felt that they should have intervened more.

This indicates that intermediaries may be aware of poor questioning but do not intervene after every question they consider inappropriate. This could occur because the intermediary may be concerned about interrupting the interviewer too frequently, a difficult task that could interrupt the interviewer's flow or cause the interviewer to feel the intermediary is being overly fastidious (Plotnikoff and Woolfson, 2007). However, the detailed planning of a police interview with the aid of an intermediary should mean most of the interview questions are already appropriate for the witness's cognitive level. That said, many of the intermediaries' suggested solutions for developmentally inappropriate questions identified in Krähenbühl's study (2011) involved remodelling the question into a closed and often forced-choice or yes/no format. These forms of questioning are discouraged in current interview guidelines. Therefore intermediaries may inadvertently make questioning simpler for vulnerable witnesses in a manner that could be disadvantageous to the quality of evidence. One solution to this would be for intermediaries to complete police interview training (as few as 9 per cent report doing so) (Plotnikoff and Woolfson, 2007) or for initial training to be extended to cover such issues.

Neither field nor experimental studies have examined the effect of intermediary presence on witnesses' recall or their well-being. However, police officers report benefits of intermediaries' work, including alerting them to the witnesses' comprehension levels (which were generally overestimated) and help with planning interviewee-appropriate questions (Plotnikoff and Woolfson, 2007; Cooper, 2009). Additionally, Ridley *et al.* (2015) conducted a study in which mock jurors, barristers and police officers evaluated two versions of a transcript of a fictitious child witness interview conducted by a police officer. One version of the transcript included the presence of an intermediary who requested clarification of a number of questions posed by the officer. The second version did not have an intermediary present. Overall, intermediary presence had a generally positive or neutral effect on perceptions of various aspects of the interview, particularly among the police and barristers, and no negative effects on the perceived credibility of the child witness.

Despite the generally positive views the police have of the use of intermediaries, Plotnikoff and Woolfson (2007) highlighted that they very rarely request intermediaries for witnesses based on age alone (14 per cent); instead they are mostly requested for children with additional vulnerabilities (such as learning disabilities) and for vulnerable adults (approximately 76 per cent of requests). This is despite children being the largest group of witnesses eligible for intermediary presence (Plotnikoff and Woolfson, 2007). However, the number of requests for intermediaries for all vulnerable witnesses appears to be increasing, with 3,318 requests between 2009 and 2012 compared to approximately 2,000 requests between 2004 and 2009 (Cooper, 2012). This increase in overall numbers is likely to include more children's interviews.

As this review highlights, research on the impact of intermediaries on child interviews and the criminal justice process is limited. Further research would help to establish the effectiveness of the intermediary scheme both in terms of its stated objective of enhancing communication with vulnerable witnesses and the unintended consequence of providing emotional support.

Interview supporters

According to ABE (Ministry of Justice, 2011), all vulnerable witnesses are eligible for interview supporters. However, to our knowledge, there is little research and no recent data addressing the frequency and quality of interview supporter use in investigative interviews in England and Wales. We have therefore largely turned to other countries for evidence from similar schemes.

In the US, victim/witness assistants (VWAs) are professionals who either act as supporters for children themselves, or who, through their professional role, should be in a position to comment on the extent to which other persons (such as relatives) support child witnesses. McAuliff *et al.* (2013) carried out a survey of 414 VWAs. They felt that supporters were used 'rarely' to 'sometimes' during investigative interviews, despite believing that their presence decreases stress for the child witness and increases the accuracy and credibility of the child. In Scotland, Plotnikoff and Woolfson (2000) reported that children were accompanied by supporters in 25 of the 45 police interviews examined, but the child witnesses were not always asked whether they wanted a supporter present.

The experimental literature on this topic seems limited entirely to the use of peers as interview supporters (see Greenstock and Pipe, 1997; Moston, 1992). Although these studies have generally found neutral or positive effects of peer presence, the practical and legal difficulties of including another child in an investigative interview means this is not a viable way of supporting children.

There has, however, been one field study in Finland of 27 cases in which children's relatives acted as interview supporters. Santtila *et al.* (2004) found that the presence of relatives had negative effects on both interviewee and interviewer behaviours. Interviewers asked more suggestive questions and spoke more whereas children said less, provided fewer details and descriptions and gave more meaningless answers when their relative was present compared to interviews where a child was interviewed alone. Additionally, negative behaviours by parental interview supporters themselves were reported in McAuliff *et al.*'s (2013) study. VWAs generally perceived that parents who supported their children in legal settings did not have a positive impact on the children's stress levels, often interfered in children's testimony and had inadequate training for acting as a support person. These neutral effects on children's well-being and negative effects on their testimony may be caused by embarrassment and increased anxiety due to their relatives' presence and their prior relationship with that person. However, this may not mean that interview supporters other than parents would also have negative effects on children's performance in investigative interviews. In a study conducted in Wales, Aldridge and Wood (1998) suggest 'attached' adults (i.e. someone with a personal connection to the child, such as their parent) find it difficult not to participate in the interview, either through volunteering information or because the child expects them to provide it. They therefore suggest that an attached adult's presence may be detrimental to not only the child's but also the supporting adult's emotional well-being and the perceived quality of the evidence. To avoid this, they propose that a 'detached' adult's presence (e.g. a social worker) may be more beneficial.

However, these studies have some limitations: McAuliff *et al.* (2013) acknowledge limitations with the sampling of VWAs and possible response biases due to the self-report nature of the study. Santtila *et al.* (2004) point out that their Finnish sample was unrepresentative, being drawn from a source of interviews whose quality had been questioned and involving a quasi-experimental design, meaning there may have been significant differences between the children interviewed with and without interview supporters. Aldridge and Wood's (1998) recommendations are based on a sample of 100 child interview transcripts, with no details as to how many included interview supporters.

From our review of the limited research available on interview supporters, there is evidence that the use of parents or relatives may not be appropriate. At the very least, simple guidelines for witness supporters in England and Wales, along with a move towards greater professionalisation of this service (in line with the VWA scheme in the US) need to be considered.

Implications for research, policy and practice

- Based on sound psychological research, effective protocols for the questioning of adults and children in investigative interviews have been developed and are widely adopted in England and Wales.
- Relatively little research has been conducted to ensure that the *social support* provision for child witnesses during investigative interviews is both fit for purpose and actually fulfils the dual purpose of making the child feel comfortable and either improving or at least not diminishing the quality of the evidence provided.
  - Comparisons of rapport-building in different interviewing protocols would clarify the relative benefits and disadvantages of longer rapport-building times and more emotionally involved rapport-building (i.e. greater empathy and interest in children's lives).
  - Research regarding the effects of intermediary and interview supporter presence on child witnesses' well-being and recall is necessary. The opportunity for this research exists as these *special measures* are already in operation in the criminal justice system.
- The use of continuous socially supportive behaviours, including non-verbal behaviours such as smiling and frequent use of eye contact, during the substantive phase of an interview should be encouraged. Their inclusion in police interview training would be a relatively easy way to increase the social support provided to child witnesses and victims.
- Extended training for intermediaries to include interview techniques is advocated to ensure appropriate balance between the need for the child to

understand the question while avoiding (as far as possible) closed or leading questions. This would benefit both intermediary input into planning the investigative interview and the interview itself.

- From the existing research, there appears to be a need for information or training for interview supporters. An alternative would be to introduce a professional interview supporter role for all child interviews, in a similar manner to the US's victim/witness assistant.

Notes

1. The ABE guidelines are the basis for level two specialist interview PIP training and as such embrace the general principles of good interviewing and the Enhanced Cognitive Interview detailed above.
2. The National Institute of Child Health and Human Development (NICHD) interview protocol; for details see Lamb *et al.* (2011) and La Rooy *et al.* (2013).
3. New Zealand and the USA offer similar support to their child witnesses (McAuliff *et al.*, 2013; New Zealand Ministry of Justice (NZMoJ), 2010).

References

Ahern, E., Hershkowitz, I., Lamb, M. E., Winstanley, A. and Blasbalg, U. (2014) *Interviewer Support and Alleged Child Abuse Victim Reluctance in the Pre-substantive Phase of Investigative Interviews: Revised vs. Standard NICHD Protocols.* Paper presented at the meeting of the American Psychology-Law Society, New Orleans, Louisiana.

Aldridge, M. and Wood, J. (1998) 'Establishing rapport', in M. Aldridge and J. Wood, *Interviewing Children: A Guide for Child Care and Forensic Practitioners.* Chichester: Wiley & Sons, pp. 25–69.

Almerigogna, J., Ost, J., Akehurst, L. and Fluck, M. (2008) 'How interviewers' nonverbal behaviors can affect children's perceptions and suggestibility', *Journal of Experimental Child Psychology*, 100: 17–39.

Almerigogna, J., Ost, J., Bull, R. and Akehurst, L. (2007) 'State of high anxiety: how non-supportive interviewers can increase the suggestibility of child witnesses', *Applied Cognitive Psychology*, 21: 963–74.

Association of Chief Police Officers (2009) *National Investigative Interviewing: Briefing Paper.* Retrieved from: http://www.acpo.police.uk/documents/crime/2009/200901 CRINSI01.pdf.

Bull, R. and Corran, E. (2003) 'Interviewing child witnesses: past and future', *International Journal of Police Science and Management*, 4: 315–22.

Carter, C. A., Bottoms, B. L. and Levine, M. (1996) 'Linguistic and socioemotional influences on the accuracy of children's reports', *Law and Human Behavior*, 20: 335–58.

College of Policing (2013) *Investigative Interviewing.* Retrieved from: http://www.app.college.police.uk/app-content/investigations/investigative-interviewing/.

Collins, K. (2012) 'Rapport Building in Child Investigative Interviews'. Unpublished doctoral dissertation, University of Stirling, Scotland.

Collins, R., Lincoln, R. and Frank, M. G. (2002) 'The effect of rapport in forensic interviewing', *Psychiatry, Psychology and Law*, 9: 69–78.

Cooper, P. (2009) *Tell Me What's Happening: Registered Intermediary Survey 2009*, Project Report. Retrieved from http://eprints.kingston.ac.uk/26963/.

Cooper, P. (2012) *Ten years of Registered Intermediaries in England and Wales*. Retrieved from: http://www.city.ac.uk/__data/assets/pdf_file/0010/150688/Ten-years-of-Registered-Intermediaries-in-England-and-Wales-Jun-2012.pdf

Dando, C., Wilcock, R. and Milne, R. (2008) 'The Cognitive Interview: inexperienced police officers' perceptions of their witness/victim interviewing practices', *Legal and Criminological Psychology*, 13: 59–70.

Dando, C., Wilcock, R. and Milne, R. (2009) 'The Cognitive Interview: novice police officers' witness/victim interviewing practices', *Psychology, Crime and Law*, 15: 679–96.

Davies, G. M., Westcott, H. L. and Horan, N. (2000) 'The impact of questioning style on the content of investigative interviews with suspected child sexual abuse victims', *Psychology, Crime and Law*, 6: 81–97.

Davis, S. L. and Bottoms, B. L. (2002) 'Effects of social support on children's eyewitness reports: a test of the underlying mechanism', *Law and Human Behavior*, 26: 185–215.

Greenstock, J. and Pipe, M. (1997) 'Are two heads better than one? Peer support and children's eyewitness reports', *Applied Cognitive Psychology*, 11: 461–83

Hanna, K., Davies, E., Henderson, E. and Hand, L. (2013) 'Questioning child witnesses: exploring the benefits and risks of intermediary models in New Zealand', *Psychiatry, Psychology and Law*, 20: 527–42.

Henderson, E. (2010) 'Innovative practices in other jurisdictions', in K. Hanna, E. Davies, E. Henderson, C. Crothers and C. Rotherham, *Child Witnesses in the New Zealand Criminal Courts: A Review of Practice and Implications for Policy*. Auckland, NZ: Institute of Public Policy.

Henderson, E. (2012) 'Alternative routes: other accusatorial jurisdictions on the slow road to best evidence', in J. R. Spencer and M. E. Lamb (eds), *Children and Cross-examination: Time to Change the Rules?* Oxford: Hart, pp. 43–74.

Hershkowitz, I. (2009) 'Socioemotional factors in child sexual abuse investigations', *Child Maltreatment*, 14: 172–81.

Hershkowitz, I., Lamb, M. E., Katz, C. and Malloy, L. C. (2013) 'Does enhanced rapport-building alter the dynamics of investigative interviews with suspected victims of sexual abuse?', *Journal of Police and Criminal Psychology*, 30: 6–14.

Hershkowitz, I., Orbach, Y., Lamb, M. E., Sternberg, K. J. and Horowitz, D. (2006) 'Dynamics of forensic interviews with suspected abuse victims who do not disclose abuse', *Child Abuse and Neglect*, 30: 753–69.

Imhoff, M. C. and Baker-Ward, L. (1999) 'Preschoolers' suggestibility: effects of developmentally appropriate language and interviewer supportiveness', *Journal of Applied Developmental Psychology*, 20: 407–29.

Korkman, J., Santtila, P., Drzewiecki, T. and Sandnabba, N. K. (2008) 'Failing to keep it simple: language use in child sexual abuse interviews with 3–8-year-old children', *Psychology, Crime and Law*, 14: 41–60.

Krähenbühl, S. (2011) 'Effective and appropriate communication with children in legal proceedings according to lawyers and intermediaries', *Child Abuse Review*, 20: 407–20.

La Rooy, D. J., Brown, D. and Lamb, M. E. (2013) 'Suggestibility and witness interviewing using the cognitive interview and NICHD protocol', in A. M. Ridley, F. Gabbert and D. J. La Rooy (eds), *Suggestibility in Legal Contexts: Psychological Research and Forensic Implications*. Chichester: Wiley-Blackwell.

Lamb, M. E., La Rooy, D. J., Malloy, L. C. and Katz, C. (2011) *Children's Testimony: A Handbook of Psychological Research and Forensic Practice*, 2nd edn. Chichester: Wiley-Blackwell.

Leander, L., Christianson, S. Å., Svedin, C. G. and Granhag, P. A. (2007) 'Judges', lay judges', and police officers' beliefs about factors affecting children's testimony about sexual abuse', *Journal of Psychology*, 141: 341–58.

McAuliff, B. D., Nicholson, E., Amarilio, D. and Ravanshenas, D. (2013) 'Supporting children in U.S. legal proceedings: descriptive and attitudinal data from a national survey of victim/witness assistants', *Psychology, Public Policy, and Law*, 19: 98–113.

Memon, A., Meissner, C. A. and Fraser, J. (2010) 'The cognitive interview: a meta-analytic review and study space analysis of the past 25 years', *Psychology, Public Policy, and Law*, 16: 340–72.

Milne, R. and Bull, R. (1999) *Investigative Interviewing*. Chichester: Wiley.

Ministry of Justice (2011) *Achieving Best Evidence in Criminal Proceedings: Guidance on Interviewing Victims and Witnesses, and Guidance on Using Special Measures*. Retrieved from: http://www.justice.gov.uk/downloads/victims-and-witnesses/vulnerable-witnesses/achieving-best-evidence-criminal-proceedings.pdf.

Ministry of Justice (2012) *Registered Intermediary Procedural Guidance Manual*. Retrieved from: http://www.cps.gov.uk/publications/docs/RI_ProceduralGuidanceManual_2012.pdf.

Moston, S. (1992) 'Social support and children's eyewitness testimony', in H. Dent and R. Flin (eds), *Children as Witnesses*. Chichester: Wiley & Sons, pp. 33–46.

National Society for the Prevention of Cruelty to Children (2014) *The Criminal Justice Response to Child Sexual Abuse*. Retrieved from: http://www.nspcc.org.uk/globalassets/documents/research-reports/how-safe-children-2014-criminal-justice-response-child-sexual-abuse.pdf.

New Zealand Ministry of Justice. (2010) *Alternative Pre-trial and Trial Processes for Child Witnesses in New Zealand's Criminal Justice System*. Retrieved from: http://www.justice.govt.nz/publications/global-publications.

Peter-Hagene, L., Bottoms, B. L., Davis, S. L. and Nysse Carris, K. L. (2014) *Social Support Effects on Children's Suggestibility After One Year*. Poster presented at the meeting of the American Psychology-Law Society, New Orleans, Louisiana.

Plotnikoff, J. and Woolfson, R. (2000) *An Evaluation of Child Witness Support*. Edinburgh: Scottish Executive Central Research Unit.

Plotnikoff, J. and Woolfson, R. (2007) *The 'Go-Between': Evaluation of Intermediary Pathfinder Projects*. London: Ministry of Justice.

Quas, J. A. and Lench, H. C. (2007) 'Arousal at encoding, arousal at retrieval, interviewer support, and children's memory for a mild stressor', *Applied Cognitive Psychology*, 21: 289–305.

Quas, J. A., Bauer, A. and Boyce, W. T. (2004) 'Physiological reactivity, social support, and memory in early childhood', *Child Development*, 75: 797–814.

Ridley, A., Van Rheede, V. and Wilcock, R. (2015) 'Interviews and interventions: barristers', police officers' and mock jurors' perceptions of a child witness interview with and without an intermediary', *Investigative Interviewing Research and Practice*, 7: 21–35.

Santtila, P., Korkman, J. and Sandnabba, N. K. (2004) 'Effects of interview phase, repeated interviewing, presence of a support person, and anatomically detailed dolls on child sexual abuse interviews', *Psychology, Crime and Law*, 10: 21–35.

Shepherd, E. and Milne, R. (2006) '"Have you told management about this?" Bringing witness interviewing into the twenty-first century', in A. Heaton-Armstrong, E. Shepherd, G. Gudjonsson and D. Wolchover (eds), *Witness Testimony: Psychological, Investigative and Evidential Perspectives*. Oxford: Oxford University Press, pp. 131–51.

Teoh, Y. S. and Lamb, M. (2013) 'Interviewer demeanor in forensic interviews of children', *Psychology, Crime and Law*, 19: 145–59.

Tickle-Degnen, L. and Rosenthal, R. (1990) 'The nature of rapport and its nonverbal correlates', *Psychological Inquiry*, 1: 285–93.

Westcott, H. L. and Kynan, S. (2006) 'Interviewer practice in investigative interviews for suspected child sexual abuse', *Psychology, Crime and Law*, 12: 367–82.

Wood, J. M., McClure, K. A. and Birch, R. A. (1996) 'Suggestions for improving interviews in child protection agencies', *Child Maltreatment*, 1: 223–30.

Youth Justice and Criminal Evidence Act 1999. Retrieved from: http://www.legislation.gov.uk/ukpga/1999/23/contents.

10 Interviewing witnesses in Estonia

Kristjan Kask

Introduction

Estonia is a country in the Baltic region of Northern Europe with a population of 1.3 million. In 1991 independence was restored from the Soviet Union and reforms in the judicial system began to take place. The Estonian judicial system is based on the German model with which it has historical links. In the first instance (i.e. county courts) criminal matters concerning criminal offences in the first degree shall be heard by a court panel consisting of the presiding judge and two lay judges (who have all the rights of a judge in a court hearing). Matters concerning criminal offences in the second degree and criminal matters in which simplified proceedings are applied shall be heard by a judge sitting alone (Code of Criminal Procedure (CCP) §18, RT I, 04.10.2013). A criminal offence in the first degree is an offence the maximum punishment prescribed for which in this Code is imprisonment for a term of more than five years, life imprisonment or compulsory dissolution whereas a criminal offence in the second degree is an offence the punishment prescribed for which in this Code is imprisonment for a term of up to five years or a pecuniary punishment (Penal Code (PC) §4, RT I, 04.04.2012).

A significant change to the legislation occurred in 2002 when a new Penal Code replaced the previous Code of Criminal Conduct (whose roots lay in legislation made during the Estonian Soviet Socialist Republic era, when the country was part of the Soviet Union). Under the new Penal Code several fundamental aspects were changed. For example, adversarial elements were integrated into criminal procedures.[1] Estonian legislation states that the victim has the same rights and obligations as the witnesses in the interview (although in general the rights of victims are broader). In the pre-trial procedure victims and witnesses are interviewed according to the CCP.

In this chapter current interviewing practices with adults and children in Estonia are introduced along with some insight into the legislation. How investigators are trained will be described. Then, relevant literature concerning best practices (i.e. published in peer-reviewed international journals) and emerging practices (i.e. published in local scientific journals in Estonian and relevant student theses) is reviewed. Finally, the implications for research, policy and practice are given.

Current interviewing practices

The CCP gives no indication as to which techniques or methods (such as the cognitive interview (Fisher and Geiselman, 1992)) should be used when interviewing adults or children. Lindmäe (1998) has pointed out that the interview should begin with preparation, then procedure should be followed (date, time, participants, rights and obligations); the collection of all necessary parts of the evidence (who, when, how, with what, for what) is followed by clarification of the details using questions. Similar guidelines have been given by Krüger (2008) who also notes that the interviewer should introduce him/herself, explain the goal of the interview, demonstrate trustfulness, introduce and explain rights and obligations, thank the interviewee for the answers provided, provide contacts after the end of the interview and control his/her non-verbal communication.

According to Krüger (2008) there are some additional issues which the investigator should take into consideration. It must be explained to the witness whether the interview is video- or audio-recorded. The investigator has to answer the interviewee's questions about the interview. When interviewing, appropriate language should be used which corresponds to the level of language used by the witness as words can have different meanings for different persons. If this is the case then the meaning of words should be clarified. Questions should be asked which can be answered with full sentences, i.e. favouring open questions; 'why' questions and suggestive questions should be avoided. The witness should be encouraged first to tell everything he/she knows about what happened; verbal prompts should be used to urge the witness to tell more. When asking questions, the first account given by the witness should be taken and the questions should be asked only about that account before going on to the next account. Different elements of the account should be examined one by one. Caution should be kept in making conclusions and also deductions based on the statements.

Sometimes an informal interview (i.e. explanation) takes place (which cannot be used as evidence later in the proceedings). The witness has to agree to participate to give an explanation but it cannot prejudice the witness's fundamental rights and freedoms. When an adult witness is interviewed then the officer usually simultaneously writes a protocol on a computer. Concerning interviewing technique, both free recall is used along with the question-answer format. In the protocol statements may be modified into a chronological story of what happened with whom and when. There are also guidelines concerning the format of writing a protocol (Krüger, 2008).

Interviewing children

The special treatment of child witnesses is covered in several sections in the CCP, for example declaring the trial to be closed (i.e. removing all persons from the courtroom who are not part of the trial – this can be used for both minors and adults) and taking regard of the specialities of interviewing children in the pre-trial procedure and in court. In redaction of some elements in the CCP in

September 2011 several aspects concerning interviewing were introduced. The effects of the changes in the law are now discussed in more depth based on the analysis of Kask (2011a).

Interviews with children should be video-recorded if the child's statements that are given during the pre-trial procedure are to be used in court as evidence in criminal proceedings. However, video-recorded statements given during the pre-trial procedure are allowed to be used in court as evidence only if the child is younger than 10 years and repeated interviewing can have a negative effect on the child's psychological state; if the child has disabilities (i.e. hearing or speaking difficulties or is mentally challenged); or if the child is younger than 14 years but the crime has been related to a sexual offence or family violence. The suspect has the right during the pre-trial procedure to examine the interview recording and then has five days to submit an application concerning his/her questions to the witness. The prosecutor's office then decides whether the application is approved or not (i.e. whether these questions have already been answered in the initial video-recorded interview or whether another video-recorded interview with the same child should take place). Another procedure using statements given during the pre-trial procedure in court as evidence is statement depositing (i.e. when a witness is interviewed in the preliminary investigation in the presence of a preliminary investigation judge and under the rules of cross-examination; this can be used also for adults). However, this means that the person is interviewed in the pre-trial procedure in a courthouse accompanied by a preliminary investigation judge and parties by the rules of cross-examination.

Before September 2011, interviews with children were video-recorded but in the context of the pre-trial procedure only, which could result in a situation where the child witness still has to testify in court and repeat the testimony given during the pre-trial procedure unless forensic psychiatry and/or psychology experts have advised that remembering the events again would traumatise the child and therefore the statements given in the pre-trial procedure can be used in the court.

Currently, there are special interviewing rooms with video-recording equipment for children in all prefectures. The first special unit for investigating serious crimes (sexual and physical abuse, family violence) against minors was formed in 2004 in the capital, Tallinn, and was the starting point of video-recording child witnesses' statements. The interviewing procedure can be partly or fully video- or audio-recorded but the witness should be informed by the CCP that the interview is recorded. In the video-recording the child has to be informed that he/she has a right not to testify against those closest to him/her and it should be confirmed that the child understands that only the truth should be told (and that the child understands the difference between truth and lies).

The legislation also allows either audio- or video-recording of interviews with adult witnesses. However, this is not conducted that often as such recordings cannot be used as evidence in court. Most often video-recording is used in the event of connecting statements with the conjuncture where both child and adult witnesses are taken back to the crime scene so they can explain to investigators (by virtue of being there) the circumstances of the crime. There are also possibilities to use tele-hearing in court by means of which the witness, who may be in a separate room in the court or other location, can be interviewed via video-link. Tele-hearing can be used when it is too expensive or difficult to bring the witness to court; it is also used to protect the interests of victims and witnesses. With regard to children, on some occasions a portable screen has been used in practice (to prevent the witness from seeing the accused), while a video link from a safe house to a court has also been used by child witnesses.

If the police officer has received no particular training in interviewing children then it is obligatory to involve a specialist (i.e. child protection worker, social worker, psychologist, teacher) in the pre-trial procedure if the child is younger than 10 years where repeated interviewing can have a negative effect on the child's psychological state; the child has disabilities (i.e. hearing or speaking difficulties or is mentally challenged); or the child is younger than 14 years but the crime has been related to a sexual offence or family violence.

The use of a specialist comes from the historical position in which the investigators were not trained in how to interview children and the duty of the specialist in the pre-trial procedure and in court was (and still often is) mainly to protect the child's rights (for example, rephrasing difficult questions). Before the change in the CCP in September 2011, using a specialist was also obligatory in misdemeanours (e.g. theft of mobile phones), which created difficulties in rapidly organising the interviewing after the crime. At present, if the investigator still needs the help of a specialist in interviewing, then he/she can be asked to assist. The main role in interviewing still relies upon the investigator but the specialist can help get better contact with the child. The child is also provided with the service of a specialist in court where he/she observes the child's age and capabilities and rephrases the questions if needed. Lately, the Ministry of Justice has put together printed leaflets about what is going to happen in court which can be sent or distributed to the child witness before the hearing.

When the child gives his/her statement in court the judge advises the child to tell everything he/she remembers about what happened. When the child has done so, he/she will then be asked questions by both prosecution and defence counsels. Once the child has provided his/her testimony he/she is dismissed from the court room. Also, the court can interrupt the hearing and ask questions in its own right or based on written questions prepared by the different parties. In the pre-trial procedure the child or adult witnesses are not allowed to be asked suggestive questions (i.e. confronting a child with information which he/she has not mentioned yet). With regard to children, suggestive questions can, however, be asked if the court allows it in order to clarify some points which the child may have difficulty answering or understanding. In court, the child witness can sit near the prosecutor or parent or specialist instead of standing in the witness stand as the court rooms are still mostly inquisitorial although procedure has changed to adversarial. Finally, cross-examination can be not used if it is considered by the court to affect the mental or physical state of the witness; it is also not allowed in any circumstances for witnesses younger than 14 years.

Training of investigators

During their training police officers acquire basic skills in interviewing in the Police College or in the Academy of Security Sciences. The provision of basic training in the Police College provides vocational secondary education and successful candidates can continue their studies at the Police College of the Academy of Security Sciences in Tallinn at undergraduate and Master's levels.

Investigators are taught about the techniques of interviewing witnesses, although this is mainly from the legislative point of view (based to some extent on the principles of the cognitive interview – see Krüger, 2008). Also, the practice sessions are mainly targeted at interviewing to obtain good evidence and to follow legal procedure. The research in interviewing has suggested that structured interviewing methods such as the cognitive interview (Fisher and Geiselman, 1992) or the NICHD Protocol (Orbach *et al.*, 2000) result in a more detailed description of what happened. However, the investigators do not receive special structured interview training, such as the cognitive interview, as part of their education, though there have been some adult training sessions in cognitive interviewing for investigators already working but these training sessions are very infrequent.

The special training for investigators interviewing children lasts for three weeks. Within this training period one day is devoted to trainees being taught the theoretical principles of applied memory research as well as the basics of the NICHD Protocol (Orbach *et al.*, 2000) and one day is given over to video-based role-play training with feedback from the other participants and the lecturer. In some prefectures supervision groups take place once or twice a year where investigators, specialised in interviewing children, watch several video-recorded interviews from their practice and discuss how the interviewing was undertaken both from the tactical side and from the legislative side, and what can be done better in future if similar cases occur. Training sessions are also given to prosecutors and judges concerning how to interview children (in both criminal and civil cases).

Best practices

Kask (2011b) examined the knowledge of eyewitness testimony of 69 Estonian law enforcement officials (judges, prosecutors, investigators, juvenile police officers) using a questionnaire based on Kassin *et al.* (2001), and Wise and Safer (2004). Some statements concerning interviewing and memory in this Estonian sample were consistent with the findings of previous scientific research such as the effect of attitudes and expectations on memory, the effects of post-event information, the forgetting curve, the wording of questions and child suggestibility. However, some statements contained larger discrepancies between the law enforcement officials' evaluations and the experts. For example, with regard to child witness accuracy ('Young children are less accurate as witnesses than are adults') 47 per cent agreed and 44 per cent disagreed with the statement; for elderly witnesses ('Elderly eyewitnesses are less accurate than are younger adults') 52 per cent agreed and

28 per cent disagreed. There were no major differences in the ratings to the statements between the professionals which indicates unity in their education process. The statement ratings of law enforcement officials were similar to those of lay people which indicates that there is still room for training to increase knowledge concerning issues in eyewitness testimony (as current knowledge may lie mainly in common-sense principles).

Estonian investigators' knowledge of the principles of the cognitive interview and question types have been studied (Kask, 2012a). Kask examined which techniques of the cognitive interview the investigators (who were specialised in criminal procedure investigating crimes against minors and/or adults) use most and how effective these techniques were considered. Further, investigators' knowledge of question types in investigative interviews was analysed. Kask found that investigators tended to use those techniques they thought to be effective and which were more related to the communication and process of the interview rather than techniques which involve cognitive memory improvement. Techniques investigators used most frequently and thought to be effective included establishing rapport and providing a last chance to recall followed by explaining the goals and advising the witness to give their account in their own words. Children were asked whether they discriminated between truth and lies, and were also told if they did not know the answer or understand the question they could say so. The least frequently used techniques were change perspectives and imagery. Regarding the question types, investigators were correct in identifying explanations and verbal affirmations. Direct and option-posing questions created more difficulties and invitations and suggestive questions were most difficult to correctly identify.

Kask and Kübard (2014) have examined eyewitnesses' memories of a shooting incident in Estonia where multiple eyewitnesses saw the attempted murder of a man which resulted in the death of a schoolgirl. They concluded that the witnesses should be quickly separated and skilfully interviewed to preserve all the details and minimise the effects of co-witness information.

Concerning children, Kask (2012b) examined the dynamics of using different question types in Estonian police interviews of children in cases of physical and/or sexual abuse. The transcriptions of investigative interviews with 66 children conducted between 2004 and 2008 (mean age 8 years 10 months, range 4 to 14 years) were analysed. It was found that forced-choice and direct questions were most frequently used; however, free recall produced significantly more information. Age differences emerged as four- to seven-year-old children were asked more suggestive questions than older children (as the interviewer may have wished to guide them to talk). Also, multiple questions per interviewer utterance were present. A large proportion of interviews started with specific questions and the free narrative phase ended too quickly.

When different parts of the interviews were compared, the average number of explanations and free recall questions per interview decreased as the interviews progressed, whereas the number of suggestive and forced-choice questions increased. Interestingly, Kask also found that regardless of children's age similar types of questions were being asked by investigators, which suggests that the police officers may structure their interviews in a similar manner, although as previously noted, younger children were asked more suggestive questions than older children. It was concluded that the investigators may feel pressured by the legal demands associated with investigative interviews (e.g. if they do not get a good quality statement from the child, the perpetrator may not be prosecuted).

Emerging practices

With regard to more recent developments in practice there have been some overview papers where issues in interviewing children have been discussed from the legal perspective (e.g. which issues to consider in interviewing to create an acceptable evidence in court (Rammo, 2006)) and from the psychological perspective (e.g. the benefits of structured interviewing methods in interviewing child witnesses (Kask, 2007)). Next, the results of the relevant studies from the Academy of Security Sciences are introduced.

Raudmets (2011) examined the issues of memory in pre-trial procedure and in court, and found that in 14 of her sample of 15 cases (between 2005 and 2010) errors in memory occurred. When the time delay between the event and hearing in court was shorter then it decreased the number of errors in the memory. The legislation states that if the event is not remembered in accordance to the statements in the pre-trial procedure then these statements cannot be used in the court as evidence. The main sources of errors concerned the timing and sequence of what happened in the event, as well as with numbers and names (comparing the facts with the corroborating evidence).

Suggestive questions during the cross-examination in court resulted in errors in one-third of the cases. In two-thirds of the cases the witnesses stated that in the pre-trial procedure they remembered the event better (or did not remember the event at all) as too much time had passed. It is noteworthy that the mean time delay between the pre-trial procedure and hearing in court was 12 months; between the event and interview in the pre-trial procedure the mean time delay was on average three days. Concerning legislation, the victim (but not a witness as the victim is a participant in the proceedings) may read the file of pre-trial procedure and therefore his/her statements can be influenced by the information from the file in the court (Kergandberg *et al.*, 2004).

Lehtlaan (2007) has examined the possibilities of introducing the cognitive interview (CI) into the practice in a survey of 30 investigators across Estonia. He found that almost three-quarters of the participants did not know about the cognitive interview as an interviewing method. Half of the respondents thought that the CI method would increase interviewing time. When asked about the possibilities of applying CI it was pointed out that the conditions of interview rooms at any point in time do not encourage better remembering. One-third of the investigators answered that they are able to use special interviewing rooms; however, witnesses are still interviewed mainly in the investigator's office where there is access to a computer to write a protocol of the statements.

A quarter of the respondents did not type when the statements were being given while others typed simultaneously.

Thal (2009) analysed 25 interviews video-recorded between 2005 and 2008 in the South Prefecture and found that the regulations were often violated, for example the child was not informed of their right not to testify against their next of kin (i.e. stepfather). The quality of the interview depended largely on the skills of the interviewer. Sometimes promises were given to the child which could not be kept ('You never have to tell this again'). Also signs of little preparation emerged (possibly as a result of the limited interview training at that time). Thal argued that the errors in following the rules emerged due to recklessness – sometimes the people who participated in the interview were not introduced, the purpose of the interview was not clarified or the issues concerning rights and obligations were introduced superficially. However, she noted that the compatibility of the interviews to the regulations (i.e. about which issues the witness should have been informed to create evidence) was better in 2008 than in 2005. Sometimes the child can be informally interviewed (in juridical terms an explanation is taken) before the official video-recorded interview which may result in repeating what is already said or even a refusal to talk.

More recently, Paluoja (2012) has investigated how video-recording is used in interviewing and found that besides interviewing children, most video-recording is used outside of the police station when connecting the statements with the conjuncture (a procedure done both with witnesses and suspects). It is thought by the officers that the protocol should be a transcript of the recording of the interview (which would be very time-consuming to register); however, neither legislation nor prosecutors require it (National Audit Office, 2003).

Tagu (2013) has proposed that in some cases the video-recorded interviews should be obligatory and should be used as evidence in court. Tagu argues that such a development could well increase the level of the credibility of the evidence (particularly where cross-examination is not possible). However, it is acknowledged that there are concerns that such an approach can violate the defendant's right to defence.Also, using partial statements as evidence should be allowed – at the moment, the statement is considered as a whole and if there are inconsistencies the whole statement is dismissed.

Otsing (2011) examined similar topics and found that video-recording interviews was rarely used. The National Audit Office (NAO, 2003) found that prosecutors and judges are overwhelmed by long and short-of-content protocols and this may encumber judicial procedure. Otsing's findings contrasted with the NAO results, indicating that the statements in the protocols are skeletal. The practices differ greatly which influences the quality of the interview protocols. All the answers can be registered in the protocol and therefore the protocols can be long and include unnecessary details from the procedural point of view. Otsing found that the expert interviewees (prosecutors) were not satisfied with the quality of the protocols; interviews were superficial and important details were not obtained. The planning of the interviewing was weak. The interviewers pointed out that the best tactic was to first let the witness recall the situation freely and then ask specific questions which are also put down in the protocol. Interviewers stated that it is important to record the exact wording of questions. It is not recorded to which question the witness has not answered, for example. There was little criticism to longer and detailed interviews as often it is not known on which basis the statements are formed. Prosecutors and heads of the investigation units favoured the use of recording equipment. In the case of children it was pointed out that later transcribing of the interview helps to preserve important verbal and non-verbal information. In summary, there are shortcomings in the necessary recording equipment, training and also with progress in audio- or video-recording statements.

Implications for research, policy and practice

The laws concerning interviewing both adult and child witnesses have been greatly reformed in recent years (Kask, 2011a). Shortcomings can be pointed out in the terms of the applicability of the legislation. Training on better application of the CCP is encouraged as these are not used in full. For example, the investigators may still type the protocol of the witnesses' accounts although the interview can be recorded and the protocol written afterwards. However, the latter will require more time and resources but the quantity and quality of the information acquired may increase.

There are guidelines on how to interview witnesses from the legal point of view with the aim of forming good-quality evidence (Krüger, 2008). However, there is a lack of literature in Estonia, particularly with regard to memory and other psychological issues which can have an effect on the witnesses' accounts (Kask, 2007). To make the investigative interviews more effective, good examples and best practices of interviews should be used in training sessions where investigators have to evaluate the question types used or evaluate the question types in their own interviews. Also, follow-up sessions for and supervision of investigators are strongly supported to maintain the skills learned in the training.

The NICHD Protocol is used in the training of those more experienced investigators who have already finished their studies and later in their career have begun working in those few units which specialise in interviewing children. However, structured interviewing methods for interviewing adults such as the cognitive interview should also be added to the curriculum of the basic training of police cadets.

There is also a need for a better witness support system in Estonia. At the moment, it is the prosecutor who largely looks after the needs of the witnesses in court. With regard to children, these rights can be monitored and also protected by a specialist who, however, may not be familiar with court procedures. However, a support person is also needed in the case of vulnerable adults in court in which circumstances he/she would make sure to explain to the witness the structure of the court system and how to prepare him/herself for the hearing etc.

Future research should be focused on the methods of interviewing adult witnesses. The findings from surveys (Kask, 2012a) indicate that knowledge about eyewitness issues is poor and also it is not known how adult witnesses are interviewed in practice in Estonia. As in recent years training for investigators interviewing children has increased it would be beneficial to examine whether more recently conducted interviews with children differ from those conducted in the first decade of the twenty-first century.

Acknowledgements

The author of the chapter wishes to thank Urmas Krüger from the Academy of Security Sciences and Saskia Kask from the Northern District Prosecutor's Office for their valuable comments.

Note

1. In the chapter the term 'interview' is used instead of 'interrogation' (which is used in the Estonian language for interviewing both victims/witnesses and suspects). Also, the term 'witness' is used constantly to cover also the term 'victim'.

References

Code of Criminal Procedure – RT I, 04.10.2013, 4 (in Estonian).

Fisher, R. P. and Geiselman, R. E. (1992) *Memory Enhancing Techniques for Investigative Interviewing: The Cognitive Interview*. Springfield, IL: Charles C. Thomas.

Kask, K. (2007) 'Arengupõhiselt sobivad meetodid laste küsitlemiseks' ['Developmentally appropriate interviewing techniques of children'], *Juridica*, 4: 229–38.

Kask, K. (2011b) 'Comparison of knowledge of law enforcement and lay people regarding eyewitness testimony', *Juridica International*, 18: 161–72.

Kask, K. (2012a) 'I use what I use: Estonian investigators' knowledge of investigative interviewing', *Juridica International*, 19: 161–9.

Kask, K. (2012b) 'Dynamics in using different question types in Estonian police interviews of children', *Applied Cognitive Psychology*, 26: 324–9.

Kask, K. and Kübard, K. (2014) 'An analysis of the eyewitnesses' memories of a shooting incident', *Investigative Interviewing: Research and Practice*, 6: 32–41.

Kask, S. (2011a) *Lapstunnistaja erikohtlemine kriminaalmenetluses* [*Special Treatment of Child Witnesses in Criminal Proceedings*]. Master's thesis, Tallinn University, Institute of Social Work.

Kassin, S. M., Tubb, V. A., Hosch, H. M. and Memon, A. (2001) 'On the "general acceptance" of eyewitness testimony research: a new survey of the experts', *American Psychologist*, 5: 405–16.

Kergandberg, E., Järvet, T., Ploom, T. and Jaggo, O. (2004) *Kriminaalmenetlus. Teine, muudetud trükk* [*Criminal Procedure*], 2nd edn. Tallinn: Academy of Security Sciences.

Krüger, U. (2008) *Ülekuulamine kohtueelses menetluses: Õiguslikud aspektid* [*Interrogation in the Preliminary Proceedings: Juridical Aspects*]. Tallinn: Sisekaitseakadeemia.

Lehtlaan, A. (2007) *Kognitiivne intervjuu ja selle rakendamine Eesti Politseis* [*The Applicability of Cognitive Interview in Estonian Police*]. Bachelor thesis, Academy of Security Sciences, Tallinn.

Lindmäe, H. (1998) *Menetlusmetoodika* [*Methods of Procedure*]. Tallinn: Juura.

National Audit Office (NAO) (2003) *Kuritegude kohtueelne menetlemine* [*Pre-trial Procedure of Crimes*], Audit raport no. 2-5/03/133. Retrieved from: http://www.riigikontroll.ee/tabid/206/Audit/1735/Area/14/language/et-EE/Default.aspx (11 December 2013).

Orbach, Y., Hershkowitz, I., Lamb, M. E., Sternberg, K. J., Esplin, P. W. and Horowitz, D. (2000) 'Assessing the value of structured protocols for forensic interviews of alleged abuse victims', *Child Abuse and Neglect*, 24: 733–52.

Otsing, M. (2011) *Uurimistoimingu käigus antavate ütluste kajastamine ja talletamine Põhja Prefektuuri näitel* [*Saving and Preserving Statements in Investigative Activities in the Example of Northern Prefecture*]. Bachelor thesis, Academy of Security Sciences, Tallinn.

Paluoja, E. (2012) *Videosalvestis ütluste talletamise moodusena Põhja prefektuuri näitel* [*Videorecording Statements as a Method in the Example of Northern Prefecture*]. Bachelor thesis, Academy of Security Sciences: Tallinn.

Penal Code – RT I, 04.04.2012, 1 (in Estonian).

Rammo, R. (2006) 'Alaealise ülekuulamine kriminaalmenetluse kohtueelses staadiumis' ['Interrogation of minors in preliminary proceedings of criminal procedure'], *Juridica*, 5: 317–28.

Raudmets, P. (2011) *Mäletamise arvestamine isikulise tõendi kogumisel* [*Remembering in Collecting Evidence*]. Bachelor thesis, Academy of Security Sciences, Tallinn.

Tagu, A. (2013) *Tunnistaja ütlused tõendina kriminaalmenetluses* [*Witness' Statements as Evidence in the Criminal Proceedings*]. Bachelor thesis, Academy of Security Sciences, Tallinn.

Thal, E. (2009) *Alaealise kannatanu ülekuulamine ja selle videosalvestamine kohtueelses menetluses* [*Interviewing Minor Victim and Videorecording It in the Preliminary Investigation*]. Bachelor thesis, Academy of Security Sciences, Tallinn.

Wise, R. A. and Safer, M. A. (2004) 'What US judges know and believe about eyewitness testimony', *Applied Cognitive Psychology*, 4: 427–43.

11 History, practical aspects and contemporary research on witness and victim interviewing in France

Samuel Demarchi, Anaïs Taddeï, Laurent Fanton, Hervé Fabrizi and Stefania Tamasan

Introduction and historical aspects of practices

At the end of the nineteenth century, France was the scene of several heinous crimes. In the Vacher case, for example, a day laborer murdered then raped and mutilated numerous children and young adults. He was convicted only on the description provided by eyewitnesses (for a description of the case, see Soustre de Condat, 2013).

The beginning of the twentieth century is considered the milestone of scientific research applied to eyewitness testimony. The United States of America and Europe (mainly Germany and the United Kingdom) accounted for the majority of publications. Some findings like the consecutive distortions of memory due to closed questioning, for example (e.g. Binet, 1900; Stern, 1902; Whipple, 1909, 1913), are still taken into consideration when researchers develop new interviewing methods.

With the exception of Alfred Binet's research on child suggestibility (1900), the few publications from that time period are mainly the product of historians, philosophers, lawyers, and more rarely of psychologists. Larguier de Bancels (1905), in a review about eyewitness testimony, stated "[that] there is not great damage to neglect them" (p. 159). The interest of a scientific approach to testimony by researchers and professionals of justice did not carry in France. In the opposite direction of this trend, Munsterberg's work triggered some swirls in the scientific community of America (1908; for a review, see Bornstein and Meissner, 2008). Binet (1904) criticized the unresponsiveness of his French peers about his work on the importance of the interrogation format, the questioning and memory accessibility: "[…] my book about suggestibility did not have in France any echo. I even believe that no analysis took account of it … It's in Germany that the grain germinated" (p. 130). Binet also attempted to explain: "I can say well one of the reasons of our failure: it is in the inertia with which the administrations of justice opposed to me" (p. 131).

In order to introduce the current state of the art procedures in the field of witness interviewing in France, we first discuss the scientific research existing in this field and accessed by professionals. Then we focus on field practices and the training proposed for professionals (police, *Gendarmerie Nationale*, legal medicine), and highlight the lack of exchange between researchers and professionals. Finally, we briefly describe the interviewing of victims in forensic examinations.

Main results of scientific research

Legal psychology did find some echoes among medical examiners (Lacassagne, 1906; Lacassagne and Martin, 1906a, 1906b), magistrates (Gorphe, 1924), and psychologists who regularly published reviews on testimony (e.g. Claparède (1905) who recommended, following Gross (1905), the use of the criminological term to translate the judge's psychology) or critical assessments of foreign articles which were mainly published in the review *L'Année psychologique*. Then, over several decades, only a few rare scientific articles were published in French (for example, a review by Cenac, 1951), but it is not possible to identify in the first part of the twentieth century a structured research program around the hearing of witnesses and victims in France.

This absence could be the consequence of the legal or regulatory framework's lack of information surrounding the practice of witness interviewing, or, as Cario (2008) opined, the lack and the falseness of statistics that made impossible the study of the legal world. The legal institutions do not allow the follow-up of practices for longitudinal statistical treatments. But most disconcerting is the weak interest carried by the French legislator to the question of testimony. It does not seem to have any particular weighting for this fundamental investigation procedure, except the credibility assessment/evaluation of the depositors; and yet, however, many professionals use it daily, be they investigators of judicial police, magistrates, medical examiners or social workers!

Scientific publications in French relating to eyewitness testimony reappeared in the 1990s. In France, the first work concerned a French adaptation of the cognitive interview (Ginet, 1998; Ginet and Py, 2001; Ginet *et al.*, 2014; Py and Ginet, 2001; Py *et al.*, 1997), its comparison with hypnosis (Py and Fernandes, 1995), and the evaluation of witness credibility (Biland *et al.*, 1999). Since then, several have been defended concerning the hearing of children (Verkampt, 2009), the method's adaptation to professional constraints (Colomb, 2011), and the criminal description by witnesses and victims (Demarchi, 2003).

With regard to the cognitive interview, researchers wanted the standardization of their practice, insisting on a systematization of one free recall after each instruction (e.g. Colomb and Ginet, 2012). But the practices must still be flexible and adaptive. For example, it is possible to use only a few mnemonics (e.g. Colomb and Ginet, 2012; Ginet and Verkampt, 2007), in accordance with other work (e.g. Wright and Holliday, 2007; Dornburg and McDaniel, 2006; Roberts and Higham, 2002). They also recommend always beginning by making a report followed by the *Report All* and *Mental Context Reinstatement* instructions. Then, the witness has to make a first free recall. The continuation of the interview differs according to the elements previously collected. Investigators can then use complementary mnemonics, including change of order and change perspective.

Research undertaken in France is now structured around the creation and evaluation of new instructions, which supplement the existing ones. For example, Demarchi and Py (2009) have proposed two mnemonics to enhance the description of the criminal. The first is intended to obtain general information (sex, ethnicity, corpulence, etc.) and the criminal's silhouette, whereas the other focuses on facial information. Used jointly, they make it possible to double the volume of information without a decrease in accuracy. These instructions can be easily used at the end of a cognitive interview, in particular when the investigator is questioning the witness on the criminal's appearance.

Most new instructions suggested by the French teams relate to obtaining factual information. Thus, Colomb and Ginet (2012) proposed the *Guided Peripheral Focus* instruction that can be used after a first recall. The advantage is to use retrieval clues as information which the witness already reported at the time of previous recalls. The investigator helps the witness by listing the significant components of the event which she or he has just provided, which is in agreement with the compatible witness questioning as described by Fisher and Geiselman (1992). For each element, the investigator will ask the witness to close his or her eyes and create a mental image based on the main information and the details. Colomb and Ginet (2012) proposed the following formulation: "I would like you to close your eyes, to form a very clear and detailed mental image of the scene and to focus your retrieval not only on actions and central elements but also and especially on more peripheral ones" (p. 38). The first evaluation revealed important benefits, in particular with regard to descriptions of people and places, in comparison with a minimal instruction or instructions for change of order and prospect. However, an increase in errors was also observed.

Recently, Brunel *et al.* (2013) proposed the *Open Depth* instruction (OD), which may make it possible for the witness to retrieve memories by varying the strategies of recall (Tulving, 1974). Based on the principle of the multicomponent view of a memory trace (Bower, 1967), OD allows witnesses to circumvent the problem of centering too much on the actions at the time of an account. The instruction is formulated as follows: "During a first recall, people often concentrate on certain types of details, mainly actions, and cannot report everything they have in mind. Please, tell me once again everything you saw/remember about the event, and focus your attention on all little details you did not have the opportunity to report" (p. 849). In comparison to a *motivated recall* instruction (Davis *et al.*, 2005), the OD allows an increase in the volume of correct information, without an increase in the errors. Only a drop concerning the description of people has been observed.

Some variations must nevertheless be applied when children are interviewed. In research relating to suggestibility, Verkampt and Ginet (2010; see also Verkampt *et al.*, 2010) introduced a new instruction named the *cued recall* (CR). Verkampt and Ginet proposed CR instead of the instruction of change of perspective, which is generally put aside for child interviews and which results in a loss of significant information (Hayes and Delamothe, 1997; Holliday, 2003a, 2003b). It is formulated as follows: "I would like you to recall one last time everything you remember about the painting session. But this time, you will start with the very first thing you remember, and tell me what happened right after that" (p. 1284). During the recall, non-suggestive prompts are used (e.g. "And what happened right after that?"). Authors noted that a cognitive interview including a context reinstatement, a report of all instructions and a CR instruction constituted the configuration allowing for the best performances in terms of completeness. They also suggest giving up the change order instruction because, although it makes it possible for children to resist the suggestion, it presents difficulties in comprehension. Lastly, the authors did not observe any increase or decrease in suggestibility following the use of this new version of the method.

Scientific research: access to publications by professionals

During this last period, the field of eyewitness testimony written in French was diffused through different types of publications: books (e.g. Bertone *et al.*, 1999; Guéniat and Benoit, 2013; Van de Plas and Magerotte, 2012), scientific reviews (Demarchi and Py, 2006; Py and Ginet, 1995), popular reviews (e.g. Py and Demarchi, 2004; Demarchi, 2011), and websites (e.g. http://www.pschotemoins.inist.fr). A verbatim version of the instructions of the French version of the cognitive interview, with some advice for its implementation, is available in Demarchi and Py (2006). But accessibility to certain documents and research in a foreign language (English) is sometimes difficult for professionals because of a lack of availability of the original document in specialized libraries. And English is sometimes a problem for professionals. However, they can use other publications in French, in particular Belgian, Swiss and Canadian-Quebec (Cyr and Dion, 2006; St-Yves and Landry, 2004; St-Yves and Tanguay, 2007; St-Yves and Collins, 2011)

Publications of national institutions and professionals

The *Gendarmerie Nationale* has published several accounts and expert reports, but these documents are not available to staff/others outside of the institution. Websites include documents, but their scientific quality can be challenged. More specifically, professionals have at their disposal many works written by peers which report their observations and practice (e.g. Clément and Portelli, 2001; Diaz, Fontanaud, and Desfarges, 1994; Gévaudan, 1980). But references to scientific works are quasi non-existent, which can lead us to think that the practice of interviewing is primarily done the common way, and generally is learned via contact with colleagues. In fact, the lack of procedures and standards harm the homogeneity of practices and the evaluation of performance. One experimental work revealed the low conformity of practices on the ground to international standards (Ginet and Py, 2001): the interviews carried out included many procedural biases, like the absence of a first free recall not stopped by questions from the interviewer, several speech cutoffs, and many closed and often directed questions. These results, in conformity with works on the same topic from other countries (e.g. Fisher *et al.*, 1987), attest to the need for training in interviewing methods.

Training and practice

Training

Training both initial and continuous specifically dedicated to interviewing appeared in national schools about twenty years ago. Officer cadets, executives (police chiefs) and magistrates are sensitized or trained in the practice of interviewing. The duration of training lasts for a few hours and several days. The contents are virtually identical and relate in particular to biases and practices that should be removed or reinforced. Most training centers use settings in situation to sensitize trainees with principal biases. Video demonstrations are used and documents are distributed. Some centers approach ways to improve the memory through the cognitive interview, but rarely propose a full course of training on it.

To our knowledge, for nearly ten years only the *Centre National d'Etude et de Formation de la Police Nationale* proposed and provided a week of training, beginning with an assessment of the initial and ongoing competence of investigators. A study carried out by trainers from the center and the team of scientists who created the first French adaptation of the cognitive interview showed that investigators, even those active in the field for several decades, had used less than two sentences to introduce the hearing and to explain the objectives (e.g. "I listen to you, what happens?"). In addition, only 29 percent of trainees left sufficient time for the witness to make a full account, without interruption. The first interruption occurred on average after 62 seconds, and the fastest was listed after only three seconds. On this point, researchers recorded a great deal of inter-individual variance since nearly 28 percent stopped the witness between four and ten times, and others up to 31 times in 15 minutes! With regard to the questions, researchers coded approximately 40 questions in 15 minutes (or a question every 22 seconds), of which 35 percent were directed, 11 percent were open-ended, 44 were percent closed, and 10 percent were negative. Globally, untrained investigators in a standard police interview make on average a mistake every 28 seconds (i.e. 1 every 11 seconds maximum, 1 every 50 seconds minimum).

After a presentation of the best practices in non-directive interviews, trainers carried out a thorough debriefing of the simulations based on the video records of the interviews conducted by the trainees. New simulations were then carried out to ensure the recommendations for good practical application were being used (e.g. building report, witness compatible questioning, transferring control of the interview to the witness, mental imagery). After a two-day training session, the course on the cognitive interview began. The team that developed the French version presented its scientific foundations (memory operations, memory disturbances, etc.) and various instructions, then made a sequence of videos to clarify the objectives and the various possible formulations. The formal training was concluded by a consideration of the expected advantages, based on their own scientific work.

Finally, the benefit arising from this week of training was a very significant reduction in interviewer bias and increased conformity with the structuring and the instructions of the cognitive interview, as was validated in the French version. Currently, universities and schools for justice professionals (the *École Nationale de la Magistrature*, the *Gendarmerie Nationale*, etc.) propose the same training.

Practice

How adults and children are interviewed in practical terms in France remains an open question. To our knowledge, there has been no published data on the practice of witness and victim interviews, other than a recent contribution concerning the in situ evaluation of performance and the perceptions of investigators with regard to the cognitive interview (Colomb *et al.*, 2013). Investigators found the method has better results with victims than with witnesses, and increases the volume of judicially relevant information in comparison to a structured interview (+29.3 units of information) or a standard police interview (+30.4). Moreover, investigators have stated an increase in interest for the method in the future. These results attest to the utility and utilization of the French version of the cognitive interview in the field with real cases, and are compatible with research undertaken in other countries.

In France, other professionals and medical examiners interview victims of violence as part of the forensic examination, particularly in cases of sexual aggression. Their practice is both different and complementary to that performed by the legal investigator.

Victim interviewing in forensic examinations

In France, forensic medicine is tasked with (1) forensic autopsy (thanatology) and (2) forensic examination of victims of violence (clinical forensic medicine). The 2010 reform of forensics situated in university hospital centers, thanatology, clinical forensics, medical examiner training and the organization of a "community" network (Ministère de la Justice, 2012; Ministère de la Justice et des Libertés, 2010). In parallel to the university hospital structures, a community network was set up based on healthcare structures and physicians specially trained in victim management. This set-up is different to that prevailing in other, notably English-speaking countries, where the activities of medical examiners are often restricted to forensic autopsy, with victim management consigned to emergency services or multidisciplinary reference centers (Chariot *et al.*, 2010).

The first objective of the forensic management of victims of violence is to perform as precisely as possible an assessment of the physical and psychological injury, safeguarding all elements likely to be of legal interest, especially in cases of sexual violence (French health authority, *Haute Autorité de Santé*, 2005). The second objective is to fix the duration of the victim's "complete occupational incapacity", a medico-legal measure that may influence the court judging the case and thus the severity of any sentence (Manaouil *et al.*, 2011). Finally, the court may call upon the medical examiner to assess the compatibility of the victim's version of events with the medical findings. All of the evidence resulting from the examination of the victim is passed on in a written report to the investigators or magistrate. The medical examiner may be questioned about the report during the investigation or trial.

Examination of the victim, like any other medical act, begins with an interview, which should, so far as possible, follow health authority guidelines (*Haute Autorité de Santé*, 2005). The first step is to introduce the careworkers and explain the examination procedure and what is of interest. The medical examiner then secures the victim's consent to the examination, to the taking of samples, and to any photography. Information is then collected, not only about the events but also about the medical history. Regarding the events in particular, the health authority (*Haute Autorité de Santé*, 2005) specifies, without going into detail, that they should be stated as reported speech within speech marks:

> "X claims to have been the victim of ..."
> "The victim declares ..."
> "According to the victim ..."

It is noteworthy that the actual choice of questions is left up to the medical examiner, as is the length of the interview. The victim thus initially testifies freely about the events without being interrupted; only secondarily does the examiner pose questions on matters of fact to clarify the analysis of the evidence. These questions may also serve to refine the interpretation of test results: date of last consensual sexual relations, with or without protection, aggression with armed threat, physical attack, change of clothing or douche after the events, etc. At the end of the interview, the medical examiner also explains the medical and legal follow-up and provides contact information for victim-aid associations.

However, apart from the above-mentioned health authority general guidelines (*Haute Autorité de Santé*, 2005), to the best of our knowledge there are no established good-practice guidelines setting out the precise procedure for the interview in terms of both form and content. Likewise, there have been no scientific studies addressed to the medical community seeking to assess and improve interview techniques, in contrast to the field of legal interviewing. In practice, medical examiners acquire and refine their interview techniques as part of their initial clinical training and then during multidisciplinary professional training sessions bringing together magistrates, investigators, psychologists and physicians, often run by victim-aid associations. There is, however, nothing to show that the objectives and contents of such training meet corresponding international standards (World Health Organization, 2003, 2004).

The forensic community could take up the challenge provided by this lack of specific interview methodology. Cycles of practical training could be set up, as methods of effective listening require simulation exercises with frequent feedback from trainers in order for the skills to be acquired rapidly. Such training has proved effective for investigators and magistrates.

There is, however, no relevant comparison between interviews performed by medical examiners and those performed by investigators. The objectives are not the same: investigators use the interview to clarify the course of events so as to determine responsibility in the penal sense, whereas the medical examiner is helping to establish the reality of the events. Even so, given that the forensic interview is often followed by interviews with investigators and contact with victim-aid structures, studies should be carried out to ensure that two fundamental forensic objectives are being met: firstly, to avoid worsening the psychological sequelae of violence by unsuitable behavior or words, while on the contrary taking the first steps in psychological care; and secondly, to avoid interfering with the investigation with unsuitable procedures that risk modifying victims' memories.

Conclusion

In France, interview practice remains globally empirical (i.e. untested) and based on communication and formation/training with peers. It is difficult – even very difficult – to find training that contains the latest scientific work. Moreover, the training content remains questionable because it is mainly provided by professionals who are not aware of the world of research. (Note that the exact opposite criticism can be made of the researchers by professionals concerning the practice in the field.) Nothing can ensure that training sessions comply with international regulations. Otherwise, it is very rare for evaluative research to be conducted, and when it has been conducted, it generally just assesses the perceived content that has formed and has been formative in terms of utility and applicability, more often based on common sense than on scientific sources and knowledge.

However, the scientific research concerning interview methods for witnesses and victims can be described as nascent and dynamic. More than ten scientific articles or chapters have been published since 2010, but as publications are in English, their adoption by professionals and use in the field is held back.

To overcome this, it would be necessary to ensure dynamic exchanges between professionals and researchers. With professionals having to be instructed and trained with the latest scientific advances and researchers having to propose improvements in methods, it will be possible to better evaluate training and the conformity of the work to the French regulatory and legislative frameworks.

References

Bertone, A., Mélen, M., Py, J., and Somat, A. (1999) *Témoins sous influences: recherches de psychologie sociale et cognitive*. Grenoble: Presses Universitaires de Grenoble.

Biland, C., Py, J., and Rimboud, S. (1999) "Evaluer la sincérité d'un témoin grâce à trois techniques d'analyse, verbales et non verbale," *European Review of Applied Psychology*, 49: 115–22.

Binet, A. (1900) *La Suggestibilité*. Paris: Schleicher Frères.

Binet, A. (1904) "La science du témoignage," *L'Année psychologique*, 11: 128–36.

Bornstein, B. H. and Meissner, C. A. (2008) "Basic and applied issues in eyewitness research: a Munsterberg centennial retrospective,' *Applied Cognitive Psychology*, 22: 733–6.

Bower, G. H. (1967) "A descriptive theory of memory," in D. P. Kimble (ed.), *The Organization of Recall*. New York: New York Academy of Sciences, pp. 112–85.

Brunel, M., Py, J., and Launay, C. (2013) "Cost and benefit of a new instruction for the cognitive interview: the open depth instruction," *Psychology, Crime and Law*, 19 (10): 845–63.

Cario, R. (2008) *Introduction aux sciences criminelles*. Paris: L'Harmattan.

Cenac, M. (1951) *Le Témoignage et sa valeur au point de vue judiciaire*. Paris: Masson

Chariot, P., Saint-Martin, P., and Lorin de la Grandmaison, G. (2010) "Organisation de la médecine légale dans le monde," in P. Chariot and M. Debout (eds), *Traité de médecine légale et de droit de la santé à l'usage des professionnels de la santé et de la justice*. Paris: Vuibert, pp. 24–31.

Claparède, E. (1905) "La psychologie judiciaire," *L'Année psychologique*, 12: 275–302.

Clément, S. and Portelli, S. (2001) *L'Interrogatoire*. Paris: Sofiac.

Colomb, C. (2011) "L'Entretien cognitif sous influence: Du développement d'un protocole modifié à son étude en interaction avec trois variables sociales." Unpublished doctoral dissertation, Université Blaise Pascal, Clermont-Ferrand, France.

Colomb, C. and Ginet, M. (2012) "The Cognitive Interview used with adults: an empirical test of an alternative mnemonic and of a modified protocol," *Applied Cognitive Psychology*, 26 (1): 35–47.

Colomb, C., Ginet, M., Wright, D., Demarchi, S., and Sadler, C. (2013) "Back to the real: efficacy and perception of a modified cognitive interview in the field," *Applied Cognitive Psychology*, 27 (5): 574–83.

Cyr, M. and Dion, J. (2006) "Quand des guides d'entrevue servent à protéger la mémoire des enfants: l'exemple du protocole NICHD," *Revue Québecoise de Psychologie*, 27 (3) 157–75.

Davis, M. R., McMahon, M., and Greenwood, K. M. (2005) "The efficacy of mnemonic components of the cognitive interview: towards a shortened variant for time-critical investigations," *Applied Cognitive Psychology*, 19: 75–93.

Demarchi, S. (2003) "Conception et évaluation, selon une démarche d'ingénierie psychosociale, d'un outil de recueil d'informations concernant l'apparence physique des personnes." Unpublished doctoral dissertation, Université Paris 8, Saint-Denis, France.

Demarchi, S. (2011) "Les témoignages, pièges à conviction," *Pour la science*, 72–7.

Demarchi, S. and Py, J. (2006) L'entretien cognitif: son efficacité, son application et ses spécificités," *Revue Québécoise de Psychologie*, 27: 177–96.

Demarchi, S. and Py, J. (2009) "A method to enhance person description: a field study," in R. Bull, T. Valentine, and T. Williamson (eds), *Handbook of Psychology of Investigative Interviewing: Current Developments and Future Directions*. Wiley: Chichester, pp. 241–56.

Diaz, C., Fontanau, D., and Desfarges, M. (1994) *Le livre du crime: un juge et deux commissaires enquêtent sur l'homicide*. Paris: Calmann-Lévy.

Dornburg, C. C. and McDaniel, M. A. (2006) "The cognitive interview enhances long term free recall of older adults," *Psychology and Aging*, 21 (1): 196–200.

Fisher, R. P. and Geiselman, R. E. (1992) *Memory Enhancing Techniques for Investigative Interviewing: The Cognitive Interview*. Springfield, IL: Charles C. Thomas.

Fisher, R. P., Geiselman, R. E., and Raymond, D. S. (1987) "Critical analysis of police interview techniques," *Journal of Police Science and Administration*, 15: 177–85.

Gévaudan, H. (1980) *Flic: les vérités de la police*. Paris: J. C. Latès.

Ginet, M. (1998) "Etude d'une nouvelle technique d'audition destinée à améliorer les souvenirs des témoins: l'entretien cognitif." Unpublished doctoral dissertation, Université Blaise Pascal, Clermont-Ferrand, France.

Ginet, M. and Py, J. (2001) "A technique for enhancing memory in eyewitness testimonies for use by police officers and judicial officers: the cognitive interview," *Le travail humain*, 64: 173–91

Ginet, M. and Verkampt, F. (2007) "The cognitive interview: is its benefit affected by the level of witness emotion?" *Memory*, 15 (4): 450–64.

Ginet, M., Py, J., and Colomb, C. (2014) "The differential effectiveness of the cognitive interview instructions for enhancing witnesses' memory of a familiar event," *Swiss Journal of Psychology*, 73 (1): 25–34.

Gorphe, F. (1924) *La Critique du témoignage*. Paris: Dalloz

Gross, H. (1905) *Criminal Psychology: A Manual for Judges, Practitioners, and Students*. Leipzig.

Guéniat, O. and Benoit, F. (2013) *Les secrets des interrogatoires et des auditions de police*. Lausanne: Presses Polytechniques et Universitaires Romandes.

Haute Autorité de Santé (2005) *Recommandation de bonne pratique. Certificat initial concernant une victime de violence*. Retrieved 10 October 2014 from: http://www.has-sante.fr/portail/jcms/c_1120330/fr/certificat-medical-initial-concernant-une-personne-victime-de-violences.

Hayes, B. K. and Delamothe, K. (1997) "Cognitive interviewing procedures and suggestibility in children's recall," *Journal of Applied Psychology*, 82: 562–77.

Holliday, R. (2003a) "The effect of a prior cognitive interview on children's acceptance of misinformation," *Applied Cognitive Psychology*, 17, 443–57.

Holliday, R. (2003b) "Reducing misinformation effects in children with cognitive interviews: dissociating recollection and familiarity," *Child Development*, 74: 728–51.

Lacassagne, A. (1906) *Précis de médecine légale*. Paris: Masson.

Lacassagne, A. and Martin, E. (1906a) "Les données de la statistique criminelle," *Archives de l'anthropologie criminelle*, 21: 836–50.

Lacassagne, A. and Martin, E. (1906b) "État actuel de nos connaissances en anthropologie criminelle pour servir de préambule à l'étude analytique des travaux nouveaux sur l'anatomie, la physiologie, la psychologie et la sociologie des criminels," *Archives d'anthropologie criminelle*, 21: 104–14.

Larguier des Bancels, J. (1905) "La psychologie judiciaire," *L'Année psychologique*, 12: 157–232.

Manaouil, C., Pereira, T., Gignon, M., and Jardé, O. (2011) "The total work incapacity (TWI) in the French penal code," *La Revue de médecine légale*, 2: 59–71.

Ministère de la Justice (2012) Circulaire du 25 avril 2012 relative à la mise en œuvre de la réforme de la médecine légale, April (NOR: JUSD1221959C). Paris: Ministère de la Justice.

Ministère de la Justice et des Libertés (2010) Circulaire du 27 décembre 2010 relative à la mise en œuvre de la réforme de la médecine légale, December (NOR: JUSD1033099C). Paris: Ministère de la Justice et des Libertés.

Münsterberg, H. (1908) *On the Witness Stand*. New York: Doubleday

Py, J. and Demarchi, S. (2004) "Quelle fiabilité accorder aux témoignages?" *Pour la science*, April, pp. 26–31.

Py, J. and Demarchi, S. (2006) "Utiliser l'entretien cognitif pour décrire et détecter les criminels," *Revue Québécoise de Psychologie*, 27: 197–215.

Py, J. and Fernandes, C. (1995) "L'hypnose et l'entretien cognitif: deux techniques efficaces d'amélioration de la mémoire des témoins," *Psychologie Française*, 40: 281–94.

Py, J. and Ginet, M. (1995) "L'entretien cognitif: un bilan de douze années de recherches appliquées," *Psychologie Française*, 40 (3): 255–80.

Py, J. and Ginet, M. (2001) "Évaluer l'efficacité de techniques pour améliorer les souvenirs des témoins ou victimes à l'usage des professionnels de la justice," *European Review of Applied Psychology/Revue Européenne de Psychologie Appliquée*, 51 (1–2): 121–31.

Py, J., Ginet, M., Desperies, C., and Cathey, C. (1997) "Cognitive encoding and cognitive interviewing in eyewitness testimony," *Swiss Journal of Psychology*, 56: 33–41.

Py, J., Ginet, M., Demarchi, S., and Ansanay-Alex, C. (2001) *Une démarche psychosociale d'évaluation des procédures d'instructions*. [*A Psychosocial Assessment of Judicial Investigation*]. Retrieved from La Mission de Recherche Droit et Justice website: http://www.gip-recherche-justice.fr/catalogue/PDF/syntheses/65-qualitepy.pdf.

Roberts, W. T. and Higham, P. A. (2002) "Selecting accurate statements from the cognitive interview using confidence ratings," *Journal of Experimental Psychology: Applied*, 8 (1): 33–43.

Soustre de Condat, B. (2013) *Le Saccage de la chaire*. Paris: Mosesu.

Stern, L. W. (1902) "Zur Psychologie der Aussage" ["On the psychology of testimony"], *Zeitschrift fuer die gesamte Strafrechtwissenschaft*, 22: 315–70.

St-Yves, M. and Collins, P. (2011) *Psychologie de l'intervention policière en situation de crise*. Montreal: Éditions Yvon Blais.

St-Yves, M. and Landry, J. (2004) *Psychologie des entrevues d'enquête: de la recherche à la pratique*. Montreal: Éditions Yvon Blais.

St-Yves, M. and Tanguay, M. (2007) *Psychologie de l'enquête criminelle: la recherche de la vérité*. Montreal: Éditions Yvon Blais.

Tulving, E. (1974) "Cue-dependent forgetting," *American Scientist*, 62: 74–82.

Van De Plas, M. and Magerotte, S. (2012) *Manuel de l'audition policière: technique de base Vol. 6*. Brussels: Politeia.

Verkampt, F. (2009) "Entretien cognitif: son adaptation pour l'audition des très jeunes enfants dans un cadre judiciaire." Unpublished doctoral dissertation, Université Blaise Pascal, Clermont-Ferrand, France.

Verkampt, F. and Ginet, M. (2010) "Enhancing children's testimonies using cognitive interview: which of its variations is the most efficient?" *Applied Cognitive Psychology*, 24: 1279–96.

Verkampt, F., Ginet, M., and Colomb, C. (2010) "L'entretien cognitif est-il efficace pour aider de très jeunes enfants à témoigner d'Un Événement répété dans le temps," *L'année Psychologique*, 110 (4): 541–72.

Whipple, G. M. (1909) "The observer as reporter: a survey of the psychology of testimony," *Psychological Bulletin*, 6: 753–70.

Whipple, G. M. (1913) "Psychology of testimony and report," *Psychological Bulletin*, 10: 264–8.

World Health Organization (2003) *Guidelines for Medico-legal Care for Victims of Sexual Violence*. Geneva: World Health Organization.

World Health Organization, Department of Reproductive Health and Research, UNFPA and UNHCR (2004) *Clinical Management of Rape Survivors: Developing Protocols for Use with Refugees and Internally Displaced Persons*. Geneva: World Health Organization.

Wright, A. M. and Holliday, R. E. (2007) "Enhancing the recall of young, young-old and old-old adults with cognitive interviews," *Applied Cognitive Psychology*, 21 (1): 19–43.

12 Investigative interviewing of witnesses in Germany

When law is better than practice

Renate Volbert and Bianca Baker

Introduction

Psychological research on examining witnesses has a long tradition in Germany. In 1903, William Stern founded a journal entitled *Beiträge zur Psychologie der Aussage* (*Contributions to the Psychology of Testimony*), and in 1904 he wrote a landmark article entitled "Die Aussage als geistige Leistung und Verhörsprodukt" ["Testimony as a mental achievement and a result of interview tactics"). More than 100 years ago, he had already distinguished between free narrative and questioning and found that free narratives contained fewer errors than the answers given to questions posed during an interview. Stern found this to be true for statements by both children and adults. However, the negative impact of leading questions was more pronounced in children's statements as children are more susceptible than adults. Hence the idea that the way interviews are conducted can exert a substantial influence on witness and suspect statements has been around for more than a century in Germany. Recommendations on how to design the interview format to obtain as much information as possible by using a free narrative style and open questions were already formulated more than 40 years ago (e.g. Arntzen, 1970).

Legal regulations

Like suspects, witnesses are not obliged to appear before the police in Germany. However, they are obligated by the Criminal Procedural Law (§ 161a Strafprozessordnung (StPO)) to appear before the public prosecution office or before the court upon being summoned (§ 48 StPO). One difference in the law between suspects and witnesses is, however, that witnesses are obliged to give full, truthful statements. If they fail to comply with this procedure and are 14 years or older, they are liable to prosecution. However, there are certain exceptions to this law. Persons have the *right to refuse to testify* on personal grounds if they are (a) the fiancé(e) of the accused or the person to whom the accused has made a promise to enter into a civil partnership; (b) the spouse or the civil partner of the accused, even if the marriage or the civil partnership no longer exists; or (c) lineally related or related by marriage, collaterally related to the third degree, or related by marriage to the second degree to the accused (§ 52 StPO). Some people may refuse to testify on professional grounds (e.g. clergymen, attorneys, tax consultants, doctors, psychotherapists) when asked about information that was entrusted to them or became known to them in this capacity, unless they have been released from their obligation of secrecy (§ 53 StPO). Witnesses who fall under the exceptions above and refuse to testify are not allowed to be interviewed. If such witnesses have already given a statement to the police, and then decide to exercise their right to refuse to testify afterwards, none of the contents of their prior statements given during police interviews may be used in court proceedings.

Witnesses also have the *right to refuse to give self-incriminating information*. They may refuse to answer any questions if replying would subject them or one of their relatives to the risk of being prosecuted. In this case, they may not refuse to testify completely, but can reject only answers to particular questions (§ 55 StPO).

In contrast to suspect questioning (Volbert and Baker, 2015), the Criminal Procedure Code also contains *specific regulations and laws for the conduct of witness interviewing*. Witnesses are directed to state coherently (by free narrative) everything they know about the subject of their interview. If so required, further questions can then be asked in order to clarify and complete the statement, as well as to establish the grounds on which the witness's knowledge is based (§ 69 StPO). This legal requirement applies to both police and judicial inquiries.

Interviewing practice training

According to the German constitution police jurisdiction in Germany lies primarily within the 16 states.[1] This means each state has its own *state police* with its own police laws and organization, which follow a similar yet not identical structure. Therefore the responsibility for the training of the development lies also with the states and is not uniform. For this reason training in interviewing witnesses and suspects is not homogenous across all states, because there is a lack of explicit and/or mandatory interview training curricula. Some states provide a standardized interview training, while other states offer a theoretical education combined with training on the job. This means in practice that police officers learn how to interview by working together with more experienced colleagues. Investigative interviews with witnesses (including vulnerable witnesses) are conducted by police officers.

Against the background of the legal requirements described above, German literature on witness interviewing consistently proposes that investigative interviewing should first elicit and actively support a free recall of the event by the witness. After free recall, the interviewing changes to a funnel-shaped style of questioning that moves from open questions to questions requiring specific responses (e.g. Arntzen, 1970; Brockmann and Chedor, 1999; Greuel, 2008; Heubrock and Donzelmann, 2010; Steller and Boychuk, 1992).

Probably the most extensively formulated German guidelines for police questioning of witnesses are to be found in the PCFQCE (Preparation, Contact and orientation, Free report, Questioning, Conclusion, Evaluation) model of the structured interview of witnesses formulated by Berresheim and Weber (2003) and based on the PEACE (Planning and preparation, Engage and explain, Account, clarify and challenge, Closure, Evaluation) model. This model is only briefly outlined below because of the great similarity with the English model.

- *Preparation.* The preparation stage incorporates the acquisition of knowledge about the facts and the relevant persons. It then determines the specific interview goals and evaluates the considerations for the interview setting (whether the interview is to be conducted by one or two officials, if an interpreter is needed, etc.).
- *Contact and orientation.* This step includes rapport-building, an instruction on rules (such as rights and obligations), and an explanation of the process of interrogation to make the situation transparent and easily understood.
- *Free report.* This stage of the interview includes requesting the witness to give a free report. It also includes two mnemonics (as in the Cognitive Interview), the "reinstate context" and "report everything" (Geiselman and Fisher, 1997). An important component is that there should be no interruption of the free report and no immediate questions during the witness's breaks in speech. Instead, the free report stage is meant to prompt more detail on the report from the witness.
- *Questioning.* Each piece of information produced by the witness during free recall is then assigned to single action sequences that are arranged in a chronological timeline. This timeline forms the structure for the questioning phase. How much information is needed to clarify each different action sequence depends on the circumstances of the case. During this stage, questioning once more follows the above-mentioned funnel-shaped structure. That is, it starts with broader questions, similar to free recall, but specific to certain topics. Subsequent questions are asked as openly as possible and mainly serve to clarify where, how, when, what happened exactly and with whom. Resorting to the use of closed questions is permissible only if an essential part of the relevant information has already been collected during open questioning and more information is needed. The clarification of any inconsistencies should also be made only in the final phase of the interview.
- *Conclusion.* During the conclusion, the official summarizes the information obtained, and the witness is given an opportunity to add details and to clarify any misunderstandings. Furthermore, the witness is made aware that for the remainder of the proceedings, any subsequent additions to the statement are welcome, should the witness still have any further information to provide.
- *Evaluation.* The final stage evaluates to what extent the pre-formulated interview objectives have been achieved. Furthermore, the interrogator must reflect on his or her own role in the interrogation.

However, untrained police officers often do not recognize the methodological importance of the free report. Studies have shown that untrained interviewers typically utilize prompts such as "Tell me briefly what you know about the incident" or "Give a short overview of what happened." In wording prompts this way, it is left to the witnesses to interpret what exactly the interviewer is expecting of them. This affects both the amount of information given in the free report as well as the depth of details offered. In questionings of this style, witnesses often give a short overview of the sequence of events (Berresheim and Weber, 2003; Weber *et al.*, 2011). Should witnesses terminate their short overview of the sequence of events, this is often regarded by untrained police officers as the moment to begin the questioning phase of the interview. Moreover, inexperienced police officers also frequently interrupt the free recall and switch to the questioning phase prematurely. However, such courses of interviews may well be inadequate, because the focus of information retrieval lies on the questioning and not on the free recall phase (e.g. Lipton, 1977).

Systematic training can significantly improve questioning behavior. In an *evaluation of the structured interview of witnesses*, 25 mock interviews by police officials carried out before and after training were analyzed and compared to each other (Berresheim and Weber, 2003). Results indicated that two-thirds of the participants implemented the training they had received in the actual interviews. After training, the free report was, on average, more than twice as long as before. However, even after training, the free recall still only reached 15 percent of the total examination time. The portion of speaking by witnesses increased significantly, whereas the number of questions asked, of complaints to the witness, of interruptions, and of interpretive statements by the interrogators dropped significantly. Those police officials who implemented what they had learned obtained 15 percent more detail during the interview, whereas those who did not implement training strategies into their interviews produced no significant increase in detail. Although the increase in correct detail coincided with an increase in incorrect detail, the proportion of incorrect detail in relation to the total amount of detail did not change. In a follow-up on how the implementation was employed in practice, it was found that the need to simultaneously produce written documentation (see Volbert and Baker, 2015) impeded a thorough execution of the structured interview of witnesses (Weber *et al.*, 2011). Of course, a replication of this study with a larger sample would be desirable.

Weber *et al.* (2011) further describe that police officers who are less experienced in questioning are better able to implement the structured interview than experienced interrogators. The latter apparently have more difficulty changing strategies that they perceive to be successful. However, interview novices often feel overtaxed by the complexity of the interview requirements. Therefore, during interview training, participants are handed a checklist detailing the concrete steps for each phase. In mock interviews, the specific phases are acted out repeatedly. This enables participants to gradually gain more self-confidence. Parallel to this, participants are given observer sheets so that they can learn to evaluate observed interviewing behavior adequately. These observer sheets also help participants to grasp what is expected of them in an investigative interview. In North Rhine-Westphalia (one of the 16 German states), all police interview novices have been receiving a one-week intensive training in the structured interviewing of witnesses since 2002. By late 2010, more than 1,300 police officers in North Rhine-Westphalia had completed this training. In the same state, the structured interview has now also become an integrated part of the bachelor degree program for training police officers (Weber *et al.*, 2011). In other German states, some practice in open interview strategies supporting free reporting is given in the context of education and training. However, not all training is carried out systematically.

Vulnerable witnesses

Interviews with (alleged) victims

If witnesses being interviewed have been affected directly by the events, they are granted particular rights. Witnesses who have been aggrieved by the criminal offence have to be given an opportunity to make submissions concerning the effects that the offence had on them (§ 69 StPO). All aggrieved persons may avail themselves of the assistance of an attorney or be represented by an attorney, and a legal counsel is permitted to be present at the aggrieved person's investigative interview. A person whom they trust may, at their request, also be permitted to be present, except when this could endanger the purpose of the investigation (§ 406f StPO). Persons who are aggrieved by, for example, sexual offences, human trafficking, abduction, physical abuse, assault, attempted murder, or manslaughter may also take part in a public prosecution as a joint plaintiff (§ 395 StPO). In this case, an attorney may inspect the files for the aggrieved person and can represent the aggrieved person in court proceedings. The attorney can ask questions, provide proof of evidence, hold a closing argument, or make an appeal (or ask for a review) where the case ended in an acquittal of the accused.

The police or judicial hearing of an alleged victim should, in principle, be similar to the interview of other witnesses as described in detail above. However, victims of violent and sexual offences are often particularly emotionally strained and may therefore not provide an extensive representation of the offences that occurred. In a subset of cases, there are additional challenges: although a complaint has been made, it may not be certain whether the alleged offence actually took place and whether the alleged victim is actually a victim of the reported offence. In such cases, it is not only necessary to support witnesses in their memory retrieval but also to estimate the credibility of their testimony (see below).

Establishing rapport is therefore of particular importance when interviewing (alleged) victims. On the one hand, interviewers should express understanding for the victim and their emotional strain during questioning. However, on the other hand, it is equally important for them to adopt a neutral standpoint so that an open and unbiased interview can be carried out. With this in mind, the witness should then be informed of the importance of giving a detailed representation of the criminal occurrences. Another important aspect when questioning victims of violent and sexual crimes is to be cautious with the use of context reinstatement, because this can trigger the emotions experienced during the offence (Brockmann and Chedor, 1999).

Interviews with children

In Germany, there is no minimum age for the hearing of children.[2] Theoretically, any child with whom verbal communication is possible can be questioned by the police or in court. At the same time, the aforementioned obligation to make a statement holds regardless of age – with the exception of the right to refuse to testify because of the nature of a relationship with the accused – and is thus also applicable to children.

If children have an evidentiary privilege, but due to lack of intellectual maturity have no sufficient understanding of the importance of their right to refuse to testify, a testimony may be taken from them only if they are willing to testify and if their statutory representative also agrees to the child being interviewed. If the statutory representative is the accused, he or she is not allowed to exercise this right to refuse to testify. If both parents are entitled to act as statutory representatives, the same applies to the parent who is not accused. In this case, another person (guardian) is employed who can make this decision for the child. If there is no evidentiary privilege, in principle, neither the child, nor the child's parents, nor the guardian can refuse a hearing of the child. However, because no coercive measures can be imposed on a child under the age of 14 years, the obligation to testify against children is ultimately unenforceable.

Minors who have been victims of an offence are eligible for the already described victims' rights, and this also applies to police questioning. In addition, minors under the age of 18 have specific rights in court hearings to protect them from the negative impact of testifying. It should be noted that Germany has an inquisitorial criminal justice system. This means that there are no parties that present relevant information before the court that is subsequently evaluated by a jury. Instead, the legal procedure is considered as an inquest, a court-controlled pursuit of facts directed toward establishing the truth. Although documentary presentation of evidence would be consistent with the inquisitorial model, the German version of the inquisitorial system strongly favors the oral presentation of evidence. In reaching a verdict, the only relevant information is the information introduced during the hearing (for a comparison between adversarial and inquisitorial systems, see Van Koppen and Penrod, 2003). Therefore, witnesses must also testify in a trial even if they have already been questioned extensively by the police as a witness. This also applies to children, even if they have been victims of a crime.

Special protection rules apply to the judicial hearing of children and adolescents. The court may exclude the public from a hearing if a person under the age of 18 years is being examined (§ 172 Gerichtsverfassunggesetz (GVG) (Courts Constitution Act)). The court may also order defendants to leave the courtroom during an examination of persons under 18 years of age if considerable detriment to the well-being of such witnesses is to be feared when interviewed in the defendant's presence. In this case, the presiding judge has to inform the defendants of the essential contents of the testimony given during their absence (§ 247 StPO). The examination of witnesses under the age of 18 has to be conducted solely by the presiding judge. Others involved such as the public prosecutor, joint plaintiff, defense attorney, other judges, jurors, and defendant may request the presiding judge to ask witnesses further questions. The presiding judge may also permit these persons to put questions to witnesses directly if no detriment to the well-being of the minor is to be expected (§ 241a StPO).

The "Witness Protection Law," which came into effect in December 1998, introduced the use of video-recorded statements. The court may order that witnesses remain in another place during the examination if there is an imminent risk of serious detriment to their well-being through being examined in the presence of those attending the main hearing. A simultaneous audiovisual transmission of the testimony then has to be provided in the courtroom (§ 247a StPO). In proceedings relating to sexual offences, homicide, assault, and the like, the examination of witnesses less than 18 years of age may be replaced by the presentation of an audiovisual recording of their previous *judicial* examination as long as the defendants and defense counsel were given the opportunity to participate in such an examination and to request the judge to ask the witness further questions. Supplementary witness examination in court is also admissible (§ 255a StPO).

The same interview strategies as described above may also be utilized during the interviewing of children – although their level of development has to be taken into consideration. When assessing the cognitive capacities of children to testify, it should be noted that this does not just concern whether children are in any way able to remember a past event. Children must be capable of giving their own account of the occurrences they remember, and they have to be able to respond to prompts and answer further inquiries. If recall is possible only in response to specific cues, this is not particularly problematic as long as there is no doubt that the events have indeed occurred. If there is knowledge about what exactly happened, this information can be used as supportive cues. Nonetheless, such situations do not occur regularly in forensic practice (Volbert, 2005). Instead, statements are usually made about events in which no additional information is available. If questioning has to be based on specific cues and asking specific questions, there is a major risk that it will reflect primarily the interviewer's ideas about what happened rather than being a representation of the actual events.

Interviews with learning-disabled witnesses

People with intellectual disabilities face a disproportionally high risk of becoming victims of sexual abuse (Baker, 2015; Schröttle *et al.*, 2012) and thereby becoming involved in the criminal justice system. However, there are no specific regulations for examining learning-disabled witnesses in Germany; and, in most cases, there is no special education or training for police officers or judges on interviewing these witnesses. Interviews with five police officers (Rauchert, 2008) showed that they feel poorly trained for questioning people with intellectual disabilities and complain about the lack of interview guidelines for them to follow or of further education courses in this field. The police officers stated that they tend to utilize guidelines on how to interview children when questioning learning-disabled individuals. A study conducted in Austria, Germany, and Switzerland revealed that there has been little research on this topic in all three countries, and there are only minimal or no current guidelines on questioning learning-disabled witnesses (Niehaus *et al.*, 2013). Another Swiss study interviewed intellectually disabled victims and their caregivers about their experiences with the criminal justice system (Krüger *et al.*, 2012). Results showed that they had to face the consequences of a lack of specialized knowledge in police officers. Although they pointed out that police officers had indeed been very kind, adult witnesses nonetheless felt that they were treated as children.

Assessing the credibility of a statement

When one statement contradicts another during criminal proceedings, assessing the veracity of testimony becomes crucial. This situation occurs frequently in sexual offences: the accused denies the offense, and – due to a lack of material evidence and eyewitnesses – the only evidence is the incriminating testimony of the victim. For more than five decades now, courts in Germany have addressed this issue by appointing psychological experts to deliver expert opinions on the credibility of the testimony given in a particular case. The basic method for assessing this credibility is called Statement Validity Analysis (SVA) and was developed in Germany and Sweden in the 1950s (see Undeutsch, 1967, 1982).

In a nutshell, the basic assumption is that a testimony derived from the memory of an actual experience differs in content quality from a statement based on fabrication. This is because liars cannot fall back on an event-specific representation in memory; and, through their need to appear credible, they are more preoccupied with strategic self-presentation than truth-tellers are. As a result, liars have to handle a higher cognitive load and are hence unable to achieve the same quality of testimony as truth-tellers. However, content quality is influenced not only by the veracity of the statement but also by other (personal and contextual) variables, and these have to be taken into account when analyzing the single case. Of special importance are suggestive influences that might have preceded the statement in question, because these can lead to false memories that can, in turn, produce high-quality testimony. The principal diagnostic approach is therefore to compare and contrast different models offering alternative explanations for the given data. This makes it necessary to test whether the statement in question can be explained in any other way than as being based on real experience, or whether such alternative explanations are incompatible with the available data. If all theoretically conceivable not-true hypotheses are incompatible with the available facts, they can be dismissed, and one may accept the opposite hypothesis: the assumption that the statement is true.

Hence, so-called Statement Validity Analysis delivers a comprehensive ideographic approach. Accordingly, conducting an SVA calls for more information than just the statement. In Germany, psychological experts are granted access to all files containing the results of investigations by the police, the public prosecutor, and the court; they can themselves interview the witness before the trial; and during the trial, they can further question not only the witness whose statement is being assessed but also other witnesses or the defendant (see Volbert and Steller, 2014, for a comprehensive overview of SVA).

Implications

The legal framework for examining witnesses in Germany requires that the testimony be collected as far as possible in the form of a free narrative and that questions are asked only to clarify what has previously been reported in the free account. The law thus reflects sound psychological findings indicating that information given through a free report is more reliable than information given upon questioning. However, there are problems with the practical implementation of this method, because systematic training in this interview strategy is not given throughout Germany. Without specific training, interviews are often conducted in a question-and-answer style, even though this runs counter to the legal requirements (Berresheim and Weber, 2003). Therefore, the recommendation for the future is to provide systematic training to all police officers who conduct interviews.

Notes

1. The Federal Criminal Police Office (Bundeskriminalamt), as the central police agency in Germany, coordinates crime suppression at the national and international level. In general, it is responsible for police communications with the law enforcement and judicial authorities as well as with other public authorities in other countries. The Federal Criminal Police Office thus acts as an information and communication centre of the German police. In addition, all official communications between the German police and other countries are routed through the Criminal Police Office. The Federal Police (Bundespolizei), on the other hand, is responsible for border and transportation security, the protection of constitutional organs, etc.
2. Legal age starts at 18; criminal responsibility at 14. There is no minimum age for a child to be interviewed as a witness. Witnesses under the age of 18 are considered vulnerable witnesses; specific laws were introduced to protect this group from secondary victimization.

References

Arntzen, F. (1970) *Vernehmungspsychologie* (*The Psychology of Interrogation*). Munich: Beck.

Baker, B. (2015) “Do Learning Disabled Sexual Offenders Have a Specific Victim Fixation?” Manuscript submitted for publication.

Berresheim, A. and Weber, A. (2003) “Die Strukturierte Zeugenvernehmung und ihre Wirksamkeit” (“The structured interview of witnesses and its efficacy”), *Kriminalistik*, 57 (12): 757–70.

Brockmann, C. and Chedor, R. (1999) *Vernehmung, Hilfen für den Praktiker* [*Interrogation: An Aid for Practitioners*]. Hilden: Verlag Deutsche Polizeiliteratur.

Geiselman, R. E. and Fisher, R. P. (1997) "Ten years of cognitive interviewing," in D. Payne and F. Conrad (eds), *Intersections in Basic and Applied Memory Research*. New York: Erlbaum, pp. 291–310.

Greuel, L. (2008) "Zeugenvernehmung" ["Interviewing witnesses"], in R. Volbert and M. Steller (eds), *Handbuch der Rechtspsychologie*. Göttingen: Hogrefe, pp. 221–31.

Heubrock, D. and Donzelmann, N. (2010) *Psychologie der Vernehmung. Empfehlungen zur Beschuldigten-, Zeugen- und Opferzeugen-Vernehmung* [*The Psychology of Interrogation: Recommendations for Interviewing the Accused, Witnesses, and Victims*]. Frankfurt: Verlag für Polizeiwissenschaft.

Krüger, P., Caviezel Schmitz, S., and Niehaus, S. (2012) "Geistig behinderte Opfer sexueller Gewalt im Strafverfahren – Die Sicht der Betroffenen" ["Intellectually disabled victims of sexual abuse in legal proceedings"], *Schweizerische Zeitschrift für Heilpädagogik*, 18 (11–12): 8–14.

Lipton, J. P. (1977) "On the psychology of eyewitness testimony," *Journal of Applied Psychology*, 62: 90–3.

Niehaus, S., Krüger, P., and Caviezel Schmitz, S. (2013) "Intellectually disabled victims of sexual abuse in the criminal justice system," *Psychology*, 4: 374–9.

Rauchert, K. (2008) *Polizeiliche Anhörung von (Opfer-) Zeugen mit geistiger Behinderung* [*Police Questioning of Victims with Intellectual Disability*]. Frankfurt: Verlag für Polizeiwissenschaft.

Schröttle, M., Hornberg, C., Glammeier, S., Sellach, B., Kavemann, B., Puhe, H., and Zinsmeister, J. (2012) "Lebenssituation und Belastungen von Frauen mit Beeinträchtigungen und Behinderungen in Deutschland" ["The living conditions and stress of women with impairments and disabilities in Germany"], *Journal Netzwerk Frauen- und Geschlechterforschung NRW*, 30: 60–4.

Steller, M. and Boychuk, T. (1992) "Children as witnesses in sexual abuse cases: investigative interview and assessment techniques," in H. Dent and R. Flin (eds), *Children as Witnesses*. Chichester: Wiley, pp. 47–71.

Stern, W. (1904) "Die Aussage als geistige Leistung und als Verhörsprodukt: Experimentelle Schüleruntersuchungen" ["Testimony as a mental achievement and a result of interrogation tactics: experiments with school children"], in W. Stern (ed.), *Beiträge zur Psychologie der Aussage*. Leipzig: Barth, pp. 269–326.

Undeutsch, U. (1967) "Beurteilung der Glaubwürdigkeit von Zeugenaussagen" ["Assessment of the credibility of witnesses' statements"], in U. Undeutsch (ed.), *Handbuch der Psychologie, Band 11: Forensische Psychologie*. Göttingen, Germany: Hogrefe, pp. 26–81.

Undeutsch, U. (1982) "Statement reality analysis," in A. Trankell (ed.), *Reconstructing the Past*. Stockholm: Norstedt & Söners förlag, pp. 27–56.

Van Koppen, P. J. and Penrod, S. D. (eds) (2003) *Adversarial Versus Inquisitorial Justice: Psychological Perspectives in Criminal Justice Systems*. New York: Kluwer.

Volbert, R. (2005) "Zur Entwicklung von Aussagefähigkeiten" ["The development of the ability to give testimony"], in K.-P. Dahle and R. Volbert (eds), *Entwicklungspsychologische Aspekte der Rechtspsychologie*. Göttingen: Hogrefe, pp. 241–57.

Volbert, R. and Baker, B. (in press) "Investigative interviewing of suspects in Germany: defining what not to do," in D. Walsh, G. Osburgh, A. Redlich, and T. Myklebust (eds), *Contemporary Developments and Practices in Investigative Interviewing and Interrogation: An International Perspective. Volume II: Suspected Offenders*. London: Routledge.

Volbert, R. and Steller, M. (2014) "Is this testimony truthful, fabricated, or based on false memory? Credibility assessment 25 years after Steller and Köhnken (1989)," *European Psychologist*, 19: 207–20.

Weber, A., Berresheim, A., and Capellmann, M. (2011) "Die Strukturierte Vernehmung. Die Methode für die Praxis der Polizei in NRW" ["The structured interview: the method for police practitioners in North Rhine-Westphalia"], *Kriminalistik*, 65 (3): 169–75.

13 Interviewing witnesses in Italy

Francesco Pompedda, Angelo Zappalà, Massimo Scarabello and Vittorio Maria Rossini

The situation in Italy regarding how to conduct the interview of a witness is not completely clear and, above all, the conduct and training are not nationally regulated. For this reason there are different practices (almost one for each court) that make it difficult to summarize practice as a whole. As such, while some coverage is given to interviews with adult witnesses, the main focus of this chapter will be on the interviews with children as witnesses for various reasons. The first reason is the role of the child as a witness: children have to be regarded as a particular type of witness who needs more attention and specific regulations because of their vulnerability to suggestion, misinterpretation, etc. In Italy the awareness that children have to be regarded as a special type of witness is quite strong. This is evident by the large number of guidelines and rules concerning how to conduct child witness interviews. In contrast, focusing upon adult witnesses might result in a non-exhaustive and oversimplified view of the fragmentary situation concerning the conduct of such witness interviews in Italy. This focus on child witnesses does not mean that we will completely ignore interviews of adult witnesses, but that we will give more space to the interview with child witnesses because it allows us to present the Italian situation in a clearer way for the reader.

In this chapter we will focus on the description of the techniques and methodologies used in Italy during the interview of victims and witnesses and specifically on the interviews of minors in alleged child sexual abuse, as the interviews in these cases play a central role for the investigation (Ceci and Bruck, 1995; Lamb, 1994). As previously stated, the situation regarding the procedure to use in these cases is not so clear at present; nevertheless some guidelines have recently been developed according to the most recent international literature on the field,[1] but nothing has been undertaken regarding the training of the different figures involved. Nowadays training is mostly based on individual choice of which methodologies to use. Additionally, in most police or jurist training, specific psychological training is not usually provided.

Introduction

The witness is the most important "tool" in the Italian trial because of the central role it plays in reconstructing the facts for the prosecutor or judge concerning what happened. The Italian legal system requires that any individual giving oral testimony during a trial has to recite a declaration accepting the responsibility to be truthful. The declaration translates roughly to: "I am aware of the moral and legal responsibility that I take with my statement, I undertake to tell the whole truth and not to hide anything, to the best of my knowledge,"[2] and is recited at the beginning of each witness's testimony or if the judge suspects that the deposition is false (Code of Criminal Procedure (CPP), Art. 497, 2). If a witness lies during an oral testimony he or she has committed a crime (Art. 372), but this rule is not always valid. The witness has the right to make any statement, true or false, in his or her defense[3] according to the principle known as *nemo tenetur se detegere*, which means that nobody, in any way, must be forced to say something that could lead to a legal accusation against him or her.[4] In other words, the suspect could lie for what concerns his own responsibility with no consequences (Art. 63; CPP 372, 384). After that *notizia criminis*[5] has been written on the registers, the interview of the witness can begin; usually a minor is heard by competent authorities (PM, Police Forces or by an expert called by the PM), However, after *The Lanzarote Convention*,[6] the CPP was changed in 2012 and now states that police, prosecutors or judges must take advantage of an expert in children psychology or psychiatry (lg. 172/2012; Arts 351, 362, 391). Listening to the minor is called *audizione protetta*[7] and is conducted in order to underline the importance of the well-being of the child, allowing the judge to decide when, where, and how the interview with the child is to be carried out (Art. 398, 5*bis*), making the best choice for the good of the child. Unfortunately, in too many cases, the interview is carried out by different people and on several occasions, because the Italian system gives no provision or specification at this stage for hearing the minor. It is possible to find the same lack of clarity among the experts. That is, there are no agreements between the professionals regarding which techniques are to be used when interviewing children. The consequence of this is that the ability and the expertise of the person conducting the interviews becomes of utter importance, with the whole case relying on choices lacking guidance.

History and guidelines regarding the child as a witness

Even if the *Daubert principles*[8,9] are not taken into consideration when the judges have to evaluate the evidence, the idea of the importance of a *strong* scientific basis for interviewing such witnesses is starting to be a common idea among the experts and judges. The first concrete guidelines (*Carta di Noto*) that highlighted the problem of the child witness testimony during trials were collected during 1996. Experts in the most important field involved in alleged child sexual abuse (CSA) cases (lawyers, judges, psychologists, psychiatrists, criminologists, forensic scientists) met in Noto (Italy) for a convention in order to develop a *memorandum of good practice* to use in alleged CSA cases. The paper has already been updated twice, the first time in 2002 and the second during a conference at the International Institute of Higher Studies in Criminal Sciences in 2011. Changes to the guidelines were made according to the research development and according to the legislative changes in Italy. Simultaneously with afore-mentioned guidelines, many other have been promulgated in the last few years:

- Directive regarding child sexual abuse (SINPIA, 2007)
- Directives regarding the child as witness (*Questura di Roma*, 2011)
- Listening to the child into the legal field (UNICEF Manual, 2011)
- Protocol of Cosenza (SISF, 2014).

These protocols highlight the importance of the use of:

- evidence-based methodology, tests and techniques, based on the Daubert principles (*Carta di Noto*, Art. 1 a, b);
- use of interview protocols based on the indications of international research (*Carta di Noto*, Art. 7 (Lamb *et al.*, 2008);
- video recording of the interviews (*Carta di Noto*, Art. 10).

The Legitimacy Court[10] made a declaration regarding the *Carta di Noto* that can to some extent be related to all the guidelines present in Italy. This declaration states that the suggestions made in the *Carta di Noto* are merely technical references and are not legal. In other words the violation of what is suggested in the protocol cannot affect the legitimacy of the evidence. All these different guidelines were finally combined in 2012 and, after almost two years of meetings, in the National Guidelines for listening to children. Different scientific societies represented by experts in the different fields met in Rome to draw up the paper. The scientific societies that took part in drawing up the paper were: the Italian Society of Criminology, the Italian Society of Forensic Medicine, the Italian Society of Child Neuropsychiatry, the Italian Society of Neuropsychology, the Italian Society of Psychiatry, and the Society of Forensic Psychology. One of the reasons for drawing up these guidelines is cited in the National Guidelines as follows:

> Among the reasons for drawing up this Consensus were the common concerns shared by many experts regarding the limited competence of the people (that should be called experts) who made these evaluations during the trials and the use of no evidence-based tests and methodology. (National Guidelines, 2012)

All the advice in the paper is in agreement with the latest international research findings (e.g. Lamb *et al.*, 2007; *Lamb et al.*, 2008), helping Italy to become up to date with the newest findings in this field. The first step to a radical change in the vision of the child as a witness was the adoption of the principles posted in the Lanzarote Convention. They were adopted by the Italian parliament on 12 April 2012 and ratified on 23 October 2012. Among all the new suggestions, these are the ones that concern the testimony of the child (Art. 35, Lanzarote Convention):[11]

- Interviews with the child should take place without unjustified delay after the facts have been reported to the competent authorities.
- Interviews with the child should take place, where necessary, in premises designed or adapted for that purpose.
- Interviews with the child are to be carried out, where necessary, by or through professionals trained for that purpose.
- The same persons, if possible and where appropriate, should conduct all the interviews with the child.
- The number of interviews should be as limited as possible and interviews are to be carried out only where strictly necessary for the purposes of criminal investigations and proceedings.
- The child may be accompanied by a representative or, where appropriate, an adult of the child's choice, unless a reasoned decision has been made to the contrary in respect of that person.

Among the other important changes derived from the Lanzarote Convention and the enactment of the law 172/2012 there is also an enhanced importance to the role of the expert in the interview of the child witness (Art. 351, CPP); now it is explicitly required that the police use the aid and support of external experts (compared to before when this was only suggested as an option).

Description of current practice as stated by the law

In this section we will first describe what is stated by the law concerning witness interviews and precisely what an interviewer is allowed to do or not during a witness interview. After that we will separately describe interviewing techniques and methodologies for adult and child witnesses.

As stated in the *Codice di procedura penale*[12] (Gazzetta Ufficiale, 1988) the following must be avoided:

- any methods or techniques that may influence the suspect's right to self-determination (e.g. torture);
- any methods or techniques that alter his memory or capability of evaluating facts[13] (e.g. hypnosis, narcoanalysis, polygraph);
- questions that can interfere with the truthfulness of the answers;[14]
- suggestive questions.[15]

The lack of other kinds of more strict directives is the cause of the differences among the different courts.

Interview and interrogation practices for adult witnesses

This section describes the most common technique used during the interview of an adult as a witness.

During the trial, witnesses are interviewed by direct and cross examination.[16] Direct examination is led by the party who summoned the witness to testify. During direct examination leading questions[17] are prohibited. This prohibition prevents witnesses potentially providing an answer that has been suggested by the way the question has been initially posed. In the event that a witness summoned by a party becomes hostile during the interview, the law states that in such circumstances leading questions are allowed. After direct examination the witness is cross-examined by the other party. At this point, questions are often leading as the lawyer tries to hinder the witness's recollections. Attorneys have several techniques they may utilize. For witness examinations it is particularly important for the attorney to focus on the behavioral aspects of the subject who is questioned. Everything from tone of voice and body language to how the subject reacts to questions from the different parties (i.e. the judge and the opposing counsel) is taken into consideration. It is important to remember that an attorney may also introduce documents at any time during the trial, but before the *Discussion portion*[18] of the trial. This can be used as a strategy in order to attack the credibility of witnesses' statements. Introducing documents that may contradict a witness's testimony is one of the strategies most used by attorneys in order to test the witness's reaction (mainly used if they suspect that the witness is lying). If there is a contradictory testimony between two witnesses or even two co-defendants, an attorney has the possibility to ask the judge to call on both persons simultaneously. Having both individuals present at the same time allows the judge to question them in an attempt to resolve the conflicting information. Where the conflict persists, the judge can ask the two parties to attempt to resolve it by open discussion with each other. Attorneys will evaluate each case based on the facts and individuals involved and use these techniques to create the best possible strategy for any situation.

Interview and interrogation practices for child witnesses

In this paragraph we are going to describe the current practice used in Italy to interview a child witness. As highlighted earlier in the chapter there are a different number of guidelines. However, as these are not completely regulated by law, the current situation resembles a patchwork of different techniques and methodologies, some of which are lacking in empirical evidence. Among the most often used methods for interviewing children is the cognitive interview (Saywitz et al., 1992).

The cognitive interview (CI) is a technique used to help the witness to elicit as much information as possible and is based on four different retrieval methods. Two of the methods attempt to increase the feature overlap between the memory record for the event and the memory retrieval aid while the other two encourage using many retrieval paths (Saywitz *et al.*, 1992). The standard steps of the CI are (Zulawski *et al.*, 2001) as follows:

1. *Establish rapport.* The interviewer begins by establishing rapport with the witness.

2. *Reconstruct the circumstances of the event.* The interviewer asks the witness to reconstruct how the incident began and the circumstances preceding it. The interviewer instructs the witness to think about what the environment looked like and the witness is also asked to recall his or her emotional mindset at the time of the event.
3. *Instruct the eyewitness to report everything.* The witness is encouraged to recover any detail, even if it may seem trivial.
4. *Recall the events in different order.* The interviewer instructs the witness to start from the middle or the end and move either forward or backward through the story.
5. *Change perspective.* The interviewer asks the witness to change roles or positions with another person present during the event.

A psychological assessment of the child is usually arranged in order to evaluate the credibility of his or her deposition (Mazzoni and Rotriquenz, 2012), sometimes using statement validity analysis (Yuille and Cutshall, 1989) and the criteria-based content analysis scale (Steller and Köhnken, 1989).

Scientific theoretical and practical support

The cognitive interview (CI) has been well researched in the laboratory, although less so in the field (Clifford and George, 1996; Geiselman *et al.*, 1985; Köhnken *et al.*, 1994). Generally what has been found is that the use of the Cognitive Interview enhances both the quality and quantity of the information recalled by witnesses compared with a standard police interview (Dando *et al.*, 2008). Some studies have reported a slight increase in the amount of incorrect information recalled (e.g. Memon and Higham, 1999); however, overall accuracy rates[19] have been found to be good and almost identical[20] (Köhnken et al., 1999). Among the limits of the CI that should be taken into consideration is the fact that it cannot be used with children under six years of age. This is because children younger than six do not have the cognitive capacity demanded for this interviewing technique, nor do they generally have a sufficient vocabulary (Gulotta and Cutica, 2009).

Training

In Italy, police officers and public prosecutors (POPP) do not receive any specific training in techniques or strategies (e.g. strategic use of evidence, cognitive interviews, Scharff' technique) for investigative interviewing or criminal interrogation. The training aims are to provide an intense education more on the legal framework than on the psychological. POPP do not receive any specific education regarding interrogation psychology or eyewitness testimony. POPP lack both knowledge of the theoretical background and the findings of empirically based research on which techniques and strategies work during the investigative interview and the criminal interrogation. The pedagogy of the training is largely founded on lectures and case studies. One study (Calzolari and Mestitz, 2000) conducted in the north of the country showed that 90 percent of the experts in this region lacked the required training. Role plays and other *learning by doing* methodologies are minimally used in general during the training. Concerning the investigative interview and criminal interrogation of children or adolescents, POPP usually receive a specific lecture and case-study training. However, POPP are not provided with specific training on conducting protocols. International research has shown the importance of structured protocols in order to improve:

- the degree of informativeness of child disclosure;
- the use of open questions and limiting the use of suggestive questions. For example, the NICHD protocol (Lamb *et al.*, 2007) has been found to be effective in translating professional recommendations into operating guidelines.

A possible explanation for the lack of training could be the fact that there are no strict rules guiding experts in the kind of methodology or technique; the judge is not obliged (according to the law) to decline a piece of evidence based on "general acceptance" or other evidence that is not solidly based on scientific knowledge. Following this line of reasoning further, we could state that this explains the absence of the need (of the experts) to be up-to-date and well trained. Obviously this is a general hypothesis. As said before, the choice to keep up-to-date and well trained is not compulsory but responsibility falls on the individual, which in turn means that there are both well up-to-date and trained experts in Italy with a knowledge of scientifically founded methods and those that lack this crucial knowledge.

In Italy today, there are good guidelines but not a national training program. The risk in this is that the lack of training might lead interviewers to make mistakes. As highlighted by international research, knowledge is not enough in order to interview a child witness in an effective and appropriate manner (Aldridge and Cameron, 1999; Warren *et al.*, 1999).

Next, we are going to present extracts taken from the written transcripts of interviews during trial cases of child sexual abuse (CSA), undertaken during the period from 1995 to 2006. For clarification, we will only show the wrong kinds of questions made during the interview in order to highlight how detrimental these particular wrong kinds of questions can be during child witness interviews, something which is highly likely without proper training in this conduct.

- ***Extract 1 (child: nine years old; convicted: janitor)***[21]

  I: *"Your mum told me about the bad things that happened to you … Would you like to talk about it?"*
  C: *(Stays silent)*
  I: *"If you will not tell the truth all those things will happen to other children as well"*

- ***Extract 2 (pre-school child, no one convicted)***

  I: *"Has any adult forced you to do something bad?"*
  C: *"No"*

I: *"Then you are a liar. Do you know who tells lies?"*
C: *"You"*
I: *"Then ... You are really telling lies!"*
C: *(Child stays quiet)*
I: *"Again ... Is it true that there were some people who hurt you?"*
C: *"It is not true!"*

- ***Extract 3 (pre-school child, no one convicted)***

I: *"So ... I want you to tell me the whole truth about what happened to you ... Was you father there? Was your uncle there? Was your step-brother there? Was your father there?"*

- ***Extract 4 (child: five years old; convicted: family friend)***

I: *"Where were you when he touched you? Were you at home or somewhere else?"*
C: *"At home"*
I: *"Were you alone?"*
C: *(Child keeps quiet)*
I: *"Only you two?"*[22]
C: *(Child keeps quiet)*
I: *"Was there someone else?"*
C: *"Was big"*[23]
I: *"Did he strip himself off his clothes?"*
C: *(Child stays quiet)*
I: *"Did he show you his willy?"*[24, 25]
C: *"I don't remember"*

In the first extract the interviewer has used the phrase "your mum told me". This kind of question must be avoided because it could make the child more accommodating in agreeing to what the mum said, even if it is not true. In the second extract the interviewer has started with a highly suggestive question implying that something bad really happened and then showing in a strong way that he or she did not believe what the child was saying, forcing the child to say what he or she expected to hear. In the third extract there is an example of an unclear and long question, the interviewer has used four different questions and one repetition in the same statement. In the fourth extract the interviewer has started with a suggestive and unclear question and he or she has used a suggestive questioning style throughout the extract. Another remarkable use of a unreliable questioning style is the last question "Did he show you his willy?" In using this question, the interviewer has mentioned a detail that the child had not mentioned before, incurring the risk of creating a false detail.

Conclusions

There is still much to improve concerning witness testimonies in Italy, but there are some positive aspects as well. Although the training is almost non-existent or, if available, often ineffective, it is remarkable that a large number of guidelines have been created in response to the more concerning cases that were poorly managed in the past. Also, the adoption of the Lanzarote Convention shows that there is a wide interest in this problematic and important area. It is clear that in Italy, as in other countries, the standard of interviewing is likely to be low.[26] The experts have responded to this problem by drawing up some up-to-date guidelines, but it is also really important to provide up-to-date training programs. One could argue that there are three phases of the process involved in improving the quality of child witness interviews in Italy. The first phase involves a national awareness of the problem. The second phase involves creating up-to-date and scientifically based guidelines. The third phase involves establishing an institution which guarantees high-quality training for experts involved in these cases while overseeing and updating the practice guidelines. The transition between the first and second phases requires some length of time, likewise the transition between the second and third phases, and, we argue, it is this period of transition Italy is in today.

Notes

1. Only for the child as a witness.
2. Gazzetta Ufficiale Italiana (1995).
3. Unless the statement is accusing another person of a crime and this accusation is knowingly false.
4. Self-incrimination.
5. Refers to the information regarding a crime that is formally taking over by the Pubblico Ministero (PM) (i.e. the public prosecutor).
6. Council of Europe Convention on the Protection of Children Against Sexual Exploitation and Sexual Abuse (25 October 2007).
7. Protected hearings.
8. *Daubert* v. *Merrell Dow Pharmaceuticals, Inc*. 509 US 579 (1993).
9. Federal Rules of Evidence, rule 702.
10. Cass., sez. III, 16 dicembre 2010 n. 15157, CED Cass., n. 249898 nello stesso senso anche Cass., sez.. III, 10 aprile 2008, n. 20568, CED Cass., n. 239879 e Cass., sez. III, 14 dicembre 2007 n. 6464, CED Cass., n. 239091
11. Official Journal of the European Union, L 101/9 2011.
12. Set of rules specifically dedicated to direct all the phases of a criminal proceeding.
13. This prohibition is granted even if the suspect agreed to the use of these methods. In other words, this right cannot be waived by the suspect.
14. Art. 499, subpara. 2
15. Art. 499, subpara. 3
16. Cross examination is not used if the witness is a child.
17. Leading questions are questions that lead the witness's answer.
18. Equivalent to the Closing Arguments portion of the USA trial system.
19. Proportion of correct details relative to the total amount of details reported.
20. 85 percent for the CI and 82 percent for the standard (Dando *et al.*, 2008).
21. I: Interviewer; C: Child.
22. Unclear question.
23. Without subject because the child did not mention it.
24. *Willy* (colloquial term) refers to the penis.
25. The child never mentioned this detail.
26. Sternberg *et al.* (2001).

References

Aldridge, J. and Cameron, S. (1999) "Interviewing child witnesses: questioning strategies and the effectiveness of training," *Applied Developmental Science*, 3 (2): 136–47.

Calzolari, M. G. and Mestitz, A. (2000) "Interrogatorio del minore vittima e/o testimone di reato da parte di polizia giudiziaria, pubblici ministeri e giudici nel nord Italia. Psicologia e giustizia," *Rivista Italiana on line di psicologia giuridica* (http://www.psicologiagiuridica.com).

Ceci, S. J. and Bruck, M. (1995) *Jeopardy in the Courtroom: A Scientific Analysis of Children's Testimony*. Washington, DC: American Psychological Association.

Clifford, B. R. and George, R. (1996) "A field evaluation of training in three methods of witness/victim investigative interviewing," *Psychology, Crime, and Law*, 2: 231–48.

Cornell University Law School (n.d.) Federal Rules of Evidence. Rule 702: Testimony by expert witness. Retrieved from: http://www.law.cornell.edu/rules/fre/rule_702.

Dando, C., Wilcock, R., and Milne, R. (2008) "The cognitive interview: inexperienced police officers' perceptions of their witness/victim interviewing practices," *Legal and Criminological Psychology*, 13 (1): 59–70.

Diritto e Giustizia Minorile. Year II, Vols 2–3, 2013, 112–121. Retrieved from: http://www.dirittoegiustiziaminorile.it/wp-content/uploads/2014/01/Rivista-2e3-2013.pdf.

European Union (2011) Directive 2011/36/EU of the European Parliament and of the Council of 5 April 2011 on preventing and combating trafficking in human beings and protecting its victims, and replacing Council Framework Decision 2002/629/JHA. *Official Journal of the European Union L 101/9*. Retrieved from http://eur-lex.europa.eu/LexUriServ/LexUriServ.do?uri=OJ:L:2011:101:0001:0011:EN:PDF.

Gazzetta Ufficiale Italiana (1988) *Decreto del president della repubblica 22 settembre 1988, n. 447*. Retrieved from Gazzetta Ufficiale Italiana.

Gazzetta Ufficiale Italiana (1995) *SENTENZA 4–5 maggio 1995, n. 149*. Retrieved from Gazzetta Ufficiale Italiana.

Geiselman, R. E., Fisher, R. P., MacKinnon, D. P., and Holland, H. L. (1985) "Eyewitness memory enhancement in the police interview: cognitive retrieval mnemonics versus hypnosis," *Journal of Applied Psychology*, 70: 401–12.

Gulotta, G. and Cutica, I. (2009) *Guida alla perizia in tema di abuso sessuale e alla sua critica* (Vol. 39). Giuffré editore.

International Institute of Higher Studies in Criminal Sciences (2011) *Carta di Noto III*. Noto, Italy. Retrieved from http://www.psicologiaforense.it/Noto3.pdf.

Köhnken, G., Thurer, C., and Zoberbier, D. (1994) "The cognitive interview: are the investigators' memories enhanced too?" *Applied Cognitive Psychology*, 8: 13–24.

Köhnken, G., Milne, R., Memon, A., and Bull, R. (1999) "The cognitive interview: a meta-analysis," *Psychology, Crime and Law*, 5 (1–2): 3–27.

Lamb, M. E. (1994) "The investigation of child sexual abuse: an interdisciplinary consensus statement," *Child Abuse and Neglect*, 18: 1021–8.

Lamb, M. E., Hershkowitz, I., Orbach, Y., and Esplin, P. W. (2008) *Tell Me What Happened: Structured Investigative Interviews of Child Victims and Witnesses*. Chichester: John Wiley & Sons.

Lamb, M. E., Orbach, Y., Hershkowitz, I., Esplin, P. W., and Horowitz, D. (2007) "A structured forensic interview protocol improves the quality and informativeness of investigative interviews with children: a review of research using the NICHD Investigative Interview Protocol," *Child Abuse and Neglect*, 31 (11): 1201–31.

Linee Guida Nazionali (2012) *L'ascolto del minore testimone*, Rome, Italy. Retrieved from: http://scuolasuperioreavvocatura.it/wp-content/uploads/2014/09/Linee-guida-nazionali-Lascolto-del-minore-testimone.pdf.

Mazzoni, G. and Rotriquenz, E. (eds) (2012) *La testimonianza nei casi di abuso sessuale sui minori* (Vol. 53). Giuffrè editore.

Memon, A. and Higham, P. A. (1999) "A review of the cognitive interview," *Psychology, Crime and Law*, 5 (1–2): 177–96.

Saywitz, K. J., Geiselman, R. E., and Bornstein, G. K. (1992) "Effects of cognitive interviewing and practice on children's recall performance," *Journal of Applied Psychology*, 77 (5): 744.

Società italiana di neuropsichiatria dell'infanzia, and dell'adolescenza (SINPIA) (2007) *Linee guida in tema di abuso sui minori*. Edizioni Erickson. Retrieved from: http://www.psicologiagiuridica.net/wp-content/uploads/2008/06/sinpia.pdf.

Spangher, G. (2012) *Codice di procedura penale*. G Giappichelli Editore.

Steller, M. and Köhnken, G. (1989) "Criteria-based statement analysis," in D. C. Raskin (ed.), *Psychological Methods in Criminal Investigation and Evidence*. New York: Springer-Verlag, pp. 217–45.

Sternberg, K. J., Lamb, M. E., Davies, G. M., and Westcott, H. L. (2001) "The memorandum of good practice: theory versus application," *Child Abuse and Neglect*, 25 (5): 669–81.

UNICEF (2012) *L'ascolto dei minorenni in ambito giudiziario*. Italy. Retrieved from: http://www.unicef.it/Allegati/Ascolto_minori_ambito_giudiiziario_2012_1.pdf.

US Supreme Court (1993) *Daubert* v. *Merrell Dow Pharmaceuticals, Inc*. 509 US 579. Retrieved from: https://supreme.justia.com/cases/federal/us/509/579/#annotation.

Warren, A. R., Woodall, C. E., Thomas, M., Nunno, M., Keeney, J., Larson, S., and Stadfeld, J. (1999) "Assessing the effectiveness of a training program for interviewing child witnesses," *Applied Developmental Science*, 3 (2): 128–35.

Yuille, J. C. and Cutshall, J. (1989) "Analysis of the statements of victims, witnesses and suspects," in J. C. Yuille (ed.), *Credibility Assessment*. Dordrecht: Kluwer Academic, pp. 175–91.

Zulawski, D. E., Wicklander, D. E., Sturman, S. G., and Hoover, L. W. (2001) *Practical Aspects of Interview and Interrogation*. CRC Press.

14 Interviewing witnesses in the Netherlands

Imke Rispens and Jannie van der Sleen

Introduction

In the Netherlands, in accordance with the Code of Criminal Procedure (Art. 338 Sv), it is only possible to assume that the suspect has committed the crime he is charged with if the court is convinced by the contents of the legal evidence at the hearing (the immediacy principle). As legal evidence only the following is recognised (Art. 339 Sv): observation by the court, statements of the accused, witness statements, expert statements, written documents. A witness statement means: information given in the investigation at the trial of facts or circumstances which he himself has observed or experienced (Art. 342 Sv). Since 1926, however, the immediacy principle has been greatly weakened in the Netherlands by the admission of hearsay statements (hearsay evidence) (Supreme Court Decision, December 20, 1926, NJ 1927, 85 – the hearsay judgment). In a hearsay statement, the witness testifies as to what he heard from another person. The Supreme Court ruled in 1926 that the content of that statement of hearsay may be part of the evidence. In this particular judgment, the Supreme Court also accepted as evidence a report by an investigating officer that included a witness statement.

Criminal procedural law in the Netherlands does not have the 'best evidence principle'. The judge is not required to hear a witness at the hearing if his statement is included in an official report. The court may rely solely on the official police report. Moreover, the testimony of a witness at the hearing has no more evidential value than an earlier statement that the witness gave to the police. This means that relatively few witnesses in the Netherlands are interviewed by the investigating judge or at the hearing. It is only if the defence or the prosecutor submits a motivated request that a witness is called to appear at the hearing.

The consequence of this is that great importance is attached to statements that witnesses have made to the police. A huge responsibility rests on the police to interview a witness in the correct manner and to record this as well as possible.

History

It is only since the early 1980s that attention has been paid to the training of police officers in communication skills for interviewing. Initially, they only practised a number of specific communication techniques (including attentive behaviour, open questioning, summarising, how to cope with the feelings of the interviewee). In the training of detectives, basic theory lessons were also given on perception and memory. These lessons mainly focused on detectives' awareness of the problem that witness statements are susceptible to perception and memory errors and therefore cannot simply be accepted on face value as true. Any relationship between the content of the testimony and communication techniques used by the investigator during the recording of the statement was not yet clearly established.

Because psychologists became involved with the education of the detectives, the research that was carried out in the United States by, for example, Elizabeth Loftus (Loftus, 1979) entered into the training of detectives in the Netherlands. In addition, there were a number of prominent Dutch academics, for instance Wagenaar, Crombag and Van Koppen, who had 'thrown themselves' into legal psychology, including the problems concerning witness testimony. In the textbook for detectives *Learning to Investigate* which first appeared in 1988 (Criminal Investigation College Zutphen, 1988), much attention was paid to the way a witness was to be interviewed. The importance of 'the witness's own story/free recall' was already explicitly discussed in that publication. Since then, interviewing witnesses has developed considerably. The scientific research that has been conducted in recent years, especially abroad, in conjunction with practical experience, has led to two witness examination models in which detectives are now being trained: 'the generic witness interview model' and 'the scenario model for interviewing vulnerable witnesses'.

'The generic witness interview model' was developed at the Police Academy starting in 1991 (Amelsvoort *et al.*, 2015). The scenario model for interviewing vulnerable witnesses originated with the police in Amsterdam where they laid the foundation for the interviewing of children by detectives. Initially, interviewing children in the Netherlands was done by care providers (psychologists and special educators). By 1989, however, the belief originated that interviewing children in an investigation, just as with the interviewing of adult witnesses, is a matter for the police. As a result, a training programme was developed by the police in Amsterdam, initially for a small group of vice detectives, and a child-friendly interview studio was set up equipped with audio-visual recording equipment. In 1991, training for detectives was transferred to the Police Academy and was taught throughout the country. In addition to the interviewing of children, the interviewing of mentally handicapped witnesses was also part of the training. Since 2013, attention has also been paid to other vulnerable witnesses, such as witnesses with cognitive impairments or mental disorders. More child-friendly interview studios were set up (currently there are 11 such interview studios in the Netherlands). The separate elements were merged into a structured interview model: the scenario model for interviewing vulnerable witnesses (Dekens and Van der Sleen, 2013).

Guidelines

In the legal world, people have become increasingly convinced of the importance of verifiability over the manner in which witnesses are interviewed, particularly in regard to the risk of being influenced by the interviewer. Also of importance are qualified interviewers in cases where vulnerable witnesses are to be interviewed. This has led to two major directives from the Board of Procurators General (the Board of the Public Prosecution Service): the Directive for the Investigation and Prosecution of Cases of Sexual Abuse (2010) and the Instructions for Auditory and Audio-visual Recording of Interviews of Informants, Witnesses and Suspects (2011). Since 2005 and 2006, respectively, there had already been precursors of these directives.

The Instructions for Auditory and Audio-Visual Recording of Investigative Interviews of Informants, Witnesses and Suspects (henceforth abbreviated to Directive AVR) dictates the circumstances under which an interview shall be recorded with auditory and/or audio-visual equipment. Whether an interview is or is not to be auditorily registered depends on the nature of the crime, the vulnerability of the witness/suspect or the situation during the investigative interview. Interviews of suspects and the planned interviews of witnesses and informants for offences set out in the Code of (Military) Criminal Law must, at least, be recorded auditorily:

- if there is a deceased victim;
- if the penalty carried by the offence is 12 years imprisonment or more;
- if the penalty carried by the offence is less than 12 years and there is obvious serious bodily injury;
- if it concerns a sexual offence with a maximum sentence of eight years or more, or sexual abuse in a relationship.

If there is also a vulnerable person involved or the witness interview is carried out or supported by a behavioural expert, it must be recorded with audio-visual equipment. The following are designated as vulnerable persons:

- minor children under 12 years old (for this youngest group there are special guidelines);
- minor children between 12 and 16 years old;
- persons with intellectual disabilities;
- persons with cognitive impairments.

In the Directive on the Investigation and Prosecution of Cases of Sexual Abuse (2010) it states that, in investigative interviews on sexual offences of minors under 12 years of age, persons with intellectual disabilities and persons with cognitive impairment, the interviews of witnesses and informants must be carried out by a specialist interviewer. This is an investigating officer who conducts the interview in a child-friendly studio and who is certified via the training course 'Interviewing Vulnerable Witnesses in Sexual Abuse Cases' at the Police Academy or is currently undertaking this training course. If the latter is the case, the interview takes place under the supervision of an instructor from the training course. In addition, the interviewer must be a qualified (i.e. certified) vice detective. If necessary, during the preparation of the interview, a behavioural expert who has expertise in the field of people with intellectual disabilities may be consulted. This may include help with the 'translation' of any psychological reporting on the witness to the interview situation and/or advice on the particular mode of communication during the interview. If necessary, this behavioural expert could coach the interviewer during the interview from the control room. In exceptional cases, a behavioural expert may conduct the interview him/herself, for example where the interview can only take place when very special communication techniques are employed. The public prosecutor is responsible for this decision. According to the Directive AVR children between 12 and 16 years old are considered vulnerable, but there is no guideline in that directive (or any other directive) that prescribes who has to interview these children and how.

For the interview of (vulnerable) witnesses, the guidelines in the Directive AVR apply unless it is a sexual abuse case. In this case, the guidelines in the Directive for the Investigation and Prosecution of Cases of Sexual Abuse also apply. When children or people with cognitive disabilities are possible victims of a sexual offence, there is first a so-called 'informative meeting'. This may be with the person him/herself, but in most cases this is with a counsellor, parent or guardian speaking on behalf of the person in question. After the informative meeting, there is some reflection time (about two weeks) after which the person can press charges. This is often the time when the reporting party (e.g. the child) him/herself, is interviewed. A child is interviewed in the child-friendly interview studio. People with intellectual disabilities, who are to be interviewed in a sexual abuse case as witnesses, are interviewed by a specialist interviewer. The place of the interview can be the child-friendly interview studio but may also be a 'normal' interview room.

In a non-sexual offence case, it is not regulated who may conduct the interview. In police practice, generally a specialist interviewer is brought in for interviewing the witness if capacity is available and if it is known in advance that this concerns a person with an intellectual disability.

Description of current practice

Interviewing witnesses

In the Netherlands, a distinction is made between interviewing adult 'normal' (eye)witnesses and interviewing vulnerable witnesses. For each group, there is a separate interview model.

The most commonly used method for interviewing adult witnesses/eyewitnesses is called 'the generic witness interview model' (Amelsvoort *et al.*, 2015). This interview model consists of three phases: opening, asking case-oriented questions and closing. Each phase contains a number of activities which the police officer must perform during the interview with the witness. In the opening phase, there is an explanation of the interview and what follows afterwards. The interviewer also says that he/she is going to take notes during the interview. Only after everything is clear to the witness and any questions, comments or emotions have been discussed does the case-oriented part of the interview commence. The opening and closing of this interview method are not discussed in detail here because they are pretty standard. The case-oriented section consists of six steps as follows (see Table 14.1).

1. Obtain free recall and give instruction 'report everything'

The questioning structure begins by asking an opening question in order to get free recall from the witness. This question is supplemented with the explicit instruction to the witness to tell everything he/she experienced, every detail, no matter how insignificant it may seem. As a general rule, the witness will, in fact, make a selection him/herself in his/her testimony based on what he/she thinks is important for the police. The interviewer listens actively and takes notes of the free recall of the witness. At the end of his/her story, a summary follows to check whether the story of the witness was well understood. Possibly, context reinstatement may be helpful in retrieving the memory of the witness, but this is not an explicit part of this interview method.

2. Determine the viewing conditions

When estimating the reliability of the observation of the witness, the internal and external conditions of observation are also significant. After the free recall, the interviewer questions the witness about these viewing conditions and has the witness make a situation sketch. Thus the interviewer gets a picture of what the situation was, what the witness may have observed and under what circumstances. The reason the witness is asked to make the sketch is that it often provides answers to many questions about the conditions of observation.

Table 14.1 Generic witness interview model – case-oriented questioning phase

Step	*Content*
1	Obtain free recall and give instruction 'report everything'.
2	Determine the viewing conditions under which the witness observed the incident and provide a sketch of the scene.
3	Determine what topics the witness should be further questioned about.
4	Ask questions by topic: 1st subject a. Obtain a cued free recall. b. Ask further questions on the free recall and ask control questions. 2nd subject 3rd subject, etc.
5	If necessary, ask additional questions as a result of research data and/or experience.
6	Ask what information the witness got from third-parties.

Examples determining the viewing conditions
'Can you describe and draw for me what the situation at the scene was?'
'What was the distance between you and the perpetrator?'
'What kind of weather was it at that time?'
'What kind of lighting was there at the scene?'
'How long did you see him?'
'To what extent did you have a clear view of the perpetrator?'
'How did you feel at that time?
'How is your vision?'

Figure 14.1 Examples of step 2.

The interviewer may also use, as a tool, a map of the crime scene (with no traces on it). This step can also be combined with step 1. Figure 14.1 is an example of step 2.

3. *Determine the topics for further questioning*

A witness often mentions several (sub) topics in his free recall. In the continuation of the interview, the interviewer must mention these topics and indicate that there will be further questions on each topic.

4. *Ask questions by topic*

Each topic starts with an opening question in order to obtain a cued free recall about that topic. In response to what the witness states, the interviewer asks questions and assesses the witness's statements by asking control questions (asking how he knows this) (see Figure 14.2). In this way, all the issues that the witness has stated in his free recall will be further questioned, unless the issues are not relevant to the investigation.

5. *Ask additional questions*

Thus far, the witness has made a statement which is based on his/her own experiences and frame of reference. Usually, there are remaining issues about which the interviewer must ask questions. These questions are based on investigative data or experience, or are necessary for informing police files, e.g. ViCLAS. Also, there could be specific questions that have to do with the unfurling of various scenarios in the police investigation. As these questions may well influence witness's account, the interviewer should wait to ask them until the end of the interview (after an account has been obtained), providing the witness with

Examples of cued free recall questions

'You said you saw a car. Tell me everything about the car.

'You mentioned a man with a gun. Tell me everything about the man.

'Tell me everything about the weapon.

Examples of control questions

'You say that you think that the perpetrator is a Surinamese? Why do you think that?

'You say that the perpetrator is about 1.90 m. How do you know that?

Figure 14.2 Examples of step 4.

instructions not to guess and also to indicate when he/she does not know the answer.

6. Ask what information the witness received from third parties

Finally, the interviewer must ask the witness whether or not he/she received information from third parties (post-event information). This may include information from the media, the Internet, information and/or statements from other witnesses or gossip from the neighbourhood. Reading or hearing this post-event information about the incident or talking to someone may have affected the witness's memory of the incident. This question is asked in order to obtain an insight into potential influencing.

When everything has been discussed, the interview is completed and later put into a report. This is done on the basis of the recording of the interview and/or notes from the interviewer. Sometimes this even happens during the interview for practical reasons.

Scientific, theoretical and practical support

There have been two Dutch studies in which the generic witness interview model has been examined. Thiecke (1997) compared the method of the generic witness interview model to another interview method, namely guided memory. In 2003, three methods were compared: the generic witness interview, guided memory and the cognitive interview (Van Maastricht, 2003). The comparison showed no differences in the number of correct and incorrect details obtained. However, to obtain the same number of details more questions are necessary in the generic witness interview. In spite of the limited study of the method in its entirety, the model is constructed from separate components the value of which have already been proven by foreign studies or based on how the memory works. This is done, for example, by encouraging the (cued) free recall and instruction 'report everything' (Memon *et al.*, 1997). Having a witness draw a situation sketch is effective for retrieving the memories, because the witness is forced to make use of context reinstatement (Dando *et al.*, 2011). Querying the viewing conditions is meant to allow insight into the factors that may have influenced perception, the so-called estimator variables (Cutler *et al.*, 1987). The sixth stage, asking about information from third parties, is intended to obtain insight into potential post-event information. A great deal of research has shown that seeing or hearing information after an event may affect the memory of that event (Davis and Loftus, 1997; Crombag *et al.*, 1996). As such, it makes sense to ask the witness about this so that it can be taken into account when estimating the reliability of the witness statement.

Interviewing vulnerable witnesses

The scenario model for interviewing vulnerable witnesses is a structured interview model and is used to gain the most complete and accurate testimony from a vulnerable witness. The scenario model is developed for questioning in sexual abuse cases (when there are suspicions of sexual abuse). The model is, however, also suitable for the examination of vulnerable witnesses in other cases. Depending on the case, sometimes adjustments are necessary. The model is based on scientific research summarised in two textbooks: *Children's Testimony* (Westcott *et al.*, 2002) and *Tell Me What Happened* (Lamb *et al.*, 2008). The model is also based upon 25 years of experience in the Netherlands in interviewing vulnerable witnesses in police practice. The scenario model consists of the steps shown in Table 14.2.

In the introduction phase, the interviewer collects the witness and the parents/guardians from the waiting room. They are then given a tour of the interview room and the control room and are given an explanation about the interviewing procedure to be undertaken as well as being provided with information concerning the recording equipment and the monitoring by police officers from the control room. Then the parents/guardians return to the waiting room and the

Table 14.2 Scenario model

Step	*Content*
1	Introduction
2	Case-oriented interview: • Opening question • If the witness immediately starts talking: Scenario A • If the witness does not start talking: Scenario B • If Scenario B yields no information: Scenario C: confront with case information
3	Closing

witness goes with the interviewer to the interview room. Parents/guardians do not watch the interview, as this may influence the statements of the witness. The interviewer tells the witness that even though he is not wearing a police uniform, he works with the police. He also explains that the witness can tell him everything and that the interviewer will never become angry, will never punish the witness and will never judge anything that is said as weird or unusual. The interviewer then gives the witness the choice: he/she can immediately tell why he/she came or first have a chat, draw for a bit or play a game. If the witness chooses to chat, the interviewer tries to encourage the witness as much as possible to engage in a general and cued free recall about a topic that is interesting for the witness but not case-oriented. In this way, the interviewer trains the witness to tell him what happened as comprehensively as possible. This is something that is needed during the case-oriented interview. Also, the interviewer takes the witness through a number of ground rules and tests the witness's understanding using examples. The ground rules are:

- 'If you do not know or remember something, you can tell me.'
- 'If you do not understand something, you can tell me.'
- 'If I say something wrong, you should correct me.'
- 'I might ask some questions twice. That is not because you gave a wrong answer the first time, but because I forgot the answer. You can then just tell me again what happened.'

In the case-oriented interview, the interviewer starts with a neutral opening question, for example: 'What have you come to tell me?' or 'What have you come to talk about?' Then the interviewer asks the witness to report as much as possible in his own words (free recall). If the witness immediately starts talking about details of the case, then the interviewer starts with Scenario A. In this, they repeatedly encourage the witness to tell as much and as extensively as possible in their own words. The interviewer repeatedly checks, by summarising, to make sure that he has always understood exactly what the witness told him. He then asks additional questions. The interviewer indicates that he was not there when the original incident(s) occurred and therefore does not know exactly what happened. And that is why he is asking questions. If necessary, during the questioning, the interviewer repeats the ground rules. For example, when a witness takes a really long time to answer a question, the interviewer can repeat that it is also OK to say 'I don't know'.

If the witness says he does not know why he has been called to give a statement, then the interviewer asks so-called alternative opening questions. In total, there are four possibilities. For each of these questions it is possible that the witness will start to talk on his own and then the interviewer can continue with Scenario A (see Table 14.2 above). For example, the interviewer asks who advised the witness to come to the interview room and what that person actually said about it. Or the interviewer asks: 'Do you really not know, do you find it difficult to get started, do you find it unusual, don't you feel like doing this or is there something else?' The other two alternative opening questions are: 'Is it about you or someone else?' and 'Is it about something nice or something that was not nice?' If the witness does not respond to these questions, the interviewer starts with Scenario B (see Figure 14.3 for an example). In this scenario, the interviewer tries a detour to get onto the subject about which the child may have something to say. This could be done, for example, by asking questions about the everyday life of the witness or the witness's relationship with neutral persons and with the suspect. If the witness offers information that is related to the case, then the interviewer moves on to Scenario A and asks 'free recall'. If that does not happen, then the interviewer could move on to Scenario C.

In Scenario C, the interviewer, after consultation with the people sitting in the control room, introduces relatively neutral information about the allegation. The principle is that the name of the suspect and the sexual acts mentioned in the allegation are not mentioned to the witness. Also, from whom the information comes from, the source, must not be mentioned. The reason for this is that the witness must be prevented from feeling that he is 'leaving the source in the lurch' if they say that the information is not correct. For example, it can be difficult for a child to contradict what the caregivers (if they are the source) have said. And, because of that, the witness gives incorrect information. What could be given, for example, is a location or the moment of disclosure. If the witness then begins to talk, the interviewer switches to Scenario A. If the witness says he does not know or says that the information is incorrect, then the interviewer (possibly after a short follow-up question) closes the interview.

In the closing phase, the witness is then asked if he has anything to add or have any questions, what his feelings are about the interview. He then receives a compliment, for example: 'Thank you for coming here to talk to me. You did really well.'

The scenario model rests on three pillars:

- *The avoidance of influencing the witness.* This is achieved by providing and enforcing ground rules for the hearing, asking for free recall as much as possible, asking as few closed questions as possible, and by reacting neutrally to the emotions of the witness and refraining from giving positive or negative feedback on the responses of the witness.
- *The fullest possible evidence gathering.* This means, on the one hand, that as many details as possible are collected about the alleged sexual acts about

> *Example Scenario B (witness was possibly abused by an uncle when staying there)*
>
> 'Where do you sleep at home? Who do you sometimes go to stay with? Who do you like to stay with? Who don't you like to stay with? Who did you stay with the last time? How did that go?'

Figure 14.3 Example of Scenario B.

which the witness reports but, on the other hand, alternative scenarios for the origin of the witness's story are examined. Is it possible that the witness was influenced prior to the interview? Is it possible that there may be a misunderstanding whereby innocent actions were interpreted as sexual abuse? Could the witness have fabricated the story?

- *Adapting to the witness*. For each witness, an assessment must be conducted to determine what this person needs in order to be able to tell his/her story as well as possible. For example, how long should the introduction phase take? How should the interviewer be structured? What should the pace of the interview be? How should the language of the interviewer be adapted to the witness? How long should the interview last? To what extent are breaks necessary in the case-oriented part of the interview?

Training

Training in interviewing, including witness interviewing, is given by the Police Academy. In the basic police officer training, basic knowledge of the interview model for witnesses in a simple case is included. In the training course for detectives, a total of six training days are spent on witness interviewing. Students must first study the theory on the 'generic witness interview model' and the effectiveness of perception and memory. During training, the theory is further explained, including the ZeG, the Dutch version of the Self-Administered Interview (see Gabbert *et al*., 2009). The training is further supported by practical demonstrations. Also, extracts from witness examinations are shown and discussed. Much attention is paid to the analysis of the reliability of witness statements and training for witness interviewing takes the form of role playing with actors.

The 'Professional Training in Interviewing' course, which is a training for investigative interviewing in complex cases, is undertaken over two days where the theory about witness interviewing is covered more deeply. In this course, several sub-skills are practised, including the use of context reinstatement, free recall and asking follow-up questions.

Questioning of vulnerable witnesses is addressed in the training course 'Interviewing Vulnerable Witnesses in Sexual Abuse Cases' (known in the Netherlands as 'VKGZ'). This is a specialised training course on witness interviewing that is only open to participants who have successfully completed a training course on investigative research in sexual abuse cases. The VKGZ covers a total of 252 study hours, spread over ten months. The course consists of 15 classroom days, three days of interview training, six interviews in police practice, one practical training day, two exams and one follow-up meeting. Independent study consists of studying educational materials via e-learning. During the classroom days, blended learning is used: besides e-learning, different didactic methods are used, e.g. lectures, tutorials, discussions, demos, role play. The theory is further deepened and clarified by watching interview fragments of real interviews with children and other vulnerable witnesses and the discussion of practical situations. Also, there is a great deal of practice, both among the students themselves and using actors as role models. In the interview training, the students can practise using the scenario model by carrying out conversations with real children about a non-traumatic event. In order to learn to become attuned to the target group of mentally disabled witnesses, the students must undertake an internship in an institution (one day) and also conduct interviews with residents, for example in an institution where people who are mentally disabled live or work. In the exams, they must show that they have mastered the scenario model and can apply it properly. A few months after graduating from the programme, students send one interview they carried out, along with the accompanying analysis, to an instructor. In groups of four students and one instructor, these interviews and analyses are then discussed.

Implications for research, policy and practice

In the Netherlands, thorough training is given in interviewing witnesses; the specialised training for interviewing vulnerable witnesses in particular is quite intensive. In other parts of the world, research conducted by Lamb *et al.* (2002), however, shows that interviewers (consciously or not) fall into old interviewing habits in the absence of supervision and expert feedback. In addition, they suggested that the interview skills learned dramatically deteriorated once supervision had ceased. Canadian research (Cyr *et al.*, 2012) showed that interviewers who received individual written feedback on an interview they conducted applied the interview protocol they had learned more often than interviewers who received no feedback on their interviews. Also, the interviewers who received feedback were more inclined to invite witnesses to give a free recall and the witnesses gave more central details. When supervision and written feedback cease, interviewers use fewer open questions and therefore get less information from a witness. In the VKGZ, therefore, there is one follow-up session included in the training course. After that, interviewers must organise their supervision themselves. Evaluation of one's own interviews, peer review and follow-up are essential and lead to better interviews (Smets, 2012). This should be standard police practice.

While the components of the generic witness interview model have been individually examined by researchers few studies have been conducted on the entire interview method. There have been two studies which compared different interview methods. The first study compared generic witness interview with guided memory. This study found no difference between the methods in the number of reporting details. The suggestion was that most witnesses use context reinstatement when they try to remember an incident, even when the interviewer asks explicitly not to do this (Thiecke *et al.*, 1996). The second study compared three methods: generic witness interview, guided memory and cognitive interview (Van Maastricht, 2003). The comparison showed that the generic witness interview elicited the same number of correct and incorrect details as the other methods. Moreover, no field research has been undertaken into the application of this method in practice, apart from hearing the experiences of interviewers in the training sessions and during practical advice by instructors. Because of this, there is insufficient insight into how the practical application of the generic interview model works. Instructors in the VKGZ training course coach many interviews of vulnerable witnesses in practice, which has resulted in a better insight into this area of expertise in police practice. The scenario model can, thus, still be further developed.

With the deployment of the ZeG, practical experience is gained, but there is still no question of national implementation. This tool and its application should be further developed.

Conclusion

In the Netherlands there is a long history of interviewing witnesses. In the 1980s it started with basic training in communication skills. Soon the training was further developed into an interview model for interviewing witnesses. In the 1990s training in interviewing vulnerable witnesses, especially children, was developed including a special interview model: the scenario model. Since then, these interview models have been further developed and updated according to the latest scientific results and experiences in police practice, as has been the training in these interview models: modern techniques such as e-learning are now being used. After the training in interviewing vulnerable witnesses, there is follow-up of the training to keep the competences of the interviewers up-to-date. The guidelines for witness interviewing are more recent. There are guidelines about recording the interview and about who should conduct the interview. Interviewing young witnesses of under the age of 12 years is seen as a specialty, so there are more guidelines for this kind of interview.

References

Amelsvoort, A. van, Rispens, I. and Grolman, H. (2015) *Handleiding verhoor* [*Handbook for Interviewing*]. Amsterdam: Stapel & De Koning.

Bertens, T. (2011) *Strafrecht and Strafvordering 2011/2012*, Elfde herziene editie [*Criminal Law and Criminal Proceedings 2011/2012*, 11th revised edn]. Nijmegen: Ars Aequi.

Board of Procurators General (2010) *The Directive for the Investigation and Prosecution of Cases of Sexual Abuse*. Ref: 2010A026.

Board of Procurators General (2011) *Instructions for Auditory and Audio-visual Recording of Interviews of Informants, Witnesses and Suspects*. Ref: 2010A018gp.

Criminal Investigation College Zutphen (1988) *Recherche(le)ren* (*Learning to Investigate*). Lelystad: Koninklijke Vermande.

Crombag, H. F. M., Wagenaar, W. A. and Koppen, P. J. (1996) 'Crashing memories and the problem of "source monitoring"', *Applied Cognitive Psychology*, 10: 95–104.

Cutler, B. L., Penrod, S. D. and Martens, T. K. (1987) 'The reliability of eyewitness identification: the role of system and estimator variables', *Law and Human Behaviour*, 11: 233–58.

Cyr, M., Dion, J., McDuff, P. and Trotier-Sylvain, K. (2012) 'Transfer of skills in the context of non-suggestive investigative interviews: impact of structured interview protocol and feedback', *Applied Cognitive Psychology*, 26: 516–24.

Dando, C. J., Wilcock, R., Behnkle, C. and Milne, R. (2011) 'Modifying the cognitive interview: countenancing forensic application by enhancing practicability', *Psychology, Crime and Law*, 17: 491–511.

Davis, D. and Loftus, E. F. (2007) 'Internal and external sources of misinformation in adult witness memory', in M. P. Toglia, J. D. Read, D. F. Ross and R. C. L. Lindsay (eds), *Handbook of Eyewitness Psychology: Volume 1: Memory for Events*. Mahwah, NJ: Erlbaum, pp. 195–237.

Dekens, K. and J. van der Sleen (2013) *Handleiding het kind als getuige. Derde druk*. Amsterdam: Reed Business Information.

Gabbert, F., Hope, L. and Fisher, R. (2009) 'Protecting eyewitness evidence: examining the efficacy of a self-administered interview tool', *Law and Human Behavior*, 33: 298–307.

Lamb, M. E., Hershkowitz, I., Orbach, Y. and Esplin, P. W. (2008) *Tell Me What Happened*. Chichester: Wiley.

Lamb, M. E., Sternberg, K. J., Orbach, Y., Esplin, P. W. and Mitchell, S. (2002) 'Is ongoing feedback necessary to maintain the quality of investigative interviewers with allegedly abused children?', *Applied Developmental Science*, 6: 35–41.

Loftus, E. F. (1979) *Eyewitness Testimony*. Cambridge, MA: Harvard University Press.

Memon, A., Wark, L., Bull, R. and Köhnken, G. (1997) 'Isolating the effects of the cognitive interview techniques', *British Journal of Psychology*, 88: 179–97.

Maastricht Forensic Institute (2012) *Werkboek Deskundige in Strafzaken* [*Workbook Expert in Criminal Cases*]. Heerlen: Open Universiteit/University of Maastricht.

Sijlbing, R. (1986) 'Beslissing in het rechercheonderwijs: evaluatie van een gesprekstraining' ['Decisions in detective education: evaluation of an interview training session'], *Algemeen Politieblad*, 19: 428–31.

Smets, L. (2012) *Police Investigative Interviewing: A New Training Approach*, Reeks Politiestudies nr. 3. Antwerpen/Apeldoorn: Maklu.

Thiecke, M. (1997) *Geleide herinnering versus standaard getuigenverhoor* [*Guided Memory Versus Standard Witnesses Examination*]. Zutphen: Rechercheschool [Criminal Investigation College].

Thiecke, M., Sijlbing, R. and Jackson, J. (1996) 'De opbrengst van het getuigenverhoorde relatie tussen verhoor en verklaring', *De Psycholoog*, pp. 472–7.

Van Maastricht, A. S. (2003) *Maximizing the Accuracy and Completeness of Eyewitness Reports: Which Technique Is Preferred?* Maastricht: University of Maastricht.

Westcott, H. L., Davies, G. M. and Bull, R. H. C. (2002) *Children's Testimony*. Chichester: Wiley.

15 Forensic interviewing of witnesses in Portugal

Carlos Eduardo Peixoto, Catarina Ribeiro, Raquel Veludo Fernandes and Telma Sousa Almeida

Introduction

In the past several years, many changes have occurred in Portuguese law and judicial proceedings concerning witnesses' protection, particularly with regard to the way alleged victims' statements are obtained. The Law no. 93/99 (Witness Protection Law (WPL)) addresses special measures to assure witnesses' protection in cases where their involvement may endanger their life, emotional and physical integrity, and property. By approving this law, the legislator wanted to guarantee that witnesses would be less reticent to cooperate, and more likely to provide and maintain their statements in forthcoming judicial procedures. This law establishes and regulates measures such as identity secrecy, use of teleconferencing and digital recording, police protection, and special procedures for vulnerable witnesses (e.g. children).

Nevertheless, the practical applications of such procedures seem not to achieve their main purposes, and witnesses are still the object of poor investigative approaches, especially in the context of information gathering. Also, only recently (Peixoto, Ribeiro, and Lamb, 2011; Peixoto, Ribeiro, and Alberto, 2013) has forensic interviewing received a more empirical research focus.Therefore, forensic interviewing, as an evidence-based approach, is still a new topic in the Portuguese judicial and academic contexts. Also, it has posed important challenges to criminal investigation and judicial decision-making, and began the development of an important body of psychological research. We share in this chapter some of those challenges and preliminary achievements. To date, much of the research has focused on the interviewing of child victim/witnesses and thus a majority of our review is on children and the special challenges they pose when interviewed in forensic settings.

Witnesses in the Portuguese judicial context

The Portuguese Criminal Procedure Code (PCPC) states the importance of evidence given by testimonies. For that reason, it regulates how such evidence should be obtained, stating that suggestive and intimidating questioning is not allowed. The PCPC also states that witnesses' testimony is obtained by the police, with the authorization of the Public Prosecutor Office. After a long tradition of written statements, Law no. 20/2013 recently introduced changes in the PCPC and ruled that statements should be video- or audio-recorded, and the written statement should be the exception.

Witnesses, according to the PCPC, have the right to refuse to give statements when the suspects are family members or have/had marital relations with them. The judicial authorities have the right to evaluate the capability of witnesses to testify, for example when the witnesses have cognitive impairments, psycopathologies, or are children.

Interviewing children

The Portuguese judicial system identifies children as a particular group of witnesses. A specific set of rules and procedures have been implemented to protect children during judicial proceedings. The PCPC, for example, prevents the public exposition of children during a trial concerning sexual crimes against children, by not allowing public attendance in the courtroom (No. 3, Art. 87 PCPC). Also, in those cases, the accused person is not allowed to be present in the courtroom during the alleged victim statements (Art. 352 PCPC), and the alleged victim is only interviewed by the presiding judge (Art. 349 PCPC).

In 1999 the WPL also stated that children are a vulnerable group of witnesses that should be heard in the shortest time possible (Art. 28), and that all measures must be implemented to guarantee the statement's spontaneity (Art. 26). Psychological support should be provided to the witness when necessary and the presence of a professional to support the witness is mandatory during the statement procedure (Art. 27). The WPL also states that special proceedings of anticipated evidence, called "Declarações para Memória Futura"[1,2] (DMF), should be requested.

The DMF is an early interview, conducted in the investigation stage, that can be used as evidence in a trial because it is a procedure presided over by a judge, who also, most of the time, conducts the interview. This procedure has the primary objective of preventing children from testifying in court. Since 2007, this procedure became mandatory for children who are alleged victims of sexual abuse. In the DMF, the child is interviewed by the judge, in the presence of the Public Prosecutor, the suspect's lawyer, and a psychologist who by law has the role of supporting the child. In spite of this, the law does not specify what kind of role or the level of involvement the psychologist should have during the DMF, although there have been some recommendations set to help these professionals (Caridade, Ferreira, and Carmo, 2011).

In May 2012, the Portuguese parliament approved a resolution that ratified the 2007 European Council Convention for Children's Protection Against Sexual Exploitation and Sexual Abuse. The European Council Convention advocates in article 35 that children's statements should be obtained as quickly as possible, in adapted premises, with interviews performed by specialized professionals, and, when it is necessary to repeat them, those interviews should be done by the same person. Also, the number of interviews must be limited and children, in some cases, should be accompanied by legal representatives or an adult of their choice. The Convention stresses the importance of interview video recording and its acceptance as evidence during trial proceedings.

The ratification of the Convention seems to have had repercussions on Portuguese law. Recently, there were changes in the PCPC that allowed criminal investigators to use video-recording in interviews with witnesses and suspects (Law no. 20/2013, February 21). This could be a key step in the development of forensic interviews in the Portuguese judicial context. The use of video-recording will allow full observation of the interviewer/interviewee interaction, generating data for quality assessment and supervision input. More importantly, it will allow criminal investigators to develop better interview techniques and increase the amount of reliable and comprehensive information. Hopefully, this change will reduce the number of times children are interviewed. Nevertheless, despite this change, the video-recorded interview conducted by criminal investigators is still not allowed as evidence in court, unless it is made in the presence of a prosecutor or judge. This legal requisite maintains the need, in most cases, to repeat children's interviews.

Research on interview and interrogation practices

As mentioned above, research in forensic interviewing is still in its early stages. Nevertheless, in the last ten years, a more comprehensive and empirical focus has been established on the study of testimony, particularly child interviewing.

In the case of adult witnesses, the main focus of research and public policy has been victims of domestic violence. To address this type of witness, several guidelines have been published on how to deal with and interview them (e.g. Manita, Ribeiro, and Peixoto, 2009), and police intervention (MAI, 2013). The Ministry of Home Affairs (MAI) created in 2013 a Police Work Manual in cases of domestic violence where the issue of interviewing victims and other witnesses is addressed. In the manual, investigative interviewing roles and their importance in domestic violence criminal investigation are extensively discussed. Issues such as the influence of domestic violence dynamics (e.g. feelings of guilt, fear for the consequences for their children), choice and adaptation of where the interview is conducted, and managing reluctance and retraction are addressed. Also, the manual contains an in-depth description of the Cognitive Interview, summarizing some of the underlying research, explaining the steps and giving examples of questions.

As mentioned above, children are often interviewed in criminal cases, particularly in sexual abuse cases. In 2009 Catarina Ribeiro conducted a pioneer study in Portugal into the representation of children involved in sexual abuse cases. In her study, among other important aspects, she focused on the number of interviews that children were submitted to in formal procedures. An average of eight interviews was a disturbing finding. Those interviews were done by several professionals, with different roles (e.g. police, social worker, forensic psychologist, forensic medical doctor, prosecutor, judge) and, apparently, without any particular technique or interview protocol. This study highlighted that the repeated questioning developed in the children feelings of ambivalence, distrust, and resistance towards the investigative process and the professionals involved.

Research on sexual abuse cases also demonstrated that the excessive number of interviews conducted with children happens when other types of evidence are present. Peixoto (2012) analyzed cases where biological (e.g. DNA of the alleged perpetrator found in the victim) and physical (e.g. anal or vaginal lacerations) signs were highly supportive of the occurrence of sexual abuse. Even in those cases, children were interviewed between four and nine times by several professionals.

Other important research has been conducted, mostly in the context of memory and suggestibility research. Costa and Pinho (2010) collected data suggesting that social desirability has an important role in the determination of suggestibility in nine year olds, mainly if it is related to the child's intelligence and memory deficits. Cunha (2010) also found that high levels of intelligence seem to be protective against suggestibility, decreasing the likelihood of children with better intellectual performance accepting false information.

Guidelines on child interviewing

The Portuguese scientific literature on child interviewing is characterized by general references about best practices and interview protocols. Most of these references are included in textbook chapters (Machado, 2002; Machado and Antunes, 2005; Machado, Caridade and Antunes, 2011; Magalhães, Ribeiro, Jardim *et al.*, 2010) or literature review papers (Manita, 2003; Machado, 2005; Magalhães and Ribeiro, 2007) about forensic psychological assessment or credibility assessment of child sexual abuse allegations.

In 2002, the Associação de Apoio à Vítima[3] (APAV) published intervention guidelines in sexual abuse cases. These guidelines focus on several aspects of intervention such as the current legislation and judicial procedures, advice about psychological and social support, as well as practical advice, such as how to fill out a report and conduct an interview with the child. With regard to this latter aspect, the guidelines point out important features of an interview: the development of rapport; the establishment of ground rules; being asked to tell only the truth; the use of open-ended questions to elicit a spontaneous narrative. Nevertheless, these guidelines are still only general ideas, lacking a more extensive approach to child interviewing, for example describing or citing fundamental research and interview protocols.

Other guidelines have been published, for example for police officers (CNPCJR, 2011a) and child protection professionals (CNPCJR, 2011b). These guidelines are also only general and the interview is not the sole focus. Nevertheless, the guidelines for police officers (CNPCJR, 2011a) describe the cognitive interview (Fisher and Geiselman, 1992) phases and characteristics, and advocate it as an interview protocol for child interviewing.

Adaptation of the NICHD investigative interview protocol to the Portuguese context

As we already pointed out, research-based interview protocols and practices in the Portuguese context are still scarce. To fill this gap we initiated research into the implementation of a structured interview protocol using the NICHD Investigative Interview Protocol (Peixoto, Ribeiro and Lamb, 2011; Peixoto, Ribeiro and Alberto, 2013).

Because forensic interviewers worldwide often have difficulty following recommended interview practices in the field, Professor Michael Lamb and his colleagues (Lamb, Hershkowitz, Orbach *et al.*, 2008) developed the fully structured NICHD Interview Protocol. This protocol is currently mandatory for forensic interviewers in several countries (e.g. Canada, Israel, parts of the USA), taught as "state-of-the-art" guidelines (e.g. England, Finland, Scotland, Sweden, Wales), and is being studied and adapted in others (e.g. Chile, Brazil, Korea, Japan).

For these reasons, Peixoto, Alberto and Ribeiro (2011) chose to adapt to the Portuguese context the NICHD Interview Protocol, given its ecological validity which replicates the approach used by forensic interviewers in many countries and is consistent with best-practice guidelines advocated by research and practitioner groups (Lamb, Hershkowitz, Orbach *et al.*, 2008). The adaptation process consists of a translation phase, a linguistic and cognitive review phase, an applicability phase, and a phase to test its legal usefulness.

First, the NICHD protocol was translated into Portuguese by three independent translators who individually proposed a translation and after a joint review developed a final Portuguese version of the protocol. Secondly, the authors made sure there was a connection between the verbatim language used and the cognitive processes that they intended to prompt. Translating the expression "tell me" posed a challenge, given its multiple translation options in portuguese: "conta-me", "fala-me", "diz-me". The more intuitive translation ("conta-me") is semantically similar to a word associated with fantasy and fairytale stories ("conto"), therefore further testing was required. The three translation options were compared using a sample of 109 4–15 year olds, divided into three groups. The same video was shown to each group and they were later interviewed with the Portuguese version of the protocol. The interviewer used only one of the "tell me" translation options with each group. Contrary to their hypotheses, the authors found that the expression "conta-me" prompted fewer errors and suppositions than the other translation options. It would seem that children are more familiar with this expression and are more predisposed to respond to it. So a final Portuguese version of the NICHD protocol using the expression "conta-me" was developed.

Second, the Portuguese version of the protocol was tested in actual forensic cases. In order to observe whether the Portuguese version of the NICHD Investigative Interview Protocol yielded similar results to other versions of the protocol, 33 interviews were conducted in real cases of alleged sexual abuse.

All interviews were carried out with children between four and six years old, male (N = 6) and female (N = 27), in forensic psychological assessment settings.

In this study, all interviews were transcribed verbatim from digital audio recordings. All interviewer or child utterances (including facilitative utterances such as "mmhmm" or "uh huh") were transcribed. Interviews were coded according to the scheme used and developed by Lamb and colleagues (Lamb, Hershkowitz, Sternberg *et al.*, 1996; Lamb, Hershkowitz, Orbach *et al.*, 2008). This coding scheme categorizes interviewers' utterances and children's responses. For the purposes of this study, we focused on the parts of each interview concerned with substantive information (interviewers' statements or questions and child responses that focused on anything that happened during the event being investigated), therefore excluding introductory exchanges at the beginning of the interview or within the substantive part, attempts to establish rapport with the child, digressions, and attempts at the end of the interview to discuss neutral topics.

The interviewers' utterances, which are defined as a "turn" in the discourse or conversation, were coded as invitations or *open-ended prompts* (e.g. "Tell me everything that happened from the beginning to the end."), *cued invitations* (e.g. "You mentioned [content mentioned by the child], tell me about that"), *directive prompts* (are "cued-recall" prompts, mostly wh- questions: who, what, when, where, how – e.g. "You said [child's words]. What do you mean?"), *option posing prompts* (are utterances that focus the child's attention on aspects of the account that the child did not previously mention, e.g. "Were the toys on the table when this happened?") or *suggestive prompts* (assume incident-related information that has not been disclosed by the child earlier in the interview and imply that a particular response is expected). The total number of each type of utterance used by the interviewer and the total number of words for children's responses to each type of interviewer utterance were counted.

The analysis of the 33 interviews revealed that most of the interviewers' utterances were *open-ended prompts* (48 percent), such as *invitations* or *cued invitations*, followed by *option-posing prompts* (38 percent), *directive prompts* (12 percent) and *suggestive prompts* (2 percent). Similarly, the majority of the children's words were provided in response to *open-ended prompts* (66 percent), followed by *option-posing* prompts (25 percent), *directive prompts* (8 percent), and, finally, *suggestive prompts* (1 percent). These results are similar to other studies using the NICHD protocol (Cyr and Lamb, 2009; Lamb, Sternberg, Orbach *et al.*, 2006; Orbach, Hershkowitz, Lamb *et al.*, 2000; Sternberg, Lamb, Orbach *et al.*, 2001). The data provided by our pilot study suggests that the Portuguese NICHD Investigative Interview Protocol version behaves similarly to other versions, particularly in terms of interviewer behavior and child responses. Also, our data corroborate the extensive literature describing the advantages of using open-ended questions when interviewing children about alleged abuse (Lamb, Hershkowitz, Orbach *et al.*, 2008; Lamb, La Rooy, Malloy *et al.*, 2010; Milne and Bull, 1999; Poole and Lamb, 1998; Westcott, Davies and Bull, 2002).

The final phase of the adaptation process consists of evaluating the extent to which the use of this protocol can improve Portuguese judicial procedures, thereby increasing the quantity and quality of the information provided by the children. To do so, we plan to compare interviews conducted using the Portuguese version of the NICHD protocol and DMF interviews conducted without any protocol. As we mentioned before, DMF is the only interview that can be later used as evidence in the trial and, therefore, implementing a structured interview protocol in this proceeding is likely to be extremely relevant and useful. The description of the current practices will allow us to have a baseline and to better understand the gains of using the NICHD protocol. Data (interviews conducted in DMF with 3–17 year olds, both male and female) were collected from several Portuguese judicial entities (e.g. courts, departments of criminal investigation) throughout the country and coded using the coding scheme developed by Lamb and his colleagues (Lamb, Hershkowitz, Sternberg *et al.*, 1996; Lamb, Hershkowitz, Orbach *et al.*, 2008). These data will be compared with the current child interview practices with the interviews conducted using the Portuguese version of the NICHD protocol.

In sum, with this study we hope to promote a better understanding of how children are interviewed in the Portuguese judicial context and contribute to an improvement in obtaining children's testimonies. Adapting the NICHD interview protocol to the Portuguese context is a step forward towards improving the way children are interviewed about witnessed or personally experienced crimes in Portugal. The NICHD protocol has been identified as the best example of applied science in children's interviewing (Saywitz, Lyon, and Goodman, 2011), recognition obtained through strong research empirically grounded (Lamb, Hershkowitz, Orbach *et al.*, 2008). Studies suggest that the NICHD protocol also enhances credibility assessments (Hershkowitz, Fisher, Lamb *et al.*, 2007; Hershokowitz, Lamb, and Orbach, 2008; Lamb, Sternberg, Esplin *et al.*, 1997), increasing the amount of information relevant for criminal investigation (Pipe, Orbach, Lamb *et al.*, 2013). Furthermore, recent evidence shows that when the NICHD protocol is used for interviewing young victims and witnesses, charges are more likely to be filed and suspects are more likely to be convicted at trial (Pipe, Orbach, Lamb *et al.*, 2013).

Implications for research, policy and practice

Although there are some guidelines on how witnesses' testimonies should be obtained, Portuguese interviewers do not completely adhere to the international best-practice guidelines in forensic interviewing in judicial proceedings, and professionals (e.g. judges and police officers) lack specialized training and ongoing supervision.

Also, even though professionals recognize that the forensic interview is a crucial moment in the criminal investigation process, legislation has not been implemented for mandatory procedures. In fact, there are some aspects of concern characterizing the way witnesses testimonies are currently obtained in Portugal:

- non-significant use of video-recording, use of audio recording only in DMF and court proceedings, and persistent use of written statements by the police;
- absence of a mandatory structured forensic interview protocol;
- lack of regular training (e.g. police officers undergo only general initial training on interview and interrogation techniques using the cognitive interview (Fisher and Geiselman, 1992) as a paradigm, with criminal investigators having more training on their specialty training course) and supervision;
- reliance on non-specialized interviewers;
- conducting interviews at the end of the investigation stage (most often witnesses make several statements to different people); and
- on occasions, in the case of children, requiring their statement in the trial, despite the presence of a DMF.

For these reasons, forensic interviewing in the Portuguese judicial context seems to be characterized by unsupported practices based mainly on experience and general guidelines. Although Portuguese criminal law emphasizes the importance and special care of witnesses, application of these legal statutes in real cases has met with several obstacles. Nevertheless, in the last ten years, an interest in a research-based approach to forensic interviewing, primarily with children, has grown, and important empirical data (Peixoto, Ribeiro, and Alberto, 2011) and recommendations (Peixoto, Ribeiro, and Alberto, 2013; Peixoto, Ribeiro, and Magalhães, 2013) have been generated. In this context, the study, training, and implementation of structured forensic interview protocols, such as the NICHD Investigative Interview Protocol, will have a decisive impact on the way children are interviewed in Portugal.

Acknowledgement

This chapter is supported by the Portuguese Science and Technology Foundation (FCT) (PTDC/MHC-PAP/4295/2012) and by the Operational Program for Competitive Factors (COMPETE) (CCOMP-01-0124-FEDER-029554).

Notes

1. Statement for Future Use.
2. Cf. Art. 271 of the Portuguese Criminal Procedure Code.
3. Portuguese Victim Support Association.

References

Associação Portuguesa de Apoio à Vítima (APAV) (2002) *Manual Core para atendimento de crianças vítimas de violência sexual*. Lisbon: Artes Gráficas Simões.

Caridade, S., Ferreira, C., and Carmo, R. (2011) "Declarações para Memória Futura de Menores Vítimas de Crimes Sexuais: Orientações para Técnicos Habilitados," in

M. Matos, R. A. Gonçalves, and C. Machado (eds), *Manual de psicologia forense: Contextos, práticas e desafios*. Braga: Psiquilibrios, pp. 65–85.

Comissão Nacional de Protecção de Crianças e Jovens em Risco (CNPCJR) (2011a) *Guia de orientações para os profissionais das forças de segurança na abordagem de situações de maus tratos*. Lisbon: CNPCJR.

Comissão Nacional de Protecção de Crianças e Jovens em Risco (CNPCJR) (2011b) *Guia de Orientações para os Profissionais da Acção Social na Abordagem de Situações de Maus Tratos ou Outras Situações de Perigo*. Lisbon: CNPCJR.

Costa, A. and Pinho, M. S. (2010) "Sugestionabilidade interrogativa em crianças de 8 e 9 anos de idade," *Análise Psicológica*, 28 (1): 193–208.

Cunha, A. (2010) *A sugestionabilidade interrogativa em crianças: O papel da idade e das competências cognitivas*. Braga: Universidade do Minho.

Cyr, M. and Lamb, M. E. (2009) "Assessing the effectiveness of the NICHD investigative interview protocol when interviewing French-speaking alleged victims of child sexual abuse in Quebec," *Child Abuse and Neglect*, 33 (5): 257–68.

Fisher, R. P. and Geiselman, R. E. (1992) *Memory-Enhancing Techniques for Investigative Interviewing: The Cognitive Interview*. Springfield, IL: Charles C. Thomas.

Hershkowitz, I., Lamb, M. E., and Orbach, Y. (2008) *The Effects of the NICHD Investigative Interview Protocol on the Assessment of Credibility in Child Sexual Abuse Allegations*. Paper presented to the American Psychology-Law Society Conference, Jacksonville, FL.

Hershkowitz, I., Fisher, S., Lamb, M. E., and Horowitz, D. (2007) "Improving credibility assessment in child sexual abuse allegations: the role of the NICHD Investigative Interview Protocol," *Child Abuse and Neglect*, 31 (2): 99–110.

Home Office (2011) *Achieving Best Evidence in Criminal Proceedings. Guidance on Interviewing Victims and Witnesses, and Using Special Measures*. London: Home Office.

Lamb, M. E., Hershkowitz, I., Orbach, Y., and Esplin, P. W. (2008) *Tell Me What Happened: Structured Investigative Interviews of Child Victims and Witnesses*. Chichester: Wiley-Blackwell.

Lamb, M. E., La Rooy, D. J., Malloy, L. C., and Katz, C. (2011) *Children's Testimony: A Handbook of Psychological Research and Forensic Practice*. Chichester: Wiley-Blackwell.

Lamb, M. E., Sternberg, K. J., Esplin, P. W., Hershkowitz, I., Orbach, Y., and Hovav, M. (1997) "Criterion-based content analysis: a field validation study," *Child Abuse and Neglect*, 21 (3): 255–64.

Lamb, M. E., Hershkowitz, I., Sternberg, K. J., Esplin, P. W., Hovav, M., Manor, T., and Yudilevitch, L. (1996) "Effects of investigative utterance types on Israeli children's responses," *International Journal of Behavioral Development*, 19 (3): 627–38.

Lamb, M. E., Sternberg, K. J., Orbach, Y., Aldridge, J., Bowler, L., Pearson, S., and Esplin, P. W. (2006) *Enhancing the Quality of Investigative Interviews by British Police Officers*. Paper presented at the Second International Investigative Interviewing Conference, University of Portsmouth, UK.

Machado, C. (2002) "Abuso sexual de crianças," in C. Machado and R. A. Gonçalves (eds), *Violência e vítimas de crime*, Vol. 2 *Crianças*. Coimbra: Quarteto, pp. 40–94.

Machado, C. (2005) "Avaliação da credibilidade de alegações de abuso sexual: Consensos e controvérsias," *Revista "Psicologia Educação Cultura,"* IX (2): 513–34.

Machado, C. and Antunes, C. (2005) "Avaliação de vítimas de abuso sexual," in R. A. Gonçalves and C. Machado (eds), *Psicologia forense*. Coimbra: Quarteto, pp. 207–29.

Machado, C., Caridade, S., and Antunes, C. (2011) "Avaliação psicológica de vítimas de abuso sexual," in M. Matos, R. A. Gonçalves, and C. Machado (eds), *Manual de psicologia forense: Contextos, práticas e desafios*. Braga: Psiquilibrios, pp. 91–122.

Magalhães, T. and Ribeiro, C. (2007) "A colheita de informação a vítimas de crimes sexuais," *Acta Médica Portuguesa*, 20: 439–45.

Magalhães, T., Ribeiro, C., Jardim, P., Peixoto, C., Oliveira, R., Abreu, C., Pinheiro, F., and Guerra, C. (2010) "Da Investigação inicial ao diagnóstico de abuso," in T. Magalhães (ed.) *Abuso de Crianças e Jovens: Da suspeita ao diagnóstico*. Lisbon-Porto: Lidel, pp. 147–88.

Manita, C. (2003) "Quando as portas do medo se abrem ... do impacto psicológico ao(s) testemunho(s) de crianças vítimas de abuso sexual," in *Actas do Encontro Cuidar da Justiça de Crianças e Jovens – A função dos Juízes Sociais*. Coimbra: Almedina, pp. 229–53.

Manita, C., Ribeiro, C., and Peixoto, C. E. (2009) *Violência Doméstica: Compreender para Intervir – guia de boas práticas para profissionais das forças de segurança*. Lisbon: CIG.

Milne, R. and Bull, R. (1999) *Investigative Interviewing: Psychology and Practice*. Chichester: Wiley.

Ministério da Administração Interna (MAI) (2013) *Manual de Policiamento da Violência Doméstica*. Lisbon: MAI

Orbach, Y., Hershkowitz, I., Lamb, M. E., Sternberg, K. J., Esplin, P. W., and Horowitz, D. (2000) "Assessing the value of structured protocols for forensic interviews of alleged child abuse victims," *Child Abuse and Neglect*, 24 (6): 733–52.

Peixoto, C. E. (2012) *Avaliação da credibilidade de alegações de abuso sexual de crianças –uma perspectiva psicológica forense*. Porto: FPCEUP.

Peixoto, C. E., Ribeiro, C., and Alberto, I. (2011) *The Portuguese Adaptation of the NICHD Forensic Interview Protocol: An Analysis of Some Psycholinguistic Variables*, in iIIRG International Conference, Dundee, Scotland.

Peixoto, C. E., Ribeiro, C., and Alberto, I. (2013) "O Protocolo de Entrevista Forense do NICHD: contributo na obtenção do testemunho da criança no contexto português," *Revista do Ministério Público*, 134: 181–219.

Peixoto, C. E., Ribeiro, C., and Lamb, M. E. (2011) "Forensic interview protocol in child sexual abuse. Why and what for?" in T. Magalhães (ed.), *Abuse and Neglect Series: To Improve the Management of Child Abuse and Neglect*, Vol. I. Porto: SPECAN, pp. 133–60.

Peixoto, C. E., Ribeiro, C., and Magalhães, T. (2013) "Entrevista forense de crianças alegadamente vítimas de abuso," in T. Magalhães and D. N. Vieira (eds), *Agressões Sexuais: Intervenção Pericial Integrada*, Vol. 2. Maia: SPECAN, pp. 75–102.

Pipe, M.-E., Orbach, Y., Lamb, M. E., Abbott, C. B., and Stewart, H. (2013) "Do case outcomes change when investigative interviewing practices change?" *Psychology, Public Policy, and Law*, 19 (2): 179.

Poole, D. A. and Lamb, M. E. (1998) *Investigative Interviews of Children: A Guide for Helping Professionals*. Washington, DC: American Psychological Association.

Ribeiro, C. (2009) *A criança na justiça: Trajectórias e significados do processo judicial de crianças vítimas de abuso sexual intrafamiliar*. Coimbra: Almedina.

Saywitz, K. J., Lyon, T. D., and Goodman, G. S. (2011) "Interviewing children," in J. E. B. Myers (ed.), *The APSAC Handbook on Child Maltreatment*. Newbury Park, CA: Sage, pp. 337–60.

Sternberg, K. J., Lamb, M. E., Orbach, Y., Esplin, P. W., and Mitchell, S. (2001) "Use of a structured investigative protocol enhances young children's responses to free-recall prompts in the course of forensic interviews," *Journal of Applied Psychology*, 86 (5): 997–1005.

Westcott, H., Davies, G., and Bull, R. (2002) *Children's Testimony: A Handbook of Psychological Research and Forensic Practice*. Chichester: Wiley.

16 Investigative interviewing in Scandinavia – witnesses and victims

Kristina Kepinska Jakobsen, Ivar A. Fahsing and Emma Roos af Hjelmsäter

Introduction

Scandinavia consists of Denmark, Sweden and Norway, three countries which are all highly stable welfare societies with very low crime rates and a high level of transparency. Indeed, the three Scandinavian countries do generally have very much in common – both socially, politically and culturally. This is true also when it comes to policing, legislation and many criminal investigation practices. In this chapter we will describe similarities and then describe some of the differences regarding education and research in the three countries.

Legislation and organisation of criminal investigations

The legislation when it comes to criminal law and criminal procedures law is quite similar within the region. Witnesses and victims of crime are not formally obliged to give statements to the police, but this is nevertheless how the vast majority of records and statements are collected during criminal investigations. It is required that a record is kept of all details of importance to the investigation and summaries of interviews shall be written down straight away by the investigator. The interviewee is given the opportunity to check, adjust and sign before the interview is filed. Sound and video recordings are obligatory for children and vulnerable adults.[1] For all other witnesses, recordings are not obligatory and statements might be written down as summaries by the investigator. In Sweden and Norway it is recommended that all interviews in serious crimes are taped and the recordings saved. In all three countries the prosecution service is formally responsible for leading the preliminary investigation from the time when someone can reasonably be suspected of an offence.[2] In Denmark and Norway parts of the prosecution service are integrated into the police organisation, while in Sweden it is an entirely separate organisation. The way that the responsibility for practical investigations are organised in the daily service varies between the countries and sometimes even from case to case. The court procedure in the three countries is predominantly adversarial but with inquisitorial elements. Fact-finding is primarily the prosecuting parties' responsibility, but the court can demand further investigation if it is not outside of the formal charge put forward by the prosecution service. All evidence is presented orally and directly to the court by the parties. Historically, victims of crime in Scandinavia have had the same legal position as any witness; this was, however, changed in Denmark in 2006 and in Norway in 2008 to strengthen the victim's rights, emotional welfare and evidential position before, under and after a criminal court process. Among a number of significant changes was the right to free legal counselling for all victims of sexual and violent crime prior to a formal police report. In Scandinavia, children do not have to testify in court. Instead, the child is interviewed in so-called children's houses during the pre-trial investigation and the recorded interview is shown in court. When it comes to investigative methods including interviewing, none of the countries has a general national code of conduct; nevertheless, relatively detailed and sound guidance is given in a variety of legislative documents. Even so, much of the practical responsibility of how to go about the task has been left up to the individual officer. On the other hand, when it comes to how children and other vulnerable witnesses should be interviewed, there are many specific and strict regulations.

Like many others countries, Denmark and Norway also learned hard-earned lessons through cases in the 1990s when children in therapy told stories about serious incidents of sexual assault. Three (in)famous cases were those of *Bjugn*, *Roum* and *Vadstrupgaard*, where horrific accusations of sexual abuse occurred. In two of these cases, however, almost all of the accusations were later deemed inadmissible in court and both cases have later been described as witch-hunt like processes due to the interviews with children being conducted unskilfully (Tange, 1995; Kringstad 1997).

Norway

In general the reliability of police interviews with witnesses and victims has not been met with much scepticism in Norway. However, in the so-called *Bjugn* case in 1993, the small community of Bjugn was tormented by widespread accusations of child sexual abuse. At first, the accusations were directed towards pre-school staff, but they quickly spread to include a number of leading members of the community, including the local sheriff. The local county board demonstrated its belief in some of the accusations by awarding financial compensation to the children. However, in the end none of the suspects were ever convicted and all of them were later also awarded financial compensation. Some of the children in Bjugn, but not all, have later retracted their accusations. The physical examinations, which were the most solid base of evidence that some abuse had occurred, are now no longer considered credible by unanimous expert opinion. The *Bjugn* case illustrates how administrative authorities, in contrast to the courts, are likely to believe in the truth of even outrageous accusations. Like other international cases the *Bjugn* case in Norway gave rise to a new regulation in 1998 concerning standards and the training regime when conducting interviews with children and vulnerable persons.

Training

In 2002, a basic investigative interviewing training course was commissioned by the National University College in Norway. The course is named KREATIV 1,[3] and is heavily influenced by the British PEACE course. Professor Ray Bull and DCI (retired) David Murthwaite (Merseyside Police) were brought to Norway to help educate the instructors and initiate the programme. The instructors are recruited from within the police force and since 2002 approximately 100 officers have completed the six-week trainer's course, covering topics such as pedagogy, human rights, ethical interviewing, interviewing and communication skills (the PEACE model), eyewitness memory, cognitive interviewing, interview strategy and false confessions.

The British PEACE course was evaluated by Clarke and Milne (2001) and several problems were identified. One such problem was that newly educated officers in England and Wales had to train others in the model, having only just completed a training course themselves with little or no centralised support. Over time the local trainer gradually included their own material and, as such, confusion arose as to what the PEACE model actually included. In an attempt to prevent the same problems with the KREATIV international scholars have assisted in the education of the instructors in Norway. The individual instructors are encouraged to improvise and exemplify their lessons when delivering the course in the field. However, to ensure consistency and prevent another problem that was identified in England and Wales (where some areas of interviewing were downplayed while others were overemphasised – see Clarke and Milne, 2001), the Norwegian trainers are provided with a presentation package of 22 short but mandatory PowerPoint lessons. These are reviewed on a yearly basis, evaluated by the trainers and updated by scholars in an attempt to keep KREATIV up to date with the latest scientific developments within the field.

The KREATIV course is, in line with Baldwin's conclusions (1993), pitched at a 'down-to-earth' level, free from any psychologically advanced techniques and has now been delivered to almost two thousand detectives, NCOs and members of the prosecution service. The course is, as was the original PEACE course, a five-day, intensive training programme with mandatory reading of literature in advance. This programme is now an integral part of basic police education for all Norwegian police officers – the Bachelor programme in Policing.

For further specialisation two additional postgraduate levels are available at the Norwegian Police University College. The first two levels (KREATIV 1 and KREATIV 2) focus on common knowledge and the abilities necessary for all sorts of police interviews, and there is no clear distinction between interviews with suspects, witnesses and victims. Although there are some formal and methodological differences, the idea is that all investigative interviews have very much in common.

While KREATIV 1 is a one-week training course, KREATIV 2 is a formal education programme which is estimated to comprise 280 hours of full-time study. A plan for the development of a more specialised level 3 programme is in progress.

The second formal education programme is for detectives specialising as certified interviewers of children between 6 and 16 years old and other vulnerable persons. The programme is estimated to require 420 hours full-time study. This programme of study has replaced a previous training course which was held from 1995. A new study specifically addressing pre-school children and mentally disabled persons is planned to be launched soon based on research and the theory of a sequential interview process. This programme is estimated to require 300 hours full-time study.

The theoretical foundation of all interview training in the Norwegian Police builds upon the PEACE model. What separates the two approaches is the introduction of the Dialogical Communication Method (DCM) for interviewing children developed by Gamst and Langballe (2004).

In addition to the training developments, from 2006 to 2012 a nationwide network of so-called children's houses was established, where all interviews of child victims of abuse and violence take place. During the last couple of years there have been some interesting developments also drawing upon international research. In 2010 the practical use of the Self-Administered Interview (Gabbert *et al.*, 2009) was piloted by the Oslo Police Department. The results have been encouraging as the police have obtained many useful details making them able to prioritise which witnesses should be interviewed first. It is now recommended for national use. Furthermore, in 2013 the Director for Public Prosecutions published a revision of the procedures for line-ups in criminal cases. The new recommendations are a result of comprehensive work drawing on the latest research and best practice. Sequential presentation of the suspect and double-blind administration are now recommended practice.

Research

There has in recent years been an increasing amount of research in applied forensic psychology. This research involves child interviews (Melinder, 2004; Gamst and Langballe, 2004; Myklebust, 2009), credibility rating (Bollingmo and Wessel, 2007), judges' knowledge of forensic psychology (Magnussen *et al.*, 2010) and eyewitness accuracy (Fahsing *et al.*, 2004). Among ongoing research can be mentioned police interviews involving a forensic linguistic perspective at the Norwegian University of Science and Technology, and several different projects evaluating the interviews of victims of the 22 July terror attack in Norway in 2012.

Denmark

Denmark has also experienced several cases which have led to debate about child abuse and the investigation of these cases. Two of the most controversial cases will be described here. In the first case from 1990, the so-called *Roum* case, seven persons were convicted of sexual abuse on the testimony of three teenagers, two of whom were mentally disabled. The abuse allegations arose out of hours of therapy with the same therapist. In 1995 the defendants were granted a new trial and six of the seven persons were acquitted. In the other case from 1997, a male teaching assistant was convicted of sexually abusing 23 children. He appealed and the punishment was increased. The case led to extensive public debate and despite the fact that the defendant has never been acquitted, this case contributed to the development of new regulations, standards and training regime regarding interviews with children and vulnerable persons in 2001.

Training

In 2014, the basic police officer education was raised to Bachelor's degree level and delivered by the national Police Academy. Interview training is part of students' 84 hours of education in investigation. According to the syllabus, the approach is inspired by the Norwegian KREATIV model and the cognitive interview. Prior to the revision of police officer education, the training in interviewing was mainly focused on the rules governing police interviews and how to write down a formal statement.

A one-week training course in interviewing for serving detectives was introduced in 2005 by the Police Academy in close collaboration with the national Commissioner. The training was delivered by a psychologist together with experienced detectives. The centralised training was terminated in 2010 and was then delegated to the local police authorities. Hereafter, the focus and length of the training practices seem to vary markedly. Some districts have included interviewing techniques in other training programmes, spending two hours on this issue, while other local authorities have chosen to put in place a four-day training programme. In 2014, the National Police Board initiated a project that aims to explore the current situation and future training needs. Furthermore, the intention is to draw on experiences from other countries, especially the UK and Norway. The project is expected to result in new training programmes in the near future.

Children and vulnerable persons under the age of 12 are interviewed by specially trained detectives. In 2001 a two-week training course was established for child interviewers. The training course covers child developmental psychology, legal issues and four days of practical interview training. The methodology is inspired by NICHD (Lamb *et al.*, 2008). Although the basic police education now is accredited as a Bachelor programme the further training courses are not held as university studies. Interviews of children are carried out in so-called children's houses which were established in 2012.

Research

Very little research in this field has been conducted in Denmark. Some experimental research on interviewing and witness identification line-ups (Smith, 1986) has been conducted as well as research on children's memory and suggestibility

(Thomsen, 2004; Thomsen and Berntsen, 2005). In 2006, a psychologist studied how 15 rape victims had experienced police interviews as well as whether the necessary requirements of the legal system were fulfilled (Guldberg, 2006). To the authors' knowledge, there has been no earlier, or ongoing, research concerning police interviews of children in Denmark. In 2006, one of the authors of the present chapter conducted an unpublished internal evaluation of police interviews of adult witnesses and victims (Jakobsen, 2007). The study contained an analysis of 18 interviews and the results indicated that most of the interviewers did not introduce the interviewee to the interview, did not invite the interviewee to give a free account, and used mainly closed and leading questions combined with few open questions. The impression was that these shortcomings are due to the fact that the interview is not recorded and that the police report is written contemporaneously as the interview is being conducted.

Sweden

A well-known case which has spurred much debate over the topic of witness interviews concerns the assassination of former Swedish Prime Minister Olof Palme in Stockholm in February 1986. Olof Palme was shot and killed at close range while walking home after a visit to the cinema with his wife Lisbeth Palme. The killing marked the beginning of the biggest investigation Sweden ever had seen, and naturally Mr Palme's wife became a central witness. Three years after the killing, the previous convict Christer Petterson was arrested after a somewhat vague tip linking him to an alleged earlier ownership of a gun similar to the one used in the killing (a .357-calibre Magnum pistol). Lisbeth Palme identified Petterson as the murderer in a police line-up and Petterson was convicted to life imprisonment in 1989. Later the same year, however, he was freed after an appeal court cited lack of evidence, for example the murder weapon was never found. The court also questioned the reliability of Mrs Palme's initial witness interviews and the line-up identification. Both the initial interviews of Mrs Palme and the subsequent identification have been subject to massive criticism, mainly because the interviews did not follow the protocols required under normal procedures and because the line-up construction was unfair. The suspect stood out from the others in the line-up in that he wore different clothes and had a rugged look. Moreover, it could not be excluded that Mrs Palme had learnt from rumours in the media that the police suspect was an alcoholic, and when she identified Pettersson, she did so stating that it was obvious which of the persons in the line-up was an alcoholic. Pettersson was later awarded about $50,000 in compensation for defamation by the police and for wrongful imprisonment. Shortly after the trial, the police published a report offering guidelines as to how to conduct line-ups. An updated report was published in 2005 which now provides research-based recommendations.

A more recent case which also caused some debate over procedures for witness interviews is the killing of Swedish foreign minister Anna Lindh. In September 2003, Ms Lindh was attacked in a busy shopping mall and stabbed to death.

There were plenty of witnesses to the attack, and after the attack, these witnesses were gathered in a lunch-room where they waited to be interviewed by the police. Naturally, the witnesses started to talk to each other and discuss the stabbing they had just witnessed. Moreover, when the police interviewed the witnesses, this was not done in private. That meant that some of the witnesses heard the interviews with others before they were interviewed themselves. This is very unfortunate considering that co-witness discussion and information from others may actually change what a witness reports (e.g. Granhag *et al.*, 2010; Ost *et al.*, 2008), in the sense that they report what others have said rather than what they have seen with their own eyes. In the case of Anna Lindh, incorrect information about the perpetrator's clothing was spread between the witnesses, and this incorrect information was included in the national alarm that was sent out to all police units shortly after the attack. Blood found on the murder weapon was later linked to the suspect through a DNA analysis, but if it had not been for this crucial piece of evidence the botched witness statements may have proved fatal for the investigation.

Training

As in Denmark, the Swedish National Police Board is responsible for the development of procedures within the police and for police training and the police programmes. The basic police programme is a higher education programme and is funded through student finance. It consists of five semesters, of which the first four entail full-time studies on a training course and the final semester is a traineeship within the police force. The education is based on problem-based learning aimed at enhancing the candidate's skills by means of reflection, analysis and independent review. Theory is interspersed with practical training. The curriculum for the police programme contains general descriptions of course contents and goals but no specific guidelines. Instead, it is up to each course leader to decide the specific contents of the course. While this may offer flexibility, it also leads to diversity, as a common knowledge base may be lacking. The curriculum states that upon completion of the programme, students are expected to demonstrate knowledge about 'psychological mechanisms which form the basis for individual and group behaviour in connection to police work', about 'communicative methods and strategies in police work' and about 'current research and development'. Moreover, they should demonstrate an ability to 'collect and analyse investigative material in a legally secure manner' and to 'distinguish between research, established practices, and personal values'. In addition to the basic training, there are several courses administered by the local police authorities offering further training in interview methods. The courses last between one and four weeks and although Sweden doesn't currently offer a national interview concept like the Norwegian KREATIV or the British PEACE models, most of the courses do introduce the PEACE model as well as the cognitive interview (Fisher and Gieselman, 1992). New courses in both basic and advanced investigative interviewing methods are currently under development at the National Police Academy in Sweden.

For child investigators, there are three courses of further education. These are held in collaboration with the University of Stockholm. The first is 'Investigative Methods with Emphasis on Crimes against Children and Juveniles', estimated to comprise 400 hours of full-time study, which can be followed up with 'Investigative Interviews with Children and Adolescents', estimated to comprise 200 hours of full-time study. In addition, there is a recurring 40-hour course that can be taken after completion of the first two. Child investigators in Sweden are trained in a structured interview method based on the NICHD (Lamb *et al.*, 2008). The aim is that all child interviewers should pass this training course. However, an evaluation of the children's houses in Sweden 2013 showed that only 30 per cent of child investigators at the children's houses had taken part in all three courses (Landberg and Svedin, 2013). (The first children's house in Sweden was established in 2005 and by 2013 there were 29 children's houses across the country. Approximately half of the Swedish municipalities use children's houses for legal interviews involving children.)

In 2013 the Swedish Parliament decided to reorganise the Swedish Police Service. As a result, on 1 January 2015 the former 21 county police authorities were replaced by one national police force. The aim of this reform was to ensure higher quality, cost-effectiveness, flexibility and legally consistent activities in police performance. Within the decentralised system, the education and training in interview methods differed between the different course locations and the link between basic and further training was quite weak (Granhag *et al.*, 2013).

Research

There is very little research that evaluates real-life Swedish eyewitness interviews. However, Cederborg *et al.* (2000) investigated the type of questions used in forensic child interviews. They found that more than 50 per cent of the questions were option-posing or suggestive. Only 6 per cent of the interviewers' utterances were open-ended invitations and these elicited only 8 per cent of the information obtained.

Hagborg *et al.* (2012) analysed interviews with children suspected of being sexually abused. They found that interviews with younger children (3–6 and 7–12 years) contained fewer open questions than interviews with older children (13–16 years).

Conclusion

It seems evident that serious cases involving failed investigations, such as the *Bjugn*, *Roum* and *Palme* cases have created urgency around the need for new knowledge and professionalism in investigative interviews with witnesses in general and children in particular.

Of the Scandinavian countries, as of today only Norway has a national concept for investigative interviewing. The model used is similar to the model in England and Wales, with one research-based concept running through all the different levels from the basic Bachelor programme to the higher-level specialisations. Sweden seems to have the same scientific foundation; however, the general impression is that there is a larger difference between suspect interviews and other interviews. Moreover, Sweden has not wrapped their different training packages into a national model as in Norway. In Denmark the newly established Bachelor education programme seems to have led to a recognised need for enhancing the postgraduate training, and at the time of writing, new training courses are being planned as are guidelines regarding the recording of interviews. The volume and methodology is therefore still not known.

In general it seems as if police organisations are more open to change and development in the area of interviewing witnesses than they are when it comes to suspect interviews which probably are more deeply rooted in police identity and culture.

Although there are substantial differences between the police practices in the three Scandinavian countries they all seem to be in a process of constant, albeit slow, development towards more scientifically based methods. To ensure the use of effective investigative methods, an increased collaboration between researchers and practitioners is recommended. Also, in developing new investigative models, collaboration between the Scandinavian countries is appropriate, as the cultures as well as legal systems are similar.

Notes

1. In Norway children are individuals under the age of 16, in Denmark under the age of 12 and in Sweden under the age of 15. Similar age thresholds apply with regard to vulnerable persons with mental disabilities in these three countries.
2. In Sweden the prosecutor leads the preliminary investigation from the point when a certain individual can be reasonably suspected of having committed the offence. In the case of less serious offences (e.g. shoplifting, traffic offences), the police conduct the preliminary investigations from beginning to end.
3. KREATIV is an acronym that represents the values on which it is based : communication, rule of law, ethics and empathy, awareness, transparency, information and scientifically based principles.

References

Baldwin, J. (1993) 'Police interview techniques: establishing truth or proof?', *British Journal of Criminology*, 33: 325–51.

Bollingmo, G. C. and Wessel, E. O. (2007) *The Emotional Witness: A Study of Judgments of Credibility*. Doctoral dissertation, University of Oslo, Department of Psychology.

Cederborg, A., Orbach, Y., Sternberg, K. J. and Lamb, M. E. (2000) 'Investigative interviews of child witnesses in Sweden', *Child Abuse and Neglect*, 24: 1355–61.

Clarke, C. and Milne, R. (2001) *National Evaluation of the PEACE Investigative Interviewing Course*. London: Home Office.

Fahsing, I. A., Ask, K. and Granhag, P. A. (2004) 'The man behind the mask', *Journal of Applied Psychology*, 89: 722–9.

Fisher, R. P. and Geiselman, R. E. (1992) *Memory-Enhancing Techniques for Investigative Interviewing: The Cognitive Interview*. Springfield, IL: Charles C. Thomas.

Gabbert, F., Hope, L. and Fisher, R. P. (2009) 'Protecting eyewitness evidence: examining the efficacy of a self-administered interview tool', *Law and Human Behavior*, 33: 298–307.

Gamst, K. T. and Langballe, Å. (2004) *Barn som vitner: En empirisk og teoretisk studie av kommunikasjon mellom avhører og barn i dommeravhør: Utvikling av en avhørsmetodisk tilnærming*. Doctoral dissertation, University of Oslo, Faculty of Education.

Granhag, P. A., Memon, A. and Roos af Hjelmsäter, E. (2010) 'Social influence on eyewitness memory', in P. A. Granhag (ed.), *Forensic Psychology in Context: Nordic and International Approaches*. Cullompton: Willan, pp. 139–53.

Granhag, P. A., Strömwall, L.A. and Cancino Montecinos, S. (2013) *Polisens förhör med misstänkta: Svensk utbildning i internationell belysning* [*Police Interviews with Suspects: Swedish Education in an International Context*], Report 2013:7. Stockholm: Rikspolisstyrelsens utvärderingsfunktion.

Guldberg, A. (2006) *Er det virkelig sket? En undersøgelse af kvinders reaktioner på retspraksis efter politianmeldelse af voldtægt*. Copenhagen: Center for voldtægtsofre.

Jakobsen, K. K. (2007) *Politiets vidneafhøring set i et kognitionspsykologisk perspektiv*. Copenhagen: Rigspolitiet.

Kringstad, H. (1997) *Bjugn-formelen*. Oslo: Tiden.

Lamb, M. E., Hershkowitz, I., Orbach, Y. and Esplin, P. W. (2008) *Tell Me What Happened: Structured Investigative Interviews of Child Victims and Witnesses*. Hoboken, NJ: Wiley & Sons.

Landberg, Å. and Svedin, C. G. (2013) *Inuti ett Barnahus: En kvalitetsgranskning av 23 svenska verksamheter* [*Inside a Children's House – A Quality Evaluation of 23 Swedish Facilities*]. Stockholm: Save the Children.

Magnussen, S., Melinder, A. M., Stridbeck, U. and Raja, A. Q. (2010) 'Beliefs about factors affecting the reliability of eyewitness memory: a comparison of judges, jurors and the general public', *Applied Cognitive Psychology*, 24: 122–33.

Hagborg, J., Strömwall, L. A. and Tidefors, I. (2012) 'Prosecution rate and quality of the investigative interview in child sexual abuse cases', *Journal of Investigative Psychology and Offender Profiling*, 9: 161–73.

Melinder, A. M. (2004) *Perspective on Children as Witnesses*. Doctoral dissertation, University of Oslo, Department of Psychology.

Myklebust, T. (2009) *Analysis of Field Investigative Interviews of Children Conducted by Specially Trained Police Investigators*. Doctoral dissertation, University of Oslo, Department of Psychology.

Ost, J., Granhag, P. A., Udell, J. and Roos af Hjelmsäter, E. (2008) 'Familiarity breeds distortion: the effects of media exposure on false reports concerning media coverage of the terrorist attacks in London on 7 July 2005', *Memory*, 16: 76–85.

Smith, E. (1986) *Vidnebeviset. En vurdering af afhøringsmetoder og vidneforklaringer*. Copenhagen: G. E. C. Gads.

Tange, M. (1995) *Roum-sagen: En omvendt hekseproces?* Copenhagen: Tange.

Thomsen, Y. (2004) *Førskolebørns påvirkelighed i en vidnepsykologisk kontekst*. Doctoral dissertation, University of Aarhus, Department of Psychology.

Thomsen, Y. and Berntsen, D. (2005) 'Knowing that I didn't know: preschoolers' understanding of their own false belief as a predictor of assents to fictitious events', *Applied Cognitive Psychology*, 19 (4): 507–27.

17 Contemporary developments and practices in investigative interviewing of witnesses and victims in Scotland

Annabelle Nicol, David La Rooy and Stuart Houston

Introduction

Despite the importance of conducting investigative interviews with witnesses and victims of crimes appropriately, there was a period of time in Scotland, as was the case in the rest of the UK and indeed many other countries, when there were no standardised evidence-based guidelines or formal training methods for investigative interviewers. Training procedures for police officers comprised largely of watching more experienced colleagues conduct interviews (Moston and Engleberg, 1993). It was not until the Police and Criminal Evidence Act (PACE, 1984) was passed in the UK, that the handling of criminal investigations from the initial arrest and detention, to the investigation and interview process, was formalised and guidelines for police officers were developed. PACE 1984 led to the development of the PEACE model (*P*lanning and Preparation, *E*ngage and Explain, *A*ccount, *C*losure and *E*valuation) (1992), introduced by the Association of Chief Police Officers for England and Wales (ACPO), that served as formal interview guidelines to be followed in England and Wales. (See Chapter 9 in this volume for further information on practices in England and Wales.)

Given that Scotland has its own judicial system, there are some differences to the rest of the UK, and it was not until 1996 that the PRICE model (*P*reparation, *R*apport, *I*nformation Gathering, *C*onfirming the Content and *E*valuation and Action) was introduced to the Scottish probationary police constable courses, despite it being part of the Detective Training Unit at the Scottish Police College since the early 1990s. The PRICE model is indeed very similar to the PEACE model.

Interviewing witnesses and victims

Interviewers' initial training in Scotland consists of two three-day investigative interviewer training courses. This Initial Investigator Course covers suspect and witness interviewing as well as the cognitive interview. Two further days of practical applications are used to assess the trainees upon completion. The PRICE model is expected to be followed in Scotland during investigative interviews and can be used with both suspects and witnesses. The PRICE model provides a structure for interviewers to follow, with the intention that all interviewers are guided through the process in a manner designed to elicit high-quality information, and that all interviewees are provided an equal opportunity to give their account of what happened. The key components of the PRICE model are:

1. *Preparation*. Research the case beforehand, work out the aims and objectives of the upcoming interview, anticipate potential problems that may occur during the interview and have planned strategies to overcome them.
2. *Rapport*. Put the interviewee at ease and invite a willingness to talk through use of a calm and neutral tone of voice, friendliness and appropriate non-verbal communication. Explain the purpose of the interview, how the interview will be conducted and the rights of the interviewee (e.g. to stop the interview if they need a break).
3. *Information gathering*. Use open questions to encourage the interviewee to tell their story, along with facilitators to keep the free narrative flowing. Do not interrupt the interviewee or ask unnecessary questions. Postpone any attempts to clarify the order and details of events until the whole account has been educed. Elicit as complete an account as possible of the events in question.
4. *Confirming the content*. Expand and clarify the salient points and then summarise the information that has been gathered.
5. *Evaluation and action*. Evaluate the information obtained from the interview and decide on the appropriate way to progress with the case (e.g. whether a follow-up interview is needed).

At this point in time a general consensus has been reached, following decades of research that has all pointed to the same conclusions, with regard to how best to conduct forensic interviews with witnesses and victims. Structured interview protocols have been developed to guide the interviewer through the procedure, setting out the order and providing example questions as a template for the interviewer with everything they should cover, to give them the best chance of conducting a sound interview. When structured protocols are not used, the interviewer has less control over the direction the interview will take; this means that the interview experience can vary between interviewees, with some being afforded a better opportunity than others to tell their side of the story.

Since the PRICE model was introduced, many other interview protocols have been developed in other countries in an effort to improve further the standards of police interviews and the evidence elicited from interviewees, some of which have been scientifically validated in numerous research studies e.g. the NICHD protocol (Lamb *et al*., 2007). The PRICE model has yet to be specifically evaluated, despite the PEACE model undergoing scientific evaluations on two separate occasions upon request by the Home Office (McGurk *et al*., 1993; Clarke and Milne, 1999).

Interviewing vulnerable witnesses and victims

When the standard approach to interviewing is not applicable, such as in the case of interviewing vulnerable and child witnesses, there are separate guidelines that must be followed. Vulnerable witnesses include all child witnesses (which will be covered separately) and anybody with a mental health disorder, a physical disability, an intellectual disability and/or a learning disability that causes diminished communicative or social functioning. Intimidated witnesses and victims of sexual offences are also included in the category of 'vulnerable witnesses' because the quality of their evidence may be diminished by fear or distress. This may stem from the process of giving evidence, or by behaviours directed towards the witness by the accused, associates of the accused and/or other witnesses in the case, as well as the nature of the crime.

When interviewing vulnerable or intimidated witnesses, interviewers should follow the guidance of the Vulnerable Witnesses (Scotland) Act (2004), developed in an effort to guide practitioners on how to elicit the best evidence from such witnesses. Specialist training is expected to have been undertaken by those interviewing vulnerable witnesses, including working with intermediaries. The intermediaries themselves are also expected to have completed a national training programme to the standards set by the Scottish Appropriate Adult Network.

Special measures must be taken when possible and tailored to the individual's needs. For example, those with physical disabilities may benefit from having an intermediary's assistance with many different elements of the interview, such as getting to and from the interview room and the bathroom, or to provide medication and refreshments. Interpreters should be made available for witnesses whose first language is not English, as they may choose to be interviewed in the language of their choice. For those with comprehension difficulties, intermediaries should ensure interviewees have understood their rights, and for those with mental health disorders intermediaries may request a break or stoppage if they feel that the interviewee's mental health is being compromised (e.g. if they are displaying signs of distress).

Intermediaries who are familiar to the witness can help to maximise the quality of evidence with interviewees with certain disorders such as autism and Down's syndrome, as they will be aware of the individual's specific idiosyncrasies when it comes to language and communication. However, caution must be exercised when allowing a friend, relative or carer to be present as the appropriate adult during the interview, due to the effect or influence they may have over the interviewee.

The work of intermediaries is not confined to the interview room; intermediaries may also be present to assist vulnerable witnesses in the courtroom during the trial. Special measures such as using the witness's pre-recorded statement as evidence in chief may also be applicable.

In terms of conducting the interview with a vulnerable or intimidated witness, there are no specific guidelines to be followed. The PRICE model is the interview protocol that must still be followed, unless the witness is suffering from deficits in comprehension that are severe enough for the interviewer to justify moving to the use of the Scottish Executive (2011) child interviewing guidelines.

Interviewing child witnesses and child victims

Witnesses and victims under the age of 18 fall into the category of 'child witnesses'. Much more is known about conducting interviews with children. In Scotland, the procedures for conducting investigative interviews with children are laid out in the Scottish Executive (2011) guidelines *Guidance on Joint Investigative Interviewing of Child Witnesses in Scotland*. The guidelines require that all forensic interviews with children are jointly conducted by both a social worker and a police officer. While interviewers are trained locally and the course structure varies between jurisdictions, each course is expected to be designed, delivered and run in accordance with the content and framework set out in the National Curriculum (Scottish Executive, 2007).

Training

Interviewers are trained for one week; this can be a continuous week or split into different sessions, as long as five days are completed. Training involves learning about communicative and developmental issues, familiarisation with the guidelines, conducting practice interviews with adult actors, receiving feedback on practice interviews and learning about the role of the interview in the wider context of criminal proceedings. Trainees will receive presentations from invited experts in the field and from interview trainers, aiming to educate them about the dynamics of child abuse and interviewing, and the research behind them. They will then get an opportunity to put theory into practice by conducting practice interviews with adult actors playing the role of a child.

At present, the experience trainees have varies from jurisdiction to jurisdiction, and even within jurisdictions the practice interview experience trainees have can differ as they will be given different scenarios from each other for their practice interviews. The scenarios provided for role-play vary in complexity from single incidents of physical abuse or sexual touching to repeated rape by multiple perpetrators. They also vary by age (5–15), status (victim or witness) and willingness to disclose (willing or unwilling). Some scenarios contain a 'red herring', which involves the interviewer being misled from the start by the interviewee, who will make a false allegation. Therefore, some trainee interviewers may have a much more difficult experience during training compared to some of their peers.

When interviewing children, interviewers must follow the Scottish Executive (2011) guidelines, which stress the following components:

- *Introductions*. Introduce all persons present and explain the purpose of their attendance and the purpose of the interview, without introducing the allegation. Note aspects of the interview such as the visual recording and the ground rules and make the general principles of the interview explicit from the start.

- *Rapport.* Encourage the child to talk by inquiring about neutral topics, such as things they like to do. This allows the child to get used to the interview setting and to build up a connection, so that the child will feel comfortable when it comes to talking about substantive issues later on.
- *Practice narrative.* Probe for an account of a neutral event the child has experienced, from start to finish using open prompts. This allows for an opportunity to gauge the child's language and communicative abilities and to adjust language and questioning if necessary. Probe for further detail about aspects of the event mentioned by the child using open prompts – this will familiarise the child with the level of detail they will be required to report in the substantive phase of the interview.
- *Free narrative.* Use a non-suggestive opener and then follow up on the information the child provides using open and cued prompts to elicit further details. When multiple incidents have occurred, explore each incident from start to finish. Exhaust the child's free narrative account before asking focused questions. Encourage the child to continue with their narrative by using facilitative utterances such as 'Go on' and echoing back the last few words spoken by the child. Never interrupt the child.
- *Questioning.* Once free narrative has been exhausted, use appropriate focused questions to clarify certain aspects of the child's story or to inquire about things the child has failed to mention. Prepare focused questions carefully in the planning stage and use with caution. If possible pair them with open prompts. Do not use suggestive questions, excessively long questions, double negatives, multiple propositions, abstract/hypothetical questions or questions containing legal jargon.
- *Closure.* Summarise what the child has alleged during the interview, explain to the child honestly and realistically (in an age-appropriate fashion) what will happen next, provide the child and second interviewer an opportunity to ask any questions they might have, leave the child contact details of the police or social workers and thank them for participating in the interview. Finally, end the interview by discussing neutral topics as the child should never leave in a negative frame of mind or while distressed. Even if no allegation is made or the interview is terminated prematurely, closure must always be done.

Current practice

To date, two studies have looked at field interviews conducted in Scotland. La Rooy *et al.* (2012), analysed the quality of 37 interviews with children aged 4–16 years, conducted between 2003 and 2011 (under the guidance of the Scottish Executive 2003 guidelines). They found that interviewers were asking open prompts only 8 per cent of the time. The rest of the questions were comprised of 39 per cent directives, 36 per cent option posing and 17 per cent suggestive. They also found that none of the interviewers had conducted the recommended practice interview before asking children substantive allegation-related questions. With regard to communicating the ground rules at the start of the interview, the importance of telling the truth was discussed with 43 per cent of the children, while a practice demonstration of the child's understanding of truth and lies was present in 30 per cent of interviews. Twenty-four per cent of interviewers told the child to let them know if they did not understand a question, 22 per cent of interviewers told the child not to guess but to instead say 'I don't know' if they didn't know the answer to a question and 3 per cent of interviewers conveyed that the child could and should correct them if they made a mistake.

The follow-up to this study (La Rooy *et al.*, 2013), looked at 19 interviews conducted in Scotland with children aged 4–16 years in 2012 (under the new Scottish Executive 2011 guidelines). This study found that with regard to the practice interview, no improvements had been made as there were still no practice interviews conducted in any of the interviews. The number of open prompts used had improved, rising to 15 per cent, the rest of the questions being made up of 49 per cent directives, 34 per cent option posing and 2 per cent suggestive. With regard to communicating the ground rules at the start of the interview the authors found modest improvements had been made with some of the rules, with the exception of demonstrating the child's understanding of the concept of truth and lies using a practice question which was absent in all interviews at this time. A discussion of the importance of telling the truth was present in 74 per cent of interviews, 58 per cent of interviewers told the child to let them know if they did not understand a question, 47 per cent of children were told to say 'I don't know' instead of guessing if they didn't know the answer to a question and 16 per cent of interviewers told the child to correct them if they made a mistake.

While it would appear there have been improvements made in the number of open questions being used and the communication of the basic interview principles in interviews with children in Scotland since the introduction of the new guidelines, the interviews are still of a relatively poor quality when compared with best-practice interviews.

In Scotland, the child interviewer guidelines were updated in 2011. One of the most important changes made to the guidelines was the removal of the structured interview protocol which was in the appendix. The previous guidelines – the Scottish Executive 2003 guidelines – contained a shortened version of the NICHD protocol for interviewers to follow. The NICHD protocol has been shown to elicit the longest and most accurate responses from children when followed (Lamb *et al.*, 2008).

The 2011 guidelines also say a practice narrative is recommended only where appropriate. For example, if the child appears to want to discuss the allegation straight away, it is recommended that the interviewer should skip rapport and practice. While there is no common consensus on what the appropriate course of action is if this situation arises, it fails to take into consideration the value of any alternative strategies such as confirming with the child that they will discuss substantive issues soon but that the interviewer would like to get to know them a bit better first. The practice narrative is a very important stage for both the interviewer and the interviewee. It allows interviewers to gauge the child's language and communicative abilities providing them an opportunity to adjust their language and questioning if they feel it is advanced for the child. This will be of great help in the substantive phase as they will be familiar with the child's capabilities, aiding the identification of any issues the child may be having. For example, if the child seems unable to talk about substantive issues after providing information in the practice phase, it may indicate that the issue is reluctance as opposed to lack of ability to answer questions. As well as being beneficial to interviewers, the practice interview is also beneficial to the child as being asked open questions is not common practice in real-life situations, therefore, they should be familiarised with the level of detail they will be required to report in order for the substantive information elicited to be as complete as possible. Not giving some interviewees the opportunity to engage in a practice interview could mean that some are not being afforded the same opportunity to provide high-quality evidence later on during the interview.

The Scottish Executive Guidelines (2011) contain some suggestions about conducting the interview that directly contradict the research findings on conducting interviews with children. Suggested topics for the practice interview are television programmes, which is incongruous with the research that advocates avoiding any discussion of fantasy (television, computer games, anything 'made up') (e.g. Lamb *et al.*, 2008). It is emphasised at the start of the interview that the child is expected to tell the truth and to tell the interviewer only about things that have really happened. Discussing fantasy, especially with younger children, may confuse and undermine the point of the interview. The guidelines also say to use open questions to elicit details, but they then use 'Who, What, Where, When, How' questions as examples of open questions. The research literature deems these questions as 'Directives', as they tap 'cued recall' memory. An open prompt, such as 'Tell me what happened', taps 'recall memory' and does not dictate what information the child is expected to provide. The open prompts give children the opportunity to provide lengthy narratives, where a directive question such as 'What colour was it?' dictates what information is requested and probes for only a one- or two-word answer.

Based on the Pigot Report (1989), that recommended the visual recording of all child interviews so that the video evidence could be used in court thus eradicating the need for children to appear live in court for examination-in-chief, all Joint Investigative Interviews are expected to be visually recorded. In England and Wales this measure has been in place since 1992, but in Scotland this practice has been variable between police forces, with some jurisdictions using VRI (video recorded interviewing), some audio recording and others relying on scribing (handwritten verbatim notes taken by a second interviewer present during the interview) alone. It was not until the end of 2011 that it became mandatory for all interviews in Scotland to be visually recorded.

Emerging practice

An emerging practice in some jurisdictions in Scotland is the recent engagement with research, particularly into training methods. At present adult actors are used in practice interviews to pay the role of a child. Preliminary analyses by Nicol *et al.* (2012), involving 25 police officers and social workers from one jurisdiction in Scotland, found that in practice interviews where the trainee interviewers practised with adult actors playing the role of the child, interviewers were using high numbers of the best-practice open prompts (29 per cent) and lower numbers of the riskier focused questions (27 per cent directives, 42 per cent option posing and 2 per cent suggestive). An unaddressed concern at present is that while the interviewers are being trained, the actors receive no training to play these roles. Studies in other countries such as Powell *et al.* (2008) have looked at the use of trained respondents and found that practising with a trained respondent can increase the interviewers' use of open questioning, as they provided appropriate responses and rewarded interviewers with information when they asked these best-practice questions.

The authors have been working with one jurisdiction on the introduction of actors who have extensive knowledge of child interviewing and best practice, in an attempt to enhance the experience interviewers have by working with respondents trained to promote the use of best questioning. The eventual aim is to provide training for all actors who participate in Joint Investigative Interviewers' training practice interviews.

Contraindicated practice

Anatomically correct dolls have been used since the late 1970s by interviewers, clinicians, and child protective services as an aid for facilitating children's disclosures of sexual abuse. Their use has generated a lot of controversy within the scientific community, mostly centred on the issue of suggestibility and interviewers' subjective interpretations of play. Many studies have reported children lacking the ability to report true touching and inaccurate false reporting of touching when the dolls were used (Saywitz *et al.*, 1991; Bruck *et al.*, 2000; Bruck *et al.*, 1995; Goodman *et al.*, 1997).

While the Scottish Executive guidelines state that use of anatomical dolls and body diagrams is appropriate as long as adequate training has been provided, in Scotland there is no standard protocol for appropriate use of anatomical dolls and no training in their use. Therefore, it is unknown how interviewers are actually trained to use them and the skill level of interviewers using these aids is also unknown.

Many other unsupported practices have been found in interviews conducted in Scotland. Body diagrams are used, but similar problems exist when using them with children, especially younger children. Other examples of unsafe practices that have been used include asking reluctant children to 'write down a word', requesting children to draw pictures relating to the incident, presenting materials allegedly drawn/written down by the child outside of the interview room, the use of a 'secrets jar' and the use of telepathic communication. While these practices are not common, they are detrimental to the quality of the interview and the credibility of the evidence.

Implications for research, policy and practice

Research has shown that structured interview protocols have improved the quality of information elicited from children in forensic interviews. Based on this finding, the introduction of a structured protocol for interviewing adult witnesses and vulnerable witnesses is recommended. As the child interviewing protocol available in the appendix of the Scottish Executive guidelines (2003) was based on the NICHD protocol, that has been shown in numerous studies to elicit the longest and most accurate responses from children, we recommend that it is reinstated for use in child interviews in Scotland. The current adult interviewing model (PRICE) should be evaluated scientifically, as is the case with the PEACE model which has been evaluated twice. It is essential that the quality of interviewing can be monitored and that evidence-based improvements can be made to practice. Previous research has shown that use of trained respondents in training interviews has increased the use of best-practice questions by forensic interviewers; we therefore advise that the adult actors used in such training are trained themselves to respond appropriately. Finally, we recommend the discontinuation of controversial interviewing practices such as the use of anatomical dolls and body diagrams, especially with younger children.

References

Bruck, M., Ceci, S. J. and Francoeur, E. (2000) 'Children's use of anatomically detailed dolls to report genital touching in a medical examination: developmental and gender comparisons', *Journal of Experimental Psychology: Applied*, 6: 74–83.

Bruck, M., Ceci, S. J., Francoeur, E. and Renick, A. (1995) 'Anatomically detailed dolls do not facilitate preschoolers' reports of a paediatric examination involving genital touching', *Journal of Experimental Psychology: Applied*, 1: 95–109.

Clarke, C. and Milne, R. (1999) *National Evaluation of the PEACE Investigative Interviewing Course*, Police Research Award Scheme Report no. PRAS/149.

Goodman, G. S., Quas, J. A., Batterman-Faunce, J. M., Riddlesberger, M. M. and Kuhn, J. (1997) 'Children's reactions to and memory for a stressful event: influences of age, anatomical dolls, knowledge, and parental attachment', *Applied Developmental Science*, 1: 54–75.

La Rooy, D., Earhart, R. and Nicol, A. (2013) 'Joint Investigative Interviews (JIIs) conducted with children in Scotland: a comparison of the quality of interviews conducted before and after the introduction of the Scottish Executive (2011) guidelines', *Scots Law Times*, 31: 4–10.

La Rooy, D., Nicol, A., Halley, J. and Lamb, M. E. (2012) 'Joint investigative interviews with children in Scotland', *Scots Law Times*, 30: 175–84.

Lamb, M. E., Hershkowitz, I., Orbach, Y. and Esplin, P. W. (2008) *Tell Me What Happened.* Chichester and Hoboken, NJ: Wiley.

Lamb, M. E., Orbach, Y., Hershkowitz, I., Esplin, P. W. and Horowitz, D. (2007) 'Structured forensic interview protocols improve the quality and informativeness of investigative interviews with children: a review of research using the NICHD Investigative Interview Protocol', *Child Abuse and Neglect*, 31: 1201–31.

McGurk, B. J., Carr, M. J. and McGurk, B. (1993) *Investigative Interviewing Courses for Police Officers: An Evaluation*, Police Research Series Paper No. 4. London: Home Office Police Department.

Moston, S. and Engleberg, T. (1993) 'Questioning techniques in tape recorded interviews with criminal suspects', *Policing and Society*, 3: 223–37.

Nicol, A., La Rooy, D. and Gabbert, F. (2012) *Actor Performance in Joint Investigative Interviewers' Training in Scotland: A Pilot Study*. Poster session presented at 8th National Forrest Conference (FORensic RESearch and Teaching), Abertay University, Dundee.

Pigot, T. (1989) *The Report of the Advisory Group on Video Evidence*. London: Home Office.

Police and Criminal Evidence Act 1984. Available online at: http://www.legislation.gov.uk/ukpga/1984/60/pdfs/ukpga_19840060_en.pdf (accessed 13 May 2014).

Powell, M. B., Fisher, R. P. and Hughes-Scholes, C. H. (2008) 'The effect of using trained versus untrained adult respondents in simulated practice interviews about child abuse', *Child Abuse and Neglect*, 32: 1007–16.

Saywitz, K. J., Goodman, G. S., Nicholas, E. and Moan, S. F. (1991) 'Children's memories of a physical examination involving genital touch: implications for reports of child sexual abuse', *Journal of Consulting and Clinical Psychology*, 59: 682–91.

Scottish Executive (2003) *Guidance Interviewing Child Witnesses and Victims in Scotland*. Edinburgh: Scottish Executive.

Scottish Executive (2005) *Vulnerable Witnesses (Scotland) Act (2004)*. Edinburgh: Scottish Executive.

Scottish Executive (2007) *National Curriculum Joint Investigative Interviewing of Child Witnesses Training in Scotland*. Edinburgh: Scottish Executive.

Scottish Executive (2011) *Guidance on Joint Investigative Interviewing of Child Witnesses in Scotland*. Edinburgh: Scottish Executive.

Vulnerable Witnesses (Scotland) Act 2004. Available online at: http://www.legislation.gov.uk/asp/2004/3/pdfs/asp_20040003_en.pdf (accessed 13 May 2014).

18 Gathering information from victims and witnesses in Slovenian investigation proceedings

Tinkara Pavšič Mrevlje, Igor Areh and Sabina Zgaga

Introduction

The Republic of Slovenia, located between Austria, Hungary, Croatia and Italy, became an independent state in 1991. Since 2004, it has been a full member of the European Union. After the proclamation of the new constitution in 1991, all legal provisions in force at that time stayed in force, except where they were in conflict with human rights and fundamental freedoms. New legislation, including criminal legislation based on the new constitution, gradually replaced the previous Yugoslavian legal order. A brand new Criminal Code and Criminal Procedure Act entered into force in 1995. The Criminal Code was then replaced in 2008, whereas the Criminal Procedure Act has been amended several times but has not yet been replaced by completely new legislation, although a new Act has been drafted. Both documents are consistent with the European Convention of Human Rights (ECHR).

In Slovenia, significantly more attention has been devoted to topics dealing with the interrogation of suspects than to topics dealing with gathering information from victims and witnesses of criminal acts. A lack of credible research evidence concerning the questioning of victims and witnesses makes it difficult to judge, at least with any certainty, how well police investigators undertake this task. Therefore we have deduced the techniques employed by police officers with an overview of the literature that has frequently been cited and used as study material in training criminal investigators. The first Slovenian training manual appeared in 2003 (Štirn and Podvršič, 2003), but only as an internal unpublished draft that relies heavily on the sources presented later in the chapter. It can be assumed that the information presented there was, at least in part, translated into practice. However, it should be kept in mind that the standards of scholarly writing in Slovenia and the former Yugoslavia some twenty years ago were low. Citing primary sources was an exception rather than the rule, and where citations do exist, they are frequently incomplete. With citations being rare, it is often difficult to pinpoint the sources of ideas propagated by authors at the time. Moreover, it appears that the psychological aspects of questioning victims and witnesses were mainly examined by legal professionals, not psychologists.

As with adult victims and witnesses, the field of examining children and adolescents also lacks research evidence and relevant sources.

Questioning adult witnesses and victims

One of the first relevant sources frequently cited at the time of the former Yugoslavia – and, therefore, also in Slovenia, a part of that country – was written by Austrian lawyer Roland Grassberger. Published in 1950, the *Psychology of Criminal Proceedings* was translated and introduced eight years later. Judging from the frequency of citations in other sources discussing criminal investigation, Grassberger's work seems to have exerted an important influence up until the 1980s. Today, the book reads like a manual for practitioners, full of anecdotal evidence serving as arguments for the author's presumptions.

The second influential work was published in 1973 by the psychologist Dušan Putnik. Here, the author discusses, on a few pages, the specific characteristics of questioning witnesses. A typology of witnesses is provided: emotionally unstable and stable witnesses, observers, describers, clarifiers, babblers, silent types, over-raters, under-raters and liars (Putnik, 1973). The author offers short pieces of advice on dealing with different witness types but pays no attention to gathering information from witnesses and victims. As sources for the typology are not provided and no research is mentioned on which the typology is based, it is fair to assume that it is based on the author's common-sense reasoning.

In his extensive work characterised by greater accuracy in citations, Vodinelić (1987) describes the techniques for examining witnesses who are well-intentioned or are lying. In the case of well-intentioned witnesses, the author suggests starting the interview with open questions and allowing the witness to speak freely. The investigator should listen carefully and make sure not to interrupt the interviewee. During the second stage of the interview, the investigator should first assess whether the testimony was true or false, and then proceed by asking appropriate questions – these must be short, clear, direct, specific, adjusted to the witness and arranged in an order allowing the witness's answers to form a whole. The author warns of the risk of posing suggestive questions and the need for considering the physical and mental health of the witness. It is also emphasised that the interviewers should avoid giving an impression of impatience or boredom and refrain from asking nonsensical or awkward questions. Furthermore, Vodinelić (1987) argues that memory recall in investigation proceedings is frequently initiated with the following techniques:[1]

- The interviewer asks questions seemingly unrelated to the criminal offence, yet nevertheless of interest to the interviewee because they might be related to the event.
- Questions are posed on the circumstances that existed prior to the event.
- The witness is asked to describe in detail all the things they did and experienced on the critical day, known as a mental reconstruction of preceding events.

- Exceptionally, the witness can be told certain details or shown objects connected with the criminal offence. However, the witness must not be told or shown any critical details. The statements of other witnesses may be read out to the witness, but only containing details prior to and following the event which the witness has forgotten. Importantly, the witness must not be familiarised with the statements of other witnesses about the critical event.
- The questioning is conducted at the scene of the event or, alternatively, with the use of models, maps and drawings.

Vodinelić (1987) also suggests using control questions to check for the accuracy of the information gathered. According to his advice, questions should be formulated so as to include verified information about the criminal offence or even evidence upon which the accuracy of the witnesses' or victims' verbal response is gauged. If the witness is found to be lying, the advice for conducting the interview is similar to that suggested by the Reid interrogation technique (Inbau *et al.*, 2013). The author offers some practical suggestions but, not being supported by research evidence, they remain at the common-sense advice level. Worryingly, the author recommends the use of a technique where an allegedly lying witness is forced into categorically answering a set of questions until they get caught up in their own contradictions. Once this happens, the witness is told in no uncertain terms that they are lying and are therefore facing criminal liability charges, then warned that the best course of action is to tell the truth. This technique resembles the Reid technique, which is believed to have been and, to a lesser extent, continues to be used in Slovenia. Even with interrogation of suspects, it is difficult to ascertain with any degree of certainty which techniques were actually used in practice. However, from discussions with senior and retired criminal investigators, we can assume that a transfer from textbook into practice (and vice versa) was common.

The topic of questioning witnesses was also discussed by other authors dealing with criminal investigation. For example, Aćimović (1988) draws on Trankell (1972) and, in part, Undeutsch (1982) in pointing out that the validity of each statement has to be assessed according to specific circumstances, the type of criminal offence committed and the witness's characteristics, role and motives. In his book, Aćimović devoted special attention to issues regarding eyewitness testimony, which was rare in those times.

Towards the end of the 1980s, one of the most influential works in this part of the world dealing with investigative interviewing was published. It suffers from many of the same flaws previously elucidated: inconsistent and rare citations, arguments backed up with anecdotal evidence and mostly common-sense recommendations. In his work on investigative interviewing with witnesses, Roso (1988) recommends that police investigators first chat in a relaxed manner with the interviewee, thereby establishing a confidential and constructive relationship. The initial part of the interview should last approximately 45 minutes and is followed by more relevant topics. The first pertinent question to be asked is: 'Do you know why you are here?' An analysis of the interviewee's responses is conducted immediately afterwards in order to assess their credibility. The method suggested by Roso for assessing the interviewee's credibility is similar to methods described in manuals of coercive interrogation techniques. Moreover, his recommendations often bear a resemblance to Reid's interrogation technique (see Inbau *et al.*, 2013). As a rule, the interview should start with open questions, the interviewee must be interrupted as little as possible, and the interviewer should establish a calm, empathic relationship (Roso, 1988). Finally, Roso introduces the findings of the cognitive psychologist Elizabeth Loftus who, in the context of eyewitness testimony, highlighted the importance of emotions, stress, violence, suggestibility and the subconscious transfer in identifying suspects as well as providing witness accounts (Loftus, 1979).

After Slovenia gained its independence in 1991, the questioning of victims and witnesses remained an overlooked topic. Not a single work has been published since then that can be assumed to have influenced police practices as much as previous works probably did. In his book, Maver (1997) briefly enumerates selected psychological aspects in suspect identification, but as a lawyer, he is more interested in the legal aspects. Further, Areh (2007) discusses the issue of eyewitness testimony but offers no concrete guidelines on examining witnesses and victims. Although several articles on the topic have been published in journals, it is difficult to determine their influence on police practices. The authors of this chapter managed to obtain some materials used in the internal training of Slovenian criminal investigators, but these are merely unpublished drafts. Nevertheless, the materials mentioned reveal that police officers are familiar with the principles of the cognitive interview but are not trained for its implementation and do not implement it in practice.

Questioning children and adolescents

One of the earliest works available touching upon children's testimony is the previously mentioned book by Putnik (1973). Here, the author briefly states that, in line with legal provisions, the interviewer must make an independent decision if, to what extent and when to believe children's testimony, and whether the child's age can represent an issue in doing so. Importantly, Putnik concludes that even children aged less than 7 years may convey the objective truth, provided the right conditions have been met and the questions are posed professionally. In his work, Vodinelić (1987) explains the techniques of gathering information from children and adolescents in more detail, pointing first to the issues of lying and the impact of the imagination in young children. In addition, Vodinelić argues that children aged 7–10 years can be excellent witnesses and is critical of authors who insist that the reliability of children's and adolescents' testimony depends strictly on their gender and age (pre-pubertal boys were said to be outstanding observers, whereas girls were allegedly more egocentric and less realistic due to a faster onset of pubertal changes, making them unreliable witnesses).

Towards the end of the 1980s, Yugoslavian authors also started to explore and offer practical guidelines for conducting investigative interviews with children and adolescents (e.g. Roso, 1988). They suggest that, in addition to taking the child's developmental stage into account, interviews with children should be conducted as soon after the event as possible (particularly if the child is under seven years of age), while the interviewed children should be isolated from all figures of authority in their lives. The interviewer must be well prepared and it is advisable to conduct the interview only once and to audiotape it. Preparations should include, among other things, obtaining information on the child's personality and the circumstances of her or his life by a psychologist or a psychiatrist. The directions of these professionals should primarily be used when assessing the credibility of the minor and her or his mental development. First, the child should be allowed to speak freely about the criminal offence, with non-suggestive questions following later. Finally, Roso underlines the fact that interviewers must be familiar with the theories of pedagogy, psychology and criminal investigation, and must also be empathic and patient. However, even though these elements were recognised as necessary, no special training was organised in this regard. In addition, Vodinelić (1987) stresses the importance of control questions used to verify the child's and the interviewer's understanding, and calls for the presence of a psychologist or a psychiatrist when a child is the main witness in cases involving mental or physical conditions, and in all cases involving sexual offences.

Adolescents aged 14–18 years are characterised by specific developmental processes which have to be considered when examining this age group. Yet only Vodinelić provides any guidelines for questioning an adolescent, pointing out that adolescents' egocentric predisposition and the resulting manner of experiencing events must be taken into account. An appropriate connection should first be established with the adolescent and the interview should be conducted in a calm and dignified tone of voice, but above all interviewers must be careful not to hurt the adolescent's moral and sexual feelings and not to spur their imagination (Vodinelić, 1987). Of all the authors mentioned, Vodinelić (1987) devotes the most attention to the techniques and methods of gathering information from children and adolescents in his work *Criminalistics*. He explains, albeit briefly, the criteria for assessing the credibility of child witnesses according to two authors: Arntzen (1951, in Vodinelić, 1987) and Undeutsch (1954, 1957 and 1966, in Vodinelić, 1987).

Much as is the case with adult witnesses and victims, the subject of questioning children and adolescents in investigation proceedings offers virtually no new sources following Slovenia's independence. A notable exception are the extensive recommendations (Republic of Slovenia, 2011) drafted at a specialist conference on interviewing children via video link. The introduction details proposed legislative changes and technical recommendations and goes on to specify recommendations for a child-friendly interview room. In terms of interviewing children, two chapters are particularly relevant. The first of these suggests that a child be interviewed as soon as possible following the event and specifies the appropriate professionals to be present during the interview, then recommends that the setting be a child-friendly interview room. Such a room would have bright walls, neutral furniture adapted to children in size, material and colour, and easily accessible toys designed for different developmental stages of the child. The key elements of an interview in pre-trial and criminal procedures are also listed. In the second relevant chapter, two clinical psychologists explicate the psychological aspects of working with child abuse victims in judicial proceedings (Moškrič and Ribičič, 2011). The authors first explain how abuse influences the development of a child's personality structure and point out that over one in two abused children develop post-traumatic symptomatology and other emotional and behavioural disturbances. The stress of judicial proceedings on a child is emphasised, and the characteristics of developmental stages from pre-school to adolescence are outlined. For the first time in specialist literature, the consequences for professionals working with abused children are mentioned and the key importance of clinical supervision is highlighted. Finally, the paper touches upon children's suggestibility and the credibility of a child's testimony.

In recent years, three papers have been published that shed light on selected aspects of interviews with children. One discusses the reliability and credibility of child testimony, and the key role of the interviewer (Umek, 2009). In the second, for the first time in Slovenia, different protocol types for conducting investigative interviews with children are mentioned (Areh, 2012), and in the third practical guidelines for implementing a forensic interview according to a child's psychological development are offered (Pavšič Mrevlje, 2013). Child sexual abuse investigators rarely get the opportunity to receive any training, but when they do, they mostly participate in lectures about developmental or clinical psychology with no specialised practical work demonstrated.

Witness and victim protection during questioning – legal framework

In Slovenian criminal procedure, the victim of a criminal offence can appear 'merely' as a victim or as an authorised prosecutor. That is, in cases involving criminal acts liable to private prosecution, a private prosecutor (the victim) is the authorised prosecutor. Furthermore, if the public prosecutor finds that there are no grounds to prosecute a criminal act *ex officio*, the victim has a right to prosecute the defendant as the subsidiary prosecutor. Mostly, however, in cases involving criminal acts liable to prosecution *ex officio*, the public prosecutor is the authorised prosecutor. In most cases, the victim will testify as a witness and must therefore observe the obligations of witnesses: to appear in court, to testify and to give truthful testimony (Criminal Procedure Act 1994). A witness in a Slovenian criminal procedure is obliged, as a rule, to give a statement three times: first to the police in a pre-trial procedure, then to the investigating judge for investigation purposes and finally to the panel of judges at the main hearing. Because police officers are not allowed to question witnesses (Supreme Court, 2007, I Ips 65/2005), official notes with witness statements from the pre-trial procedure may not be considered by the judges in issuing a verdict but can, however, be used in assessing witness credibility and for filling the gaps in their testimony (Supreme Court, 2013, I Ips 51335/2010-116).

Although, in general, witnesses are under an obligation to testify, there are exceptions to this rule, namely privileged witnesses are exempt from the duty to testify. Under the Criminal Procedure Act (CPA), privileged witnesses are considered to be close relatives of the accused and persons bound by the duty to keep secret what they learn in exercising their profession, except in exceptional instances (Horvat, 2004). According to the Supreme Court, the purpose of granting privileged witness status is to protect close family relationships between the witness and the accused, and to observe the principle of confidentiality (Supreme Court, 2011, I Ips 159/2010). The status is designed to benefit the witness, not the accused (Supreme Court, 2003, I Ips 259/2003).[2] Importantly, the witness must decide by themselves whether to take advantage of the privileged witness status or not (Supreme Court, 2011, I Ips 220/2010).

A witness can only be granted privileged witness status during an investigation. Therefore, police officers are under no obligation to inform potential privileged witnesses of their rights in the pre-trial procedure (Supreme Court, 2010, I Ips 47/2009). Persons in charge of an official procedure in which the witness makes a statement must not be interviewed on the content of statements made by a privileged witness to other authorities, if the witness opts to exercise his privileged witness rights. Such authorities include inspection bodies, administrative authorities, disciplinary authorities, social care institutions, etc. (Supreme Court, 2002, I Ips 197/2002). However, this does not apply in cases where a privileged witness makes a statement to other persons of their own free will, for example to a neighbour, a friend, a journalist, a foster mother, a crisis centre worker, etc. (Supreme Court, 2011, I Ips 4349/2009-96).

During an investigation and at the main hearing, a witness is interrogated by an investigating judge, at which time the accused can be present. However, the investigating judge may order the accused to be removed from the interrogation if the witness in unwilling to testify in the presence of the accused or if circumstances indicate that the witness will not tell the truth in the presence of the accused (Supreme Court, 2002, I Ips 70/99). In order for the accused to be removed from interrogation, it is not sufficient to suppose that the witness will not testify or tell the truth (Supreme Court, 2013, I Ips 34239/2010-121), nor that the witness will be uncomfortable during the interrogation, as this is the case for most testimonies, particularly if they are incriminating (Supreme Court, 2011, I Ips 162/2010). Other, more solid reasons must exist. For example, a judge can decide to consider the psychological and physical conditions of the victim on the basis of expert opinions issued by a pedagogue,[3] a neurologist and a psychiatry specialist (Supreme Court, 2013, I Ips 34239/2010-121). A favourable decision was also granted when two victims clearly stated that they did not wish to testify in the presence of the accused and gave valid reasons for their request (Supreme Court, 2004, I Ips 168/2004). In practice, such cases normally include victims of sexual assault, particularly those under 15 years of age (Supreme Court, 2005, I Ips 202/2004). In rendering a decision, a judge will consider the nature of the criminal offence, the victim's age, the possibility of reliving the criminal offence, the relationship between the witness and the accused, etc. (Supreme Court, 2013, I Ips 34239/2010-121).

Thus the Criminal Procedure Act (CPA) grants special protection to certain child and adolescent witnesses/victims (CPA, 1994). Direct questioning of these victims at the main hearing is not permitted, the records of previous questioning of such victim must first be read, and parties to the procedure may pose indirect questions through an investigating judge (Hauptman, 1999). In practice, therefore, questioning is normally conducted at this stage of investigation in the presence of the defendant's counsel, the state prosecutor, the victim's authorised representative and a court expert (Supreme Court, 2010, I Ips 260/2009). Furthermore, the CPA provides that minors (persons under 18 years of age) who are considered privileged witnesses and cannot understand the meaning of the right to decline testimony in view of their age and the stage of their intellectual development may not be examined as witnesses except where the accused himself demands it (Supreme Court, 2001, I Ips 225/98; Šugman, 2001). The issue of whether minors appearing as witnesses cannot understand the meaning of the right to decline testimony is one which should be decided by the court (Supreme Court, 2010, I Ips 260/2009). Again, the court may obtain an expert opinion to assist it in its decision (Supreme Court I, 2008, Ips 403/2007).[4] After all, the court must consider all the circumstances of the case (Supreme Court, 2008, I Ips 403/2007). For example, the court passed a decision that a victim aged 11 years was capable of understanding the meaning of the right to decline testimony against his father (Supreme Court, 1999, I Ips 282/97), whereas it is generally considered that children under 10 years of age do not understand the meaning of that right (Horvat, 2004). Even though the provisions of the CPA refer explicitly to minors with the status of a privileged witness, it is admissible to also apply them to adult victims whose intellectual development is at the stage of a child (Horvat, 2004).

Questioning a minor, especially if they have suffered harm from the criminal offence at issue, must be conducted considerately to avoid producing a deleterious effect on their state of mind. If necessary, a pedagogue or some other expert should be called to assist in the examination of a minor (Supreme Court, 2013, I Ips 34239/2010-121). In one such case, the court permitted a victim to be examined with the assistance of a pedagogue, even though the victim was an adult at the time of the questioning. The court consulted with the pedagogue on the victim's ability to testify and entrusted him to monitor the victim. In addition, the court may consult an expert in selecting a questioning method that is the least stressful or harmful to the witness/victim. The expert's active role is required in this case, as well as in formulating and posing questions (Supreme Court, 2013, I Ips 34239/2010-121).

Conclusion

It is difficult to make any definitive conclusions on the questioning of witnesses and victims conducted in Slovenia in practice. A lack of credible research evidence left us to deduce the questioning practices from specialist sources that most probably featured in the internal training of police officers and criminal investigators. In the past, much attention in criminal investigations has been devoted to suspect interrogation, with unfairly little weight being given to effective and ethical questioning of witnesses and victims. This has become clear over the past ten years, judging from the content of a police manual published in 2003 in which a total of 82 pages deal with suspect interrogation compared to only half a page devoted to eyewitness issues. In this work, Štirn and Podvršič (2003) stress the fallibility of memory recall.

Slovenian investigators interviewing children and adolescents rarely get the opportunity to participate in specialist training from the field. The previously mentioned reading material mostly summarises the findings of authors from abroad, and although they can be helpful for Slovenian investigation professionals, they are not suffice to ensure a high standard of practice. When it comes to working with children and adolescents, Slovenian criminal investigators have to rely primarily on their own resourcefulness and efforts due to a weak internal system of professional support.

From the legal perspective, especially in case law, the issue of witness examination seems to be all about finding a compromise between the right of the accused to defence, and consequently to examining a witness testifying against him, and the protection of specific witness categories. These categories receive special attention from the court and include, in particular, child victims of sexual assault – they must not be questioned in the presence of the accused – and privileged witnesses who decide themselves whether they want to testify. When establishing the ability of a witness to testify, and in examining particularly vulnerable witness categories, the court may seek advice from an expert. In terms of witness protection, all efforts are aimed at reducing the amount of direct contact between the witness and the accused and at eliminating multiple witness questionings.

Notes

1. Unfortunately the author does not specify where these techniques are being practised, leaving us to deduce from the context that the practices of investigators from abroad, not from the former Yugoslavia, were implied.
2. Case law expresses doubt over the credibility of testimonies made by such witnesses because they are motivated to influence the outcome of judicial proceedings and are testifying under pressure (Supreme Court, 2011, I Ips 1008/2010-35).
3. A person professionally involved in education or training.
4. In such cases, the court often relies on the opinion of clinical psychology experts (Supreme Court, 2010, I Ips 260/2009) or child psychology experts (Supreme Court, 2011, I Ips 159/2010).

References

Aćimović, M. (1988) *Psihologija zločina i suđenja* [*Psychology of Crime and Trial*]. Beograd: Savremena administracija.

Areh, I. (2007) *Psihologija za varnostno področje* [*Psychology and Security Studies*]. Ljubljana: University of Maribor.

Areh, I. (2012) 'Protokoli preiskovalnih intervjujev za ugotavljanje spolne zlorabe otrok' ['Investigative interview protocols with children as alleged victims of sexual abuse'], *Varstvoslovje*, 14 (1): 97–112.

Criminal Procedure Act 1994, *Official Gazette of the Republic of Slovenia*, 63/94 and later.

Grassberger, R. (1950) *Psychologie des Strafverfahrens*. Vienna: Springer-Verlag.

Hauptman, P. (1999) 'Oškodovanec v kazenskem postopku' ['The victim in criminal procedure'], *Pravosodni bilten*, 20: 63–76.

Horvat, Š. (2004) *Zakon o kazenskem postopku s komentarjem* [*Criminal Procedure Act with Commentary*]. Ljubljana: GV.

Inbau, F. E., Reid, J. E., Buckley, J. P. and Jayne, B. C. (2013) *Criminal Interrogations and Confessions*, 5th edn. Chicago: John E. Reid & Associates.

Loftus, E. F. (1979) *Eyewitness Testimony*. Cambridge, MA: Harvard University Press.

Maver, D. (1997) *Kriminalistika* [*Criminalistics*]. Ljubljana: Uradni list republike Slovenije.

Moškrič, B. and Ribičič, V. (2011) *Zlorabljeni otrok v sodnem postopku – psihološki vidiki. Priporočila: Razgovor z otrokom s pomočjo videokonference in drugih tehničnih sredstev* [*Child Abuse Victims in Judicial Proceedings – Psychological Aspects. Recommendations: Child Interview via Video Conference and Other Technical Means*]. Ljubljana: Ministry of Justice.

Musek, J., Polič, M. and Umek, P. (1992) *Uvod v psihologijo* [*Introduction to Psychology*]. Ljubljana: Ministry of the Interior.

Pavšič Mrevlje, T. (2013) 'Razvojne značilnosti otrok v okviru forenzičnega razgovora' ['Children's developmental characteristics in the forensic interview'], *Psihološka Obzorja*, 22: 167–75.

Putnik, D. (1973) *Psihologija* [*Psychology*]. Belgrade: Viša škola unutrašnjih poslova.

Republic of Slovenia, Ministry of Justice (2011) *Priporočila: Razgovor z otrokom s pomočjo videokonference in drugih tehničnih sredstev [Recommendations: Child Interview via Video Conference and Other Technical Means*]. Ljubljana: Ministry of Justice.

Republic of Slovenia, Ministry of the Interior (2003) *Gathering Information from the Suspect – Amendment to the Criminal Procedure Act*. Ljubljana: Ministry of the Interior.

Roso, Z. (1988) *Informativni razgovor i intervju* [*Informative Interview*]. Zagreb: Republički sekretariat za unutrašnjeposlove SR Hrvatske.

Štirn, M. and Podvršič, I. (2003) 'Zbiranje obvestil od osumljenca' ['Gathering Information from Suspects']. Ljubljana: Ministry of the Interior (unpublished).

Šugman, K. (2001) 'Kazenski postopki, povezani z nesrečami in nasiljem – še posebej glede na otroka' ['Criminal procedures involving accidents and violence with special emphasis on children'], in T. Samec and V. Slodnjak (eds), *Psihične travme v otroštvu in adolescenci*. Ljubljana: Inštitut za psihologijo osebnosti, pp. 184–9.

Supreme Court of the Republic of Slovenia (1999), I Ips 282/97.

Supreme Court of the Republic of Slovenia (2001), I Ips 225/98.

Supreme Court of the Republic of Slovenia (2002), I Ips 197/2002.

Supreme Court of the Republic of Slovenia (2002), I Ips 70/99.

Supreme Court of the Republic of Slovenia (2003), I Ips 259/2003.

Supreme Court of the Republic of Slovenia (2004), I Ips 168/2004.

Supreme Court of the Republic of Slovenia (2005), I Ips 202/2004.

Supreme Court of the Republic of Slovenia (2007), I Ips 65/2005.

Supreme Court of the Republic of Slovenia (2008), I Ips 403/2007.

Supreme Court of the Republic of Slovenia (2010), I Ips 206/2009.
Supreme Court of the Republic of Slovenia (2010), I Ips 260/2009.
Supreme Court of the Republic of Slovenia (2010), I Ips 47/2009.
Supreme Court of the Republic of Slovenia (2010), I Ips 60/2010.
Supreme Court of the Republic of Slovenia (2011), I Ips 1008/2010-35.
Supreme Court of the Republic of Slovenia (2011), I Ips 159/2010.
Supreme Court of the Republic of Slovenia (2011), I Ips 162/2010.
Supreme Court of the Republic of Slovenia (2011), I Ips 220/2010.
Supreme Court of the Republic of Slovenia (2011), I Ips 4349/2009-96.
Supreme Court of the Republic of Slovenia (2013), I Ips 34239/2010-121.
Supreme Court of the Republic of Slovenia (2013), I Ips 51335/2010-116.
Trankell, A. (1972) *Reliability of Evidence*. Stockholm: Beckmans.
Umek, P. (2009) 'Kako dobre priče so zlorabljeni otroci ali kako dobri spraševalci so preiskovalci?' ['How reliable are abused children as witnesses and how skilful are investigators as interrogators?'], *Revija za kriminalistiko in kriminologijo*, 60 (1): 16–24.
Undeutsch, U. (1982) 'Statement reality analysis', in A. Trankell (ed.), *Reconstructing the Past*. Deventer: Kluwer Law and Taxation Publishers, pp. 27–56.
Vodinelić, V. (1987) *Kriminalistika* [*Criminalistics*]. Belgrade: Naučna knjiga.

19 Investigative interviewing of victims and witnesses in Switzerland

J. Courvoisier, A. Schaller and M. Cyr

Introduction

To describe the Swiss practices in investigative interviewing of victims and witnesses, we will shed light on the definitions provided by the various statutses of the parties/participants in Swiss criminal proceedings. Indeed, on the 1st January 2011 a new Criminal Procedure code came into force, its primary purpose being to substitute for the 26 former cantonal codes[1] a single unified code. One effect of this unification is that the statutses of those involved in criminal proceedings have been redefined. In order to ensure a common language with the reader when addressing the practical aspects of and training in investigative interviewing, first we want to explain what is meant in Swiss criminal proceedings by the terms *victim* and *witness*. Who are they exactly? What are their attributes, their characteristics, their rights and obligations? This could allow a better understanding of who they are and the context in which they are interviewed. Moreover, this common comprehension could allow us to think about future challenges and about issues raised by these differentiations, especially in terms of training in interviewing techniques.

Statutses of interviewed people

The aim here is to describe the status of the *witness*, the disinterested observer of a specific situation, then the status of the *person called to provide information*,[2] a hybrid status and a particularity in Switzerland, and finally the status of the *injured*, the person most directly affected by the commission of a crime, and the distinction made by Swiss law between the injured, the victim and the complainant.

Witness

The Swiss Criminal Procedure Code (SCPC)[3] defines the witness as: 'Any person who did not participate in the crime, who is likely to make useful statements to clarify the facts and who is not interviewed as a person called to provide information' (art. 162). In principle, anybody could be a witness, but should not have participated in the crime; otherwise, this could mean that this person may profit from the offence and then s/he cannot be impartial in his/her statements (Perrier and Vuille, 2011). However, there are two cumulative conditions in being *capable to testify*: (1) being over 15 years of age; and (2) being capable of discernment at the time of interviewing. Any person who does not meet these conditions cannot be interviewed as a witness, but as a person called to provide information[4] (Perrier and Vuille, 2011), which will be discussed later in this chapter. The required obligations for witnesses are to testify and to tell the truth – otherwise they could be accused of making false statements (art. 307 Code Pénal Suisse (CPS)), an intentional crime – in contrast to a statement that does not correspond to reality but is unwittingly made. The competent authority[5] which conducts the investigative interview must then inform the witness of his/her obligation to tell the truth in order to not be charged for making false statements. In some cases, the person has the right to refuse to testify. In particular, this could happen to ensure a certain objectivity in case of personal relationship (art.168 CPPS), to protect oneself or somebody else (art. 169 CPPS), in relation to an official secret (art. 170 CPPS) or in relation to a professional secret (art. 171 CPPS).

Person called to provide information

A person called to provide information (PCPI) is a particular category of individuals heard in the criminal proceedings. This is laid down by art. 178 of the code. According to this article, a person called to provide information is anyone who:

(a) constituted him/herself as the complaining party;
(b) is under 15 years of age at the time of interviewing;
(c) is unable to fully understand the testimony of a witness because of a limited capacity for discernment;
(d) without being suspect, could be the offender or a participant in the case to resolve or another related;
(e) must be interrogated as co-offender of a crime attributed to him/her;
(f) is suspected in another proceedings due to an offence related to the crime to be solved;
(g) was or could be identified as representative of the company which the proceeding is against.

Thus this is an intermediate status between the suspect and the witness. As a consequence, the person called to provide information has no obligation to testify (arts. 163 and 176 CPPS). For the other rights and obligations, this status (under the direction of the prosecutor)[6] is regulated in accordance with the provisions applicable to the interrogation of suspects (Perrier and Vuille, 2011). The categories below are listed by art. 178 of the code and are presented in three distinct groups:

1. The complaining party who has a direct interest at the end of the proceedings. This status avoids him/her choosing between the defence of his/her interests

and the obligation to tell the truth. For instance, this could be the case if the person interviewed has some information to give but his/her testimony could not be objective because s/he and the suspect are relatives (Harari, 2010).

2. Individuals under the age of 15 years and incapable of discernment.[7] This status is considered because their testimony could intrinsically be suffering a lack of credibility.
3. Individuals who are or could be related to the crime as offender or participant. This status avoids them being exposed to the dilemma to self-incriminate or to contravene the obligation to testify or to tell the truth (Message, 2005; CPPS, p. 1189).

Affected persons: injured, victim, complainant

The common language considers the *victim* as a generic term, that is an individual who has suffered prejudice, regardless of its nature (e.g. moral, personal or material prejudice), but Swiss law distinguishes three types of *affected person*. These individuals would be categorised according to the *nature* of the crime suffered and whether they want to lodge a *complaint*. These specific types of *affected person* will now be explained.

Injured

We will use the term of an *injured person* in the context of 'anybody whose rights have been directly affected by a crime' (art. 115 al.1 CPPS). The person directly concerned (and this concept of *direct* attack is essential) is considered injured. However, the injured person can also be an entity. More specifically, the injured person is the one who finds damages in his/her possession. In practice, the injured person is interviewed as someone called to provide information (see below). As a consequence, s/he has the right to refuse to testify and/or cooperate with the police. For a good comprehension of the upcoming content, it should be emphasised that the victim and the complainant constitute subcategories of the entity *injured person*.

Victim

The legal language assigns the status of victim to 'the injured who, due to a crime, suffered direct damage to his/her physical, mental or sexual integrity' (art. 116 al.1 CPPS), thus it is a narrower definition than the injured person outlined above. In other words, every victim is injured, but not every injured person is a victim. Here, the condition is that the harm suffered is of a specific nature and of a 'particular' seriousness. For instance, in order to obtain the status of victim, it is not 'sufficient' if the individual has just been scared or sad. For example, a victim of common assault would not automatically be considered a victim. More precisely, Table 19.1 outlines what offences are covered by the definition given above.

Table 19.1 Offences covered by the term 'victim'

Offences against life and physical integrity	*Offences against sexual integrity*	*Offences against freedom*
Simple and serious bodily injury (122, 123 CPS)	Rape (190 CPS)	Threats (180 CPS)
Criminal negligence causing bodily harm	Sexual coercion (189 CPS)	Coercion (including forced marriage) (181 CPS)
Assault (134 CPS)	Sexual harassment (198 CPS)	Human trafficking (182 CPS)
Robbery (140 CPS)	Child sexual abuse (187 CPS)	Sequestration and kidnapping (183, 184 CPS)
	Adults having been victims during childhood	Hostage-taking (185 CPS)
	Incest (213 CPS)	

The victim enjoys special rights, differentiated by his/her age. Indeed, if the victim is under 18 years of age, which is the legal maturity in Switzerland (the sexual maturity is from the age of 16), subsequent provisions apply. These include specific arrangements that raise a better protection for the person concerned and the defence of his/her mental interests. In Switzerland, we use the term victim, or more specifically the term victim within the meaning of the Federal Act on Assistance to Crime Victims (FACV).[8] This status is defined by the FACV which entered into force in 1993. For instance, excluded from this definition is harm caused by offences against honour (defamation, slander, insult) or property (theft, fraud, breach of trust, etc.).

Complainant

The Swiss Criminal Procedure code defines the complaining party as 'the injured person who wishes to participate, as applicant, in either civil or criminal proceedings' (art. 118 al. 1 CPPS). More accurately, this would be the injured person, the victim and his/her relative (art. 116 CPPS) or legal guardian (art. 121 CPPS) (as the parent who gives written or oral notice (art. 119 al. 1 CPPS) of his/her intention to lodge a complaint on the behalf of his/her child). It could be a person or a corporate body. During police investigations, individuals who lodge a complaint have the right to refuse to testify and cooperate later in the proceedings, a right which falls under warrant in favour of an obligation to answer the questions and to tell the truth (see below).

Practices

It should be noted that police practices in Switzerland could be significantly different depending upon the global framework in which interviewing is conducted. Indeed, there can be discrepancies between whether the interview is conducted in the context of a police investigation or under a mandate issued by a magistrate (see note 6). For the sake of clarity, only the general guidelines will be discussed here.

Witness

Whichever of the authorities conducts the investigative interview, the witness must be informed that s/he has to testify in court and tell the truth. The judge will then decide if there were false statements considering all the statements made by the witness. This could be decided at the end of the interview (ATF 85 IV 79, JdT 1959 IV 79). The prosecution and/or the police must also make enquiries about the relationship between the witness and any other relevant parties involved in the investigation, being aware that any existing relationship (say husband and wife) may affect whether the witness asserts his/her right to refuse to testify. These enquiries and considerations also help ensure that his/her testimony is credible, while avoiding it being exploited at any later stages (say by the defence).

In order to consider the testimony as valid, it is necessary to notify the witness his/her obligation to testify and tell the truth. The non-validity of the testimony would give rise to the withdrawal of the case and it not being submitted to the judge. However, this evidence remains exploitable under some circumstances, which is not the case if the witness has not been informed of his/her right to testify. The status of 'witness' exists in Swiss law only if the prosecution takes charge of the case. Indeed, during investigation, the code does not allow the police to interview witnesses per se – except in cases permitted by art. 142 al. 2[9] – therefore they can only conduct interviews of people who have been advised of their requirement under the law to tell the truth. In this case, they can only conduct the interview of a person called to provide information. What investigators have to tell to them is:

> In application of articles 178 and 181 of the Criminal Procedure code, you are informed of the following rights and obligations:
>
> - You have the right to refuse to testify and to cooperate in proceedings.
> - If you know someone is innocent but accuse him/her of having committed a crime, you could be guilty of false accusation regarding article 303 of the Criminal Law code. This offence is punishable by a deprivation of liberty or a financial penalty.
> - If you denounce an offence while you know that it has not been committed, you could be guilty of misleading the justice regarding article 304 of the Criminal Law code. This offence is punishable by a maximum deprivation of liberty of three years or by a financial penalty.
> - If you help someone to avoid a criminal prosecution, you face a maximum deprivation of liberty of three years or a financial penalty according to article 305 of the Criminal Law code.

Person called to provide information

Anyone who is not a suspect is interviewed by the police for information (art. 179 al. 1 CPPS). Therefore, the police must choose and indicate in *the notice to appear* the status of those ordered to attend (PCPI or suspect). The person called to provide information has the right to refuse to testify and cooperate. This is the same right when the person called to provide information is under the direction of the prosecutor. But in addition, at any time of the proceedings under the direction of the prosecutor, this person can be assisted by a lawyer of his/her choice and at his/her own expense and s/he can ask for a translator or interpreter.

Affected persons: injured, victim, complainant

Injured

In the practice, the injured person would be interviewed as a person called to provide information (PCPI). Thus the rules of interviewing a person called to provide information described above apply (see above).

Victim

The victim would be interviewed according to the provisions that prevail for a person called to provide information (as mentioned above) including specific FACV provisions, that is to say the right:

- to information regarding help for victims (art. 305 CPPS);
- to a potential translation of the interview by someone of the same sex;
- to a closed session;
- to be accompanied by a reliable person (in addition to counsel[10]);
- to be interviewed by someone of the same sex at any time of the proceedings;
- to refuse a confrontation with the possible suspect;
- to have at least one person of the same sex in the court which will proceed to judgment;
- to refuse to answer questions related to his/her private sphere.

In the practice, the authority might offer a 'secured' framework to the interviewed victim, especially in cases of sexual offences. The room will be well set up and sometimes a special room will be chosen. Someone of the same sex as the victim will be solicited if necessary at any time during the proceedings and special attention will be necessary if intimate questions are addressed. The framework of the interview will be different according to the age of the victim. If a minor, the victim might confirm his/her consent on a recording.[11] If the interview is videotaped, it must be conducted by a trained investigator[12] and with an expert behind one-way glass (as control). This interview will be conducted in a special room without any computer.[13, 14] At the end of the interview, the authorities will clarify any remaining questions with the victim. Except in cases of road traffic offences, victims who are minors should not be interviewed more than twice.

Complainant

During a police investigation, the complaining party is interviewed as a person called to provide information (PCPI). Thus the recitals described above apply. Under the direction of the prosecutor, as for the witness, the complainant must be notified that s/he has the obligation to testify and the obligation to truthfully answer the questions. Unlike the witness, the complaining party under the direction of the prosecutor could ask for a counsel of his/her choice.

Training

For a long time, police training reflected Swiss federalism and the individualities of each of the 26 cantons. Through the Conference of Directors of Justice and Police Cantonal Departments,[15] the 'general concept of training'[16] appeared in 2002. The aim of this concept, which was finally adopted in 2004, is to ensure a common quality of training, but also a unified police doctrine as a result of the coordination of contents, methods and didactic materials. This applies especially to the initial training of police officers, which leads to the protected federal title of 'Police Officer with a Federal Diploma'. Even if initial training is provided and managed by cantons, it has to respond to the federal directives and requirements. Regarding ongoing/advanced training, the cantonal polices are free to organise and manage it. However, the different polices seem to share the same trend of practices and the same specific topics.

Initial police training

In Switzerland, there are two main kinds of police force. The first consists of uniformed police officers who mainly work as the police emergency squad and who patrol on the street. The second is the judicial police composed of different specialised squads[17] and named investigators, those who investigate and then mainly conduct interviews. There are two ways of becoming a police officer and then of joining a police force: (1) becoming a uniformed police officer, following one year of training at the police school, then completing a federal exam in order to obtain the title of police officer; (2) targeting the work of an investigator and then following the special one-year training provided by only a few cantons, for example Geneva and Vaud in the French part of Switzerland. Indeed, although some cantons offer the possibility of directly becoming an investigator, most of the cantons provide common training. This is a main issue in Switzerland that has led to several debates. Members of the public think that all police officers, whether uniformed or investigators, must receive the same training in order to be generalists and then be able to be moved (or commutable) between cantons. In addition, uniformed police officers increasingly seem to be interviewing people and require better training regarding interviewing techniques. Others think that because it is investigators who mainly conduct interviews and interrogation, they need special courses on those topics and others related to them which require different training.

As this issue of separate or common training is currently debated and because some changes will probably occur in the next few years, we will only discuss the evolution of the training in interviewing techniques in general in recent years, without making any difference between the types of training chosen. Indeed, it is interesting to note the growing interest shown by many in strengthening interviewing methods and techniques. The number of recent research papers about this topic seems to have received attention from the designers and managers of the police initial training in Switzerland (see Guéniat and Benoît, 2012). As proof, we will focus on the 'police psychology' manual of the Swiss Institute of Police, which assures a definite place to 'communicating in interviewing situations'.

While former police officers learned interviewing techniques on the ground without specific techniques (e.g. on-the-job), current training now focuses on the attitude police officers should adopt and how to consider interviews and interrogations. Indeed, the main issue is to consider the collaboration between the interviewer and the interviewee. The general training manual regarding interviewing techniques (and police psychology) of the Swiss Institute of Police states: 'The fundamental attitude of police officers should be the same regardless of who is interviewed; an attitude of respect and empathy, of acceptance of the other as a human being, the willingness to try to understand and to have an interest in people' (p. 22). Thus the challenge is to get the person conducting the interview to collaborate with the interviewee using appropriate questioning techniques. Indeed, there are some victims or witnesses who do not fully cooperate, so police officers need to be better prepared and trained to deal with such people. Thus new findings and new requirements lead us to think about a new approach in order to emphasise interviewing techniques and to increase police efficiency.

The aim of training now is to focus on the importance of the first contact and to build awareness of the art of questioning and listening, the cognitive interview,[18] suggestibility and memory functioning. Particular emphasis is being placed on the cognitive interview which aims to improve the quality and quantity of information obtained. In recent years, significant strides have been made regarding initial police training. The special issue of interviewing and interrogating according to specific criteria – for instance the person being interviewed or the kind of offence s/he has committed – is now at the core of several debates. We can therefore expect many changes and improvements in training programmes over the coming years.

Ongoing training

There seems to be a strong emphasis on the professionalisation of practices even if, as mentioned above, each canton remains free to introduce professionalisation into their teams in their own way. The different programmes proposed for actual or future ongoing training reveals an interest in interviewing methods and tactics. Overall, two major topics of ongoing training emerge. One concerns investigative interviewing of victims of sexual abuse and violence, the other is about general methods and techniques of investigative interviewing and interrogation.

Investigative interviewing of victims of sexual abuse and violence

The main training programme on this topic is provided by the Swiss Institute of Police[19] and is given by H. Van Gijseghem. The objectives are the knowledge of the legal context, child psychology, the psychology of criminal behaviour, interviewing techniques, assessment of the content of disclosures,[20] the impact of traumas and audio and video techniques.[21] The subjects taught are the criminal law, risk situations, trauma and its impact, child psychology and development, typologies of sexual perpetrators, interviewing methods in gradual stages, psychological, psychiatric and medical expertise, practical lessons and experimental studies.

For some years, another central training programme related to victims of abuse has also been given by the third author of this chapter (M. Cyr) and focuses especially on children interviewed as victims or witnesses. The main objective of this training is the protocol of the National Institute of Child Health and Human Development (NICHD) developed by M. E. Lamb and his colleagues (Cyr, 2014; Lamb *et al.*, 2008; Orbach *et al.*, 2000). This protocol was specially designed for children under 12 years old. However, with minor modifications, the protocol remains appropriate for adolescents. Mostly inspired by the cognitive interview, this protocol has a structured format, but one which is also flexible. It includes recent developments in child memory and suggestibility and relies on child abilities according to the developmental stage of children in order to allow them to provide a narrative from the age of three or four. The training lasts one week during which police officers review their knowledge concerning memory, suggestibility and the abilities and limits of children, as well as questioning techniques and, finally, the overall effectiveness of the protocol. Role-playing exercises are also conducted for each participant in order to practise the protocol. These exercises are videotaped and then viewed by the entire group so as to confirm that the structure of the protocol has been respected and to suggest new open-ended questions that could have been used. Following this training, it is recommended that retroaction sessions are provided for real investigative interviewing of victims/witnesses in order to perfect the training.

Methods and techniques of investigative interviewing and interrogation

The main training provided on this topic has been provided since 2007. This training is open to all cantonal police and mainly focuses on the comprehension of psychological mechanisms involved in interviewing and interrogation (see St-Yves and Meissner, 2014). More specifically, the goal is that police officers receive training on appropriate ways of questioning witnesses, victims and suspects, which includes the use of open-ended questions and listening without interruption and making interviewers aware of the risks associated with investigative interviewing, in particular the contamination of the account by suggestive and leading questions. Some other theoretical aspects are addressed, for instance the cognitive interview, memory functioning, good practices within investigative interviewing (see Bull, 2014; St-Yves, 2014), lie detection with the most objective truth and lie cues (see Vrij, 2008, 2014) and credibility assessment.

This training includes theoretical and practical sessions about the best ways to interview victims, witnesses and suspects. The practical exercises regarding witnesses in this training enable police officers to play the roles both as the witness – seeing a crime videotaped and then being questioned about it – and as the investigator. This allows them to practise the protocol of the cognitive interview under the supervision of observers. The role of witness provides them with a better understanding of memory functions and an awareness of the difficulty of being a *good* witness.

A new training programme is now provided by the Swiss Institute of Police (SIP)[22] since 2014. The aim of this four-day course is to increase the skills related to the different aspects of interviewing. During this training, police officers will first review the essential points regarding interviewing. Then they will address issues related to the relationship with the lawyer, deception cues and false confessions, the tactics of interviewing, memory functioning and mental illness/vulnerable personalities. The theoretical aspects are complemented with some role-playing games with professional actors in order to put into practice what has been learned. It is expected that this training will be extended over seven days. Thus there will be four theoretical days and then, a few months later, three practical days with objectives to achieve.

Conclusion

It is interesting to note that a certain paradox emerges between the various categories of people interviewed and the techniques of interviewing currently taught. Indeed, while there are many kinds of people interviewed according to the law and an important 'heterogeneity of profiles', the methods and techniques provided during training in order to interview these persons are almost all the same. Thus each witness, victim or person called to provide information is judicially defined in a precise way, and each one has some specific rights and obligations, which could be different if the person is interviewed under the direction of the prosecutor or not, or according his/her age, the offence related to the interview, etc. The formal aspects and issues of law are a big part of police training. Thus police officers have to fully understand the aspects of the law related to an interview, even before conducting it. They first have to think about formal and normative aspects of interviewing.

Afterwards, the elements constituting the offence have to be learned, and then the aspects related to the methods and techniques of interviewing, to the 'interactional' aspect of interviewing. Finally, the psychological aspect will begin. Indeed, for several years the training provided to officers in Switzerland has become more and more focused on the psychology of interviewing. This change in the perception of interviewing is a major innovation, especially due to recent research all around the world on this topic, having highlighted the importance of psychology in the interviewing room. However, while the judicial aspects of status are very specific and detailed, the psychological aspect remains quite general. The methods taught are certainly new and have proven their efficiency, but they are still global or applicable to any status of interviewee described above in this essay. There is a standardised approach to deal with the many types of situations, profiles, personalities and investigation themes.

What could be proposed next in order to take another step towards the emphasis on police training? It could be to render these psychological aspects more specific and appropriate. Problem-oriented policing might help develop appropriate and effective police responses to various types of crime and disorder.[23] It could be interesting to better understand the people interviewed and the issues related to them in order to adapt the best interviewing techniques. Moreover, techniques could be more targeted and adjusted and thus more efficient because they are more appropriate to the case.

It is essential to understand the general principles of the 'art' of interviewing, but it seems more and more necessary that it should be 'combined' with a better knowledge of the topics concerned. For instance, knowing the symptomatology related to a victim of sexual abuse could allow the conduct of a better interview, one even more adjusted and finally respectful. We believe that a better knowledge of the issues addressed[24] through research could be very helpful and lead to better adjustments in the methods taught or better efficiency in the investigative interviewing techniques used – not necessarily *more* knowing, but *better* knowing. This could be a future challenge regarding training of police interviewing in Switzerland.

Notes

1. Each of the 26 cantons of Switzerland had its own Criminal Procedure code, named the cantonal Criminal Procedure code.
2. Translated from the French 'personne appelée à donner des renseignements' (PADR).
3. Translated from the French 'code de procédure pénale suisse' (CPPS).
4. This status is a specific one between the suspect and the witness. Thus it is different from the witness because the person called to provide information could be the offender or a participant in the offence.
5. Namely the prosecution or the police.
6. It should be noted that in Switzerland, basically, the case is dealt with by the police (police investigation) or the prosecution directs the investigation (so the investigation is under the direction of the prosecutor and then conducted by the police or by the prosecution itself or by both, depending on the case and on the decision of the prosecution).
7. The decisive time is the interview, no matter the age or the state of irresponsibility (for instance being drug impaired) of the person at the moment of the crime.
8. Translated from the French 'Loi fédérale sur l'aide aux victimes d'infractions' (LAVI). This represents the law and the guidelines that specify in particular the way in which the victim must be considered in the investigation.
9. Article 142 al. 2: 'The police can interview people called to provide information and suspects. The Confederation and the cantons can designate the appropriate police officer to interview witnesses under the direction of the prosecutor.'

10. This right also applies to the victim interviewed during police investigation.
11. The audio/video-recording is then included in the file. It should be noted that, in Switzerland, only interviews of minor victims are recorded.
12. Inspired by the cognitive interview (see Geiselman *et al.*, 1985).
13. It should be noted that in Switzerland all interviews are generally typed up on a computer (witnesses, victims, suspects, PCPI).
14. However, there are some cantonal exceptions. For instance, in the canton of Neuchâtel FACV victims of a certain age (16–18 years) are interviewed on video in cases involving minor offences (according to the Criminal Code). In such cases handwritten records are not therefore required.
15. Translated from the French: 'La Conférence des directrices et directeurs des départements cantonaux de justice et police'.
16. Translated from the French: 'Concept général de formation' (CGF).
17. For instance, squads who investigate major crimes, sex crimes, robberies and crimes involving juveniles.
18. See Geiselman *et al.* (1985).
19. Translated from the French: Institut Suisse de Police (ISP). This institute was created in 1946 and focuses on the training of police managers and experts as well as ongoing training. At the national level, this institute is the largest provider of training for police.
20. For instance, the use of the 19 criteria of the Statement Validity Analysis (SVA).
21. This means how to work and conduct audio and videotaped interviews.
22. Translated from the French 'Institut Suisse de Police' (ISP).
23. For more information, see htp://www.popcenter.org.
24. As for child interviews where developmental psychology is reviewed, it could be necessary to reinforce the knowledge of investigators confronted by domestic violence, sexual abuse, psychologically vulnerable people, etc.

References

Bull, R. (ed.) (2014) *Investigative Interviewing*. New York: Springer.

Cyr, M. (2014) *Le recueil de la parole de l'enfant témoin ou victime: De la théorie à la pratique*. Paris: Dunod éditeurs.

Geiselman, R. E., Fisher, R. P., MacKinnon, D. P. and Holland, H. L. (1985) 'Eyewitness memory enhancement in the police interview: cognitive retrieval mnemonics versus hypnosis', *Journal of Applied Psychology*, 70: 401–12.

Guéniat, O. and Benoît, F. (2012) *Les secrets des interrogatoires et des auditions de police. Traité de tactiques, techniques et stratégies*. Lausanne: Presses polytechniques et universitaires romandes.

Harari, M. (2010) 'Quelques réflexions autour du droit du prévenu à la présence de son conseil', in R. Pfister-Liechti (ed.), *La procédure pénale fédérale*. Berne: Stämpfli Editions SA, pp. 79–94.

Institut Suisse de Police (2013) *Psychologie policière. Manuel de référence pour l'examen professionnel fédéral de policier/policière*. Neuchâtel: Verlag SPI.

Kruger, J. (2012) *La place des victimes dans la nouvelle procédure pénale*. Présentation faite le 7 décembre 2012 dans le cadre du congrès 'Violence domestique et système judiciaire: enjeux et perspective' organisé par le Bureau de l'égalité entre les femmes et les hommes du canton de Vaud.

Lamb, M. E., Hershkowitz, I., Orbach, Y. and Esplin, P. W. (2008) *Tell Me What Happened: Structured Investigative Interviews of Child Victims and Witnesses*. Hoboken, NJ: John Wiley & Sons.

Message du 21 décembre 2005 relatif à l'unification du droit de la procédure pénale, FF 2006.

Moreillon, L. and Parein-Reymond, A. (2013) *CPP. Code de procédure pénale. Petit commentaire*. Bâle: Helbling Lichtenhahn.

Orbach, Y., Hershkowitz, I., Lamb, M. E., Sternberg, K. J., Esplin, P. W. and Horowitz, D. (2000) 'Assessing the value of structured protocols for forensic interviews of alleged child abuse victims', *Child Abuse and Neglect*, 24 (6): 733–52.

Perrier, C. and Vuille, J. (2011) *Procédure pénale Suisse. Tables pour les études et la pratique*, 2nd edn. Bâle: Helbing Lichtenhahn.

St-Yves, M. (2014) 'Rapport in investigative interviews: five fundamental rules to achieve it', in M. St-Yves (ed.), *Investigative Interviewing: The Essentials*. Toronto, ON: Carswell.

St-Yves, M. and Meissner, C. A. (2014) 'Interviewing suspects', in M. St-Yves (ed.), *Investigative Interviewing: The Essentials*. Toronto, ON: Carswell, pp. 145–89.

Vrij, A. (2008) *Detecting Lies and Deceit: Pitfalls and Opportunities*. Chichester: Wiley.

Vrij, A. (2014) 'Myths and opportunities in verbal and nonverbal lie detection', in M. St-Yves (ed.), *Investigative Interviewing: The Essentials*. Toronto, ON: Carswell, 225–43.

North America

20 Investigative interviewing of witnesses and victims in Canada

Sonja P. Brubacher, Nicholas C. Bala, Kim Roberts and Heather Price

Introduction

As in many countries, the past three decades in Canada have seen major changes in the law and investigative practices, and much improved support for victims and witnesses in the criminal justice system. A more nuanced understanding of the limitations and capacities of victims of crime, in particular those who may be vulnerable (as in cases involving domestic violence, sexual offending or child abuse), has resulted in substantial changes in how the Canadian justice system treats victims and witnesses. Until the 1980s, the law was premised on the view that children and victims of sexual offences were inherently unreliable, and little effort was made to accommodate any witnesses, resulting in inadequate legal responses to domestic violence and child abuse cases. There has also been a substantial increase in the number and complexity of cases involving vulnerable witnesses, following the introduction in 1982 of the Charter of Rights, which augmented the protections and rights afforded to accused persons.

The Canadian criminal justice system

The Canadian criminal justice system is based on the British common law. The Supreme Court of Canada is the highest court in the country, and has the authority to bind the courts in all provinces and territories with its decisions. The Canadian Charter of Rights and Freedoms is a part of the Constitution Act that came into force in 1982, constitutionally entrenching an important set of rights to Canadians. The Charter protects fundamental freedoms, such as freedom of religion, and guarantees "equality before the law" and treatment in accordance with "principles of fundamental justice." The Charter has affected issues from abortion to same-sex marriage, but has had the greatest impact on criminal law and the rights of suspects and accused persons (Stuart, 2014).

The Criminal Code of Canada is the primary source of criminal offences and criminal procedure in Canada, and is applied in all ten provinces and three territories. Prosecutions under the Criminal Code are governed by the rules of evidence found in the Canada Evidence Act and the common law. While the federal government has jurisdiction over the enactment of laws governing criminal offences, procedure and evidentiary issues, the provincial and territorial governments have responsibility for the administration of justice, including most issues related to the investigation, interviewing, and prosecution of offences against persons and property. Thus there is significant variation in practice in the administration of justice and the treatment of suspects, victims and witnesses.

Policing in Canada

There are national, provincial, and municipal police services in Canada. The Royal Canadian Mounted Police (RCMP) is a national service that provides policing across the country related to certain offences, such as drug charges and some national security issues. Further, in much of the country, with the agreement of provincial and territorial governments, the RCMP provides most direct policing, including for sexual offences, domestic violence, and other crimes against the person or property. In the two most densely populated provinces, Ontario and Québec, as well as Newfoundland (for largely historical reasons), there are provincial police services that have responsibility for most policing. Most large and mid-size (pop. 50,000+) cities, as well as some smaller cities, also have municipal police services. Canada's Aboriginal peoples are served by a tripartite policing agreement via the First Nations Policing Program (FNPP), whereby some First Nation and Inuit communities manage their own police services in accordance with provincial and national regulations. As of 2013, the FNPP funds police officers working in 400 of these communities (Public Safety Canada, 2014).

Though not mandatory for recruitment, it is becoming increasingly common in Canada for those who want a career in policing to take a related college-level program (e.g. Police Foundation course, Criminal Justice degree), and many who make it to the rank of detective have university degrees. New recruits generally complete 4–6 months of training provided by their force to prepare them for general police patrol. (This training is broad and includes components such as basic crime scene investigation, note-taking, police policy, and lessons in conflict management.) RCMP recruits undergo six months of training at the Training Depot in Saskatchewan; Ontario Provincial Police and municipal services (who sponsor recruits in Ontario), as well as those from remote locations train at the Ontario Police College; while other services conduct training at provincially operated facilities (e.g. British Columbia Justice Institute, École nationale de police in Québec). It is generally accepted that detectives, however, need more specialized interview training than what is provided for new recruits. Additional specialized training for police takes place through provincial and regionally based training centers such as the Canadian Police College in Ottawa, the Toronto Police College, the Atlantic Police Academy (in the province of Prince Edward Island), as well as many others. Although there is a variety of programs, most include specific courses (e.g. Forensic Interviewing) that run one or two weeks.

Historical developments and current practice in victim/witness interviewing

Victims and witnesses

There have been a number of public inquiries into improper police investigative practices (e.g. failure to pool known information across departments) that have resulted in perpetrators of violence not being apprehended and therefore continuing victimization (Campbell, 1996). As Justice Campbell highlighted in his review, well-trained and highly skilled interviewers are only part of successful case management: "The work of the most dedicated, skillful, and highly motivated investigators and supervisors can be defeated by the lack of an effective case management system" (p. 8).

Concerns about inadequate police investigations are especially pronounced in regard to victimization in Canada's Aboriginal and immigrant populations. Differences in language and culture between non-Aboriginal police investigators and Aboriginal victims (e.g. see Lithopoulos and Ruddell, 2011, for discussion) can affect how the interview proceeds and may impact case outcomes. Further, a considerable portion of Canada's Aboriginal population lives in remote northern communities that must be accessed by aircraft, boat, or ice roads that are only useable in winter (Health Canada, 2009). In these locations there may be a lack of resources and training to investigate reports of violence and abuse in a timely and effective way.

A recent high-profile inquiry into notorious serial killer, Robert Pickton, who targeted women in Vancouver's sex trade, resulted in a scathing report issued by Inquiry Commissioner, Wally Oppal, regarding police attitudes towards vulnerable populations (Oppal, 2012). Pickton was convicted of murdering six women, charged with an additional 20 murders, and reportedly confessed to killing 49 women over a 20-year period. Police did not adequately follow-up on reports of the disappearances of these marginalized women, almost all of whom were Aboriginal. In one case that occurred during the disappearances, a woman escaped from the perpetrator during an attack and reported her brutal assault to the police, identifying her assailant. She was only interviewed once and, because she was a drug addict, was considered to be lacking credibility as a witness. Charges against Pickton were not pursued and no serious effort was made to conduct a thorough investigation of the information revealed in the woman's interview, resulting in further deaths in the five years between the woman's interview and his eventual arrest and conviction.

Inquiries, reports, and recommendations have resulted in increased awareness of the importance of thorough and fair investigations, and better support for socially marginalized and other vulnerable victims. However, they have not resulted in consensus for national standards to improve the quality of investigative interviewing more broadly. Indeed, Snook and colleagues (Snook *et al.*, 2010; Snook and Keating, 2011) noted that Canadian police officers receive perfunctory training in interviewing witnesses and there is a paucity of empirical data to characterize the interview training and practices where adult witnesses are involved in the Canadian justice system. An exception comes from Snook and Keating's (2011) study of a sample of adult-witness interviews conducted in one Canadian police organization. The interviews were most commonly conducted with closed-ended and probing questions, but the characteristics of interviewers and interviewees had little effect on interview dynamics. Snook and Keating recommended increased training of forensic interviewers and suggested that such training should be widely available. There are certainly places in Canada where police training is conducted to a high, evidence-based standard (some of which has been subjected to empirical scrutiny, e.g. Cyr and Lamb, 2009; Price and Roberts, 2011), but the lack of consistent protocols, standards, timelines, and monitoring is notable.

Interviewing in cases of domestic violence investigations

Prior to the 1970s, domestic violence was generally viewed as a "private matter" in Canada, and charges were only laid in the most serious cases. The women's movement of the 1970s helped create an environment where female victims of sexual assault and spousal violence as well as adult survivors of childhood abuse began to feel sufficient support to come forward with first person accounts of their traumatic experiences. In the early 1980s, policies were adopted that required police officers to lay charges in any domestic violence case where there was a reasonable prospect of conviction.

There has been a series of coroner's inquests and public inquiries into responses to domestic violence (Ontario Coroner, 2014), which have identified problems of poor investigative techniques and dismissive attitudes by police towards victims of spousal violence. Such reports have resulted in substantial changes in legislation, investigative practices, and victim supports.

In some larger centers there are special units that deal with domestic violence or sexual-offence cases. In many communities, Domestic Violence Court Programs have been established to facilitate prosecution and interagency collaboration for better responding to domestic violence cases. Their purpose is to process cases swiftly, provide early intervention, and increase the support to victims and the accountability of offenders. Including these achievements, these programs have also resulted in more cases being reported to police, greater arrest rates, improved risk assessment, and a lower attrition rate of cases in courts (Johnson and Fraser, 2011).

Interviewing child victims and witnesses

Until the 1980s few cases of child abuse were prosecuted in Canada (Bala, 1990), and children rarely testified. Awareness of child sexual abuse in Canada increased substantially after the release of the Badgley Committee Report (1984). This government-commissioned report was the first national effort to document the extent of child sexual abuse in Canada, and revealed major failings in responses to abuse, and made many recommendations for legal and social reforms. These reports revealed that children were physically, sexually, and emotionally abused at the hands of teachers, coaches, and supervisors, many of whom were ministers, priests, or nuns (Law Commission of Canada, 2000). Many of the cases involved some of society's most vulnerable children: those without parents to protect them, placed by the state in child welfare institutions, and in the now-closed residential schools for Aboriginal children. There was also a growing consciousness that much child abuse is perpetrated by family members, close family friends, or trusted community figures.

At the same time as genuine cases of child abuse were being reported in Canada (both contemporary and historic), there were widely publicized international cases of false allegations (e.g. the McMartin case). Although the number of cases of false allegations was very small compared to the number of true allegations, these cases raised concerns about poor investigative techniques by under-trained police investigators, therapists, and child welfare staff. The most infamous Canadian case of unfounded sexual abuse allegations occurred in 1992 in the small town of Martensville, Saskatchewan, as a result of overzealous, inadequately trained interviewers engaging in inappropriate questioning to "encourage" young children at a daycare center to "disclose" suspected sexual abuse (Harris, 1998). More than a dozen adults, including some members of the local police service, were charged but eventually cleared of abusing several young children. Several investigative interviewing and child development experts testified that the interviewing techniques in the investigation were known to elicit unreliable reports. Although relatively small in number, cases of unfounded allegations impose immense burdens on those falsely accused of abuse, and serve as important reminders of the need for careful interviewing by properly trained investigators, and for a fair trial process that allows accusations to be properly tested.

Around the same time as other common law countries (e.g. Australia, the US, the UK) were making changes to their child-witness procedures, Canada's Parliament began a process of legislative reform, amending the Criminal Code and Canada Evidence Act to facilitate the provision of testimony by children. The 1988 amendments abolished the requirements for corroboration of children's testimony in order to convict accused persons, permitted children to testify via closed-circuit television from outside the court, and allowed support persons to accompany children in court. These reforms also allowed for the admission into evidence of video-recorded police interviews with a child, provided the child testified, adopted the contents of the video, and could be cross-examined about the statement. During this period, Canadian courts also began to change some of the common law evidentiary rules relating to children. Notably, the Supreme Court in 1990 in *R.* v. *Khan* modified the hearsay rule, to facilitate the admission of out-of-court statements about a child's disclosures of abuse. If a child is unable to testify in court, and the out-of-court statements are found to be both reliable and necessary, a *Khan* application can be made to admit these statements as evidence.

While the 1988 amendments were significant, there was a continuing reluctance by prosecutors and judges to use some of the accommodations for child witnesses, especially closed-circuit television. In 2006, Parliament again amended the law to create a presumption that witnesses under 18 years, if requested, may testify via closed-circuit television or behind a screen, and a support person may accompany the child in court (Bala *et al.*, 2010). Provisions were also enacted to require the appointment of counsel to cross-examine child witnesses in cases where the accused is self-represented. Further, the 2006 amendments established a presumption that children under 14-years-old are competent to testify. The use of the oath was abolished for children, who can now testify after promising to tell the truth. The only test for competence is whether a child is "able to communicate" in the proceedings; children are not to be asked questions about their understanding of the meaning of the "promise to tell the truth" as part of the assessment of their competence to testify. A recent survey of Canadian judges from four provinces found that most believe these reforms facilitate the giving of evidence by child witnesses without compromising the rights of the accused (Bala *et al.*, 2011). The constitutionality of these laws has been upheld by the Supreme Court of Canada (Bala *et al*, 2010; Bala, 2014).

While Parliament and the courts have changed the laws governing criminal *proceedings* involving child witnesses in Canada, there continues to be much variation in how investigations are conducted. As with adult witnesses, there is no national standard in Canada for the training of professionals in the interviewing of children. Even within the same province or territory, vulnerable victims can have very different experiences with the police and legal system (London Family Court Clinic, 2002).

The Cornwall Public Inquiry (Glaude, 2009) provided a detailed report on the failure for more than a decade of police and child protection agencies to respond adequately to allegations of child sexual abuse, resulting in multiple further victimizations of boys and young men. That inquiry included the following recommendation:

> The government of Ontario should fund joint speciality training for child welfare workers and police officers on investigating cases of child sexual abuse. Efforts should be made to expand this training to include other relevant professionals who could be involved in investigations or in supporting the victim or his or her family (Glaude, 2009).

The extent of collaborative training between child protection workers and police varies geographically and historically. There is no commonly accepted provincial or national model of joint training (and procedures even vary within provinces and territories), and social workers and police have different mandates and minimum standards to which they must adhere. Some scholars have suggested that standardization of investigative procedures could be best achieved through legislative change (Somji, 2009), although that will be a significant challenge in a country as physically large as Canada with many isolated communities.

For example, there are 292 remote communities with a total population of more than 194,000 people which are not connected to the North American electrical grid or to the piped natural gas network (Government of Canada, 2011).

When abuse is reported to police in Canada, they conduct an interview with the child (now almost always videotaped) and other witnesses or persons who may have knowledge of the events, and make an initial decision about whether criminal charges are appropriate. Sometimes the case is referred to police by a child protection agency. In such cases police and social workers may conduct a joint interview, according to an interagency protocol; these protocols provide that the police officer will usually take the lead in initial interviewing of the child although the child protection worker may also do so. In a few locales, young victims and witnesses are interviewed at Child Advocacy Centers (CACs), where a multidisciplinary team including legal and medical professionals coordinate procedures. The CACs are non-profit agencies and receive funding from both private agencies and different levels of government. The federal government of Canada has provided funding to establish or enhance centers in major cities (Department of Justice, 2014). As of spring 2014, there were 15 CACs nationwide.

Many victims of abuse, especially children, delay disclosures for many years. When disclosed to the police, the investigations into "historic abuse" cases pose special challenges as the memories of victims and witnesses are often limited, and records may have been destroyed. However, there has been some success in Canada in prosecuting historic abuse cases, especially those involving multiple victims in institutional settings as their statements may corroborate each other (Connolly and Read, 2006; Law Commission of Canada, 2000).

The two primary interviewing procedures used with child witnesses in Canada, and supported by empirical research, are the Step-wise Guidelines (Yuille *et al.*, 2009) and the NICHD Protocol (Lamb *et al.*, 2007). In most regions of the country, however, interviewers are simply encouraged to use a structured interviewing format that they can defend in legal proceedings (e.g. the Calgary Multidisciplinary Manual). That is, most police interviewers of vulnerable witnesses are instructed to conduct "good interviews" according to "best practices" (e.g. build rapport, avoid leading questions, and conduct the interview in an open manner) but without specific and detailed interview procedures.

Interviewing adult victims and witnesses with developmental disabilities

Tharinger *et al.* (1990) estimated that, in the US, only 3 percent of abuse incidents involving adults with intellectual disabilities are reported to authorities, while Sobsey and Doe (1991) reported that despite the fact that the alleged offender was known in 95.6 percent of cases involving adults with developmental disabilities, only 22.2 percent were charged and only 8.5 percent convicted. There are no reliable Canadian statistics on the abuse of adults with intellectual disabilities. However, for a number of years researchers and advocates in Canada have been aware that persons with intellectual disabilities are at high risk of victimization and face special challenges in the court process (Bala, 1990). A recent study of Canadian Crown prosecutors suggests that many justice system professionals remain unaware of how to effectively investigate and prosecute these cases (Hurley, 2013).

The 2006 Amendments to the Criminal Code extended to vulnerable adults some of the accommodations previously made in 1988 only for children. Adults are now permitted to testify via closed-circuit television from outside the courtroom and have a support person present if they "have difficulty" in testifying "by reason of a physical or mental disability." Since 2006, judges have also had the discretionary power to allow accommodations for vulnerable adults such as appointing counsel to cross-examine a vulnerable witness rather than allowing cross-examination by a self-represented defendant, if considered necessary to obtain a "full and candid account" from the witness.

The 2006 amendments to the Canada Evidence Act prohibit asking children under 14 about their understanding of the meaning of the truth or an oath. In a significant 2012 decision, the Supreme Court of Canada recognized both the vulnerability and capacity of adults with developmental disabilities to testify (*R.* v. *D.A.I.)*. The Chief Justice Court held that there is an "equivalency" between the tests for assessing the competence of children and mentally disabled adults:

> When it comes to testimonial competence, precisely what, one may ask, is the difference between an adult with the mental capacity of a six-year-old, and a six-year-old with the mental capacity of a six-year-old? Parliament, by applying essentially the same test to both ... implicitly finds no difference. In my view, judges should not import one (para. 52).

The Supreme Court in *R.* v. *D.A.I.* significantly extended the range of cases in which mentally disabled adults can testify about their victimization, and hence increased protection available to this vulnerable population. Although changes to the law, court preparation programs, testimonial supports, and improved investigative interviewing have helped to ameliorate experience of victims in the legal process, it remains a difficult, and sometimes traumatic, experience for adults with developmental disabilities to be involved with police and the criminal courts. Further, despite these advances in accommodating special needs during in-court experiences, similar advances have not been extended to the investigation stage.

Implications for research, policy, and practice

The criminal justice system is not only concerned with ascertaining the truth but also with fair process, public accountability, and protection of the constitutional rights of the accused. In Canada there is an onus on the prosecution to prove the guilt of an accused beyond a reasonable doubt, and inevitably there will be some true allegations of victimization that cannot be proven in the criminal court.

Further, while most reports of abuse and victimization are well-founded, there are also a relatively small number of unfounded allegations. The role of the criminal justice system, starting with the police investigation and ending in court, is to balance the rights of the accused and result in fair prosecution.

Over the past 30 years, there have been substantial increases in the understanding of the capacities and needs of vulnerable witnesses and victims of family violence, which have led to enhancements in the levels of support provided by the Canadian justice system. Yet improvements are still needed in some areas, such as maintaining prosecutorial continuity in the carriage of cases and resolving cases within a reasonable timeframe. Progress is hampered by the little information there is about the experiences of witnesses as interviewees and in the broader legal system. Further legislative reform is also required. For example, while the common law rules governing the admission of children's disclosures of abuse have significantly improved, there are still many cases in which the trier-of-fact may not hear evidence of the child's initial, often graphic, disclosures of abuse, and the court is left to hear only the statements the child makes months or even years after the events in question.

As is evident from this chapter, the majority of reforms for victims and witnesses in Canada over the past few decades have focused on educational awareness (e.g. enhanced understanding of the capabilities of children and adult witnesses with intellectual disabilities; recognition of the severity of spousal abuse) or on facilitating in-court participation. Police, prosecutors, and judges generally have a much better understanding of how to treat vulnerable witnesses than 30 years ago. This awareness has spurred on the development and acceptance of appropriate provisos (e.g. removal of the competency test for children, the creation of domestic violence courts). With greater awareness among legal professionals and systemic supports in place, these changes have set the stage in Canada for improvements in investigative interviewing procedure. There is now a need for increased efforts by Canadian academics to conduct translational research, in cooperation with police, social workers, lawyers, and judges, to facilitate the incorporation of high-quality standardized interview training for professionals working with victims and witnesses, especially those who are vulnerable. This work can be followed by efforts to standardize procedure across the country, which has remained a challenge because of Canada's large size (the world's second largest country by total area – geographically larger than the US but with a population half that of the UK).

As they have done over the past three decades in other areas, researchers and policy-makers should continue to reform and improve Canada's justice system with the aim of standardizing high-quality interviewing, and interview training, across the country. Such reforms will promote the fair and thorough conduct of investigations, with due regard for the needs of victims and witnesses, as well as the rights of suspects and accused persons. Further improvements will require careful study of experiences in other countries, as well as more empirical research in Canada about the experiences of victims and witnesses in investigative interviews, and on the long-term effects of involvement in the justice system.

References

Badgley, R. F. (Chair) (1984) *Report of the Committee on Sexual Offences Against Children and Youths*. Ottawa: Supply and Services Canada (referred to as the Badgley Report).

Bala, N. (1990) "Double victims: child sexual abuse and the Canadian criminal justice system," *Queen's Law Journal*, 15: 3–30. Retrieved from http://queensu.ca/lawjournal/index.html.

Bala, N. (2014) "Canada's empirically-based child competency test and its principled approach to hearsay," *Roger Williams University Law Review*, 19: 513–45. Retrieved from: http://rogerwilliamslawreview.org.

Bala, N., Evans, A., and Bala, E. (2010) "Hearing the voices of children in Canada's criminal justice system: recognizing capacity and facilitating testimony," *Child and Family Law Quarterly*, 22: 21–45. Retrieved from: http://www.jordanpublishing.co.uk/practice-areas/family/publications/child-and-family-law-quarterly.

Bala, N., Paetsch, J. J., Bertrand, L. D., and Thomas, M. (2011) *Testimonial Support Provisions for Children and Vulnerable Adults (Bill C-2): Case Law Review and Perceptions of the Judiciary*. Ottawa: Department of Justice Canada.

Campbell, A. (1996) *Bernardo Investigation Review: Report of Mr. Justice Archie Campbell*. Toronto: Ontario Ministry of the Attorney General.

Connolly, D. A. and Read, J. D. (2006) "Delayed prosecutions of historic child sexual abuse: analyses of 2064 Canadian criminal complaints," *Law and Human Behavior*, 30: 409.

Cyr, M. and Lamb, M. E. (2009) "Assessing the effectiveness of the NICHD investigative interview protocol when interviewing French-speaking alleged victims of child sexual abuse in Quebec," *Child Abuse and Neglect*, 33: 257–68.

Department of Justice Canada (2014) *Backgrounder: Child Advocacy Centers*. Retrieved from: http://news.gc.ca/web/article-en.do?nid=815929.

Glaude, N. (2009) *The Cornwall Public Inquiry*. Toronto: Ontario Ministry of the Attorney General.

Government of Canada (2011) *Status of Remote/Off-grid Communities in Canada*. Retrieved from: https://www.bullfrogpower.com/remotemicrogrids/presentations/status_of_remote_off_grid_communiites_in_canada_2013-118_en.pdf.

Harris, F. (1998) *Martensville: Truth or Justice: The Story of the Martensville Daycare Trials*. Toronto: Dundern Press.

Health Canada (2009) *A Statistical Profile on the Health of First Nations in Canada: Determinants of Health, Vol. 1993–2003*. Ottawa: Health Canada.

Hurley, P. (2013) *Vulnerable Adult Witnesses: The Perceptions and Experiences of Crown Prosecutors and Victim Services Providers in the Use of Testimonial Support Provisions*. Ottawa: Research and Statistics Division Department of Justice Canada.

Johnson, H. and Fraser, J. (2011) "Specialized domestic violence courts: do they make women safer?" *Community Report: Phase, 1*. Retrieved from: https://contrevff.ca/sites/default/files/dvc-do-theymake-women-safer.pdf.

Lamb, M. E., Orbach, Y., Hershkowitz, I., Esplin, P. W., and Horowitz, D. (2007) "A structured forensic interview protocol improves the quality and informativeness of investigative interviews with children: a review of research using the NICHD investigative interview protocol," *Child Abuse and Neglect*, 31: 1201–31.

Law Commission of Canada (2000) *Restoring Dignity: Responding to Child Abuse in Canadian Institutions*. Ottawa, Canada: Canada Minister of Public Works and Government Services.

Lithopoulos, S. and Ruddell, R. (2011) "Policing isolated Aboriginal communities: perspectives of Canadian officers," *Policing: An International Journal of Police Strategies and Management*, 34: 434–53.

London Family Court Clinic (2002) "Child witnesses in Canada: where we've been, where we're going," *Child Witness Project, Center for Children and Families in the Justice System*. London, Canada: London Family Court Clinic.

Ontario Office of the Chief Coroner (2014) *Domestic Violence Death Review Committee: 2012 Annual Report*. Toronto: Ontario Office of the Chief Coroner.

Oppal, W. T. (2012) *Forsaken: The Report of the Missing Women Commission of Inquiry*. Vancouver: Missing Women Commission of Inquiry.

Price, H. L. and Roberts, K. P. (2011) "The effects of an intensive training and feedback program on police and social workers' investigative interviews of children," *Canadian Journal of Behavioural Science*, 43: 235–44.

Public Safety Canada (2014) *Aboriginal Policing*. Retrieved from http://www.publicsafety.gc.ca/cnt/cntrng-crm/plcng/brgnl-plcng/index-eng.aspx.

R. v. *D.A.I.* [1990] SCC 5.

R. v. *Khan* [1990] 2 SCR 531.

Snook, B. and Keating, K. (2011) "A field study of adult witness interviewing practices in a Canadian police organization," *Legal and Criminological Psychology*, 16: 160–72.

Snook, B., Eastwood, J., Stinson, M., Tedeschini, J., and House, J. C. (2010) "Reforming investigative interviewing in Canada," *Canadian Journal of Criminology and Criminal Justice/La Revue Canadienne de Criminologie et de Justice Pénale*, 52: 215–29.

Sobsey, D. and Doe, T. (1991) "Patterns of sexual abuse and assault," *Sexuality and Disability*, 9: 243–59.

Somji, N. (2009) "When will the law catch up to science? A call for legislating identification procedures," *Criminal Law Quarterly*, 54: 299–331. Retrieved from: http://www.carswell.com/product-detail/criminal-law-quarterly/.

Stuart, D. (2014) *Charter Justice in Canadian Criminal Law*, 6th edn. Toronto: Carswell.

Tharinger, D., Horton, C. B., and Millea, S. (1990) "Sexual abuse and exploitation of children and adults with mental retardation and other handicaps," *Child Abuse and Neglect*, 14: 301–12.

Yuille, J. C., Cooper, B. S., and Hervé, H. F. (2009) "La nuova generazione delle linee guida step wise per l'intervista dei minori" ["The step-wise guidelines for child interviews: the new generation"], in M. Casonato and F. Pfafflin (eds), *Pedoparafilie: Prospettive psicologiche, forensi, psichiatriche*. Milan: Franco Angeli, pp. 120–41.

21 Forensic interviewing of child witnesses in the United States

Training protocols and practices

Kyndra C. Cleveland, Jodi A. Quas and Stephanie Denzel

In the United States, like most other countries, witness accounts of alleged crimes play a critical role in the pursuit of justice. Witnesses may be questioned shortly after an event, though more often they are questioned days, months, or even years later, as details regarding a crime surface and investigations narrow on particular suspects. A continuing challenge concerns how to obtain the most reliable and complete reports possible from witnesses, without introducing suggestions or false details, so that justice can be served for all parties involved.

In the United States, this challenge has been especially pervasive when the alleged victim or witness is a child.[1] When children are asked to provide eyewitness accounts of a crime, they are most often being questioned about alleged maltreatment (Goodman *et al.*, 1999). In fact, annually, approximately three million reports are made in the United States to social services regarding suspected child maltreatment (US Department of Health and Human Services, 2012), making it a widespread and significant problem. It is also one with devastating consequences for children, families, and society. When suspicions of maltreatment arise, most children must be interviewed to establish whether it actually occurred, and if so, to identify the perpetrator and determine the event details (National Kids Count, 2013). Maltreatment, moreover, tends to occur in secrecy and often lacks corroborative evidence (Bruck and Ceci, 1999; Lamb *et al.*, 1994; Lewis *et al.*, 2014). As such, similar to crimes in which adults are the only witnesses, when children are the only witnesses, their reports can dramatically influence the progression and outcome of a legal case, placing considerable demands on children to be as complete and accurate as possible.

Broad concerns, however, exist about whether children are capable of providing accurate accounts of maltreatment. These concerns, or at least the extensiveness of them, can be traced historically to the late 1980s and early 1990s when several highly publicized and controversial legal cases involving alleged child sexual abuse dominated headline news. In these cases, daycare providers were accused of sexually abusing sometimes scores of children. The children's claims often included bizarre acts of ritual abuse, kidnapping, and even animal sacrifice (e.g. *Commonwealth of Massachusetts* v. *Cheryl Amirault LeFave*, 1990; *People* v. *Buckey*, 1990; *State* v. *Michaels*, 1993; see Ceci and Bruck, 1995). A majority of the cases ended in convictions, often based exclusively or nearly exclusively on the children's reports. At first, the media raved about the abhorrent behavior of the alleged perpetrators. Over time, however, scientific evidence on the harmful effects of suggestive interviewing on children's accuracy accumulated, and media attention shifted to highlighting the ways in which suggestive interviewing could lead to false memories of maltreatment in children and to the consequences of those false memories for innocent adults (Nieves, 1994; Stout, 1995). Most of the convictions have since been overturned under the assumption that the methods used to elicit the children's reports may have induced errors and false reports. Most professionals today believe that all or nearly all of the children's allegations in the high-profile cases emerged not from actual experience but instead from false suggestions planted by well-meaning parents and overzealous professionals.

In part, as a result of these high-profile cases and their aftermath, scientists, practitioners, and legal and social service professionals in the United States and abroad have sought to determine how best to question suspected child victims to ensure that the information they provide is accurate and complete. These efforts have led to an enormous literature concerning children's eyewitness capabilities, suggestibility, and proneness to false memory, including a set of well-supported recommendations regarding how to and how not to question children to elicit complete and accurate accounts (e.g. Bjorklund *et al.*, 1998; Lyon *et al.*, 2012; Memon *et al.*, 1996; Thompson *et al.*, 1997; see Bruck and Ceci, 1999; Goodman *et al.*, 2010; Lyon, 2005, for reviews). The purpose of the present chapter is not to review this expansive literature or describe best-practice recommendations, as this could not easily be done in a brief chapter. Instead, our purpose is to begin to address two general questions that directly follow from the literature. These are, quite simply: what forensic interviewing guidelines are most prevalent in the United States and how closely do these guidelines conform to best-practice recommendations? How frequently do these guidelines get into the hands of front-line interviewers in the United States?

Answering these questions, though, is incredibly difficult. For one, there is no single or uniform protocol that forensic interviewers are recommended or required to use. Instead, each state can adopt its own distinct set of formal guidelines or rules to guide interviewer practices, but only a few states have done so (e.g. Michigan: http://www.michigan.gov/documents/dhs/DHS-PUB-0779_211637_7.pdf; Washington: http://depts.washington.edu/hcsats/PDF/guidelines/WA State Child Interview Guide 2009 2010.pdf; Oregon: http://www.doj.state.or.us/victims/pdf/oregon_interviewing_guidelines.pdf). Second, in many states, policies are determined at the county or city level, leading to variability in practices even within a single state. Third, although interviewers often attend workshops, conferences, and seminars where best-practice interviewing guidelines are presented, the content of these programs varies considerably, potentially leading to very different interviewer beliefs and behaviors when questioning suspected child victims. Fourth and finally, even when interviewers are trained to use best practices, it is not known how closely they follow these practices, and how their adherence changes over time.

As such, rather than attempt to review each state's interviewing guidelines, we next describe several protocols currently available in the United States. We explain how the protocols emerged, their main tenets, and, when possible, how widely the protocols are distributed. We close with recommendations regarding how to improve interviewer training. Overall therefore, our chapter, though not comprehensive in terms of reviewing all practices available in the United States, does provide insight into professionals' putative knowledge of currently available protocols.

Widely known and currently available protocols

The NICHD Protocol and the Ten-Step Investigative Interview Protocol

The National Institute of Child Health and Human Development Structured Interview (NICHD) Protocol and Lyon's Ten-Step Investigative Interview Protocol are quite similar, and in fact one grew out of the other. They are also arguably the most widely known and respected protocols globally by scientists, practitioners, and policy-makers. They are thus described here together.

The NICHD Protocol was developed by Michael Lamb and colleagues (Lamb *et al.*, 2008; Sternberg *et al.*, 2002) based on the large body of science on children's social, cognitive, and emotional development, and the research team's long-standing expertise in conducting developmental research and applying that work to legal settings. The protocol distilled and integrated knowledge from these literatures to create a set of concrete recommendations about how to structure a forensic interview with a suspected child victim (Lamb *et al.*, 2007). The protocol has been adopted formally in several countries and is widely used in many others. It is, in addition, taught in mandatory training programs for interviewers across the globe.

The NICHD Protocol is described in dozens of scientific publications, book chapters, and edited and written books (Lamb *et al.*, 2011; Lamb *et al.*, 2007; Lyon *et al.*, 2009; Stewart *et al.*, 2011). As such, it is incredibly accessible and easy to distribute. In addition, its efficacy has been rigorously investigated for 15 years, and many of the articles describing the protocol are freely available online (http://nichdprotocol.com/). The protocol begins with an instruction and rapport-building phase during which interviewers should give children instructions so that they know they can say, "I don't understand" or "I don't know." Interviewers should also have children practice narrating about past events. During the substantive phase, the protocol contains instructions regarding how to introduce the allegation and how to ask follow-up invitations to elicit details of the abuse. Other instructions concern how to ask about the frequency of abuse (Lamb *et al.*, 2007) and how to interview reluctant children (Hershkowitz *et al.*, 2006; Orbach *et al.*, 2007). Finally, the NICHD Protocol includes a summary phase during which the interviewer concludes by discussing a neutral topic.

Lyon's Ten-Step Investigative Interview Protocol emerged from the NICHD Protocol and is thus similarly strongly rooted in developmental science

(Lyon, 2014). Several slight modifications were made, though, to increase the protocol's efficacy and ease of use. For one, the Ten-Step Protocol recommends eliciting a promise to tell the truth from children (Lyon and Dorado, 2008; Lyon *et al.*, 2008) and informs children that the interviewer does not know what has happened. These are designed to reinforce the importance of honesty and empower children as the primary source of knowledge. Second, the Ten-Step Protocol provides explicit instructions regarding the content of the rapport-building conversation. Children should be asked about what they like to do and what they don't like to do. This not only gives the interviewer some insight into the children's linguistic competence but also serves to prepare children to narrate about potentially negative experiences. Third, the Ten-Step Protocol contains specific recommendations about asking open-ended and follow-up prompts during rapport building so that children learn how to provide detailed responses to these types of prompts.

Fourth and finally, the Ten-Step Protocol provides more instruction than the NICHD Protocol concerning questioning children about repeated maltreatment. Children should be asked first if the allegation happened once or more than once. If the latter, children should then be asked to describe the time they remember most, the first time, and the last time. This approach helps establish that maltreatment occurred at least three times when a child cannot produce an exact number regarding how often maltreatment occurred. Children in general have considerable difficulty recounting temporal details (e.g. when, how many times) for events in the distant past, including those that were repeated and may have been quite salient (e.g. Wandrey *et al.*, 2012). The courts are often sensitive to developmental limitations in children's temporal abilities (*Bradshaw* v. *State*, 2012; *People* v. *Vasquez*, 1996; *State* v. *Otis*, 2011) and at times allow such temporal questions, combined with children's responses, to support charges of repeated maltreatment.

With regard to the utility of the NICHD and Ten-Step Protocols, evidence consistently reveals benefits from employing both protocols. For example, when the behavior of interviewers prior to NICHD training is compared to their behavior after being intensively trained with the protocol, via multiple training sessions along with practice, feedback, and supplemental trainings, interviewers ask more open-ended questions and fewer direct and suggestive questions (Lamb *et al.*, 2002). Children in turn provide more abuse-relevant information, particularly in response to open-ended invitations rather than direct questions. Because the children are providing details without being prompted, fewer concerns are raised about suggestibility than are often raised with children questioned in a traditional manner (e.g. see Bruck and Ceci, 1999). It is perhaps not surprising as well that children who are interviewed with the NICHD Protocol appear more credible and reliable (Lamb and Fauchier, 2001; Orbach and Lamb, 1999, 2001), which may lead to quicker interventions on the children's behalf.

The Ten-Step Protocol appears similarly beneficial. Eliciting a promise to tell the truth has been shown to increase children's disclosure of laboratory-based events, even events that negatively implicate children (Lyon and Dorado, 2008; Lyon *et al.*, 2008; Talwar *et al.*, 2004). Open-ended rapport building has been linked to greater productivity in field studies (Hershkowitz, 2008), particularly among children who have already disclosed maltreatment (Sternberg *et al.*, 1997). Analogue studies, especially in relation to increasing children's willingness to disclose negative events, have not revealed similar benefits of rapport building (Lyon *et al.*, 2014), but rapport has not been shown to increase errors.

The CornerHouse Forensic Interview Protocol

The CornerHouse Forensic Interview Protocol (CFIP) is widely available in the United States. Its evolution, though, diverges somewhat from the evolution of the NICHD and Ten-Step Protocols, even though many of the CFIP's current recommendations overlap. The CFIP was created by CornerHouse, a non-profit multidisciplinary child advocacy center in Minnesota that identifies and intervenes on behalf of victimized children. The CFIP began as a program called Rapport, Anatomy Identification, Touch Inquiry, Abuse Scenario, and Closure (RATAC) (Anderson *et al.*, 2009), which was developed by staff members at CornerHouse based on their personal experiences questioning alleged victims. Because RATAC was used to train large numbers of interviewers around the country and because it formed the initial basis for the CFIP, it is useful to review RATAC here. It should be noted, however, that RATAC's materials and training are proprietary. It is thus difficult without having completed the formal training to obtain precise details of its format and procedures.

Anderson and colleagues (2009) provide one of the most useful overviews of RATAC for those who have not completed the training. RATAC begins with general recommendations regarding interviewer demeanor and dress, and interview location. These recommendations are consistent with what scientific research suggests is optimal for increasing children's accuracy (Anderson *et al.*, 2009). The first stage of RATAC, Rapport, instructs interviewers to build rapport, having the child practice answering questions and having the child make drawings to facilitate her comfort. During the second stage, Anatomy Identification, anatomical diagrams are presented to ascertain how well the child can distinguish genders and identify a common language that can be used to label body parts. RATAC then recommends the diagrams remain visible throughout the rest of the protocol to use as a reference. In the third stage, Touch Inquiry, interviewers are instructed to ask about touches that are and are not okay, including who should and should not touch the child. The purpose of these questions is to evaluate how well the child understands and can talk about body touch. Once a child makes a possible disclosure, the interview transitions to the Abuse Scenario stage, during which interviewers should ask questions to gather abuse details. Finally, in the Closure stage, interviewers discuss personal safety, answer the child's questions, and thank the child.

Although RATAC encourages interviewers to build rapport, it does not recommend interviewers provide ground rules or instructions at the outset of an interview. Instead, it suggests incorporating instructions during the interview when appropriate, such as reinforcing children (e.g. providing positive feedback) for saying "I don't know." RATAC recommends not engaging in formal truth/lie discussions or eliciting a promise to tell the truth, stating that empirical evidence has failed to reveal consistent benefits of such strategies (Anderson *et al.* 2009). Finally, RATAC supports asking direct or closed-ended questions about having been touched as a means of eliciting a disclosure of abuse. It does not, as other protocols do, recommend first approaching the topic of abuse via open-ended invitations. According to Anderson *et al.* (2009), the clinical expertise of their interviewers revealed that direct questions are effective at obtaining abuse-relevant information from children.

While some aspects of RATAC overlap with best-practice recommendations derived from scientific research, RATAC, as a whole, did not emerge from research findings. Several RATAC recommendations, such as the use of anatomical diagrams and direct questions to elicit disclosures, are inconsistent with what research reveals is most effective (e.g. see Lyon, 2014). In addition, very few peer-reviewed empirical studies have tested the protocol's validity, including whether the use of RATAC can induce false reports from children. Instead, evaluations of the protocol have been undertaken primarily by its developers and published in agency-sponsored manuals or law reviews (e.g. Anderson *et al.*, 2009). The lack of empirical support for some of RATAC's recommendations, combined with the lack of public availability of details on its training methods and the lack of peer-reviewed scientific tests of its utility, have made RATAC controversial, although this controversy is playing out more among scientists and practitioners than in the courts. Legal challenges regarding potential flaws in RATAC have, for the most part, not been met with success (e.g. *Mooneyham* v. *State*, 2005; *State* v. *Gaona*, 2012; *State* v. *Wells*, 2009).

In 2013, CornerHouse significantly revised its training protocol, replacing several components of RATAC with more widely accepted interviewing techniques. For instance, the RATAC recommendation that direct questions be used initially to elicit disclosures was eliminated, and instead open-ended invitations are recommended (Anderson, 2013). With the revisions, CFIP aligns more closely with the highly respected NICHD and Ten-Step Protocols. CFIP includes four interview stages (Anderson, 2013). First, during Building Rapport, interviewers engage in narrative practice to teach the child how to provide lengthy responses and provide instructions that establish ground rules. Second, during Seeking Information, allegation details are sought via open-ended prompts that begin by asking why children are at the interview rather than by directly asking about touching. Third, in Exploring Statements, open-ended invitations and follow-up prompts are used to elicit further details about abuse. And finally, during Ending Respectfully, the interviewer closes and answers children's questions.

It should be noted that the CFIP still allows for the use of anatomical diagrams, dolls, anatomy identification, and touch inquiry questions, techniques that continue to be quite controversial given that they may induce errors and are believed, at least by some, to contribute to false allegations of sexual abuse (Bruck, 2009; Lyon, 2012; Poole and Dickinson, 2011). However, the CFIP recognizes the controversy surrounding these techniques and states that they are "possible methods that may be used with particular children to gather sufficient details about abuse," and are not standard practice.

Like RATAC, there is a lack of research testing the efficacy of the CFIP on children's memory accuracy and propensity to err. Nonetheless, given that the CFIP is moving closer to best-practice recommendations based on research and that it appears more closely aligned with widely respected protocols, using the CFIP in an interview should represent an improvement over standard interviewing tactics. Of course, such a possibility should still be confirmed with rigorous, independent scientific evaluations in order to assess directly the utility of the CFIP.

Developmental Narrative Elaboration Interview

Though not a formal training protocol per se, it is useful to comment on one other set of instructions available for questioning suspected victims, the Developmental Narrative Elaboration (DNE) Interview, developed by Saywitz and Camparo (2013). DNE, like the NICHD and Ten-Step Protocols, grew out of scientific research. It is designed to facilitate narrative productivity in suspected victims not only via open-ended prompts but also via cue cards that remind children to report information in specific topical areas (Saywitz and Snyder, 1993, 1996). The DNE manual, of note, contains age-specific recommendations, highlighting its sensitivity to the role of development in influencing children's coping, memory, suggestibility, and performance in a forensic interview.

The DNE manual begins by explaining what should occur in the preliminary phase of an interview. The interviewer should review the ground rules (e.g. let children know that they can say "I don't know") and build rapport. The manual distinguishes between a supportive interview context and selectively reinforcing specific answers, and explains the utility of the former to increase accuracy. The manual also lists several age-specific activities that can be done to help children understand the ground rules and feel comfortable. During the preliminary phase, DNE recommends the interviewer "demystify the legal process and interview" based on evidence that children rarely adequately understand the legal process or their case, and that this lack of understanding serves as a source of distress (Goodman *et al.*, 1992; Quas *et al.*, 2009). By reducing children's distress early on, their comfort and accuracy can be increased (Nathanson and Saywitz, 2003; Quas and Lench, 2007).

What is perhaps most unique about DNE, though, is the narrative elaboration strategy, first introduced in the preliminary phase. Specifically, after children have been asked to recall everything they can about a target (non-abuse) event and have exhausted their response, they are given cue cards reflecting specific topics (e.g. participants, setting, actions, conversation/affective states, consequences) and are taught to elaborate on each one with additional event details (Brown *et al.*, 2013; Camparo *et al.*, 2001). The cue cards represent non-suggestive ways of prompting children to discuss topics that they may not know or remember are important.

Once children are comfortable with the cards, the DNE manual suggests transitioning to the substantive phase. A list of non-specific prompts is provided to elicit an abuse disclosure (similar to prompts recommended by the NICHD and Ten-Step Protocols). Disclosures should be followed with open-ended prompts to elicit additional details. Once children have exhausted their reports, they are given each cue card and asked, "Does this card remind you to tell something else?" Analogue studies reveal that children interviewed with the DNE Protocol provide a larger amount of narrative information (which reduces concerns about suggestibility) than children interviewed with standard questioning tactics (e.g. Peterson *et al.*, 2013; Saywitz *et al.*, 1996). A vast majority of the information (about 95 percent) is accurate, suggesting that DNE increases children's productivity without reducing accuracy.

The DNE manual also offers guidance about the closure phase of the interview. According to the manual, closure is important because it can increase the likelihood that children will be open with interviewers in the future and it gives children an opportunity to correct errors and ask questions. Closure tasks (along with developmentally appropriate activities) are provided to guide interviewer behavior.

As mentioned, the use of the cue cards has been shown to increase children's productivity in laboratory studies without reducing accuracy (Saywitz and Camparo, 2013). However, DNE has not been examined in field research. Nor have tests been conducted concerning the effects of other aspects of the protocol, such as the legal process explanation or closure activities. Nevertheless, these components were developed based on scientific research concerning children's coping and experiences in legal cases and are consistent with the results of studies concerning stress, interview context, legal understanding, and memory (e.g. Nathanson and Saywitz, 2003; Quas and Lench, 2007; Quas *et al.*, 2009). Moreover, none of the DNE recommendations involve controversial interview tactics or those that have been shown to lead to errors or false reports. Thus DNE would likely be considered consistent with best-practice recommendations.

Field exposure to currently available protocols

Given variations in the way interview training occurs across the United States, it is challenging to determine how often the different protocols are taught, and how many front-line interviewers know about the protocols or about best practices. Some insight can be gleaned, though, by evaluating how frequently workshops, seminars, and training programs are conducted with individual protocols and by reviewing advertisements for training opportunities.

As mentioned, the NICHD Protocol is likely the most widely followed and respected protocol for questioning suspected child victims around the globe. In fact, it is mandated in some countries. Somewhat surprisingly, it is not as widely known in the United States, although it has certainly become more so in recent years, due in part to growing efforts to present it at training sessions in the states, and the development of the Ten-Step Protocol. For instance, multiple three-day NICHD training sessions have been held in Salt Lake City for the past several years that are attended by child protective service workers, detectives, clinicians, forensic interviewers, and prosecutors from around the country. The Salt Lake

City training team has provided similar training programs in other states as well (e.g. Virginia, Pennsylvania, Louisiana, Maryland, California, Colorado). According to informal estimates, approximately 2,000 professionals in the United States have been exposed to the intensive workshop (H. L. Stewart, personal communication, 7 January 2015).

In addition, the American Professional Society on the Abuse of Children (APSAC), a leading national organization concerned with protecting and intervening on behalf of maltreated children, incorporates several important components of the NICHD protocol into its training, such as rapport building, and eliciting narratives via recall and open-ended invitation prompts. The training also addresses how to interview reluctant children and what to do about children who are at risk for recantation, topics that have led to recent modifications and additions to the NICHD protocol as well. APSAC conducts two five-day intensive training sessions per year in Virginia and Washington, each with approximately 40 participants, and each providing ample opportunity for practice and feedback (M. Haney, personal communication, 6 February 2015). Research has shown that multi-day training that gives participants hands-on experience and feedback are ideal in terms of ensuring that interviewers truly understand the protocol (Lamb *et al.*, 2007; Westcott *et al.*, 2003). Those who cannot attend training sessions (e.g. because of distance or cost), however, can still access all NICHD Protocol materials for free, along with multiple free videotaped lectures and seminars on the NICHD website.

The Ten-Step Protocol was initially promoted primarily by its developer Dr Thomas Lyon and his colleagues, though many other professionals now include its components in their forensic training programs. Access to the protocol is available via several methods. First, the written protocol can be downloaded for free (http://works.bepress.com/thomaslyon/) and is available in English, Spanish, and Russian. To date, the protocol has been downloaded over 10,000 times, presumably by those who carry out forensic interviews and are interested in the guidelines. Second, interviewers have received training on the protocol via presentations and workshops, and Lyon and colleagues have presented the protocol at training programs around the country. In California, for example, virtually all of the forensic interviewers affiliated with California Child Advocacy Centers have learned about the technique, and several hundred professionals have completed three-day workshops through the California Child Abuse Training and Technical Assistance Center that have incorporated portions of the Ten-Step Protocol. Third, webinars are easily accessible through the Midwest Regional Child Advocacy Centers. Finally, all of the approximate 900 emergency response workers in Los Angeles have received training on the protocol. In addition, each month, variable numbers of forensic interviewers (e.g. from five to twenty) take part in interactive webinars in Los Angeles within which they gain additional feedback and have the opportunity to discuss actual cases. Of importance, many of these opportunities and materials are free, increasing the ease with which professionals have access, though if certification is required a fee may be charged.

RATAC and then the CFIP, both of which are proprietary, have been marketed broadly, and fees are required to be trained with the protocols. While it is unclear how many professionals have received training with RATAC versus CFIP, according to CornerHouse (http://www.cornerhousemn.org/training.html), one or the other has been taught via multi-day workshops to over 29,000 professionals in the United States and abroad who have paid to attend the training. Training has also been given to professionals attending national conferences for District Attorneys Associations and at the National Child Protection Training Center. Once the initial training has been completed, CornerHouse offers supplementary training (e.g. peer reviews, updates to protocols). In addition, CornerHouse has created curriculum packages so states can create their own certified CFIP program (Gundersen National Child Protection Training Center, 2015). States apply and pay for this status, and, if approved, receive certification to train their own personnel as long as they remain in compliance with the certification requirements. According to CornerHouse, as of 2014, 19 states have completed this certification (Gundersen National Child Protection Training Center, 2015). Given that several aspects of the CFIP now align with recommended interviewing techniques and with the other scientifically based protocols, interviewer exposure to the CFIP is positive. However, it is unknown how many of the interviewers formerly trained with RATAC have received updated CFIP training, and continued reliance on RATAC is potentially concerning from a scientific perspective.

Briefly, although DNE is a promising interviewing strategy, to date, there is no formal hands-on training program regarding its use. Instead, the scientists who developed DNE often discuss the protocol at conferences and workshops, such as at the San Diego International Conference on Child Abuse and Neglect, and instructions on its use are well articulated in Saywitz and Camparo's (2013) recent manual. It will be important in the future to track whether interviewers' knowledge of DNE practices increases, as well as whether and how they elect to use the protocol's components.

As mentioned, states vary considerably in their policies regarding the interviewing of suspected child victims. Some have more detailed, formal guidelines about interviewing, while others merely recommend that interviewers receive training. Moreover, although some of the state policies make reference to specific protocols, most are hybrids and do not conform to one protocol. Two brief examples from different states give some insight into the types of policies that have been created to guide interviewers within certain states.

Beginning in 1998, Michigan required each county to implement a standard child abuse and neglect interview protocol. The protocol was initially developed based on recommendations from a task force created by the state (DHS Publication 794, Michigan Model Child Abuse Protocol). The task force took into account scientific research in part thanks to input from Professor Deborah Poole, a well-known expert in the field, and has been revised twice since its creation, each time incorporating findings from newly available research (DHS Publication 779, Forensic Interviewing Protocol). Thus interviewers in Michigan should have basic knowledge of how children should be interviewed and what constitutes good (and bad) questioning tactics.

In Washington, a 1999 law requires that all persons responsible for investigating child sexual abuse receive specialized state-wide training that describes research-based practices (Wash. Rev. Code § 43.101.224). Training must include the opportunity to practice interviewing skills and to receive feedback, and is based on the American Professional Society on the Abuse of Children (APSAC) Handbook (see their 2012 Handbook, authored by several leading scholars in the field) and the Washington State Child Interview Guide, which itself makes reference to the NICHD Protocol several times (Washington Child Interview Guidelines, 2009). Thus, interviewers are gaining some exposure to recommended strategies for interviewing suspected child victims.

Improving best-practice guideline use in the United States

Given the availability and promotion of multiple protocols, the array of training opportunities, and different state policies, it is quite likely that interviewer behavior in the United States varies considerably. To the extent that protocols such as the NICHD and Ten-Step continue to be available and promoted, forensic interviewers should become more familiar with what they should and should not do when questioning a suspected child victim. Moreover, to the extent that DNE can be more widely promoted, and the CFIP or other proprietary protocols continue to move toward incorporating optimal, scientifically supported interviewing tactics, larger numbers of professionals should have opportunities to learn about recommended interviewing practices.

Even though we commend efforts to expand exposure to protocols that are consistent with best practice, this exposure is not sufficient. For the protocols – and best practices generally – to be implemented successfully, individuals must receive not only training but also feedback and multiple opportunities to practice their skills. Over time, as well, refresher courses are needed to maintain skills. Some feedback opportunities are available via conference calls that allow interviewers to discuss cases on a monthly basis (e.g. with the Ten-Step Protocol). These opportunities should be expanded to ensure continued adherence to best practices over time. Finally, interviewers trained with protocols not supported by scientific research need to be targeted to correct misconceptions that could be compromising the veracity of children's reports. Overall, by expanding best-practice training, feedback, and refreshers, interviewers can better identify those children who have truly been victimized and minimize incorrect identification of children who have not. Doing so will serve to protect children, families, and others involved in legal cases as a result of alleged maltreatment.

Note

1. Certainly, adults are often asked to provide eyewitness accounts of alleged crimes, and adults' reports are not immune from error, especially adults with mental disabilities. Some interview protocols have been developed to increase how much information adult witnesses provide (e.g. the cognitive interview, Fisher and Geiselman, 1992). Such protocols, though, are not mandated in any one State, and controversies regarding suggestibility and false memory are often far greater with children than adults, particularly when there is heavy reliance on children's statements as evidence of the occurrence of

a crime (for example, see Bruck and Ceci, 1999). One exception, though, concerns line-up identification and risks of false identifications (which span across all age ranges). Controversy has been particularly heated in recent years on this topic as a result of new evidence concerning the benefits and costs of sequential versus simultaneous line-up procedures. A detailed discussion of this controversy, along with its potential effects on police behavior across the United States, can be found in the National Academy of Sciences report, *Identifying the Culprit: Assessing Eyewitness Identification* (2014).

References

American Professional Society on the Abuse of Children (APSAC) (2012) *Practice Guidelines: Forensic Interviewing in Cases of Suspected Child Abuse*. Retrieved from: http://www.apsac.org.

Anderson, J. (2013) *The CornerHouse Forensic Interview Protocol: An Evolution in Practice for Almost 25 Years*. Retrieved from: http://www.cornerhousemn.org/images/Anderson_2013_CornerHouse_Forensic_Interview_Protocol.pdf.

Anderson, J., Ellefson, J., Lashley, J., Miller, A. L., Olinger, S., Russell, A., and Weigman, J. (2009) "The Cornerhouse Forensic Interview Protocol: RATAC," *Thomas M. Cooley Journal of Practical and Clinical Law*, 12: 193–331.

Bjorklund, D. F., Bjorklund, B. R., Brown, R. D., and Cassel, W. S. (1998) "Children's susceptibility to repeated questions: how misinformation changes children's answers and their minds," *Applied Developmental Science*, 2: 99–111.

Bradshaw v. *State*, 2012 Tex. App. LEXIS 6193 (Tex. App., July 26, 2012).

Brown, D. A., Lamb, M. E., Lewis, C., Pipe, M. E., Orbach, Y., and Wolfman, M. (2013) The NICHD Investigative Interview Protocol: an analogue study," *Journal of Experimental Psychology: Applied*, 19: 367–82.

Bruck, M. (2009) "Human figure drawings and children's recall of touching," *Journal of Experimental Psychology: Applied*, 15: 361–74.

Bruck, M. and Ceci, S. J. (1999) "The suggestibility of children's memory," *Annual Review of Psychology*, 50: 419–39.

Camparo, L. B., Wagner, J. T., and Saywitz, K. J. (2001) "Interviewing children about real and fictitious events: revisiting the narrative elaboration procedure," *Law and Human Behavior*, 25: 63–80.

Ceci, S. J. and Bruck, M. (1995) *Jeopardy in the Courtroom: A Scientific Analysis of Children's Testimony*. Washington, DC: American Psychological Association.

Commonwealth v. *LeFave*, 407 Mass. 927 (Mass. 1990).

Cornerhouse (2014) Training. Retrieved from: http://www.cornerhousemn.org/training.html.

DHS Publication 779. *Forensic Interviewing Protocol*, 3rd edn. Retrieved from: http://www.michigan.gov/dhs/0,4562,7-124-7119_25045---,00.html.

DHS Publication 794. *A Model Child Abuse and Neglect Protocol with an Approach Using a Coordinated Investigative Team*. Retrieved from: http://www.michigan.gov/dhs/0,4562,7-124-7119_25045---,00.html.

Fisher, R. P. and Geiselman, R. E. (1992) *Memory Enhancing Techniques for Investigative Interviewing: The Cognitive Interview*. Springfield, IL: Thomas.

Goodman, G. S., Quas, J. A., and Ogle, C. M. (2010) "Child maltreatment and memory," *Annual Review of Psychology*, 61: 325–51.

Goodman, G. S., Quas, J. A., Bulkley, J., and Shapiro, C. (1999) "Innovations for child witnesses: a national survey," *Psychology, Public Policy, and Law*, 5: 255–81.

Goodman, G. S., Taub, E. P., Jones, D. P., England, P., Port, L. K., Rudy, L., and Melton, G. B. (1992) *Testifying in Criminal Court: Emotional Effects on Child Sexual Assault Victims*, Monographs of the Society for Research in Child Development, pp. i–159.

Gundersen National Child Protection Training Center (2015) *Child First*. Retrieved from: http://www.gundersenhealth.org/ncptc/childfirst.

Hershkowitz, I. (2008) "Socioemotional factors in child sexual abuse investigations," *Child Maltreatment*, 14: 172–81.

Hershkowitz, I., Orbach, Y., Lamb, M. E., Sternberg, K. J., and Horowitz, D. (2006) 'Dynamics of forensic interviews with suspected abuse victims who do not disclose abuse," *Child Abuse and Neglect*, 30: 753–69.

Lamb, M. E. and Fauchier, A. (2001) "The effects of question type on self-contradictions by children in the course of forensic interviews," *Applied Cognitive Psychology*, 15: 483–91.

Lamb, M. E., Hershkowitz, I., Orbach, Y., and Esplin, P. W. (2008) *Tell Me What Happened: Structured Investigative Interviews of Child Victims and Witnesses*. Hoboken, NJ: Wiley.

Lamb, M. E., La Rooy, D. J., Malloy, L. C., and Katz, C. (2011) *Children's Testimony: A Handbook of Psychological Research and Forensic Practice*, 2nd edn. Chichester: John Wiley & Sons.

Lamb, M. E., Orbach, Y., Hershkowitz, I., Esplin, P. W., and Horowitz, D. (2007) "Structured forensic interview protocols improve the quality and informativeness of investigative interviews with children: a review of research using the NICHD Investigative Interview Protocol," *Child Abuse and Neglect*, 31: 1201–30.

Lamb, M. E., Orbach, Y., Sternberg, K. J., Esplin, P. W., and Hershkowitz, I. (2002) "The effects of forensic interview practices on the quality of information provided by alleged victims of child abuse," in H. L. Westcott, G. M. Davies, and R. Bull (eds), *Children's Testimony: A Handbook of Psychological Research and Forensic Practice*. Chichester: Wiley, pp. 131–45.

Lamb, M. E., Sternberg, K. J., and Esplin, P. W. (1994) "Factors influencing the reliability and validity of statements made by young victims of sexual maltreatment," *Journal of Applied Developmental Psychology*, 15: 255–80

Lewis, T. E., Klettke, B., and Day, A. (2014) "The influence of medical and behavioral evidence on conviction rates in cases of child sexual abuse," *Journal of Child Sexual Abuse*, 23: 431–41.

Lyon, T. D. (2005) "Speaking with children: advice from investigative interviewers," in P.F. Talley (ed.), *Handbook for the Treatment of Abused and Neglected Children*. Binghamton, NY: Haworth, pp. 65–82.

Lyon, T. D. (2012) "Twenty-five years of interviewing research and practice: dolls, diagrams, and the dynamics of abuse disclosure," *APSAC (American Professional Society on the Abuse of Children) Advisor*, 24: 14–19.

Lyon, T. D. (2014) "Interviewing children," *Annual Review of Law and Social Science*, 10: 73–89.

Lyon, T. D. (2015) http://works.bepress.com/thomaslyon/.

Lyon, T. D. and Dorado, J. S. (2008) "Truth induction in young maltreated children: the effects of oath-taking and reassurance on true and false disclosures," *Child Abuse and Neglect*, 3: 738–48.

Lyon, T. D., Ahern, E. C., and Scurich, N. (2012) "Interviewing children versus tossing coins: accurately assessing the diagnosticity of children's disclosures of abuse," *Journal of Child Sexual Abuse*, 21: 19–44.

Lyon, T. D., Lamb, M. E., and Myers, J. (2009) "Authors' response to Vieth (2008): legal and psychological support for the NICHD Interviewing Protocol," *Child Abuse and Neglect*, 33: 71–4.

Lyon, T. D., Malloy, L. C., Quas, J. A., and Talwar, V. A. (2008) "Coaching, truth induction, and young maltreated children's false allegations and false denials," *Child Development*, 79: 914–29.

Lyon, T. D., Wandrey, L., Ahern, E., Licht, R., Sim, M. P., and Quas, J. A. (2014) "Eliciting maltreated and nonmaltreated children's transgression disclosures: narrative practice rapport building and a putative confession," *Child Development*, 85: 1756–69.

Memon, A., Holley, A., Wark, L., Bull, R., and Koehnken, G. (1996) "Reducing suggestibility in child witness interviews," *Applied Cognitive Psychology*, 10: 503–18.

Mooneyham v. *State*, 915 so. 2d 1102 (Miss. 2005).

Nathanson, R. and Saywitz, K. J. (2003) "The effects of the courtroom context on children's memory and anxiety," *Journal of Psychiatry and Law*, 31: 67–98.

National Academy of Sciences (2014) *Identifying the Culprit: Assessing Eyewitness Identification*. Retrieved from: http://www.nap.edu/download.php?record_id=18891#.

National Kids Count (2013) *Children Who Are Subject to an Investigated Report*. Retrieved from: http://datacenter.kidscount.org/data/tables/6220-children-who-are-subject-to-an-investigated-report?loc=1andloct=2#detailed/1/any/false/868,867,133,38,35/any/12940,12955

NICHD Protocol. Retrieved from http://nichdprotocol.com.

Nieves, E. (1994) "Prosecutors drop charges in abuse case from mid-80's," *New York Times*, 3 December. Retrieved from: http://www.nytimes.com/1994/12/03/nyregion/prosecutors-drop-charges-in-abuse-case-from-mid-80-s.html.

Orbach, Y. and Lamb, M. E. (1999) "Assessing the accuracy of a child's account of sexual abuse: a case study," *Child Abuse and Neglect*, 23: 91–8.

Orbach, Y. and Lamb, M. E. (2001) "The relationship between within-interview contradictions and eliciting interviewer utterances," *Child Abuse and Neglect*, 25: 323–33.

Orbach, Y., Shiloach, H., and Lamb, M. E. (2007) "Reluctant disclosers of child sexual abuse," in M. E. Pipe, M. E. Lamb, Y. Orbach, and A. C. Ceberborg (eds), *Child Sexual Abuse: Disclosure, Delay, and Denial*. New York: Routledge, pp. 115–34.

Oregon Interviewing Guidelines (2012) Retrieved from: http://www.doj.state.or.us/victims/pdf/oregon_interviewing_guidelines.pdf.

People v. *Buckey*, No. A750900 (Super. Ct., Los Angeles County, Cal. 1990).

People v. *Vasquez*, 51 Cal. App. 4th 1277 (Cal. Ct. App., 1996).

Peterson, C., Warren, K. L., and Hayes, A. H. (2013) "Revisiting Narrative Elaboration Training with an ecologically relevant event," *Journal of Cognition and Development*, 14: 154–74.

Poole, D. A. and Dickinson, J. J. (2011) "Evidence supporting restrictions on uses of body diagrams in forensic interviews," *Child Abuse and Neglect*, 35: 659–69.

Quas, J. A. and Lench, H. C. (2007) "Arousal at encoding, arousal at retrieval, interviewer support, and children's memory for a mild stressor," *Applied Cognitive Psychology*, 21: 289–305.

Quas, J. A., Wallin, A. R., Horwitz, B., Davis, E., and Lyon, T. D. (2009) "Maltreated children's understanding of and emotional reactions to dependency court involvement," *Behavioral Sciences and the Law*, 27: 97–117.

Saywitz, K. J. and Camparo, L. B. (2013) *Evidence-based Child Forensic Interviewing: The Developmental Narrative Elaboration Interview*. Oxford: Oxford University Press.

Saywitz, K. J. and Snyder, L. (1993) "Improving children's testimony with preparation," in G. S. Goodman and B. L. Bottoms (eds), *Child Victims, Child Witnesses: Understanding and Improving Testimony*. New York: Guilford Press, pp. 117–46.

Saywitz, K. J. and Snyder, L. (1996) "Narrative elaboration: test of a new procedure for interviewing children," *Journal of Consulting and Clinical Psychology*, 64: 1347–57.

Saywitz, K. J., Snyder, L., and Lamphear, V. (1996) "Helping children tell what happened: a follow-up study of the narrative elaboration procedure," *Child Maltreatment*, 1: 200–12.

State v. *Gaona*, 293 Kan. 930 (Kan. 2012).

State v. *Michaels*, 625 A.2d 489, (N.J. Sup. Ct. App. Div. 1993).

State v. *Otis*, 2011 Wisc. App. LEXIS 98 (Wisc. Ct. App., February 1, 2011).

State v. *Wells*, 298 Kan. 1219 (Kan. 2009).

Sternberg, K. J., Lamb, M. E., Esplin, P. W., Orbach, Y., and Hershkowitz, I. (2002) "Using a structured interview protocol to improve the quality of investigative interviews," in M. L. Eisen, J. A. Quas, and G. S. Goodman (eds), *Memory and Suggestibility in the Forensic Interview*. Mahwah, NJ: Erlbaum, pp. 409–36.

Sternberg, K. J., Lamb, M. E., Hershkowitz, I., Yudilevitch, L., Orbach, Y., Esplin, P. W., and Hovav, M. (1997) "Effects of introductory style on children's abilities to describe experiences of sexual abuse," *Child Abuse and Neglect*, 21: 1133–46.

Stewart, H., Katz, C., and La Rooy, D. J. (2011) "Training forensic interviewers," in M. E. Lamb, D. J. La Rooy, L. C. Malloy, and C. Katz (eds), *Children's Testimony: A Handbook of Psychological Research and Forensic Practice*. Chichester: John Wiley & Sons, pp. 199–216.

Stout, D. (1995) "Virginia McMartin dies at 88; Figure in case on child abuse," *New York Times*, 19 December. Retrieved from: http://www.nytimes.com/1995/12/19/us/virginia-mcmartin-dies-at-88-figure-in-case-on-child-abuse.html.

Talwar, V., Lee, K., Bala, N., and Lindsay, R. C. L. (2004) "Children's lie-telling to conceal a parent's transgression," *Law and Human Behavior*, 28: 411–35.

Thompson, W. C., Clarke-Stewart, K. A., and Lepore, S. J. (1997) "What did the janitor do? Suggestive interviewing and the accuracy of children's accounts," *Law and Human Behavior*, 21: 405–26.

US Department of Health and Human Services, Administration for Children and Families, Administration on Children, Youth and Families, Children's Bureau (2012) *Child Maltreatment*. Retrieved from: http://www.acf.hhs.gov/programs/cb/resource/child-maltreatment-2012.

Wandrey, L., Lyon, T. D., Quas, J. A., and Friedman, W. J. (2012) "Maltreated children's ability to estimate temporal location and numerosity of placement changes and court visits," *Psychology, Public Policy, and Law*, 18: 79–104.

Wash. Rev. Code §43.101.224.

Washington State Child Interview Guide (2009) Retrieved from: http://depts.washington.edu/hcsats/PDF/guidelines/WA%20State%20Child%20Interview%20Guide%202009%202010.pdf

Westcott, H. L., Davies, G. M., and Bull, R. (2003) *Children's Testimony: A Handbook of Psychological Research and Forensic Practice*. Chichester: John Wiley & Sons.

South America

22 Witness interviewing in Brazil

Lilian Milnitsky Stein, Gustavo Noronha de Ávila and Luis Roberto Benia

Introduction

Over the past 30 years, investigative interview techniques in Brazil have undergone development. This development can best be understood in view of the great socio-political changes which have occurred in the country. From 1964 to 1985, Brazil was under the rule of a military dictatorship. During the 1980s, a transition to democracy occurred, which culminated in the elaboration of a new Constitution in 1988. The congressmen who took part in the creation of the constitutional text had been elected directly by the people two years before. Brazilian citizens also participated in the elaboration of laws, through public hearings held in the National Congress (Codato, 2005). The 1988 Constitution was a milestone for citizenship and human rights.

The Brazilian legal system is rooted in the Roman-Germanic tradition, and as a result, national law practice is strongly based on federal legislation. The legislation is hierarchically divided into the Federal Constitution (1988) and the Criminal Procedure Code (CPC) (1941) which are the current main sources of guidelines for forensic interviews in the country. There are two police forces in Brazil with different roles, namely the frontline uniformed military police responsible for ostensive street patrol, and the civilian police force in charge of the investigation of crimes. Since the end of the military government, the country has tried to recover human rights through modern democratic processes. The democratic changes that took place in Brazil were initially slow, but in the last ten years have increased more rapidly. This historic background might help us understand why Brazil has delayed incorporating the scientific advances in best practice in investigative interviewing. In the last decade, there has been more progress with respect to interviewing children and adolescents as compared to adults.

In the first part of the chapter we focus on child interviewing practices in the Brazilian system. In the second part of the chapter, we present the results of the first nationwide research on current practices with respect to investigative interviewing of adult victims and witnesses. We introduce each section with an overview of the legal and institutional organization for a better understanding of the current interviewing practices as there are remarkable differences in practice for those under 18 years and those older.

Interviewing child witnesses/victims

In 1989, Brazil ratified the Convention on the Rights of the Child (CRC). By doing so, the country committed itself to act in the best interest of the child (Brazil, 1990a). One year later, the Brazilian Congress enacted the Statute of the Child and Adolescent (SCA). The SCA is a set of laws and regulations with the goal of ensuring full protection of the population below 18 years of age. The SCA also regulates the protective and legal procedures related to children, which must be followed by every state in the Brazilian federation. Thus Brazil was the first country in Latin America to have national legislation following the principles of the CRC (Carvalho, 2001).

In accordance with the SCA, Guardianship Councils (GCs) were created in every Brazilian city. GCs are composed of lay people elected by the community to monitor any violation or suspicion of violation of children's and adolescents' rights by detecting signs of negligence, abuse, or mistreatment against minors (Brazil, 1990b). The guardianship councilor is not a member of the police or the justice system. He or she has the power to demand action from the public authorities to guarantee the protection of minors' rights. As can be seen in Figure 22.1, a typical joint action of the GC and a public authority (such as the police) takes place in the following manner: when there are reports of a crime or violation of rights against a child, the GC is called to assist him or her. The GC evaluates the situation and takes the necessary measures to protect the child. These measures usually include notifying the police and/or the prosecutor's office and monitoring the child and his or her family during the necessary technical (e.g. forensic assessment) and legal procedures that might follow (Milani and Loureiro, 2008).

The protection of child victims of negligence, abuse, and mistreatment is accomplished through the collaboration between the GCs, the police and the Centers for Referral of Social Services (CREAS) (Brazil, 2005). The CREAS are state-run units with a multidisciplinary team of professionals, such as social workers, educators, and psychologists. The main purpose of the CREAS is to provide specialized assistance to families, children, and adolescents whose rights may have been infringed upon whether by negligence, abandonment, mistreatment, abuse, or sexual exploitation. In 2012, there were 2,155 CREAS distributed in every state in Brazil (Brazil, 2012).

With respect to investigative interviewing of young victims, the interviews are held in three phases (see Figure 22.1): first there is an initial phase, when the GC counselor will interview the child to find out what has happened; second is the evidence-finding phase conducted by the police; and third is the criminal process phase presided over by a judge. In the Brazilian legal system there are no specific regulations defining how children should be interviewed. Thus, throughout the initial, investigative, and trial phases, a child might be interviewed more than once by ill-trained interviewers. The number of times the child is interviewed depends upon the number of agencies involved in his or her protection and on the specific characteristics of the fact-finding task for each case (Froner and Ramires, 2008). For instance, when there a is suspicion that a crime might have been

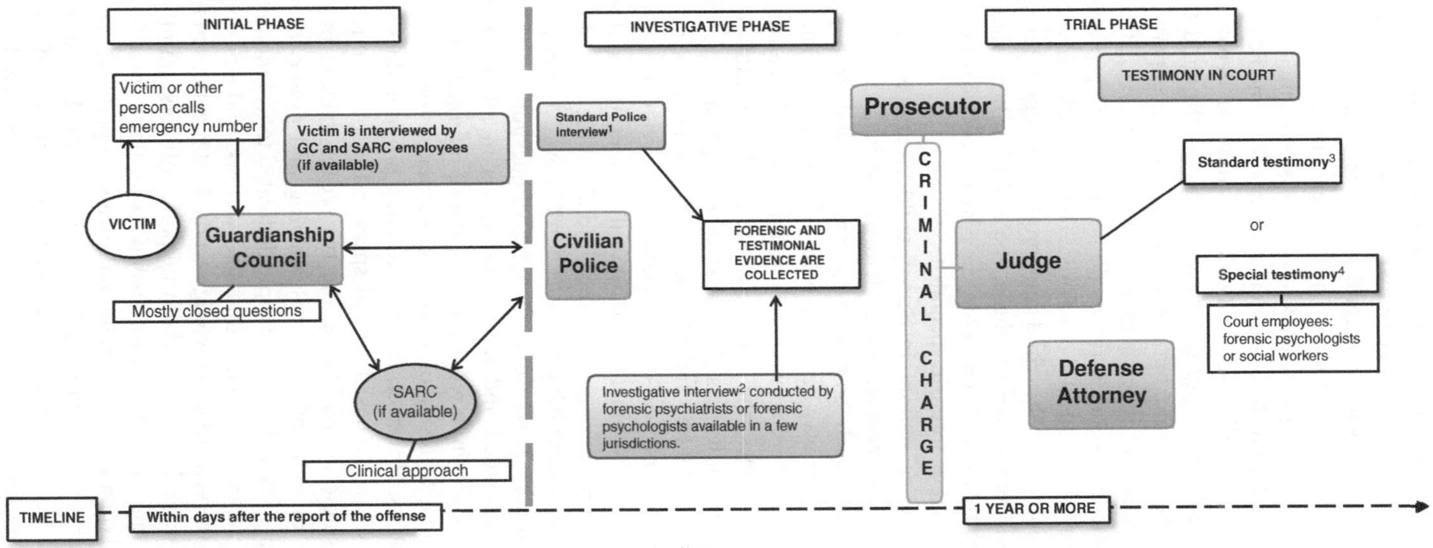

Notes:
1 Lack of interview training on best practices, mostly closed-ended questioning.
2 Interviews follow best practices to some extent, mostly open-ended questioning, interviews are recorded in audio in a few services.
3 Lack of interview training on best practices, mostly closed-ended questioning.
4 Interviews follow best practices to some extent, mostly open-ended questioning, interviews are recorded in audio and video.

Figure 22.1 Timeline of typical children's interviewing in Brazil.

committed against a child, the first action is generally taken by the GC. The GC counselor will interview the child to find out what has happened. The child is then brought to the police station, where the child will be interviewed again. In most cases, the police authority requests forensic medical examination and psychological assessment of the child. The physical examination is performed by specialized physicians from the local state forensic department called medical-legal institutes. In some states, the Medical-Legal Institutes' forensic departments have forensic psychiatrists and psychologists who will interview the child and conduct a mental health assessment. Some, but not all, of the forensic experts have basic training in the best practices of investigative interviewing (Gava, 2012). In most cities, however, the medical-legal institutes do not have such professionals and children are therefore evaluated at a CREAS. The CREAS's psychologist or social assistant will interview the child and produce a report for the police. Hence, during the evidence-gathering phase, the child has been interviewed at least three times: once by the GC counselor, once by the police officer, and once by a CREAS professional or forensic specialist.

At the majority of police stations in Brazil, child victims and witnesses are interviewed in the same manner as an adult involved in a crime (Froner and Ramires, 2008). The approach employed is intuitive, and each professional conducts the interview in the way he or she believes to be appropriate for gathering the information. Since there is no specific training in evidence-based investigative interviewing techniques, the interviews are conducted more like regular conversations between an adult and a child. A study in a specialized police department on the assistance of children and adolescents in Southern Brazil has shown that police officers with several years of experience in interviewing children relied upon contraindicated interview practices. Most of their interviews did not include any rapport. No instructions were given to the child about the ground rules of the interview, such as that it is acceptable to say "I don't know," "I don't remember," or to correct the interviewer. In respect to the types of questions, results showed a predominance of closed-ended and leading questions in all interviews (Pisa, 2006), which have been shown to reduce the amount of information gained.

In 2009, the Brazilian Ministry of Justice reformulated the syllabus for the training of police officers. However, this new training program does not include investigative interview techniques designed specifically for interviewing child victims. There is a single course during the two years training in the Police Academy devoted to all type of evidence-gathering and preservation (Brazil, 2009). During the course there is a single topic dedicated to testimonial evidence and to the approach to interviewing witnesses, victims, and suspects (Brazil, 2009). That is to say, the scientific knowledge on the best practices in the field of child interviewing is scarcely introduced during police officers' training process.

Likewise, the training for the guardianship councilors (members of the Guardianship Councils) on interview techniques is also superficial. The syllabus of the training program for councilors includes a topic named "Listening Skills" (Brazil, 2014), but it does not provide the councilors with specific knowledge related to investigative interview techniques, even at a theoretical level.

Social workers and psychologists working at the CREASs do not receive systematic training in investigative interviewing techniques. Each professional works according to his or her personal background training, generally using a clinical approach. In 2009, the Brazilian Federal Council of Psychology published a set of guidelines for psychologists assisting in cases of child sexual abuse and maltreatment (Conselho Federal de Psicologia, 2009). These guidelines state that the interview with the child should be conducted in a non-suggestive manner, within adequate physical space, and use a more spontaneous level of dialogue suitable for each child with respect to his or her developmental level. They also recommend that the psychologist evaluate the child's ability to differentiate truth from lies, his or her grasp of the meaning of secrecy, and the importance of telling the truth. The text does not contain any other specific recommendation on how the interview should be conducted or regarding a recommended protocol (e.g. NICHD) to adopt (Conselho Federal de Psicologia, 2009).

After gathering all available evidence, the police bring the case to the public prosecution office (Figure 22.1). If the prosecutor considers there is enough evidence to charge the offender, the prosecutor will initiate a trial. In the trial phase, the child victim will undergo an inquiry by the judge (usually in the courtroom) in the presence of the prosecutor and the defense attorney and sometimes the defendant. These inquiries, mostly closed-ended questions, usually do not follow the basic recommendations of best-practice interviewing guidelines (Di Gesu, 2008). Generally when the victim is an older child or an adolescent, she or he will be submitted to direct examination in court (Silva *et al.*, 2013). Judges are also able to request further assessments from forensic psychiatrists or forensic psychologists in order to produce evidence to substantiate his or her decision process.

Although the Brazilian scenario of investigative interviewing with children may seem less advanced in comparison with other countries included in this volume, during the last decade some efforts have been initiated to introduce evidence-based interviewing practices. Changes in interview practices during the investigative phase are seen mostly in the work done by the forensic psychiatrists and forensic psychologists of the medico-legal institutes or similar state departments. In 2012, at least seven medical-legal institutes from seven different Brazilian states have introduced investigative interviewing protocols: two reported they were using the cognitive interview (Fisher and Geiselman, 1992), and five reported they were conducting semi-structured interviews consisting of rapport, free recall, open-ended questions and closed-ended questions (Gava, 2012).

Furthermore, there are changes in the way children are interviewed during the trial phase in some jurisdictions. In 2003, the Court of Justice of the State of Rio Grande do Sul (a state in southern Brazil) developed a project called "Special Testimony" designed specifically for minors' testimony in court (Daltoé-Cezar, 2007; Santos and Gonçalves, 2008). This method of children's testimony consists of a forensic interview conducted in a separate room of the court house with closed-circuit television (CCTV) communication. The interviews are conducted by a forensic interviewer, mainly psychologists and social workers. Regarding interviewing practices, 32 percent of the Special Testimony interviewers reported using the cognitive interview; 21 percent described an interviewing method consisting of rapport building, free recall followed by open questions and closed questions; 14 percent reported conducting interviews based on the NICHD protocol; 8 percent reported interviews based on a portion of the cognitive interview techniques, and 25 percent reported other practices. However, these data should be taken with caution since there has been no systematic assessment on the compliance with each of those interviewing methods by the "Special Testimony" interviewers. In addition, regarding training of the "Special Testimony" interviewers, Santos *et al.* (2013) reported that although 84 percent of the interviewers have received some special training, most have received such training in a non-systematic, non-uniform fashion. Only 3 percent of the forensic interviewers have received continuous training.

In 2012, there were 42 Special Testimony rooms in use in Brazil with another 35 rooms being built (Santos *et al.*, 2013). The majority of those rooms (72 percent) are concentrated in the Southern and South-Eastern regions of the country; 20 percent are located in the North-Eastern region and 8 percent in the Middle-Western and Northern regions.

The "Special Testimony" program represents an important step in the Brazilian system in terms of bringing the attention of forensic professionals to the differences between evidence-based interviewing practices (e.g. rapport and the use of uncontaminated questions) and practices that are not recommended (e.g. suggestive questions, use of anatomical dolls). For the past ten years there have been several initiatives regarding both the training of forensic interviewers and improvements in court facilities (e.g. special interviewing rooms that have been built, video-recording) sponsored by Brazilian governmental agencies such as the National Council of Justice (Conselho Nacional de Justiça (CNJ), 2013) and NGO organizations such as Childhood Brazil (2014).

In 2010, the National Council of Justice published Recommendation 33, stating that all courts of justice in Brazil should create special services for interviewing children and adolescents, whether they are victims or witnesses (Brazil, 2010). The recommendation suggests that professionals who conduct interviews should be trained to use the basic principles of the cognitive interview (Brazil, 2010). This initiative of the National Council of Justice may contribute to the dissemination of best interviewing practices in the country.

Interviewing adult witnesses/victims

Adult witnesses or victims, defined by law as those aged 18 or older, are questioned and interviewed usually in three phases, namely the initial investigative, investigative, and trial phases (see Figure 22.2 below). In the first, initial investigative phase, military patrol police officers try to obtain information from the witnesses/victim mainly for the purposes of indentifying the culprit. In the next two phases, interview procedures are formally prescribed in the CPC.

In the investigative phase, the aim of the investigative interview conducted by civilian police officers with witnesses/victims is to gather evidence for the

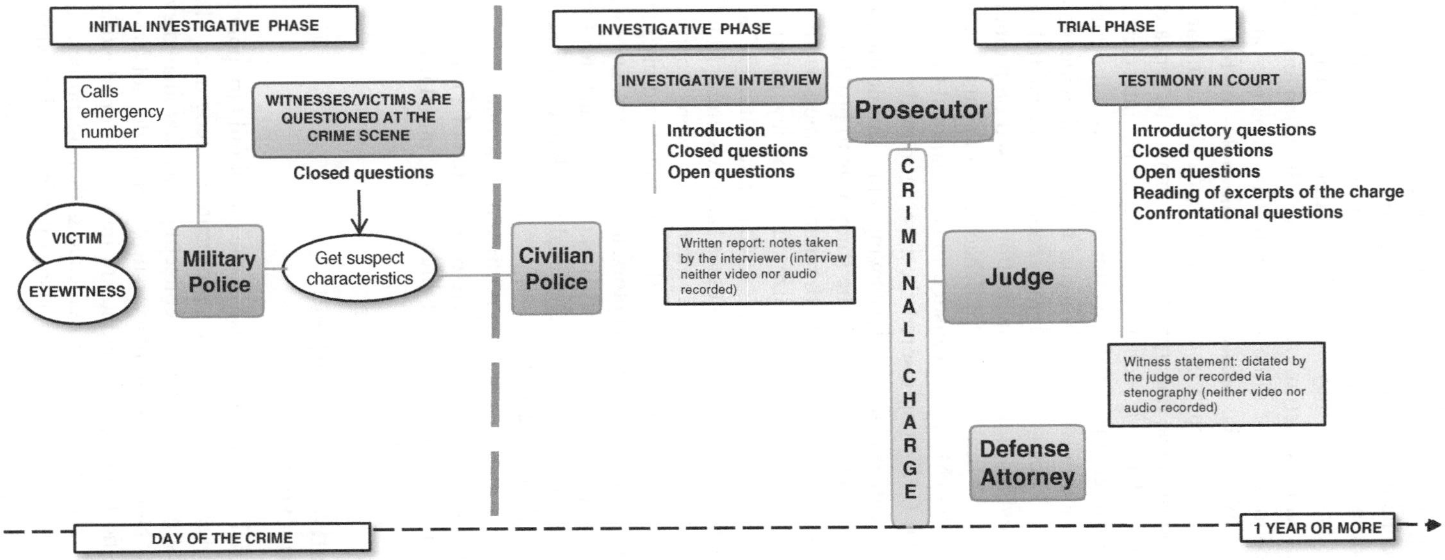

Figure 22.2 Timeline of typical adult's interviewing in Brazil.

judicial proceedings and to initiate a criminal process if the evidence is deemed sufficient. The second phase is the criminal trial presided over by a judge. During the trial phase, witnesses/victims are questioned in court by the prosecutor and defense attorney. The judge may also ask questions to clarify the information presented by the witness/victim. According to Brazilian criminal law, only evidence presented in court by witnesses/victims has probative value based on the constitutional principle of the preservation of the rights of both parties in the litigation. Testimonial evidence is considered repeatable compared to forensic evidence (e.g. blood samples, fingerprints) which cannot be repeatedly collected. Since testimonial evidence is considered repeatable, interviewing the same witness/victim in different phases of the criminal process is the current, common practice. The presumption of repeatability of testimonial evidence embedded in Brazil's outdated CPC does not take into account the substantial body of scientific psychological evidence about how testimony based on memory works and can fail (e.g. Reyna and Brainerd, 2005; Schacter and Loftus, 2013).

In 2014, the Brazilian Ministry of Justice and the National Institute for Applied Economic Research (IPEA) sponsored the first nationwide study in regard to current practices in witness/victim interviewing and identification procedures in Brazil (Stein, 2014). The main goal of the study was to provide a general diagnosis of the Brazilian judicial system with regard to witness/victim interviewing and identification procedures to subsidize future policy reforms. This study employed a qualitative method to explore the experiences of 88 law-related professionals when interviewing witnesses and victims. Individual, semi-structured and audio-recorded in-depth interviews were conducted with all participants including: 18 police officers (both military and civilian), 22 public and private defense attorneys, 22 prosecutors, and 26 judges. Data were collected from all five geographical regions of Brazil from June to October 2014. Interviews were transcribed verbatim and analyzed based on inductive content analysis procedures (Bardin, 2006).

The overall results of the study are portrayed as a timeline in Figure 22.2. When a crime has been committed or there is suspicion of a crime, the investigation and trial include the above described three phases: initial investigation phase, investigative phase and trial phase.

Initial investigative phase: military patrol police interviewing

Regarding the initial investigative phase of the patrol military police, our results indicated that judges, attorneys, and prosecutors recognized that whatever happens in this first phase is crucial for collecting uncontaminated evidence from witnesses/victims. Nonetheless, military patrol police do not have any formal protocols or specific training for conducting interviews or identification procedures. Despite its relevance for the evidence-gathering process in a criminal investigation, this initial investigative phase is not included in Brazil's CPC and not even formally recognized as part of the criminal process.

When a crime has been committed, the military patrol police are generally the first to make contact with the witness/victim, sometimes through an emergency call. According to our data, patrol officers tend to ask the witness/victim mostly close-ended questions (e.g. "Did he have any tattoos?"). The interaction between the patrol police officer and the witness is usually short and takes place at the crime scene or somewhere close by (e.g. inside the patrol police car, a shop). The main purpose of this interaction is to quickly collect information to indentify the suspect and thus allow immediate search to start. There is no formal recording (audio, video, or written) of the information obtained from the witness/victim who is usually then taken or sent to a civilian police station for a formal interview.

Investigative phase: civilian police interviewing

In accordance with the CPC, the formal investigation of a crime starts at the civilian police station (see Figure 22.2). Witnesses/victims are formally required to be interviewed by the police chief (who has a law degree) or by any of the investigative team members (i.e. police investigators, clerks and interns). In a few cases, a public prosecutor responsible for the case may participate in the interview.

Civilian police participants who have reported using a specific interviewing strategy with a witness/victim indicated that police interviews typically start with a brief introduction (including collecting identification information from the witness such as name, address, age, profession, etc.). This brief introduction is followed by a few open-ended (e.g. "What did you see at the bar?") and mostly closed-ended questions (e.g. "Was the guy pointing his gun at you?"). About one-third of the participants (28.5 percent) acknowledged the use of confrontational questions, such as: "You have told the patrol police at the scene that you have seen another guy and now you do not remember that?"

Our results have indicated that the police officers have little or no specific training in scientific investigative interviewing techniques (like the cognitive interview). Training at the police academy is limited to an overall presentation of interviewing focused on the current legislation (which does not include information about how to conduct the interview or about question format). One of the police participants in our study expressed his concern in regard to training as "we learn from practice and from more experienced officers." Guidelines on how interviews should be conducted are also unavailable.

Interviews at the investigative phase take place at the police station. The interviews are usually conducted at the chief's office. However, due to limitations of the facilities at a great number of police stations in Brazil, interviews with witnesses/victims are sometimes conducted in a busy main hall or corridor of the civilian police station.

Interviews are rarely recorded in audio or video format. Following the CPC, the witness/victim information is registered in the form of notes taken by the interviewer or a police clerk that is reduced to a written statement. The note taking process is rarely able to reproduce verbatim information given by the witness or questions placed by the interviewer (Lamb *et al.*, 2000). The written statement is included in the formal police report.

With regard to timing, witness interviews may take place several days or months after the alleged crime has been committed. According to Brazilian legislation, investigations must be completed within ten days if the accused is in jail and 30 days otherwise. However, the number of days for an investigation may triple if the case involves illegal drugs, which represents 50 percent of crimes committed in Brazil (Departamento Penitenciário Nacional, 2014). However, according to one study (Vargas and Nascimento, 2010) conducted in one of the main cities in Brazil (Belo Horizonte), the mean length of criminal investigations was 245 days, far exceeding the legal recommendation.

In crimes such as homicide, in which eyewitness testimony is essential to securing a conviction, it is often difficult to find witnesses willing to testify. Many witnesses fear retaliation from criminals who live in the same socially vulnerable communities as they do. There is a high prevalence of crimes (such as drug trafficking) in these communities (Waiselfisz, 2013). In 1999, a "Witness Protection Program" regulation was issued by the federal government to protect the anonymity and lives of people who face danger as a result of agreeing to testify in court. Nonetheless, the efficiency of this law was questioned by many of our study participants. They observed that participating in the protection program seems to make witnesses/victims feel more vulnerable and afraid of retaliation.

The challenge of having witnesses come forward to present their testimony to the police in the investigative phase has important implications for the next stage of the criminal process – the trial phase. In the absence of witnesses' evidence, the military patrol officer who first responded to the crime scene is frequently called to testify in the next phase in court. Evidence presented by the military patrol officer is considered indirect testimony, since in most cases he did not witness the crime itself.

When there is enough evidence collected during the investigative phase, the civilian police chief officer recommends that the suspect be charged. The police investigation report is sent to the public prosecutor's office. If the evidence is judged to be sufficient to incriminate the suspect, the case will be brought to the trial phase.

Trial phase: interviewing in court

Witnesses/victims are also interviewed during court hearings. Usually the prosecutor is the one who starts questioning the witness/victim followed by the defense attorney. The CPC determines that questions asked to the witness should not be leading or repetitive. The judge is responsible for monitoring the validity of the questions asked throughout the trial (Giacomolli, 2008). However, there is no definition in the CPC or guidelines in respect of the types of questions to be avoided.

Regarding question format during court hearings, contrary to recommendations in the literature (e.g. Powell *et al.*, 2005), interviews in court tend to begin with close-ended questions although open-ended questions are also used in questioning the witnesses. Law professionals rarely ask questions that encourage answers such as “I don’t know” or “I don’t remember” (Scoboria and Fisico, 2013). In fact, the opposite pattern is often observed, as judges normally begin the court session by warning witnesses about the penalties associated with giving false testimony.

The presiding judge may include some clarifying questions at the end of the witness examination (Gomes Filho, 2008). Frequently the judge’s questioning is restricted to clarifying information included in the civilian police report collected during the investigative phase. Witnesses are asked if they are able to verify what was said to the police by reading the police report. According to our study, due to extended time delays of several months or even years between the event and the court testimony, prosecutors may read excerpts of the complaint to the witness as a way of trying to help them remember the facts.

Law professionals in this research recognized that they learn to interview witnesses/victims by practice alone, that is while performing their duties. Given their poor training regarding best questioning practices, prosecutors, and especially defense attorneys, report frequently avoiding questioning the witnesses during the trial out of fear of aggravating the situation for the accused (in the case of the defense) or for the victim (in the case of prosecutors).

Audio- and video-recording are very rarely used during trial. Legal proceedings are therefore documented either using indirect methods (whereby the judge dictates the witness statements to a registrar) or by stenography. The majority of Brazilian courthouses do not have facilities to properly accommodate victims, witnesses, and defendants. For example, normally, prosecution and defense witnesses are seated in the same place (e.g. a waiting room or hall) waiting to be called to the courtroom. In addition, the defendant might sometimes be waiting in the same room or hall as the victim and witnesses.

Witness testimony plays an important role in the outcome of criminal legal disputes in Brazil (Ávila, 2013) since forensic evidence is not always available due to limited resources for the police investigation. Hence, court decisions often have to rely on witness/victim evidence. For reasons such as witnesses not complying with a formal requirement to testify in court, in a number of cases the only witness available to testify may be the military patrol officer who first responded to the scene at the time of the incident. If requested by one of the parties, it is mandatory by law that the patrol officer testifies in court. Unfortunately, the patrol police testimony does not usually convey crucial evidence. The reasons for this may include the length of time since the crime occurred (usually at least five months up to one year) as well as repeated exposure to similar situations (e.g. the same patrol officer investigating similar cases of young men involved in gang shootings in one particular community). According to our data, the length of time and repetition tend to make it almost impossible for the patrol police officer to retrieve reliable details about a particular case. In fact, unless the incident was particularly noteworthy, police officers are quite unlikely to remember crime scene details.

In sum, data from the first national study on witness evidence in the criminal system in Brazil yielded several results specifically relevant to the present chapter. Adult witness/victim interviewing occurs not in two phases of the criminal process as described in the CPC, but in three phases: the initial investigative, the investigative, and the trial phases. Best-practice interviewing (Milne and Powell, 2010) does not seem to be implemented by interviewers in all three of these phases, largely due to a lack of formal training.

Concluding remarks: implications for research, policy, and practice

Witness testimony plays a crucial role at all stages of the criminal process in Brazil. Witnesses/victims of any age often provide information which cannot be reconstructed from physical evidence alone, or in cases for which physical evidence is not available. In our study of interviews with adult witnesses/victims, the number of military police officers requested to testify in court was found to be high, especially since adult witnesses are often reluctant to go to the police or testify in court because they fear retaliation from suspects.

In Brazil, it is apparent that more efforts have been made to achieve better and more scientifically based results when interviewing children and adolescents in court as opposed to interviewing adults. Our study revealed that adult interviewing practices currently being used by the police and forensic professionals seem to be quite intuitive and based on common sense rather than hard science. Most Brazilian police and law professionals do not yet have access to the current literature in eyewitness testimony regarding best practices investigative interviewing which is mostly published in English.

Police officers, prosecutors, attorneys, and judges seem to realize that long periods of time and other factors such as witnesses' emotional states impact on the quality of testimony. However, very few of those professionals realize that their own interviewing strategies (e.g. mostly close and suggestive questions) also impact on the quality and amount of evidence they get from a witness/victim.

As in other non-European countries (for example, in Australia – Powell and Barnett, 2014), there are several challenges for the successful implementation of best-practice interviewing guidelines with children and adults in Brazil. Future research is required to address the substantial challenge of developing and testing a suitable training program for Brazil's huge territory and large population (over 200 million people: IBGE, 2015). A key direction for future research would be to examine alternative forms of training and continuous supervision to overcome limited economic and human resources in a developing country of such huge dimensions as Brazil. Particularly regarding human resources, at the present moment there are very few well-trained Portuguese-speaking supervisors that could conduct a training program in Brazil. Alternative forms of training and supervision (such as online training: Guadagno and Powell, 2012) should be considered.

In terms of policy, any substantial change in the way witnesses/victims are interviewed (for instance, adopting a best-practice guideline) would require legislative reform since Brazil is under federal regulation. State institutions are unable to enact such provisions on their own. In the last few years, there have been initiatives undertaken in Brazil to promote more substantial changes with regard to the interviewing of witnesses/victims in general. For instance, recently the Ministry of Justice (with the support of the IPEA) sponsored a meeting which was held in the Brazilian parliament to discuss possible changes in the legislation. Two leading researchers in eyewitness psychology (i.e. Ray Bull and Roy Malpass) were invited to this meeting to discuss the preliminary results of our study on adult witness interviewing and point to possible venues for a legislative change process.

References

Ávila, G. N. (2013) *Falsas memórias e sistema penal: A prova testemunhal em xeque*. Rio de Janeiro: Lumen Juris.

Azambuja, M. R. F. (2010) *Violência sexual intrafamiliar e produção de prova da materialidade: Proteção ou violação de direitos da criança?* Doctoral dissertation, Pontifícia Universidade Católica do Rio Grande do Sul, Porto Alegre, Rio Grande do Sul, Brazil.

Bardin, L. (2006) *Análise de Conteúdo*. Lisbon: Edições 70.

Brazil (1988) Constituição da República Federativa do Brasil de 1988. *Diário Oficial da União*, Brasília, DF, 15 out. From: http://www.planalto.gov.br/ccivil_03/constituicao/Constituicao.htm.

Brazil (1990a) Decreto no. 99.710, de 21 de novembro de 1990. Promulga a Convenção sobre os Direitos da Criança. *Diário Oficial da União*, Brasília, DF, 22 nov. From: http://www.planalto.gov.br/ccivil_03/decreto/1990-1994/D99710.htm.

Brazil (1990b) Lei no. 8.069, de 13 de julho de 1990. Dispõe sobre o Estatuto da Criança e do Adolescente e dá outras providências. *Diário Oficial da União*, Brasília, DF, 13 jul. From: http://www.senado.gov.br/legislacao/ListaPublicacoes.action?id=102414.

Brazil (2005) *Política Nacional de Assistência Social*. Brasília, DF: Ministério do Desenvolvimento Social e Combate à Fome. From: http://www.mds.gov.br/assistenciasocial/secretaria-nacional-de-assistencia-social-snas/cadernos/politica-nacional-de-assistencia-social-2013-pnas-2004-e-norma-operacional-basica-de-servico-social-2013-nobsuas.

Brazil (2009) *Matriz Curricular Nacional Para Ações Formativas dos Profissionais da Área de Segurança Pública*. Brasília, DF: Ministério da Justiça/SENASP. Disponível em: http://portal.mj.gov.br/services.

Brazil (2010) National Justice Council – DJE/CNJ no. 215/2010, pp. 33–4.

Brazil (2012) *Centros de Referência Especializado de Assistência Social*. Brasília, DF: Portal Brasil. From: http://www.brasil.gov.br/cidadania-e-justica/2011/10/centro-de-referencia-especializado-de-assistencia-social-creas.

Brazil (2014) *As Escolas de Conselhos*. Brasília, DF: Secretaria de Direitos Humanos da Presidência da República. From: http://www.sdh.gov.br/assuntos/criancas-e-adolescentes/programas/as-escolas-de-conselhos.

Carvalho, D. B. (2001) "Política social e direitos humanos: Trajetórias de violação dos direitos de cidadania de crianças e adolescentes," *Revista SER Social*, 8: 143–70.

Childhood Brazil (2014) Retrieved 22 February. From: http://www.childhood.org.br/ceajud-lanca-curso-depoimento-especial-e-a-escuta-de-criancas-no-sistema-de-justica-em-parceria-com-a-childhood-brasil.

Codato, A. N. (2005) "Uma história política da transição brasileira: Da ditadura militar à democracia," *Revista de Sociologia Política*, 25: 83–106.

Conselho Federal de Psicologia (2009) *Serviço de proteção social a crianças e adolescentes vítimas de violência, abuso e exploração sexual e suas famílias: Referências para a atuação do psicólogo*. Brasília: CFP.

Conselho Nacional de Justiça (2010) Recomendação no. 33, de 23 de novembro de 2010. Depoimento Especial. *Diário da Justiça Eletrônico*, 215: 33–4. From: www.cnj.jus.br/images/portarias/2010/port_gp_33_2010.pdf.

Conselho Nacional de Justiça (2013) *Cresce o numero de experiências destinadas a coleta de depoimento de crianças e adolescentes*. Brasília, Distrito Federal, Brazil. Retrieved 15 January 2015. From: http://www.cnj.jus.br/noticias/cnj/26987:cresce-o-numero-de-experiencias-destinadas-a-coleta-de-depoimento-de-criancas-e-adolescentes.

Daltoé-Cezar, J. A. (2007) *Depoimento sem dano: Uma alternativa para inquirir crianças e adolescentes nos processos judiciais*. Porto Alegre, Brasil: Livraria do Advogado.

Departamento Penitenciário Nacional. *Relatório Anual*. Retrieved 9 January 2015. From: http://pt.scribd.com/doc/249169479/Relatorio-DEPEN-Sistema-penitenciario-no-Brasil-dados-co-pdf#scribd.

Di Gesu, C. C. (2008) *Prova Penal e Falsas Memórias*. Master's thesis, Pontifícia Universidade Católica do Rio Grande do Sul, Porto Alegre, Rio Grande do Sul, Brazil.

Fisher, R. P. and Geiselman, R. E. (1992) *Memory-Enhancing Techniques for Investigative Interviewing: The Cognitive Interview*. Springfield, IL: Charles C. Thomas.

Froner, J. P. and Ramires, V. R. (2008) "Escuta de crianças vítimas de abuso sexual no âmbito jurídico: Uma revisão crítica da literatura," *Paidéia (Ribeirão Preto)*, 18 (40): 267–78. From: http://www.scielo.br/pdf/paideia/v18n40/05.pdf.

Gava, L. L. (2012) *Perícia psicológica no contexto criminal em casos de suspeita de abuso sexual infanto-juvenil*. Doctoral dissertation, Universidade Federal do Rio Grande do Sul, Porto Alegre, Rio Grande do Sul, Brazil.

Giacomolli, N. J. (2008) "Resgate necessário da humanização do processo penal contemporâneo," in A. Wunderlich (ed.), *Política criminal contemporânea*. Porto Alegre: Livraria do Advogado, pp. 331–44.

Giacomolli, N. J. and Di Gesu, C. C. (2010) "Fatores de contaminação da prova testemunhal," in *Processo penal contemporâneo*. Porto Alegre: Núria Fabris, pp. 11–40.

Gomes Filho, A. M. (2008) "Provas," in M. T. R. A. Moura (ed.), *As reformas no processo penal: As novas Leis de 2008 e os projetos de reforma*. São Paulo: Revista dos Tribunais, pp. 246–97.

Guadagno, B. and Powell, M. (2012) "E-simulations for the purpose of training forensic (investigative) interviewers," in D. Holt, S. Segrave, and J. Cybulski (eds), *Professional Education Using E-Simulations: Benefits of Blended Learning Design*. Hershey, PA: IGI Global, pp. 71–86.

IBGE (2015) *Projeção da população do Brasil e das Unidades da Federação*. Brasília. Retrieved 25 January. 2015. From: http://www.ibge.gov.br/apps/populacao/projecao/index.html.

Lamb, M. E., Orbach, Y., Sternberg, K. J., Hershkowitz, I., and Horowitz, D. (2000) "Accuracy of investigators' verbatim notes of their forensic interviews with alleged child abuse victims," *Law and Human Behavior*, 24: 699–708.

Milani, R. G. and Loureiro, S. R. (2008) "Famílias e violência doméstica: Condições psicossociais pós ações do conselho tutelar," *Psicologia Ciência e Profissão*, 28 (1): 50–67.

Milne, B. and Powell, M. (2010) "Investigative interviewing," in J. Brown and E. Campbell (eds), *The Cambridge Handbook of Forensic Psychology*. Cambridge: Cambridge University Press, pp. 208–14.

Núcleo de Estudos da Violência da Universidade de São Paulo (2013) *Report of the Center for the Study of Violence*, 12th edn. Retrieved 9 January 2015. From: http://www.nevusp.org/downloads/down273.pdf.

Pisa, O. (2006) *Psicologia do testemunho: Os riscos na inquirição de crianças*. Master's thesis, Pontifícia Universidade Católica do Rio Grande do Sul, Porto Alegre, Rio Grande do Sul, Brazil.

Powell, M. B. and Barnett, M. (2014) "Elements underpinning successful implementation of a national best-practice child investigative interviewing framework," *Psychiatry, Psychology and Law* [online 21 August 2014].

Powell, M. B., Fisher, R. P., and Wright, R. (2005) 'Investigative interviewing," in N. Brewer and K. Williams (eds), *Psychology and Law: An Empirical Perspective*. New York: Guilford, pp. 11–42.

Reyna, V. and Brainerd, C. (2005) *The Science of False Memory*. New York: Oxford University Press.

Santos, B. R. and Gonçalves, I. B. (2008) *Depoimento sem medo? Culturas e práticas não-revitimizantes*. São Paulo: Childhood Brasil.

Santos, B. R., Gonçalves, I. B., Vasconcelos, M. G. O. M., Barbieri, P. B., and Viana, V. N. (2013) *Cartografia Nacional das Experiências Alternativas de Tomada de Depoimento Especial de Crianças e Adolescentes em Processos Judiciais no Brasil: O Estado da Arte*. São Paulo: Childhood Brasil-CNJ.

Schacter, D. L. and Loftus, E. F. (2013) "Memory and law: what can cognitive neuroscience contribute?" *Nature Neuroscience*, 16: 119–23.

Scoboria, A. and Fisico, S. (2013) "Encouraging and clarifying 'don't know' responses enhances interview quality," *Journal of Experimental Psychology: Applied*, 19: 72–82.

Silva, L. M. P., Ferriani, M. D. G. C., Beserra, M. A., Roque, E. M. D. S. T., and Carlos, D. M. (2013) "A escuta de crianças e adolescentes nos processos de crimes sexuais," *Ciência and Saúde Coletiva*, 18 (8): 2285–94.

Stein, L. M. (2014) *Avanços Científicos em Psicologia do Testemunho Aplicados ao Reconhecimento Pessoal e aos Depoimentos Forenses*, Projeto Pensando Direito. Brasília, DF: Ministério da Justiça/IPEA– Instituto de Pesquisas Econômicas Aplicadas.

Vargas, J. D. and Nascimento, L. F. Z. (2010) "Uma abordagem empírica do inquérito policial: O caso de Belo Horizonte," in M. Misse (ed.), *O Inquérito Policial no Brasil – Uma Pesquisa Empírica*. Rio de Janeiro: Booklink/FENAPEF/NECVU, pp. 102–90.

Waiselfisz, J. J. (2013) *Mapa da violência 2013: homicídios e juventude no Brasil*.CEBELA.

23 Interviewing victims of sexual offences in Chile

Towards a transformation of practice and meaning

C. Navarro, D. Mettifogo and F. García

Introduction

Criminal investigation into sexual abuse is challenging because of the already known difficulties in providing proof of evidence. These difficulties are determined by the characteristics of the phenomenon itself: large numbers of victims (especially child victims), absence of material evidence, and the lack of witnesses (UNICEF and UDP, 2006; Navarro, 2011). This is why, in these cases, the victims are such crucial witnesses for the legal system, and the ultimate success of the investigation depends heavily on the information provided by them (Powell *et al.*, 2005; Navarro *et al.*, 2012).

Victims of sexual offenses in Chile are now interviewed under a new criminal procedure started in 2000. This revision has implied a significant improvement in the overall system however, has failed to highlight the role of victims (Navarro *et al.*, 2012).

In terms of public policies and interviewing techniques, Chile may be considered backwards: specifically, there are no legal requirements for video-recording of testimony, therefore, we do not know how or even what guidelines are being applied (Ministerio del Interior, 2013). What we do know is that, in Chile, children are subject to multiple forensic assessments, face hostility from some of the officers and doubts about the truthfulness of their account, and have inadequate facilities to provide testimony, especially when they have to provide it repeatedly (UNICEF and UDP, 2006).

This reveals an area of interest in the treatment of victims and the methods of investigation that they are subjected to during the investigation process, due to the high possibility of retraumatization, especially the interviews (Mide UC, 2009; Navarro *et al.*, 2012). Consequently, the interviewing of victims involves the need to manage technical and ethical issues regarding their experience as well as the evidential requirements of the system. This is particularly relevant in the case of child victims because of their doubly vulnerable condition: being victims and also in the throes of development (Navarro, 2011). Furthermore in Chile, as in the rest of the world, the phenomenon of sexual abuse mainly affects children. As a matter of fact, in 2013 there were 24,142 victims of sexual crimes, out of which 77.86 percent were under age in Chile (Ministerio Público, 2014).

Moreover, according to the results from the Fourth Study of Child Maltreatment (UNICEF, 2012), it is estimated that 8.7 percent of all children and youths have suffered some type of sexual violence.

Equally alarming is the exponential rise in the number of child sexual abuse reports filed during recent years. Between 2011 and 2012 there was a 3.7 percent rise in sexual abuse crimes, while for minors of 14 years in particular there was a registered rise of 22.2 percent (Ministerio Público, 2013). This tendency is repeated in 2013 (19.1 percent) (Ministerio Público, 2014). Consequently, this increase in reporting has produced an increase in the number of children involved in the criminal investigation process for sexual abuse crimes, which translates into a greater number of children being interviewed.

In this context, in the past few years have emerged not just social movements demanding improvements in this area, but also diverse institutional and legal efforts, all of them related to young victims. That is not the case for adult victims, which is a subject that remains unseen. In addition, interviewing practices with child victims of sexual abuse crimes in Chile are currently in a process of transformation toward the implementation of new models based on international agreed-upon standards and perspectives of human rights. Therefore the main focus of this chapter will be on child victim interviewing.

Interviewing practices with child victims

Secondary victimization and judicial investigation

The consequences of the primary experience of victimization are often worsened by the harmful effect of inadequate responses within the victim's surroundings, known as secondary victimization (Escaff *et al.*, 2006; Gutiérrez de Piñeres Botero *et al.*, 2009). This phenomenon, understood as the suffering that victims experience while passing through the criminal justice system, has been recognized by the United Nations (1999) as one of the most harmful effects of victimization. The harmful potential of secondary victimization is exacerbated when it affects vulnerable victims, such as children, who, for their developmental level and typical defenselessness, are more likely to suffer the adverse effects that can be provoked by the inappropriate responses of the social system. The aforementioned is especially harmful for children who have suffered sexual violence when they are asked to tell their traumatic experience repeatedly, remembering the event of abuse each time (Navarro *et al.*, 2012).

In the last decade, countries such as the UK, Canada, Australia, New Zealand, Israel, and the United States, among others, have been taking measures to decrease secondary victimization without foregoing procedural or administrative objectives. These measures involve the decrease in the number of statements and interviews which victims are exposed during the investigation process, as well as limiting contact victims have with the various expert professionals in the justice system. These plans have implications for changes in the legal norms that regulate the criminal investigation procedures involving children, as well as the use of new technical tools (Powell *et al.*, 2005; Powell, 2011).

The situation of sexually abused children in the context of the Chilean justice system was initially characterized through a study from 2006 that identified the route they take and the treatment they receive through the legal process (UNICEF and UDP, 2006). The study revealed that the child's testimony is fundamental to the investigation, and must be recounted several times in various forms and stages of the judicial process, in situations involving the following: police, detectives, prosecution, medical examination, sexual assault medical forensic examination, psychiatric inquiry, credibility assessment, inquiry of psychological harm, and finally at the trial. Some of these described instances may involve more than one interview with the child, in addition to reiterated "informal" interrogations by officials, as well as other formal practices, including additional assessments by the defense. The study demonstrated the tension between the objectives of investigating versus protecting the victim. That is, in the desire to prosecute offenders, the system can sometimes inadvertently cause harm to child victims.

A subsequent study allowed a better understanding of the perception that caregivers have with regard to secondary victimization within this population (Mide UC, 2009). The study interviewed 390 caregivers of children who had been victims of sexual abuse and found that more than half perceived the judicial process as generating harm in children who must pass through it, with a quarter feeling it caused great harm. The stages of the process that mainly contribute to this perception are the filing of the report, physical inquiries, and giving a statement at trial. The study also revealed that children who participated in a greater number of interviews had higher levels of perceived harm, particularly when the number of interviews exceeded five.

Correspondingly, the national studies discussed above acknowledge a criminal investigation system in Chile by which overexposure to ongoing questioning and expert examination of a child victim of sexual abuse is the norm. At the same time, victims and their families indicate that having to provide a reiterated account of the abuse experience on various occasions constitutes one of the greatest sources of suffering during the judicial process (Mide UC, 2009). This is the result of a lack of connection between the various institutions that are part of the process, an inadequate infrastructure, as well as functionaries with low levels of expertise in conducting interviews with children (Navarro *et al.*, 2012).

On the basis of the aforementioned research, there is evidence that justifies the need to modify the current interviewing practices of child sex abuse victims in Chile in order to decrease the level of secondary victimization they often suffer as a result of the judicial process.

Legal and regulatory framework of interviewing practices with children

The adversarial criminal justice system is relatively new in Chile. On 16 June 2005, the Criminal Procedure Reform was fully implemented. This process took five years to complete and signified the end of an inquisitorial criminal prosecution system. This change was in response to a series of criticisms of the old system, which maintained little transparency, a lack of impartiality, and overall inefficiency (Ministerio Público de Chile and Vera Institute of Justice, 2004). In this sense, there existed a certain level of victim invisibility, because they did not have any formal recognition in the process. This implied a lack of concern for their needs, without any type of special protection or institutions concerned for their well-being (Ministerio de Justicia, 2010).

The new institutions formed under the framework of the Criminal Procedure Reform were the Office of the Public Prosecutor (OPP), the Office of the Public Defender (OPD), the Guarantee Judge, and the Criminal Oral Trial Court Judges. The OPP is responsible for conducting the investigation, exercising public criminal proceedings, and providing protection to victims and witnesses (Ministerio de Justicia, 2010).

In Chile, the OPP has a constitutionally established autonomy therefore prosecutors exclusively direct the criminal investigation. In the case of child sex abuse victims, it has been established that only OPP professionals are able to interview them. This means that child interviewers include prosecutors, prosecutor assistants, psychologists, and, in some cases, police (Ministerio Público, 2009). In addition, there is no limit to the amount of expert opinions about the victim that could be required during the criminal proceeding, resulting in a higher number of interviews that the child victim must undergo. The reform of criminal procedure is making progress in incorporating the victim as an important actor in the criminal justice system. Nevertheless, it is seen as a maze-like process for children, especially those victims of sexual abuse who require substantial modifications (UNICEF and UDP, 2006; Mide UC, 2009).

It is worth highlighting that, not only does a law of comprehensive child protection that would guarantee effective compliance with the Convention on the Rights of the Child (CRC) not exist in Chile, nor does a central and articulating policy that would provide an integral sense of meaning (UNICEF, 2012). There is also no figure who serves as an ombudsman for children, or a well-articulated response for such in the criminal justice framework under the requirements for protection and relief. As a result, the right of the child to be heard in any judicial or administrative process in which s/he is involved, understood as respect for and consideration of the opinions of the child, does not have an effective mechanism in Chile (UNICEF, 2004).

The Chilean system does not take into consideration conditions under which children are able to provide testimony nor does it provide safeguards against interventions used by the State in the criminal justice framework. From this perspective there is a paradox – whereas the State presents itself as the guarantor of children's rights, it is in turn the direct source of infringement of those rights through the criminal proceedings, and is therefore responsible for the accompanying secondary victimization. The regulation of interviews that subject children to criminal investigation contributes to the action being taken by the State, oriented to guarantee the full exercise of rights and provide protection to this population. In order for a proposed law which regulates interviews with child victims to comply with its objectives, it must be fundamentally linked with efforts aimed at improving technique and infrastructure, as well as an alignment with best practices.

Proposed changes in the interviewing of children

After a progressive process of awareness regarding deficits in interviewing practices with children and its secondary victimization effect, Chile today presents a noticeable setting of diverse efforts for improvement. These labors, although lacking articulation, reveal a common concern for the well-being of children and a desire to modify former interviewing practices. The improvement initiatives currently under development for interviewing child victims include specific programs in some institutions that have contact with victims, as well as a legal project on this subject and contributions from the academy.

Institutional initiatives

In Chile during recent years, the various public institutions that have direct contact with young victims have developed pilot programs that seek to modify procedures to improve conditions in which interviews are carried out and to train the people responsible for them. These initiatives are based on the use of interviewing guides, training programs in a traditional format (time-specific, in groups, mainly in the classroom), as well as procedures and special physical conditions for children providing testimony in the judicial environment. Some of these have been put in to practice at the local sphere, while others have been implemented at the national level (see Table 23.1).

Although these initiatives constitute important advances, they end up insufficient for providing an effective answer to the problem of secondary victimization

Table 23.1 Current institutional initiatives for interviewing children

Initiative	*Institution*	*Objective*
Gesell Rooms chambers (2011)	Family Court	Promoting the right of the child to be heard by granting special interviews in Gesell Rooms
Guide for investigative interviewing	Office of the Public Prosecutor (OPP)	Offering to prosecutors a guide of good practices for interviewing victims
Police training courses (2012–14)	Police	Generating police officers especially trained in methods for interviewing children
Special room for the testimony of child in Criminal Oral Trial Court (2013)	Judiciary	Creating a protected place for testimony child during the trial

that child sexual abuse victims suffer because of their lack of articulation. More specifically, there are no protocols that define and coordinate the intervention of the various institutions involved in the areas of justice, health, education, police, and social services. This leads to a non-integrated solution for improvement that does not resolve the systemic origin of secondary victimization, maintaining the risk of children being subject to multiple interviews and expected to re-tell their experiences repeatedly. Another missing aspect is the lack of an evidence-based public policy in investigative interview procedures. None of the mentioned initiatives has a system of evaluation that has demonstrated evidence of effectiveness and that justifies implementation at the national level.

One last aspect relates to how well-equipped people are for interviewing children. This applies to task specialization as well as the necessary training process. Concerns arise with task specialization when the role of the interviewer becomes an add-on to other responsibilities, as is the case for prosecutors and judges. Moreover, the training processes included in the initiatives mentioned are not based on components that the specialized literature considers indispensable for the development of interviewer competency, including: a focus on practical skills, proficiency in specific knowledge, expert supervision, individual feedback, opportunities for practice (Guckian and Byrne, 2011; Wright and Powell, 2006; Bull, 2013).

In sum, the current institutional initiatives for interviewing child victims in Chile appear insufficient when presented as a whole. Nevertheless, they represent a promising scenario for an early implementation of new investigation methods in the framework of a necessary regulation of such practices.

Legislative initiatives

The implementation of a new system for interviewing child victims of sexual abuse requires a series of both legal and procedural modifications. Until now, specific laws which regulate interviewing practices of child victims have not existed in Chile. Yet there does exist greater consciousness for the need to legislate, and steps have been taken in this direction.

At the beginning of 2014, the executive power proposed a new project on this matter, which originated in a cross-sector working group that brought together government representatives, individuals from the main institutions working with victims, as well as those from the academic field.[1] This gathering provided a forum to develop the proposal for a system of videotaping the interviewing of child and adolescent victims of sexual abuse.

The core idea of this recommendation is the establishment of an integrated system at the national level. Such a system would articulate, coordinate, and regulate the actions of the distinct institutions that are involved in the criminal investigation process, while installing a new mechanism for investigation: the videotaped interviewing of child sexual abuse victims. The objectives of the proposal include: reducing the number of interviews to which children are subject; ensuring that all child victims of sexual abuse are only interviewed by personnel who are trained and specialized in doing so; and reducing the need for the child to appear at the oral trial (Navarro *et al.*, 2012).

The contents of this proposal have been the subject of broad discussions at the national level. There has been an overall agreement regarding its central aspects. Yet there are some elements of the proposal that have given rise to skepticism and reticence that has enhanced the tension between the objectives for investigating versus protecting victims.

Lastly, the topic still under discussion at the Congress, despite having no certain knowledge of the final contents of the law, is the fact that no one in Chile today doubts that there will soon be a law that seeks to improve the condition of child victims of sexual abuse in their progression through the justice system.

Academic and scientific initiatives

In 2011, the Childhood and Justice Research Group was formed at the University of Chile. This is an interdisciplinary group of investigators whose objective is to study children in the context of the national legal system and develop procedures to reduce and prevent secondary victimization. Simultaneously, this team has participated actively in advising the design of public policies for victims in Chile.

Firstly, one of the lines of investigation has been the development of instruments for the prevention of secondary victimization that children of sexual abuse suffer, specifically regarding the investigative interview and the development of interview protocols (i.e. Fisher and Geiselman, 1992; Home Office, 2011; Lamb *et al.*, 2008; Powell, 2014; State of Michigan, 2011). The first initiative has been the adaptation of the NICHD protocol (Lamb *et al.*, 2008) to the Spanish language, a work currently in progress that involves collaboration with Professor Michael Lamb.

Secondly, State sponsored research[2] is also in progress, which aims to generate a prototype model for conducting investigative interviews for child victims of sexual abuse. This model contains two components: an interviewing protocol adapted to the Chilean context; and an interviewer training program the effectiveness of which will be tested in a population of Chilean children who have been sexually abused. The second stage of this study (2015–16) contemplates the implementation of the model generated at the national level. It is hoped that this study will contribute to the development of the technical advances that will be required for successful implementation of the new law regulating the interviewing of child victims. The development of this study relies upon the permanent advisory position of Professor Martine Powell and her team at the Center for Investigative Interviewing at Deakin University in Australia.

The investigation initiatives described above represent the first scientific studies for interviewing young victims seeking to make an impact at the public policy level in Chile. The expectation is that such actions will support the transformation of the system of applied justice in Chile toward greater respect for the rights of children and adolescents.

Implications for research, policy and practice: cultural adaptation and scientific collaboration

To summarize, the situation in Chile with regard to the interviewing of child victims of sexual abuse in the judicial investigation is in the process of profound change. This is a process in which regulatory and technical aspects have not yet been established. In contrast, the objectives and principles that require a response through the transformation are clear: the reduction of secondary victimization and the adjustment of government procedures to meet the needs and rights of children. In addition, it is hoped that this transformation will improve the quality of witness testimony overall (e.g. becoming more accurate and more complete), a key component of this type of crime investigation.

From a technical point of view, the transformation of the investigative system that Chile is attempting to achieve has as its precedent well-documented international experience, both in terms of scientific development and public policy. The solid body of scientific knowledge that supports the technical component of the investigative interviewing of victims, such as the interviewing protocols and interviewer training systems developed in Anglo-Saxon countries, serve as a reference for the development of technical scientific proposals in Chile.

Nevertheless, the implementation of interviewing procedures developed in different cultural contexts and for distinct judicial systems may not readily apply. This could happen in the Latin American context with the use of protocols developed in the Anglo-Saxon world, where the interference of cultural variables must be considered. More specifically, it is important to consider possible cultural differences and the specific linguistic and para-linguistic codes that regulate interpersonal relations in each culture (Sharifian, 2011), due to the investigative techniques that are implemented in interactive contexts. The aforementioned invites researchers to reflect on the idiomatic and cultural barriers that are faced in the dissemination of knowledge in this subject area.

When considering the cultural issues, there are at least two aspects involved. The first is the linguistic effort that Spanish-speaking countries must make to access cutting-edge knowledge on interviewing victims. This involves actions in the direction of the translation of knowledge and techniques. However, recognition of the existence of cultural differences leads to the second issue: the need to adapt such knowledge to the cultural and linguistic contexts of Latin American countries. This second aspect raises the question about the appropriate and necessary actions to produce an effective process of cultural adaptation.

The answer to this question has brought us to consider that the process of translating techniques and procedures (protocols, guides, manuals, among others), as well as their mechanical application, in the Chilean context are insufficient. Thus we have started a pathway that is based on the articulation of two elements that together deal with the need for adaptation: raising local empirical evidence and partnership with international investigation teams.

Firstly, we aspire for public policy issues related to the treatment of child victims of sexual abuse in the Chilean justice system to be based on scientific evidence. This requires a systematic investigation of the subject matter through empirical studies with the national population, in order to verify the findings of international studies in this area. At the same time it allows for the identification of local characteristics that require consideration (e.g. differences in the evolving development, linguistic, etc.). Secondly, we believe that association with primary investigation teams at the international level is a key element. This association provides us with the opportunity to include the Chilean experience within a research line of long-standing data about interviewing victims. It supports the technical references and methodologies that allow for the design of research developed in Chile. This also opens the possibility for both the transformation of policy and technique in Chile, taking advantage of the international experience for its mistakes and the wisdom learned, while maximizing the results obtained.

Thus we believe that the articulation of these two elements allows the co-construction of new knowledge that will reflect the Chilean context. This new knowledge is generated from close collaborative relationships with first-rate international investigators in the field of interviewing victims and training interviewers, using an approach that enhances and respects local characteristics. We believe that from this articulation it is possible to have reciprocal opportunities for strengthening and development.

Notes

1. The Childhood and Justice Research Group from the University of Chile was part of this cross-sector working group as technical consultant.
2. Funding agency grant CONICYT-FONDEF CA13I10238.

References

Bull, R. (2013) "What is 'believed' or actually 'known' about characteristics that may contribute to being a good/effective interviewer?" *Investigative Interviewing: Research and Practice*, 5 (2): 128–43.

Escaff, E., Rivera, M., and Salvatierra, M. (2006) "Estudio de las variables asociadas a retractación en menores víctimas de abusos sexuales," *Revista de Victimología ILANUD*, pp. 117–31. Retrieved from: http://www.ilanud.or.cr/A111.pdf.

Fisher, R. P. and Geiselman, R. E. (1992) *Memory Enhancing Techniques for Investigative Interviewing: The Cognitive Interview*. Springfield, IL: Charles C. Thomas.

Guckian, E. and Byrne, M. (2011) "Best practice for conducting investigative interviews," *Irish Psychologist*, 37: 69–77.

Gutiérrez, de Piñeres Botero, C., Coronel, E., and Pérez, C. A. (2009) "Revisión teórica del concepto de victimización secundaria," *Liberabit. Revista de Psicología* [online], Vol. 15. Retrieved from: http://www.redalyc.org/pdf/686/68611923006.pdf.

Home Office (2011) *Achieving Best Evidence in Criminal Proceedings Guidance on Interviewing Victims and Witnesses*. Home Office: London.

Lamb, M. E., Hershkowitz, I., Orbach, Y., and Esplin, P. (2008) *Tell Me What Happened: Structured Investigative Interviews of Child Victims and Witnesses*, 1st edn. Chichester: Wiley.

Lamb, M. E., Orbach Y., Hershkowitz, I., Esplin, P. W., and Horowitz, D. (2007) 'A structured forensic interview protocol improves the quality and informativeness of investigative interviews with children: a review of research using the NICHD Investigative Interview Protocol," *Child Abuse and Neglect*, 31 (11–12): 1201–31.

Mide UC (2009) *Percepción de los Procesos de Investigación y Judicialización en los casos de agresiones sexuales infantiles en la Regiones Metropolitana, de Valparaíso y del Bío-Bío*, Informe de Estudio para la Fundación Amparo y Justicia, Mide UC.

Ministerio de Justicia (2010) *A 10 años de la Reforma procesal Penal: los desafíos del nuevo sistema*. Santiago de Chile: Gráfica Puerto Madero.

Ministerio del Interior (2013) *Política Nacional de Víctimas de Delito*. Retrieved from: http://goo.gl/qBCFOz.

Ministerio Público de Chile (2009) *Instrucción General que imparte criterios de actuación en delitos sexuales*, Oficio FN No. 160. Retrieved from: http://www.fiscaliadechile.cl/Fiscalia/archivo?id=843ypid=71ytid=1yd=1.

Ministerio Público de Chile (2013) *Boletín Institucional Anual 2012*. Retrieved from: http://www.fiscaliadechile.cl/Fiscalia/archivo?id=8995andpid=140andtid=1andd=1.

Ministerio Público de Chile (2014) *Boletín Institucional Anual 2013*. Retrieved from: http://www.fiscaliadechile.cl/Fiscalia/archivo?id=13002andpid=159andtid=1andd=1.

Ministerio Público de Chile and Vera Institute of Justice (2004) *Analizando la reforma a la justicia criminal en Chile. Un estudio comparativo entre el nuevo y el antiguo sistema penal*. Santiago de Chile: LOM Ediciones.

Navarro, C. (2011) "Evaluación de Credibilidad Discursiva en Víctimas de Agresiones Sexuales." In "Compendio mejores tesis, Magíster en Psicología Mención Psicología Clínica Infanto-Juvenil", Universidad de Chile. Ediciones Andros, Santiago, Chile.

Navarro, C., Mettifogo, D., Henríquez, S., Mandiola, S., Sepúlveda, E., Lathrop, F., and García, F. (2012) *Fundamentación Técnica. Proyecto de Ley que establece un Sistema de Entrevista videograbada para niños, niñas y adolescentes víctimas de delitos sexuales*. Santiago de Chile: Universidad de Chile.

Powell, M. B. (2011) *Entrevista Única Investigativa: Consideraciones Técnicas y Metodológicas*. Santiago: III Seminario Internacional sobre Agresiones Sexuales Infantiles.

Powell, M. B. (2014) "Standard Interview Method." Unpublished manuscript.

Powell, M. B., Fisher, R. P., and Wright, D. B. (2005) "Investigative interviewing," in N. Brewer and K. D. Williams (eds), *Psychology and Law: An Empirical Perspective*. New York: Guildford Press, pp. 11–42.

Sharifian, F. (2011) *Cultural Conceptualisations and Language: Theoretical Framework and Applications*. Amsterdam/Philadelphia: John Benjamins.

State of Michigan (2011) *Forensic Interviewing Protocol*. State of Michigan Governor's Task Force on Child Abuse and Neglect and Department of Human Services. Retrieved from: https://www.michigan.gov/documents/dhs/DHS-PUB-0779_211637_7.pdf.

UNICEF (2004) *Manual de aplicación de la Convención sobre los Derechos del Niño*, edición española enteramente revisada. Ginebra: Atar Roto Presse.

UNICEF (2012) *Cuarto Estudio de Maltrato Infantil*. Santiago de Chile.

UNICEF and Universidad Diego Portales (2006) *Niños, Niñas, Adolescentes Víctimas de Delitos Sexuales en el Marco de la Reforma Procesal Penal*, Informe Final, Instituto de Investigación en Ciencias Sociales, Universidad Diego Portales, Santiago, mimeo.

Retrieved from: http://www.unicef.cl/unicef/public/archivos_documento/173/Informe%20final.pdf.

United Nations (1999) *Guide For Policy Makers*. Retrieved from: http://www.uncjin.org/Standards/policy.pdf.

Wright, R. and Powell, M. (2006) "Investigative interviewers' perceptions of their difficulty in adhering to open-ended questions with child witnesses," *International Journal of Police Science and Management*, 8 (4): 316–25.

Conclusion

Interview practices for victims and witnesses – realising our potential

Trond Myklebust, Gavin E. Oxburgh, David Walsh and Allison D. Redlich

Until the release of this book, little was known about interview and interrogation practices around the world, especially in non-Western countries like the Middle and Far East and especially in an integrated manner. There also appears to be a strong link between the countries where researchers are from and the amount of scientific knowledge we previously held about a particular country's practice. Furthermore, a clear correlation exists between the lack of knowledge and those countries which are alleged (with strong anecdotal evidence) to use torture and other degrading forms of treatment. Thus the training of interviewers is absolutely vital in every aspect and this is an area that many chapters have highlighted.

Forensic interviews

We might trace the scientific perspective on investigative interviewing back to the German scientist William Stern (1903/1904), presented in Chapter 12 in this book. Stern was occupied with techniques to achieve the most valid information from interviewed children and he subsequently introduced the difference between open (*bericht*) and closed (*verhör*) questions. In his research, he clearly demonstrated the superiority of open questions, gaining more valid information compared to closed questions. Today, there exists a large number of scientific studies that investigate several components in the investigative interview, focusing on the interviewer, the interviewee and the context where the interview takes place, or the dynamic between these factors.

There are also several traditions that exist, all with different aspects to consider. One such tradition, which focuses on the interviewer, examines the effect of interviewer manner, competence and training. Another tradition, focusing on the interviewee, investigates the understanding of memory and forensic practice. A third tradition focuses upon vulnerable witnesses while a fourth focuses on interviewee deception. A fifth tradition studies practices where the interview takes place, such as the examination in court. Taken together, the amount of information in these scientific studies might appear overwhelming to the practitioner conducting the interview. To some, these studies might suggest that it is almost impossible to gain valid and reliable information from interviewees. However, since the first scientific studies by Stern (1903/1904), almost all the scientific efforts illuminate potentials in the interviewing process.

Training of forensic interviewers

Initial studies in the USA by Fisher *et al.* (1987) observed that interviewers' level of competence affected the responses of adult interviewees. The authors recommended formal, scientifically based training of police officers at the institutional level. Fisher and Geiselman (see Fisher *et al.*, 1989) introduced the cognitive interview (CI) and found that interviewers trained in this technique obtained longer responses in interviews of adults compared with interviewers without such training. They suggested that future training programmes would be most effective if they were divided into intensive short sessions rather than one large session. This would also keep the presentation component relatively short with the efficacy of the training programme profiting by extended feedback to the individual interviewers (Fisher and Geiselman, 1992; Fisher *et al.*, 1987).

In one of several studies to establish the efficacy of the CI, training programmes were conducted in four, 60-minute group sessions, including lectures describing various components of the procedure, together with demonstrations of good and poor interviewing techniques (Fisher *et al.*, 1989). However, other research has found that long-term improvement in the quality of investigative interviews are observed only when the training is distributed over a longer period of time (see, for example, Lamb *et al.*, 2000; Lamb *et al.*, 2002). In these studies, the length of training varied between three to five full-day sessions, followed by supervision and feedback to the interviewers (Lamb *et al.*, 2002; Orbach *et al.*, 2000; Sternberg *et al.*, 2001). As demonstrated in the chapters presented above, the way in which the training of interviewers is conducted varies from country to country. For example, in the US, courses are relatively shorter compared (for example) to England and Wales, where longer, more structured programmes appear to be more prevalent. However, what are the most useful interviewing skills for eliciting extensive, accurate accounts from interviewees?

As outlined in the chapters presented above and in the literature (see Oxburgh *et al.*, 2010), there is strong international consensus that the use of open (or appropriate) questioning techniques are the most effective forms, with leading and other forms of inappropriate questions being the most ineffective at producing longer and more detailed answers. It is not yet clear which specific (or combined) training elements are the most effective for improving interviewer performance. However, Powell *et al.* (2005) compared elements of those training protocols that were deemed to be successful in investigative interviews of children with those of most other training programmes. They found the successful elements to include the use of:

- structured interview protocols;
- multiple opportunities to practise over an extended period;
- expert feedback and ongoing supervision;
- internal motivation by the interviewer to enhance their individual performance.

However, consideration should also be given to the interviewing of victims and witnesses who have learning difficulties and/or mental health disorders. More is required to understand which interviewing and questioning techniques are the most effective with this vulnerable group who may have profound difficulties in their receptive and expressive communication. We must also ensure that they are able to provide their best evidence throughout the criminal justice process. In some countries there are guidelines in place to assist in this. For example, in England and Wales, there is the 'Achieving Best Evidence in Criminal Proceedings: Guidance' on interviewing victims and witnesses (Ministry of Justice, 2011). One special measure is the use of a Registered Intermediary – a communication specialist that makes the vulnerable person's journey through the criminal justice system more inclusive and, arguably, less of an ordeal. This is an area that requires additional research to establish the efficacy of such measures, but also to establish the various decision-making procedures that are in use.

Decision-making procedures

A system evaluating children's statements of alleged abuse that has been used by German courts since the German Supreme Court raised the question in the 1950s is presented (see Chapter 12 by Volbert and Baker, this volume). The German scientific community, represented by the psychologist Udo Undeutsch (1967, 1982), developed a method for content analysis of the children's statements based upon the assumption that free narratives of children increase the amount and validity of the information obtained. This assumption was later denoted 'the Undeutsch hypothesis'. The scientific work conducted by Undeutsch was further developed by the German psychologist Gunther Köhnken (2004) and the Swedish psychologist Arne Trankell (Trankell, 1972, 1982). Unfortunately, their efforts were seldom published in English journals, hence the distribution of their scientific work was limited.

Several decades have passed since the introduction of Statement Validity Assessment (SVA) and Criteria Based Content Analysis (CBCA) as methods for evaluating interviews presented for court. It is vital both for the interests of society and the protection of the defendant's human rights that there is a robust and effective means of testing oral evidence. The editors find the evaluation and development of analytic methods for the decision-makers during the investigations and presented as evidence in court to be an important area for further research and focus in the years to come. Whether or not a victim or witness gives a quality statement depends not only on their limitations but also on the interviewers' limitations and the interviewers' ability to, in a sense, take advantage of the interviewee's strength and get them to function to the best of their ability.

Conclusion

This book has brought together a collection of chapters from over 25 countries, explaining the practices used, together with contemporary developments, hitherto unreported in any current interview or interrogation book. What has become apparent from the chapters is that the aim of modern-day investigative interviewing with victims and witnesses is to gather comprehensive, accurate, relevant and reliable information within the legal framework defined by national and international legislation (see Oxburgh *et al.*, 2015). We believe that the investigative interviewing domain must continue to evolve in such a manner that protects and fosters the important practitioner/academic relationship, to ensure that practitioners are well informed and involved in academic research. However, that said, researchers and practitioners should always ensure that, before any potential changes are made to policy and practice, they are underpinned by a robust evidence base (Oxburgh and Dando, 2011).

References

Fisher, R. P. and Geiselman, R. E. (1992) *Memory-enhancing Techniques for Investigative Interviewing: The Cognitive Interview*. Springfield, IL: Charles C. Thomas.

Fisher, R. P., Geiselman, R. E. and Amador, M. (1989) 'Field test of the cognitive interview: enhancing the recollection of actual victims and witnesses of crime', *Journal of Applied Psychology*, 5: 722–7.

Fisher, R. P., Geiselman, R. E. and Raymond, D. S. (1987) 'Critical analysis of police interview techniques', *Journal of Police Science and Administration*, 15 (3): 177–85.

Köhnken, G. (2004) *Statement Validity Analysis and the 'Detection of the Truth'*, in P. A. Granhag and L. A. Strömwall (eds), *The Detection of Deception in Forensic Contexts*. Cambridge: Cambridge University Press, pp. 41–63.

Lamb, M. E., Sternberg, K. J., Orbach, Y., Esplin, P. W. and Mitchell, S. (2002) 'Is ongoing feedback necessary to maintain the quality of investigative interviews with allegedly abused children?', *Applied Developmental Science*, 6 (1): 35–41.

Lamb, M. E., Sternberg, K. J., Orbach, Y., Hershkowitz, I., Horowitz, D. and Esplin, P. W. (2000) 'The effects of intensive training and ongoing supervision on the quality of investigative interviews with alleged sex abuse victims', *Applied Developmental Science*, 6 (3): 114–25.

Ministry of Justice (2011) *Achieving Best Evidence in Criminal Proceedings: Guidance on Interviewing Victims and Witnesses, and Guidance on Using Special Measures*. London: Ministry of Justice.

Orbach, Y., Hershkowitz, I., Lamb, M. E., Sternberg, K. J., Esplin, P. W. and Horowitz, D. (2000) 'Assessing the value of structured protocols for forensic interviews of alleged child abuse victims', *Child Abuse and Neglect*, 24 (6): 733–52.

Oxburgh, G. E. and Dando, C. J. (2011) 'Psychology and interviewing: what direction now in our quest for reliable information?', *British Journal of Forensic Practice*, 13: 135–44.

Oxburgh, G., Myklebust, T. and Grant, T. (2010) 'The question of question types in police interviews: a review of the literature from a psychological and linguistic perspective', *International Journal of Speech Language and the Law*, 17 (1): 45–66.

Oxburgh, G., Fahsing, I., Haworth, K. and Blair, J. P. (2015) 'Interviewing suspected offenders', in G. Oxburgh, T. Myklebust, T. Grant and R. Milne (eds), *Communication in Investigative and Legal Contexts. Integrated Approaches from Psychology, Linguistics and Law Enforcement*. Chichester: Wiley Blackwell.

Powell, M. B., Fisher, R. P. and Wright, R. (2005) 'Investigative interviewing', in N. Brewer and K. D. Williams (eds), *Psychology and Law: An Empirical Perspective*. New York: Guilford, pp. 11–42.

Stern, W. (1903/1904) *Beiträge zür Psychologie der Aussage*. Leipzig: Verlag von Johann Ambrosius Barth.
Sternberg, K. J., Lamb, M. E., Davies, G. M. and Westcott, H. L. (2001) 'The memorandum of good practice: theory versus application', *Child Abuse and Neglect*, 25: 669–81.
Trankell, A. (1972) *Reliability of Evidence – Methods for Analyzing and Assessing Witness Statements*. Stockholm: Beckmans.
Trankell, A. (1982) *Reconstructing the Past – The Role of Psychologists in Criminal Trials*. Stockholm: P. A. Norstedt & Söners förlag.
Undeutsch, U. (1967) 'Beurteilung der Glaubhaftigkeit von Aussagen', in U. Undeutsch (ed.), *Handbuch der Psychologie Bd.11: Forensische Psychologie*. Göttingen: Hogrefe, pp. 26–181.
Undeutsch, U. (1982) 'Statement reality analysis', in A. Trankell (ed.), *Reconstructing the Past: The Role of Psychologists in Criminal Trials*. Stockholm: P. A. Norstedt & Söners förlag, pp. 27–56.

Index

Page numbers in italic refer to figures and tables. Added to a page number 'n' refers to notes.